HUMAN RIGHTS ETHICS

Purdue Human Rights Studies Series

Clark Butler
Editor

Human Rights Ethics

A Rational Approach

CLARK BUTLER

PURDUE UNIVERSITY PRESS
WEST LAFAYETTE, INDIANA

176861339

Library of Congress Cataloging-in-Publication Data.

Butler, Clark, 1944-
Human rights ethics : a rational approach / Clark Butler.
p. cm.
ISBN 978-1-55753-480-4
1. Human rights--Moral and ethical aspects. I. Title.
JC571.B883 2008
172'.2--dc22
2007043142

CONTENTS

DEDICATION

To Chaïm Perelman, Jürgen Habermas, and Georg Wilhelm Friedrich Hegel. A brief article by the first in justification of human rights opened the way to this book with astonishingly sudden power. The second, more than anyone contemporary, has publicly advanced the world towards a new rationally motivated consensus in the philosophy of international human rights law. The third continues to recall the continuing relevance of the dialectical method.

"Since the man of common sense makes his appeal to feeling . . . he is finished and done with anyone who does not agree. . . . [H]e tramples under foot the roots of humanity. For it is the nature of humanity to press onward to agreement with others; human nature only really exists in an achieved community of minds."

Georg Wilhelm Friedrich Hegel, *The Phenomenology of Spirit*, trans. A.V. Miller (Oxford: Oxford University Press, 1971), p. 43.

FOREWORD

Human Rights Ethics makes an important contribution to contemporary philosophical and political debates concerning the advancement of global justice and human rights. Butler's book also lays claim to a significant place in both normative ethics and human rights studies in as much as it seeks to vindicate a universalistic, rational approach to human rights ethics. Butler's innovative approach is not based on murky claims to "natural rights" which supposedly hold wherever human beings exist; nor does it succumb to the traditional problems of justification associated with utilitarianism, Kantianism, and other procedural approaches to human rights studies. Instead, Butler proposes "a dialectical justification of human rights by indirect proof" that claims not to be question begging. Very much in the spirit of Hegel and Habermas, Butler proposes to vindicate a "totally rational account of human rights," but one that depends concretely and historically on a dialectically constructed "right to freedom of thought in its universal modes."

If successful, Butler's account would also expand a non-circular justification of human rights into a justification of human rights ethics, with rules grounded in "no other obligation but the obligation to respect the right to freedom of thought." Butler argues persuasively that freedom of thought/speech must be recognized as "the one basic right in human rights ethics" and as "the necessary condition of justifying anything, including any other ethical theory." Having established human rights ethics out of what Butler sees as the historically constructed "story of freedom," and through "the self-criticism emerging in the pursuit of any final chosen standard other than full dialogical rationality," Butler then examines the complex relation between human rights and international law. He concludes his study by applying "human rights ethics" to the contemporary international scene and to a number of contemporary world problems, and he explores the distinction between what he sees as the "increasingly present world governance" and the absence of an effective world government. *Human Rights Ethics* aims to appeal to a wide audience, not just to specialists, and it should prove invaluable to anyone who seeks a deeper, more comprehensive understanding of the important issues surrounding human rights education and the advancement of global justice.

Steven V. Hicks
Queens College, City University of New York

ix

PREFACE

I address moral philosophers and human rights researchers, holding that right action means creating and respecting rights. The first four chapters analyze concepts of natural and human rights. Chapters Five through Seven seek to justify human rights. Chapters Eight through Eleven show human rights ethics as a position in normative ethics. Taking a *rational* approach to such ethics, I highlight the *error* of human rights violations. Others have widely documented their frequent *horror*. The remaining chapters examine the relation between human rights and international law. As a human rights *ethicist* I write as student of international human rights law, but speak at times with less caution than international human rights lawyers in the system of sovereign states.

The first chapter explores the redundant phrase "equal human rights." Here I counter arguments against human rights based on supposed unequal human abilities. Chapters Two through Four distinguish senses of "natural" and "human rights," reviewing the history of natural rights and human rights theories. I uphold the primacy of human over natural rights. Chapters Five and Six critically examine two contemporary human rights ethicists, Jürgen Habermas and Karl Popper. Chapter Seven gives a dialectical justification of human rights by an indirect proof that claims not to be question begging. Chapter Eight expands justification of human rights into justification of human rights ethics, with rules based on no obligation but respect for the universal right to freedom of thought, once that right exists. Chapter Nine offers a model of moral education in which agents discover human rights ethics through self-criticism in the pursuit of any final chosen standard other than full dialogical rationality. In Chapter Ten, I argue from the standpoint of human rights ethics against other theories in normative ethics: human rights ethics is the end of the history of normative ethics.

In Chapters Eleven and Twelve, I address alleged conflicts between human rights. I solve conflict between, for example, the right to property and to health care by having only one basic human right, the right to freedom of thought in a public context. This right stands alone among human rights as necessary for the maximal justification of anything. The justification of human rights is not that of many rights, but of a single right—of which other allegedly distinct human rights are only the same basic right in one or another of its modes. Solving a conflict between your right to this house and my right to the same house finally depends on seeing how as many as possible can effectively exercise the basic right.

Chapter Thirteen treats the United Nations Universal Declaration of Human Rights. I hold that human rights are moral ideals, not yet existing rights. International human rights law, unlike hard law, is a legal heaven that still awaits full descent to earth. Chapter Fourteen treats world problems, contrasting existing world governance and the absence of world government.

ACKNOWLEDGMENTS

This book has been several years in the making, and I have both institutions and people to thank. I started it during a sabbatical from Purdue University at the Indiana University-Purdue University Fort Wayne Campus in 1994–1995. I spent that year as a student at the International Institute of Human Rights founded by René Cassin in Strasbourg, and as a guest scholar in the libraries of the Council of Europe and of the European Court of Human Rights. I subsequently taught human rights ethics at the Fort Wayne campus at regular intervals. During 2001–2002 I spent another sabbatical in Strasbourg, teaching human rights ethics at the Institut d'Etudes Politiques in the Spring Semester. In Summer 2006 and 2007 I lectured on human rights ethics at the René Cassin Institute. I thank these institutions for affording the assistance of numerous students as I tried to refine my position. I am also grateful for opportunities provided by conferences for the presentation and discussion of various chapters. The final manuscript benefited greatly from the advice of Professor Steven Hicks. For copyediting, the manuscript has benefited both in substance and in form from careful readings by three students, Jennifer Caseldine-Bracht, Jonathan Sholl, and Bradley Turflinger.

Part One

CONCEPTS OF NATURAL RIGHTS
AND HUMAN RIGHTS

One

EQUAL HUMAN RIGHTS

1. Human Rights: Ancient, Modern, and Contemporary

Those who believe in a natural or acquired superiority of some over others regardless of the field of inquiry oppose equal human rights. In their self-satisfaction, they sneer at the masses. They are "elitist" in a bad sense. An elitist denial of universal rights norms based on the superiority of some in a given problem area is a mistake. To argue for human rights is not to deny the objective superiority or inferiority of individuals in any area of endeavor. Yet a non-elitist equality of the opportunity to reply, provided by universal human rights ethics, is essential if any elite is to be legitimate. Responding to elitists from Plato to Friedrich Nietzsche—passing through Aristotle, Augustine of Hippo, Edmund Burke, Joseph-Marie de Maistre, Auguste Comte, and Jeremy Bentham—I will endorse their denials that human rights in fact exist, differing only where they argue that human rights cannot and ought not to exist.

Nietzsche, the most crucial recent opponent of egalitarian rights, deplored their increasing influence in the West, fearing they would have a leveling effect, blocking individual creativity as it strove to rise beyond the masses.[1] We who retain the liberal creed must show how we can uphold such rights in the face of elitist objections. We must show why Nietzsche, if he is rational, must *either* forsake publishing *or* admit the humans rights norm of universal freedom of thought and let his books to meet their fate with whatever elite of critiques that enjoys the egalitarian endorsement of the general public ("the wretched and the botched!") down through future generations.

Perhaps surprisingly for his detractors, Georg Wilhelm Friedrich Hegel made the essential liberal case for human rights in the *Preface* to the *Phenomenology of Spirit*:

> Since the man of common sense makes his appeal to feeling . . . he is finished and done with anyone who does not agree. . . . [H]e tramples underfoot the roots of humanity. For it is the nature of humanity to press onward to agreement with others; human nature only really exists in an achieved community of minds. . . . [I]t is the nature of truth to prevail when its time has come, and . . . it only appears when this time has come, and therefore never appears prematurely, nor finds a public not ripe to receive it; also we must accept that the individual needs that this should be so in order to verify what is as yet a matter for himself alone, and to experience the conviction, which in the first place belongs only to a particular individual, as something universally held. But in this con-

3

nection the public must often be distinguished from those who pose as its representatives. . . . [W]e must often distinguish the more gradual effect which corrects the attention extorted by imposing assurances [by the author] and corrects, too, contemptuous censure [by critics], and gives some writers an audience only after time, while others after time have no audience left. . . . [A]t a time when the universality of Spirit has gathered such strength . . . the share in the total work of Spirit which falls to the individual can only be very small. Because of this, the individual must all the more forget himself, as the nature of Spirit implies and requires. Of course, he must make of himself and achieve what he can; but less must be demanded of him, just as he in turn can expect less of himself, and may demand less for himself.[2]

We find here a duty-based concept of the human right to freedom of thought. This right is a historically constructed universal right to the real freedom of thought with which to put members of the universal audience, still under construction, in debt to us for their power of reply. Yet the concept is as much in the spirit of Karl Popper as in that of Hegel. Reasonable members of an elite must also be egalitarian in agreeing to test the legitimacy of elitist positions in discussion by maintaining an equal opportunity of reply for all. Human rights serve to identify, not those whom a restricted circle takes to be elite, but those who are objectively elite on a given question in the universal community. A demonstrated ability to correct publicly established target beliefs is what confirms individuals as members of an elite. This is how egalitarian human rights in the Popperian open society advance the quest for truth.

Historically, three concepts of human rights exist: ancient, modern, and contemporary. Ancient human rights are rights to the sympathy of other persons, while modern and contemporary human rights are rights to freedom of speech and action.[3] Slaves do not have as extensive a right to freedom of action as free men. Yet a prominent ancient view held that, like any other human being, we ought to regard slaves kindly. Though the ancients did not use the term "human rights," ancient human rights go back to a right to dignity and fellowship as a rational being along with all other such beings. We can trace this idea of human rights to less known figures in classical Athens to whom Plato and Aristotle reacted. If we put aside legendary figures like the first Cynics and the still earlier figures in the Periclean generation, the ancient right to be treated with dignity, because of a spark of reason in each person, first forcefully arose among the Stoics. The right evolves into the Stoic right to be respected by our fellows as free even in chains—though we should, if possible, assist others in breaking free of chains.

Pre-Socratic philosophers anticipating such a human right include Pythagoras, Empedocles, Democritus, and Protagoras. *The Persians* by Aeschylus could show compassion for a defeated enemy. Euripides's *Trojan Women* also introduces compassion for the enemy. Socrates held a similar concept of human rights in the *Meno* when he showed that a slave boy knew geometry without anyone teaching him. The slave boy enjoys a dignity that comes not from potentially instructing us but from already having our knowledge.

Socrates did not reserve reason, and the dignity that goes with it, for an elite. Even those very lowly placed have a power of reasoning which gives them a right to enjoy the company, conversation, and respect of the educated. Respect for ancient human rights is not so much respect for freedom of action and thought as for what, as rational beings, human beings already are. Socrates' followers likewise embraced the human rights ideal—followers such as Antisthenes, the Cynics, and the Stoics. Earlier, major figures of the Athenian golden age like Herodotus and Sophocles also understood this early concept of human rights. Yet Aristotle and Plato, two far more influential thinkers, opposed this ancient ideal.

Modern rights arose in the seventeenth century and surrounded the French Revolution. The right to freedom of action without interference captures their essence. The ancient cultivation of sympathy from and for others is no longer here part of respect for human rights. We are now indifferent as to how others use their freedom as long as we enjoy a similar freedom from interference. Thomas Hobbes illustrates the concept. Human rights are the civil rights required for peaceful relations between individuals—the right to be left in peace. From these rights follows a duty of non-intervention in the exercise of civil rights like the right to the product of labor. John Hospers writes in the spirit of such human rights: "To claim a right is to claim a certain amount of moral space on which others may not trespass. A right is like a 'No Trespassing sign.' . . ."[4]

Distinct from ancient and modern human rights are contemporary rights focusing on an individual right to freedom of thought as a potential dialogue partner before a now emerging global audience. This emerging audience is what makes such rights contemporary. We derive actively respected contemporary rights from passively respected ancient rights by adding the technological potential of contemporary society. Yet we can find the seed of such rights in ancient human rights. If we strip Stoicism of its quiescent resignation, what remains is a positive duty to develop wherever possible universal communication among human beings.[5] Others become solicitous, no longer indifferent.

According to the contemporary concept of human rights, only those who know prior to any discussion that they have nothing to learn from some persons on any issue can justify a denial of human rights. Opponents of human rights claiming to know this have always existed. The egalitarian reply to such elitism insists that we must establish the superiority of any argumentation, not prior to discussion as determined by the established authority of a particular speaker, but by the discussion itself. We determine this superiority by seeing who has the better argument, the argument that wins over the others in dialogue undistorted by uneven distributions of economic, political, or informational power between participants and by arbitrary restrictions in the range of discussants. Human rights cast the net as widely as possible in the recruitment of talented and diverse fellow discussants.

Jürgen Habermas asserts "basic rights to equal access to processes of opinion and will-formation."[6] He also admits subjective freedom of choice even if it plays no dialogical role, so dialogue is a right and not a duty. All valid rights except the right of access to discussion are modes of that one substantial right. Non-dialogical freedom of choice is not frivolous, since such freedom creates an environment in which dialogical contributions can arise.

Diversity is now an idea surrounding us everywhere. We read in a university handbook: "The University believes that variety among its members strengthens the institution, stimulates creativity, promotes the exchange of ideas, and enriches campus life."[7] Yet emergency situations temporarily justify distorted discussion—like cockpit discussions in an airplane limited to those competent to discuss. In non-emergency situations, the rational authority of an expert does not extend beyond his or her ability to convince non-expert participants. We might suppose that the participation of a medical doctor in a discussion about health would *a priori* have more authority prior to entry into the discussion than that of an untutored layman or glib con artist. We must interpret what a person says in the discussion through its context, which may show that a medical doctor has special training.

Yet the records of discussion participants cannot alone establish the credibility of their contributions in a new discussion. The discussion itself shows who has the better argument. Yet we can only determine who provisionally has this better argument by the provisional rationally motivated consensus that results, and such a consensus results from negotiation in which lay discussion partners have a right to understand before they consent.

Human rights ethics, associated with contemporary human rights, seeks to counter the uneven distribution of economic, political and rhetorical power between discussion partners. Such an uneven distribution prevents equal participation in discussion by all concerned. The only valid elite is one that emerges from an even playing field. Lacking such a field, human rights ethics endeavors to equalize power upward, empowering the weak without disempowering the strong. Such ethics allows each discussion group to recruit as many discussion partners as it can to increase the likelihood that the best argument will emerge in that group. When a limited expert audience reaches a conclusion, we refer the matter to the closest thing to the universal audience we have succeeded in constructing. The public which funds schools and universities, and which the rational authority of biologists either convinces or does not convince, decides until further notice the acceptability of Darwinism, not the biologists themselves.

2. Habermas and Contemporary Human Rights

The distinction between ancient and modern rights is between communal rights and coexistence rights.[8] Habermas views contemporary human rights as flowing from a self-imposed duty to inquire in the public sphere before a rights-empowered audience: "the public use of one's reason must always be free, and it alone can bring about enlightenment among men."[9] The three concepts of rights are different, but also show a resemblance. All three arose in Western civilization at different stages. All three express respect for individuals, whether in quiet fellowship with kindred spirits, as a condition of peaceful coexistence, or as a condition of successful truth seeking through discussion.

The third concept connects human rights intimately with a democracy that depends on public discussion in order to reach majority decisions. Democratic discussion—like rational discussion generally—ideally equalizes economic and rhetorical power upward, so that only the "force of the better argument" prevails, not the power of money or superior natural gifts. In a polis, discussing matters of state is the prerogative of citizens.[10] The cosmopolis of the Stoics implies universal citizenship, which contemporary human rights would realize. Cosmopolitan discussion occurs within a republic of thinkers floating abstractly above material concerns unless the cosmopolis becomes a terrestrial polis.

In the framework of contemporary human rights, we no longer say that individuals may behave anyway they wish, exercising or not exercising their rights so long as they do not violate the equal rights of others or disturb the public peace. Promotion of the exercise of contemporary human rights has become an object of avid interest. In the place of coexistence rights, whose exercise others merely tolerate with indifference, persons now have dialogical rights whose exercise we actively invite. The intersubjective nature of inquiry requires communication with others. Modern human rights preserve mutually insulated individuals from destruction, restraining and even eliminating war. Contemporary human rights go beyond this, creating a worldwide forum for discussion. Peace is indispensable, but is not the final end.

Critics of contemporary rights like Barbara Hernstein Smith argue that Habermas is naive to suppose that "the force of the stronger argument" can determine the result of public discussion. For discussion takes place in a market of ideas in which players come with differing abilities, depending in part on the price paid for their effective abilities.[11] Efforts to realize human rights are an impossible attempt to force the marketplace to yield to the demands of an ideal exchange of ideas on merit. Can the marketplace with its economic and political constraints accommodate rationally motivated discussion?

Consider the market exchange of thought that Smith questions. In a market society that protects civil rights, some earn money from espousing politically unpopular ideas. In the courtroom of ideas, capable lawyers who remain equally well paid defend the idea that offers the best opportunity for novel, arresting defense. They seek to offer a new and challenging defense of some idea. Universities and the media realize this courtroom of ideas more fully, where professors and journalists earn their keep by mining the better argument. A faculty member protected by academic freedom becomes an unattached intellectual ready to pounce on the opportunity of a better argument waiting for a public defense. When some suffer violation of human rights in silence, an academic, journalist, attorney, or writer becomes the mouthpiece for those abused. Professional spokespeople, much as Karl Marx spoke for the proletariat, empower the weak.

Smith is right that a vast seminar conducted in cognitively ideal conditions will never swallow the informal adversarial pursuit of truth in the market of products and services, politics, and the arts. Despite the countervailing power of professional spokespersons, the uneven playing field on which this pursuit unfolds distorts the discussion. The public pursuit of truth and rights must ride piggyback on economic and political interests. On occasion this occurs, while often interests indifferent to the cause of rights prevail over it.

In reply to Smith, we may criticize and reduce, if not eliminate, the distortion of discussion under the influence of economic and political interests. This may occur by riding on other interests, while in other cases human rights discourse itself becomes an interest. Occasionally a global rational consensus arises at a certain level of abstraction. Many think that after 1948 such a consensus arose surrounding the Universal Declaration, even if below the surface Cold-War discord between the signatory states showed that it meant different things to different camps and that the consensus was a compromise.

We may question whether the self-imposed duty behind contemporary human rights securely grounds such rights. A right to something seems to give a right to demand it.[12] Yet if my right depends on your self-imposed obligation to dialogue, I am indebted to you for my right. I cannot demand respect for my right, since you may freely suspend the duty you have freely imposed on yourself. Any demand for respect of my rights would suppose that I take your self-imposed obligation to seek truth by discussion for granted. We must grant that contemporary rights are contingent in this way. They are neither self-evident nor inalienable. They are a gift from others for which we should express gratitude. To say that I can demand respect for my dialogical rights would imply that you pursue truth dialogically by nature. Yet, if your nature merely allows dialogical truth seeking in a way in which an animal's nature does not, your obligations in inquiry depend on your voluntary commitment.

3. Platonic and Aristotelian Objections to
Ancient Human Rights

Some common objections to human rights turn out to be objections to them only in their ancient or modern form, leaving rights in their contemporary form untouched. Some object that, within ancient human rights, no single human brotherhood exists because aptitudes and ways of life are so different. Plato's body-soul dualism excludes ancient human rights by denying community of nature between philosopher-kings and others, "[P]hilosophers only are able to grasp the eternal and unchangeable, and those who wander in the region of the many and variable are not philosophers. . . ."[13] Some have strong physical aptitudes, while others have special intellectual gifts. Can manual workers and potential philosopher-kings belong to one community? In Plato's aristocratic milieu, it did not seem so.

The modern world has broken down barriers between intellectual and manual labor, showing how theoretical knowledge depends on experimentation, and how technology depends on theoretical knowledge. One universal society of inquiry emerges. Plato's denial of universal fellowship is a misunderstanding of science. We find knowledge in conjectures subject to open public experimentation and discussion, not in exclusive and infallible intuitions.

Ancient human rights through universal fellowship denied caste differences, but never led to an active construction of particular rights: civil rights, political rights, public works/public service rights, legal rights, and welfare rights. Antisthenes, Gorgias, Alicidemas and others whom Plato repudiated respected a tacit right to dignity in a quietist spirit of universal fellow-feeling viewed as an end in itself.[14] Contemporary human rights advocates also acknowledge fellowship within the human family, but rationally motivated compassion now moves us to actively empower a universal audience and network of discussion circles. Commiseration becomes activism. Empedocles recognized a common nature between human beings, and even between human beings and animals. Honoring the dignity of living beings that were also rational expressed respect for our own rationality.

Empedocles believed in a natural justice and injustice common to all, even to those who have no association or covenant with one another. Sophocles's Antigone intends this natural justice when she says that the burial of Polyneices was just, though forbidden by human law. Empedocles illustrates this justice by invoking an obligation not to kill any living creature.[15] A natural kinship between species implies an obligation, whether consciously recognized or not. According to this ancient concept, the duty of a human being is not chiefly one of forever developing one's rationality as a prospective dialogue partner with others, but one of commemorating the established fact of our common rationality. This rationality was understood to include animals.[16] It lay in the individual's ability, as a microcosm of the cosmos, to internalize natural law through sympathetically communing with all other individuals.[17]

Plato and Aristotle denied an already existent ancient belief in human rights.[18] By opposing communal human rights, Plato and Aristotle rejected the pre-Socratic panentheistic philosophers of nature. God for Plato was no longer the cosmos, the logos of nature, but was the form of forms beyond nature. The ability of philosopher-kings to grasp immaterial forms set them apart. Inequality between the castes was as natural as that between species. Plant-like people could not—by education, equipment, or other artificial means—perform as philosopher-kings any more than dogs could perform as cats. The quest for knowledge makes no claim on their testimony.

Though all Aristotelian material substances were intrinsically goal-directed, only human beings had a contemplative capacity likening them to God. Only some could govern themselves and others too. The others were at most weakly rational, needing government by strongly rational individuals.[19] By the account of Karl Popper, Plato was an aristocrat appalled by democracy, who by his literary genius, ultimately by the trickery of art, sought to seduce even common Athenians into a reactionary retreat into a "closed society" ruled by racially separate philosopher-kings. Plato offers what is still perhaps the most common objection to human rights, namely, that the equality of intellectual ability is an illusion.

According to the Platonic view, those who are superior deserve special resources. They may not deserve more money, but in view of what they can offer as philosopher-kings, they deserve special education. They do not receive more as a reward for being superior. They receive what they need if they are to play their governing role in the state. We sometimes think of human rights theory as egalitarian in that it supposes all human beings to be equal in ability, if not in accomplishment. If we have human rights because of the intelligence that sets us apart from other species, must we not be equal in intelligence? Otherwise, we cannot have equal rights.

The case for human rights I develop makes no such claim. The practical force of human rights is to first acknowledge inequalities, and then distribute greater resources to empower the weak, so that they become more capable of participating in discussions that affect them. An argument against human rights would then have to show that natural inequalities are so great that no technology or therapeutic resource could help equalize them. Yet we do not know how far we can equalize upward unequal abilities unless we make an unrelenting effort to do so. Only after we have seriously made this effort can we accept an unequal distribution of power between discussion partners whose maximum rationality necessarily requires this attempt.

The weaker are enabled to interact more equally with the stronger, on a more even but artificially created playing ground, symbolized by handicapped parking and specially reconstructed curbs. Disabilities call for greater help, more public services and public works. One day, eugenics may equalize all individuals upwards. Potential philosopher-kings may have a less limited range of persons with whom to discuss what concerns them. We do not owe greater help tender-mindedly out of pity for the weak, but tough-mindedly out of our interest in possible enlightenment by those receiving assistance.

In human rights ethics, we assert that, as a matter of principle, we should try to help others by helping to construct and respect rights. Yet helping one visible victim is a fleeting drop in the bucket in the face of systematic violations or the simple absence of rights. General respect for rights requires institutions to reward respect and punish disrespect. The overarching rule of constructing and respecting the right to freedom of thought embraces countless secondary rules, such as a rule protecting individuals from torture. The very threat of torture strips individuals of freedom of thought, and leads to coerced speech acts lacking in credibility.

Both Plato's rejection of human rights and my proposed defense of them assume that the goal in distributing resources should be to facilitate knowledge. Yet we use different models of knowledge. For Plato, knowledge is intellectual recollection and intuition facilitated by elitist dialogue, while Popper and other contemporary writers view it as testable by discussion that extends an invitation to all who feel themselves concerned. By his concept of the human species' essence as rational animality, Aristotle made fellow feeling and the recognition of human dignity possible across boundaries of nationality, sex, and occupation. Yet he did not oppose slavery like Antisthenes, the son of a slave mother and an intimate of Socrates. He made invidious comparisons contrary to ancient human rights between Greeks and Barbarians, men and women, slaves and masters, and, more generally, weakly and strongly rational animals. Such distinctions, along with the concern they express about who should rule, forestall any return to the ancient universal egalitarian fellowship of reason. They also block progress to the contemporary idea of a fellowship embracing discussion partners representing diverse theoretical and applied specializations.

Aristotle believed that Easterners were weak in the spirit of freedom and easier to subjugate than German barbarians not accustomed to obedience.[20] Yet Germans were inferior to Easterners by being ungovernable. If practical reason lies in self-government, the acceptance of government over oneself by superiors is better than a refusal of any government at all. Yet because Aristotle distinguished between weak and strong rational animals based on the observation of a species accident and not a species essence, he opens the door to observations showing that the distinction is one of nurture, not nature. Even if Greeks and barbarians by nature could not exercise the right to freedom of thought equally, we would have to consider the potential of medical technology to equalize barbarian abilities upwards.

Materials for constructing a concept of human rights may lie in the concept of human beings as rational animals. The classification of human beings into strongly and weakly rational beings may fade into the innocuous assertion that some are incapable of guiding their conduct, and can exercise no right to do so. A right is quite empty if we cannot exercise it. The problem is

drawing the line between the two groups. As long as Aristotle excludes barbarians and women from the rights of the strongly rational, we may suspect
that he has no concept of human rights. Even if barbarians, women, and slaves
perform at a lower level now, they might come to merit the rights of Greek
males if we overcame their intellectual debilitation by first addressing their
physical disabilities through environmental alteration, technology, or medical
intervention. Nothing in Aristotle precludes this. Such external intervention
might compensate for non-essential inequalities, even if genetically based.

Even deep retardation might respond to medication or diet. Weakly rational human beings form a species accident, not a species essence. The species makes it possible for its members to move into an opposite condition by
accidental change. Yet even if weakly rational beings are essentially weak,
the acquisition of strength might still be possible by artificial means.

4. A Creationist Objection to Human Rights

Within Christian theology, Augustine expresses an objection to modern human rights, especially to the priority of rights consciousness over duty consciousness. I call it the creationist objection. The Creator is absolute power,
the Lord of lords on whom the world depends, so that the divine image is
emphatically present wherever, in human society, legitimate ruling power
under the authority of the Lord is present. Christ is manifested as divine only
as the Risen Lord, not in a slavish condition like Jesus of Nazareth in tattered
clothes on a donkey.[21] The chief duty is obedience to a lawful higher power,
to divine law—not a duty of respect for egalitarian rights:

> [P]eace between man and God is the well-ordered obedience of faith to
> eternal law. Peace between man and man is well-ordered concord. Do-
> mestic peace is the well-ordered concord between those of the family
> who rule and those who obey. . . . For they who care for the rest rule—
> the husband the wife, the parents the children, the masters the servants.[22]

Augustine had but a meager idea of modern individualistic human rights
based on mutual non-intervention, or the peace of mutual indifference. Yet his
creationist theology has survived. The divine image of lordship is visible in an
emperor, Pope, father, or even in a legitimate employer. All rightful power
comes from divine power and shares proportionately in the rights of the
higher power. We see the creationist view expressed in the alliance of altar
and throne. The church teaches what despotism wills: obedience to external
authority.[23] God may strip power from one emperor or nation (like Rome), but
he transfers it to another temporal embodiment of Lordship. In himself, God
is reason, not just power, but we submit to power in our fallen state because
our reason is too weak to penetrate divine reason. In a state of sin, God is a
power to command, restricting errant freedom of choice.

Writers after the French Revolution such as Burke and de Maistre echoed such views. Burke emphasized the arrogance of a fallen humanity overturning the wisdom of the ages by trying to reconstruct society from the bottom up with modern abstract metaphysical concepts of human rights. Human beings are not wise enough to reconstruct a rational state from scratch, throwing overboard the accumulated experience of the ages. Human rights resulted from an impudent revolt against a divine order, throwing to the wind the slow historical growths responsible for the rights of Englishmen. The freedom to think and do what we want so long as we do not interfere with the same freedom of others is a freedom to ignore what God wants.

De Maistre paralleled Burke's critique of human rights and the French Revolution, defending hierarchical rule modeled on Biblical theocracy. The Revolution and human rights represented a revolt against this divine rule. His faith is in the precedence of the Father from whom the divinity of the Son and Spirit proceed. The priority of individual rights in the French Revolution, with derivative duties, atomizes members of a community into separate individuals without essential bonds. Rights consciousness, suppressing duty consciousness, ends in anarchy. The Revolution, reversing the natural order by replacing divine sovereignty with popular sovereignty, produced individual rights that in effect gave society many heads. No such monstrosity can endure. Democratic human rights, assigning a separate vote to each individual, splinter the state, replacing the sovereignty of the state with that of the individual.[24]

Despite de Maistre, Christianity is compatible with human rights, whether modern or contemporary. From the standpoint of humanity sunken in sin, the divine image is that of the Father who commands law with a power to back it up with punishment. From the non-Augustinian, but still Christian, standpoint of a redeemed humanity collectively reborn in Christ, in the spirit, we find the divine image in everyone, not just those who rule. Many rooms exist in Christianity, which is not opposed to egalitarian rights. Even Christians who are creationists would not all view God pre-eminently as Creator. They are not all hyper-creationist. Some view God chiefly as the historical Jesus, others as infinite love or the spirit. If every human being exists in the divine image, the spirit may have the power to lead everyone to understand and judge, and to proceed into all truth. Variations of power are partly due to accidents of conquest and inheritance rather than to irremediable disabilities.

We may understand Christian love as intelligent help, which we can construe as constructing and respecting contemporary rights. Hyper-creationist Christian theology grants that the divine law is one of love, but holds that a fallen humanity cannot understand it and so must merely obey. Christian ethics enlightened by understanding of the law can thrive within a universal human rights ethics, reinforcing this universal secular ethics in Christian communities. Christian ethics would differ from dialogical human rights ethics by a non-universal faith in an infinite power backing up the intelligent help supported, according to human rights ethics, by finite human energies. Some non-Christian faith-based ethical frameworks also dwell locally in the universal framework of human rights ethics, while others do not.

5. Comte's Technocratic Objection to Human Rights vs. Discussion Rights without Diplomas

Comte also opposed human rights in the form that they took in the French Revolution, where they illustrated a stage of metaphysical thinking fixated on uniform atomic individuality. The institutions of subordination in the Middle Ages were in reality more favorable to the moral development of true fraternity than the anarchical equality which for a time followed them.[25] This individualism was due to an empirically unverifiable fixation and fetish of abstract thinking—analogous to atomism in physics. Plato's opposition to ancient human rights was biological, but Comte's opposition to modern rights was equally sociological: your debt to society is greater than any obligation society has to you as an individual. The individual is what he or she is through society far more than society is what it is through the individual. Since what we are we owe to social tradition and not just to biology, we ought to feel gratitude to society and not clamorously insist on individual rights.

One has the general right to perform one's duty. Yet, since different individuals with different stations have higher and lower duties, they have no uniform human rights. The rights over those below derive from duties to those above with still higher rights. Your standing and rights depend on your intellectual standing in the hierarchy of applied and theoretical sciences. Comte was a servant of Napoleon's *grandes écoles* created with bureaucratic elites in mind. Superimposed on the Revolution with its egalitarian rights was the regime of the *fonctionnaires* in which rights depend on diplomas.

The ideology of modern human rights brought to fruition a corrosive, non-organic, critical epoch of world history. Human rights were metaphysical fictions because they asserted an unobservable human equality. What we are we owe to tradition and biology. Entrepreneurs achieve nothing if they do not grow up in a certain society, receiving a certain education, and enjoying the market that society provides for goods and services. Others owe their failure to society. The question is whether human rights can emerge based on the rationally motivated acknowledgment of universal claims. Technocrats deny that we should recognize the validity of human rights by a rational commitment to address the universal audience. They hold that acknowledgment of expert claims to freedom of thought is alone justifiable.

Comte is a Western example of duty consciousness taking precedence over rights consciousness. Yet the primacy of gratitude, or duty consciousness, does not exclude human rights. The reason for Comte's rejection of human rights is that duties and rights vary according to our station in the social division of labor.[26] Comte denies human rights, except for the right to be tested, because he is convinced of differences in ability as shown by tests. Human rights ideology undermines respect for certified superiors.

Comte compartmentalizes dialogue into different groupings of specialists. Restricted audiences with credentials are the final authority. His faith in the distribution of individuals by competitive examinations between different rankings eliminates the need for the countervailing power of human rights, of public dialogue inviting universal participation. Comte criticized modern human rights, by which we view the individual as an atomic island unto her- or himself, claiming only non-interference. Sociology, as founded by Comte, taught the functional interdependence of individuals, hence the impossibility of freedom from intervention by others. Yet Comte would also oppose contemporary human rights through which we try to de-compartmentalize discussion and bring specialized discussants to address, in some form, the universal audience. His positivistic society, where empirical scientists and positivists have authority, is a closed ideological society. Yet without a human right to contest positivism itself, is there any possibility of maximally confirming it? Habermas writes:

> [T]he idea of an ideally extended communication community is paradoxical in that every known community is limited and distinguishes members from non-members through rules of inclusion. Precisely this difference would have to be effaced through the extension of social space and historical time. But the image of an ideal audience (Chaïm Perelman) is still too concrete. The model of a public sphere accessible to all participants, issues, and contributions comes closest to the notion envisaged.[27]

I want to uphold Perelman's concrete image of a universal audience because, unlike the "public sphere," we can address an audience. The difference between the public sphere and the universal audience is that we can think the public sphere, though we cannot adequately represent it in imagination. Yet pictorial representation can give wings to thought. The image of that audience, and of oneself as a speaker before it, serves human rights ethics. Habermas does not show that an unprecedented all-inclusive audience is impossible. That audience must be possible if contemporary human rights are possible.

6. The Utilitarian Definition of Human Rights vs. the Human Right to Judge Utilitarianism

Jeremy Bentham, responding to the Declaration of the Rights of Man and the Citizen, viewed rights as pious wishes, "nonsense on stilts," fictitious metaphysical postulates, not as "inalienable" and "imprescriptible" possessions.[28] If they were truly inalienable, we would not need to defend them. Like Comte, he rejected the modern self-evident rights of the isolated individual, the right to do what we choose unchecked by interference. Bentham is quite right that inalienable rights do not exist. For a right is a socially, and perhaps even legally, recognized claim, and those who recognize a claim can withdraw its recognition and alienate the right.

The most that utilitarians can say is that particular alienable human rights, such as the freedom of thought defended by John Stuart Mill in *On Liberty*, ought to exist by the utilitarian standard of "the advantage of society."[29] Freedom of thought and action is a way of discovering what promotes the greatest good. Yet when this is not the case, utilitarians place the rights of experts above human rights. What is unclear is why freedom of thought cannot be used to challenge and not merely serve utilitarianism. Were it to do so, its justification would be its service in uncovering truth without any presupposition that utilitarianism is true.

Mill did not give a utilitarian justification of freedom of thought as a *universal* human right, since, due to their underdevelopment, he excluded colonized non-Westerners from such freedom, at least for the present. The utilitarian justification of rights, unlike justification of rights simply by the quest for truth, is that they advance general welfare, although to complete this justification we need to know what justifies utilitarianism. Yet if we place freedom of thought in a utilitarian harness, when we ask it to testify we will have stacked the cards. We can vindicate utilitarianism only by discussion governed by a respect for human rights justified by the promotion, not of general happiness, but of the discovery of truth. To justify utilitarianism is ultimately to justify a human rights ethics of justification which cannot, without circularity, define human rights as utilitarians define them.

Bentham distinguished "right" as an adjective and as a noun.[30] To say that everyone has a right to a roof over his head because everyone having a roof over his or her head is *right* is a fallacy of equivocation. That everyone having a roof over his head is right means at most that all ought to have the right, not that they all do have it. If we hold that human rights exist because they ought to exist, we will find that most societies operate in blatant defiance of them. We may then succumb to anarchic revolt against existing states because of systematic human rights violations with the resulting social strife working against general welfare. Utilitarians condemn the myth of inalienable human rights.

Bentham's elitism shows in his belief that the rights of individuals should not depend simply on their claims. We cannot rely on anyone to claim all and only rights that maximize general welfare. Few can discern which rights, granted to all, benefit the greatest number. Human rights ideology wrongly places specialized questions of ethics and government in everyone's hands. A consensus of all may be as incompetent to treat such matters as it would be to handle questions of particle physics.

Utilitarianism is as elitist as Comte's positivism. Empirically, the aptitude of individuals for science varies. We should have only those universal rights that utilitarian experts recognize as promoting general welfare. This makes the justification of human rights depend on the truth of utilitarianism. What utilitarianism excludes are rights independent of utilitarianism, rights by which to discuss, judge, and evaluate utilitarianism. If we suddenly refuted utilitarianism, either human rights would collapse or we would have to modify these rights through justification by some other doctrine. I suggest that human rights norms do not depend on the truth of any particular doctrine. Rather, the procedures by which we investigate all doctrines presuppose them.

7. Nietzsche's Heroic Objection to Human Rights vs. the Egalitarian Justification of Elites

The most strident opponent of modern human rights is Nietzsche.[31] Some have also proclaimed him the father of post-modernism.[32] If modernist culture, including modern human rights, is Enlightenment culture, Nietzsche located the historical *other* of Enlightenment modernism in aristocratic pagan Greece. If we assume that the human rights movement which began as a reversal of aristocracy in the Periclean age, and which gained momentum with Christian tender-heartedness toward the humble and the meek, now continues in the contemporary human rights movement, Nietzsche called for a reversal of that reversal of values, reestablishing pagan aristocratic values. His post-modernism would be pre-modernism except for the massive historical presence of modernism that blocked a simple return, though it allowed a negation:

> All the world's efforts against the "aristocrats," the "mighty" the "masters," the "holders of power," are negligible in comparison with what has been accomplished against those classes by *the Jews*—the Jews, that priestly nation which eventually realized that the one method of effecting satisfaction on its enemies and tyrants was by means of a radical transvaluation of values, which was at the same time an act of the *cleverest revenge. . . .* It was the Jews who, in opposition to the aristocratic equation (good = aristocratic = happy = beloved of the god), dared . . . to maintain with the teeth of the most profound hatred (the hatred of weakness) this contrary equation, namely, "the wretched are alone good, the poor, the weak, the lowly are alone the good; the suffering, the needy, the sick, the loathsome are the only ones who are pious, the only ones who are blessed. . . ." [It] was . . . with the Jews that the *revolt of the slaves* begins in the *sphere of morals*; that revolt which has been behind it a history of two millennia, and which today has only moved out of our sight, because it—has achieved victory.[33]

Nietzsche's critique of human rights resembles others in questioning equality. How do those lacking superior talent contribute in universally open dialogue? The reply in part is that ability is relative to the task, to the question asked. The questions are so numerous that everyone may be able to contribute to the answer of some question. Among the questions that we can ask, elitists believe some are more crucial. How do we establish that a question is objectively more crucial, not just subjectively for those who ask it?

Even if philosopher-kings alone can answer the crucial questions, interbreeding may have so interspersed that race that we may find its heirs unpredictably anywhere. A right of all to respond needs protection to locate the occasional incisive answer. Can any universal aptitude test reliably do this? If philosophers capable of knowledge on agreed-upon all-important subjects constituted a localized human sub-variety, they would have a claim to special rights. Human rights would be less justifiable. Yet if talent remains dispersed due to the fallibility of universal testing, and if we know no question to be objectively more crucial without general discussion, dialogical human rights become justifiable. Such rights put all to the test regardless of past test scores, isolating both the crucial questions and present talent in addressing them. Without them, we fairly test no one's ability to contribute. Such rights do not exclude elites. They exclude both closed elites assumed to require no further testing and restrictions on recruiting new elites addressing new problems.

A Nietzschean objection to encouraging all to address a potentially universal audience of interested individuals is that it assumes (1) indulgence for the pursuit of trivial or pedestrian truth and (2) the ability of all to contribute in the pursuit of significant truth. Believing that all can contribute equally to dialogue is tender-minded. An egalitarian human right to discuss wrongly assumes that more easily accessible truth about canning fruit is as significant as truth about global warming or the meaning of life.

Elitists, to justify denying contemporary human rights, must show that some questions, which only a minority has talent to answer, are infallibly known by a limited audience to be objectively more crucial without appeal to a universal audience. Yet excluding voices beyond existing elites is arbitrary. If a given elite is not arbitrary, it must justify the significance of its questions and privilege by a universal egalitarian consensus that uses universal human rights to test the priority of its questions and the privilege of its members. We justify elites by egalitarian rational discussion (not by the sway of mass opinion) in which those outside an elite have a right of reply. If the criterion of truth is some approach to universal rationally motivated consensus, that criterion is also the one with which to test what elites we can justify. The further we remain from a universal rational consensus among rationally motivated inquirers about a given elite, the more that elite's position remains in doubt.

If some truth—say, of medicine or economics—is objectively more crucial than another truth in realizing human rights, we can fully know this to be true only by a universal consensus including all in active or passive agreement, not merely by a consensus between physicians or economists. Since ideally we can vindicate elites only by an egalitarian consent in which all are invited to speak, an egalitarian presupposition in the course of this very vindication eclipses the contrary claims of any elite. Elites will continue to exist, but if general public consensus legitimates them, elitism will not.

Any question asked by speakers in open dialogue is significant to those speakers. It may be equally significant to but a fraction of hearers in the universal audience. Yet none can know before discussion which fraction. We cannot exclude hearers capable of active interest in any locality, though obliging others to show interest is oppressive. Advancing human rights is tough-minded. Extending literacy and otherwise working to empower a universal audience out of which to recruit motivated dialogue partners is tough-minded.

8. Confucius and Rights under the Sway of Duty Consciousness

To advocate an egalitarian justification of elites is to adopt an intermediary position between extreme egalitarianism and elitism. We generally think of Confucius and China as elitist, but Confucianism implies something close to such an intermediary position. China has difficulty not so much with rights as with rights consciousness. I suspect that Confucianism and China, while rejecting the modern concept of human rights, should be able to adopt contemporary human rights. The Confucian philosophy of education holds that schools are for the egalitarian recruitment of the meritorious and for equal opportunity, in particular equal opportunity for serving the state. "In teaching there should be no class distinctions."[34] In China this opportunity is a political right, whereas I would assimilate it to the basic human right of freedom of thought—the right to an equal opportunity of reply.

Confucius discerned the higher type of man from the lower. The higher type shows natural ability and studiousness. His authority is not mysterious or beyond appeal to his peers. He acts out of responsibility for those with whom he enjoys relationships. Capable of more, he owes more to others. The lower type of man has a duty to respect superiors. "Are not filial respect and devotion and respect for elders the very foundation of the unselfish life?"[35] He urges the unselfish life for both types of man: "Virtue is denial of self."[36]

Beyond a right to equal opportunity in civil service, Confucius granted a right to be treated with dignity. Practicing the virtue of *jen* or humanity, we accord courteous and sympathetic treatment to all. In a well-regulated society, all enjoy such treatment, especially those who are through no fault of a lower type. The ancient human right of fellowship is present here. The higher type of man is no less self-effacing than the lower type, and neither parades demands. "The higher type of man is modest in what he says, but surpasses in what he does."[37] Confucius says that the higher type is an inspiration to the lower type in the performance of duty. "If a ruler is himself upright his people will do their duty without orders; but if he himself be not upright, although he may order, they will not obey."

Neither the higher nor the lower type makes any demand that others respect any "rights" of his. No exact pre-nineteenth century term exists in Chi-

nese for "rights" or "person."[38] The formal concept of human rights entered
Chinese from modern Western languages.[39] Yet Confucius understood modern individual rights, which he tacitly criticized. He understood modern individual rights pursued in litigation: "I can try a lawsuit as well as other men,
but surely the great thing is to bring it about that there be no going to the
law."[40] He substituted for rights consciousness a strong sense of duty. "He
who demands much from himself and little from others will avoid resentment."[41] Resentment marks people who demand little of themselves and much
of their superiors, proclaiming that their superiors have not respected their
rights. They are envious of superiors. By daring to criticize their superiors,
they betray an overweening ambition to replace them. Yet when inferiors
yearn to be superiors, superiors have already failed in superiority of virtue.
When superiors are truly virtuous, "he who does not occupy the office does
not discuss its policy."[42] Traditional China recognizes no human right to freedom of discussion and reply. The state that admits such a freedom would
admit its own inadmissible fallibility.

Confucius, believing in a sage king, sees no need for democracy:

> When good government prevails in the Empire, civil ordinances and pu-
> nitive expeditions issue from the Emperor. When good government fails
> in the Empire, civil ordinance and punitive expeditions issue from the
> nobles [warlords]. . . . And when there is good government the people
> do not even discuss it."[43]

Cosmopolitan discussion in the West supposes a right of anyone to discuss
anything. This is not a right to have dialogue partners made available against
their will, but is a right, limited by the existing technology, to publicize one's
views as broadly as is consistent with a similar right of others, and to discuss
with any who wish to reply. For Confucius, democratic public discussion of
policy defined by such a human right is second best, a compensation for failed
government. Yet Confucius concedes a possible case for democracy and resis-
tance to authority if government by virtuous example fails: "The wise man is
intelligently, not blindly loyal."[44] "He upon whom a moral duty devolves
should not give way even to his Master."[45]

The right to contribute as a partner in discussion, conceived as the basic
human right, conflicts with the Confucian ideal of virtuous monarchy, but is
compatible with the recognition that a sage king is an unattained ideal. The
ideal of discussion is not foreign to China. Mao Tse Tung called upon a hundred flowers to blossom, and we know of the age of the Hundred Schools in
Chinese philosophy, though it ended in the preeminence of one school, Confucianism. Human rights in China will require Chinese recollection of native
non-Confucian ideals of discussion.

Discussion exhibits a surface conflict of protagonists, but is a form of
cooperation. China's discovery of contemporary human rights from its own

sources would require more than the Confucian ideal of humanity (*jen*). It would require comfort with cooperation by way of surface conflict. It would require that China rid itself of nostalgia for an unfailingly virtuous, wise leader. If we remain within the still widespread Confucianism of China, friendship alone is non-patriarchal among five essential Confucian social relations (subject/king, son/father, wife/husband, younger brother/older brother, friendship). Friendship is the one potentially universal relationship of the five, though Confucius, unlike Mo Ti (fifth century BC), viewed it as a selective response to persons with whom one stands in special relationships, not primarily as universal. Virtue begins in filial respect for one's father, not all fathers.

The duties of universal friendship express native Chinese appreciation of ancient human rights. The Confucian ideal of equal educational opportunity is a basis for contemporary human rights once education is not just state-sponsored. Inequality between superior and inferior persons in wisdom pertaining to one question is consistent with equality as friends. Dialogue itself establishes in what domain a person is superior or inferior. Competition does not express an unfortunate disharmony reflecting a failed model emperor. Even if we recognize the ideal of a sage- or philosopher-king, once we can find none the second-best ethics of discussion replaces that of silence in the face of a king.

Official China, like Confucius, does not easily accept an ideal of free discussion, although the Chinese already approach that ideal in domestic and international scientific exchanges, in universities, in international negotiations, and in discussion by players in the market economy. Still, traditional China has something to give to the West, not just something to take. Independently of the justifiability of individual human rights, we can distinguish between a society that lives primarily in the consciousness of rights, such as the West, and one that lives chiefly with a consciousness of duties, such as China. China may help the West to a duty-based ethics of respect for human rights superior to modern Western rights-based theories of human rights:

> For the early Confucians there can be no me in isolation, to be considered abstractly. "I" am the totality of roles I live in relation to specific others. . . . A fuller account of the early Confucian ethical alternative to rights-based moralities. . . can be of direct and immediate relevance to the many issues, which currently divide the members of our own culture.[46]

The justification of individual human rights is not a justification of uninterrupted rights consciousness. A society exhibiting such consciousness without interruption, as has been the case much of the time in France, exhibits more litigation, grievances, and antagonism than a society that comes to rest in duty consciousness, in a grounding of individual rights from the standpoint of those who respect them, not from that of the right-holder. We hold rights *against* others. Rights consciousness, uncorrected by duty consciousness, views others as posing threats of encroachment.[47] Duties are duties *toward* others, breeding solidarity. Contemporary human rights presuppose a conscious duty to inquire. If others protect the rights of the individual voluntarily through their consciousness of self-imposed duty, the individual need no longer so vociferously defend his or her rights. In the face of globalization, China is facing a threat to its ancient duty consciousness. Globalization emerges from applications of science, which derive from rights to freedom of thought and action. If globalization brought to China an open society based on an interest in truth underlying the interest in profit, and if China's traditional duty consciousness were to adopt this new interest, China could develop a strong contemporary human rights culture.

China's steady duty consciousness makes it difficult for it to appreciate modern Western rights consciousness, but such rights consciousness is flawed. A more justifiable concept of human rights relegates rights consciousness to a secondary role and is consistent with over-arching duty-consciousness. No imperious modern right to have freedom respected justifies the duty to respect it. The self-imposed duty to seek truth justifies respect for the liberties of others. Despite doubt in the West that China understands human rights, we may hope that Chinese influence might someday attenuate unbridled rights consciousness in the West, and so contribute to a deeper understanding in the West of its own cherished right to free discussion:

> [Modern] human rights, such as we know them in the West, are not easily understood by the Chinese. It is first necessary to underscore the greatness of Confucius's teaching, and especially the depth and ardor of the Chinese people's attachment to his teaching. . . . His great humanism was in part spoiled by misogyny, by a very acute sense of hierarchy . . . . What is perhaps even more important is that he was rigorously opposed to a regime of law. For him law is too inhuman to procure a realm of true order; only morality could keep the people on the straight path (see *Analects* 2, 3). A human being has the moral duty to be good, and thus to love his neighbor (*ibid.* 12, 22; 1, 5–6). This distrust of laws and law in general has penetrated the Chinese soul deeply, to the point where intellectuals today, even those taken with democracy, have difficulty in accepting the concept of "human rights." Human beings have duties to their neighbors. What "rights" can they claim? Many thousands of years of Confucian thought have nourished this attitude, which reflects the finally distant relations between the State and the subject in traditional China. It is not the attitude of people who live without individual liberty. Over against the modern State, the Chinese will surely learn to claim their "rights"; we may bet they will not forget the duties to others learned from Confucius.[48]

The above passage too easily assumes that human rights aim merely at defending individuals against the state. Our neighbors, not merely the state, violate our rights, and when they do the laws are an asset, enforcing moral duty when conscience alone fails. Still, the author clearly sees rights respected by a ready sense of duty as preferable to rights respected by an insistent defense of one's own rights necessitated by an absent sense of duty on the part of others. Rights that we have to defend every time someone violates them have no solid basis.

What blocks a Confucian embrace of human rights based on Popper or Habermas is not duty consciousness but the nature of the duty. Confucian duty is not one of public inquiry and dissent but of deference to the dignity of all, to respect for tacit ancient human rights. Etiquette (*li*) blocks the competition of ideas. Politeness upholds traditional community, smoothing rough edges. Rulers and ruled have a right to dignity in the community, but the right is unspoken because the Chinese have respected it with less need for people to expressly claim it. Since some rulers in other traditional cultures, in Islam and Africa, also deny free thought despite complaint among the ruled, universal rights centering on freedom of thought are a moral ideal, but do not yet exist.

9. The Interaction of Rights Consciousness and Duty Consciousness in Human Rights Ethics

Human rights ethics, unlike Confucianism, operates under the sway of a duty to respect the individual right to competitive freedom of thought and action. Such competition requires the periodic return of individual rights consciousness. We can justify the return of individual rights consciousness by a duty to oneself to pursue truth. Consciousness of that duty by the requirements of that very duty yields at times to rights consciousness. Acting out of moral duty may mean losing ourselves for a while in the competitive fray, returning to duty consciousness only to correct distortions of rationally motivated discussion. The mark of a badly governed state is not, as Confucius held, that its subjects dare discuss policy. The etiquette of discussion, protected by the contemporary state, is one of openness, encouragement, and solicitude, even in the discussion of policy. The etiquette is the ethics of what Americans call "diversity."

In large impersonal societies, individuals steeped in duty consciousness often lack a sufficient knowledge of others and their claims to guarantee protection of their rights even when they would wish them protected. However conscientious individuals are, they are often unconscious of the secondary consequences of actions. The undercurrent of continuous duty consciousness is compatible with periodic justified eruptions of rights consciousness. Yet a significant difference exists between the rights consciousness of individuals who must arouse a non-existent sense of duty and that of individuals who can call on a pre-established sense of duty in others.

10. A Non-Elitist View of Universal Dialogue

Elitists privilege the pursuit of significant truth, of which they claim to be competent judges, over lower truth significant to others. Butterfly catching may be most significant to butterfly catchers. Yet the only truth whose pursuit is alone objectively commendable is truth without qualification all truth, including truth about better mousetraps or making jam. We maximally justify privileging truths initially significant to only some only if we concur, in a rationally motivated consensus of the universal audience, that those truths are indeed more significant. Then, contrary to any elitism infringing on human rights, the supposed truth about the greater importance of medical knowledge compared to knowledge of chess will enjoy recognition by an egalitarian consensus of all inquirers.

A group's belief that its truths are more crucial is not by itself elitist. To validate that belief, we need a consensus that extends beyond the members of any specialized elite, and that supports the belief that the truths in which some specialized elite is expert are more crucial. Any elite validated in this way is an egalitarian elite if it respects the equal right of non-specialized discussants to decide which authoritative judges to follow. Such vindication of a circle of authoritative experts invalidates bad elitism by the very method of vindication, since an egalitarian universal consensus is needed to vindicate an elite. If a universal consensus supports the target belief that medical knowledge is crucial, the medical profession's belief in its crucial nature may be non-elitist.

Creation of a universal audience requires a reduction of the distortions of rationally motivated discussion due to unequal distributions of social, economic, and political power. We all have an ideal right of access to discussion of issues that affect us—to consult a maximum of voices. A redistribution of resources to those who are the worst off by being the least audible is a resource in discussion, "[W]hile human rights are presumed to be universal, the important test for particular societies lies in their treatment of the worst off."[49] Those facing less deprivation need less assistance to become active in discussion, which makes for bargains in the creation of new discussion partners. If the worst off at times deserve to be intimidated into silence, we ought not to decide so *a priori* by the initial conditions of dialogue. We can only decide by the outcome of discussion itself.

Two

NATURAL RIGHTS, HUMAN RIGHTS

1. Three Motives for Respecting Human Rights

"Natural rights" mean different things. I will stress the relation to human rights of Thomas Hobbes' idea of "natural rights," of rights to do whatever a person cannot help doing by the laws of human behavior. Human rights gain enforcement by human beings rather than by impersonal causal law.

Compassion moves many to respect for universal rights. Identification with the suffering of others, leading us to feel their suffering, removes some obstacles to respect for human and animal rights, such as hunger, disease, and poverty. Yet compassion is consistent with an unjust distribution of its works because it relies on chance encounters with sufferers. Moreover, compassion only motivates relief from suffering, which is insufficient for human rights. This is apparent whether we consider ancient, modern, or contemporary rights. The reasons for creating human rights apply even in the case of those who do not suffer, who may also have basic rights violated. A child's right to education can suffer violation without any complaint from the victim.

The motive for respecting ancient human rights was a desire for *fellowship with all rational beings*. The motive for respecting modern human rights was the *desire to live one's life in peace*, free of encroachment. Advocates of modern human rights viewed such rights as evident, from which they inferred duties. The motive for respecting contemporary human rights is the *recruitment of possible dialogue partners* from all quarters. The universal duty to be open to discussion is more nearly evident than individual rights, rights that we only infer. Contemporary rights are non-theological, though theological justification in a restricted community can combine with a non-theological justification of universal dialogical rights.

A wish for *fellowship* with all rational beings, a motive for respecting unspoken rights, arose in antiquity. Empedocles, asserting an ascendancy of love over strife and the idea of transmigration, felt a duty to cultivate community with all kindred spirits in nature, even animals. These feelings became overt in vegetarianism, but not in a movement for political or social change.

Another motive for respecting human rights, a desire for *perpetual peace* through universal *tolerance*, is associated with rights-based non-theological natural and human rights theories. The chief motive in the Preamble to the United Nations Charter is peace, minimally by mutual tolerance. Live and let live. Yet tolerance can slide into mutual *indifference, isolation*, and *non-intervention* in the suffering of others. Peace as co-existence then dispenses with the fellow feeling of ancient human rights. The contemporary motive, *collaboration in dialogue*, arises from non-theological duty-based human rights. This motive grounds the human rights ethics discussed in these chapters. The duty to respect others for our own possible instruction is more evident than their moral right to freedom of choice.

2. Theological vs. Non-Theological Justification of Rights

We distinguish human rights theories by the type of justification of such rights. Some justifications suppose the validity of a particular *doctrine*, theological or otherwise. Some hold that persons merit respect for their divine nature, or for exhibiting an image of God or divine presence in human beings. "I am endeavoring to see God through service of humanity, for I know that God is neither in heaven, nor down below, but in every one."[1] Validation of such a doctrine by unrestricted public inquiry presupposes a prior human right to freedom of thought supposing no particular doctrine. In advancing theological human rights, a non-theological *background human right* emerges. This background right is my main concern. Any fully justifiable doctrine is justifiable before the universal audience that legislates the canons of its own operation, not merely before adherents of a particular doctrine.

Justification of rights to a faith community may reinforce secular justification before a universal audience, but never subtract from it. Christian morality commands selfless love of all to avoid sin. Suppose that love is help, and that help begins only by counseling others by their standard, not by that of those who help. Then to love them is to respect freedom of choice. A person who lives in Christ—in whom we find neither Gentile nor Jew, neither male nor female—will seek to empower others spontaneously, without the language of rights and duties. If that person falls from grace, help then becomes a duty and others may appeal to duty-bound Christians with imperious human rights. We do not exclude such Christian argument for rights. Yet validation before a restricted audience is insufficient if not all are Christians but are expected to respect rights. Not all local theologies support human rights. Islamic scholars say Medina verses of the Koran support them less than Mecca verses. Faith-bound justifications need to accompany justifications addressed to all. Human rights ethics is a universal ethical minimum.

3. Rights-Based vs. Duty-based Human Rights Theories

Rights are *duty-based* when others have rights *because* we more evidently have duties to respect those rights. They are *rights-based*, based in rights consciousness, when we have duties *because* others more evidently have rights. Modern human rights are rights-based, while contemporary human rights are duty-based. China's potential contribution to human rights in this century is to recall the priority of duty consciousness over rights consciousness. A society exhibiting rights consciousness falls into more litigation, strikes, grievances, and antagonism than one based in a duty consciousness that grounds but limits rights. The justification of individual human rights supposes a self-imposed *duty to oneself* to justify belief by adopting a *duty to others* to respect their right of reply. "The true source of rights is duties. If we discharge all our duties, rights will not be hard to seek. If leaving our duties unperformed we run after rights, they will escape us like a will-o'-the-wisp."[2]

4. Three Meanings of "Natural Rights"

Many have confused human rights and natural rights. "Natural rights" pass as a quaint way of referring to human rights. Thomas Hobbes "based sovereignty on natural rights (today called human rights)."[3] Gregory Vlastos expresses himself similarly.[4] But the concept of "natural rights" is confused. Talk of universal "natural rights" fails to recognize that rights enjoy recognition of their validity and enforcement only by convention, not by natural law.

Yet we may salvage something useful from Hobbes's idea of natural rights enforced by natural laws of motivation. He holds that we have a natural right to self-defense. The fact to which he refers, under a false description, is the fact that we have a *natural inability not to defend ourselves*. Generally, if nature enforces natural rights, they are not rights. If a merely local convention enforces them, they are not universal rights. If the action to which we have a right is unjustifiable, a right exists without being a moral right. We can interpret "natural rights" alternatively in Sophoclean, Aristotelian or Hobbesian ways. Yet, in every case, they turn out *either* not to be rights, *or* not to be universal rights, *or* not to be moral rights:

(1) *Non-Artificial Rights*. "Natural" can mean non-artificial. Natural rights are pre-legal, predating written law. They are natural because the state, a relatively recent artificial institution, does not enforce them. Instead, natural institutions like the family understood as customary practice from time immemorial enforce natural rights. Children have a non-artificial right to parental care, and a brother fallen in battle has such a right to a burial.[5] Yet family institutions vary, so non-artificial rights are not universal. Further, why is a right commendable by virtue of not being artificial? A father's right to sacrifice daughters has also been a non-artificial age-old custom. This concept of natural rights cannot establish universal moral theory.

(2) *Species Nature Rights*. A second concept of natural rights has its source in an Aristotelian view of human nature. We have a natural right to do what actualizes the potential of our species nature. Neither the Stoics nor their predecessors used "right" as a noun, although it appears in the Justinian codes and Magna Carta. Marsilius of Padua and William of Ockham are among the first philosophers to speak of "rights."[6] Yet Aristotelians conceive certain actions as morally permissible in realizing the potential of our species. Such actions, without human nature necessitating them, actualize its purpose. We may call such rights *species nature rights*. Birds have a right to fly.

Yet why should actions realizing a person's species nature be moral? Do sharks have a moral right to bite, and germs to kill, because to do so realizes their potential? *Discussion is good because discussion is the best way for finite minds to pursue truth, not because discussion is natural to any species, even to ours.* Discussion works best by being functional with respect to the possession of truth over error. If discussion is best, it is also best for cats, not because cats ought to do what they cannot do, but because it would be best if they could do it. Discussion would be best for us even if we were only capable of feline behavior, or of reciprocal genocide. If we recognized that discussion is good but that we are less capable of it than another species, we ought to admire such a species. Yet if its discussion cannot regulate our choices, we should still value human discussion with all its limitations.

Even if our natural species potentials are good in themselves (not merely because they belong to us), no right to realize them exists if someone does not claim such a right and if recognition of that claim does not exist in some society. A slave's right to be free in a slave society, due to the slave's human species nature, may be only a desirable universal claim that we ought to recognize as universally valid. A species-essence natural right would then be merely a potential human right.

(3) *Involuntarily Enforced Rights.* In a third sense common in the modern world, natural laws enforce "natural rights." Such laws imply the natural inability to do otherwise than what you have a "natural right" to do. You cannot do otherwise than to try to get your next breath, so, in a manner of speaking you have a natural right to seek to do so. Laws of behavior make exercise of the right inevitable. Our nature protects the right because by our nature we can do nothing but exercise it. The shark may have no moral right to bite, but it has a moral right to seek to bite. Given its physiology, it can do nothing else. We must manage our proximity to sharks.

Such natural rights do not imply determinism. We cannot help but seek food, but that does not mean that we cannot help all that we do. If we are determined to seek food because we cannot help seeking it, we are not determined to eat bread and not rice. A natural right may exist to seek to die; biologically there comes a time when we cannot do otherwise. Most are not yet in a position to claim a right to seek to die, but the one who is dying, and who claims a natural right to die, may enjoy such a right.

Natural rights in this third sense we contrast to *voluntarily enforced rights*, not to artificial rights. Individual conscience, custom and the state—not causal laws--enforce voluntarily enforced rights. To use custom and the state to preserve the life of a person who has claimed a natural right to seek to die may not prevent exercise of the right, but only hassle the right-holder, and at most to get the right-holder to exercise that right differently.

We have an involuntarily enforced natural right to seek to defend ourselves. Yet we cannot do so merely in general. The general involuntary right is a natural right to defend ourselves in one or another particular way. Which way depends on the situation, without being specified by the general right. Yet if free will does not exist and our situation pushes us into a corner that allows us only one way of defending ourselves, we have a natural right to defend ourselves in that way, even if it is uncivil. If free will does exist, we exercise a *natural liberty*, not just a natural right, to choose between alternative ways of exercising a more general natural right. Operating within an involuntarily enforced natural right to seek food, we are at liberty to choose bread or rice.

Determining what laws of behavior hold we best leave to natural and social scientists, not to Hobbes or any philosopher. Natural rights are not, like human rights, presuppositions of public inquiry found by reflection on such inquiry. A natural right exists to seek food. A hunger strike is a food-seeking behavior in the form of a delay. In all situations, we have a natural right to act in any way required by natural law. Note that a Hobbesian theory of inalienable natural rights allows for an *alienable natural right* to do what we cannot avoid doing in a *transient situation*. Exercise of an alienable natural right can be a way of exercising the inalienable right. A natural right is alienable when the right is inalienable only in a transitory state. Pursuing security by attacking others is inalienable in the state of nature, but alienable in civil society.

5. Involuntarily Enforced Natural Rights and International Terrorism

Exercise of an involuntarily enforced natural right is permissible because the right-holders can only do what they implicitly claim a right to do. Yet an involuntarily enforced natural right to do what we cannot help doing in any given situation is troublesome. Does a license to commit genocide and not take moral responsibility exist if the genocidal party cannot help itself? The United Nations holds that genocide violates a moral law known to all (Preamble, 1948 Universal Declaration). That genocide should be permissible and not subject to international human rights law seems abominable—even if members of an ethnic group reach a point where they cannot do otherwise and no one can fault them.

Suppose a *causal law* according to which an ethnic group that intermingles with a smaller but growing second group, and that perceives the second group to be a potentially overpowering threat to the first, will attempt genocide unless an external power (for example, international law) intervenes. Perhaps more plausibly, suppose that some other law holds by which genocide will regularly occur as a result of given conditions. Such a law might hold even if determinism is false, since free will might decide what kind of genocide occurs, not that it occurs. The first group is not morally responsible, since genocide occurs inevitably given the antecedent conditions. Yet the world community may lead members of the first ethnic group to *take* responsibility even when they are not responsible.

If genocide in general resulted from free will, how could a terrorist be any more responsible than in a deterministic universe? If a specific act is an incompletely determined choice, an act of free will, the act is also incompletely undetermined *by* the terrorist. Any substantial self that can harbor either of two contradictory choices is insufficient to cause either choice and cannot be fully responsible for either choice. Richard Taylor writes:

> An agent, which is a substance and not an event, can nevertheless be the cause of an event. Indeed, if he is a free agent then he can . . . cause an event to occur—namely, some act of his own—without anything else causing him to do so.[7]

Yet such a substantial self is not a sufficient cause of its act, since the same self could have acted otherwise. It follows that this self is not wholly responsible for its act. Members of an ethnic group accepting responsibility for atrocities may feel guilt. Objectively they may not be fully guilty, even if making them feel guilty is justifiable. Individuals often take responsibility for actions for which they are not objectively responsible. Do-gooders take responsibility for the ills of the world. We require judgment to tell when doing so expands a narrow self-identity rather than crushing a weak ego. Better than human rights tribunals that try individual members of the ethnic group is subjection of the whole group to international human rights law. If genocide becomes inevitable in a situation, the solution is to change the situation, leaving behind a state of nature in which ethnic groups are sovereign.

The dire consequences of holding someone who has committed atrocities blameless due to involuntarily enforced natural law need not follow. We should try, capture, and convict the individual, but justification of the punishment need not suppose moral responsibility. Our future rehabilitation, or the deterrent effect on violators of the rights, justifies our assumption of the terrorist's responsibility. In civil cases, individuals take responsibility without holding that they are responsible. Unintended damages are regrettable. In criminal cases of terrorism, we try, even without succeeding, to bring terrorists to feel horrified for intending what we hope they will later see as evil. Ultimately, we ought to eradicate situations in which any individual acquires a natural right to commit terrorism.

6. Involuntarily Enforced Natural Right and Voluntarily Enforced Human Rights

Thus we should not join Antigone in advocating natural rights as non-artificial customary rights. Some customs are evil. Nor should we defend natural rights as rights of our species nature: the moral permissibility of realizing our nature is an open question. Instead, morally tolerable natural rights are rights whose involuntary exercise the laws of behavior enforce, as Hobbes understood.

If human rights are voluntarily enforced conditions of the possibility of maximum justification by discussion, they are not Hobbesian natural rights. Human rights both limit and extend morally permissible expressions of natural rights. They are no mere reformulation of natural rights. Since we cannot violate natural rights, human law does not need to enforce them. Human rights do not demand respect for every exercise of every natural right. Respect for a person's human rights channels the exercise of natural rights in morally desirable ways, promoting respect for dialogical human rights. For example, contrast a *natural right to strive for health* with a *human right to health*. The human right would block one way of exercising the natural right to seek health, namely, *illness*. Illness is a failed pursuit of health. A human right to health extends exercise of the natural right to unprecedented levels of health.

The Universal Declaration does not declare involuntarily exercised natural rights. A declaration of natural rights might promote tolerance of their inevitable exercise. According to the Stoics and Descartes, we have a natural right to exercise thought. As long as we remain conscious, we exercise this faculty and cannot eliminate it. Human persons who are more than just human organisms, who are awake but cannot think, are an impossibility controverting natural law. We should put our will in conformity with natural law and not try to bend the natural order to our will. No natural right exists to act any way we want without being disturbed, but only to do whatever we cannot help doing.

The Helsinki Accords, stressing opening lines of communication in the Soviet bloc, reinforced the dialogical role of human rights.[8] Action "realizes" the exercise of such rights as a morally optimal selection from among available ways of exercising natural rights. "[S]tates should encourage popular participation in all spheres as an important factor in the development," and "in the full realization of all human rights."[9]

"I may ascribe a predicate to an object if and only if every other person who *could* enter into a dialogue with me *would* ascribe the same predicate to the same object [Jürgen Habermas]."[10] Yet this can be true only if "every other person who *could* enter a dialogue with me" is rights-protected. Maximal justification of my belief requires that everyone concerned by the issue can reply to my invitation to enter into dialogue with me by exercising freedom of thought, and that all *do* ascribe the same predicate to the object. What I would win thereby is a universal rational consensus that the belief, even if not objectively true, has become a *target belief* for all who inquire further.

Universal public service rights, public works rights and welfare rights may make it possible to consult as wide an audience as possible. Moral rights depend on reason, not on vagaries of compassion. Countless persons cannot instruct us because they do not enjoy rights. Environmental or inborn inequalities do not justify further rewards for those who are already fortunate; rationally and morally, they call for resources to amplify the voices of those currently inaudible discussion partners. We justify human rights from our perspective as inquirers who respect rights as sources of our possible enlightenment, not from the perspective of those who claim them.

We owe the exercise of a human right to no one. Refraining from exercising a right to marry, for example, is not blameworthy. The exercise of such a right answers an invitation extended by all to select from a list of actions necessarily or contingently empowering discussion. The invitation is sincere insofar as those whom we invite are free of preventable forces blocking or imposing the invited actions. Only a self-imposed obligation imposes the obligation to exercise a human right.

If human rights exist, they are always at risk. Only involuntarily enforced natural rights are inalienable. Laws of behavior enforce the Hobbesian natural right to pursue security. "The right of nature, which writers commonly call *jus naturale*, is the liberty which each man hath, to use his own power, as he will himself, for the preservation of his own nature; that is to say, of his own life. . . ."[11] If, in suicide, one pursues survival unsuccessfully, failure of the pursuit is the pursuit itself in another form. We do not blame a tiger for its stripes, or a bird for trying to fly, and we perhaps ought not to blame all who seek shelter in winter for breaking into our house. We may not like it, but we forgive agents acting by inescapable laws of behavior.

"Natural rights" exist. They are permissions to pursue satisfactions when the pursuits cannot be avoided according to the laws of behavior of the species. Since we do not enforce natural rights, which only natural law enforces, a natural right disappears only by the disappearance of the right-holder. Yet we can, consistent with the natural right, enforce the non-permissibility of some ways in which we exercise the right, so long as we allow other ways. So long as the right-holder survives, non-respect of *all* exercises of a natural right only obstructs its exercise but does not cancel it. A person who breaks into a home to escape the cold is possibly excercising a natural right.

Toleration of inescapable pursuits does not always enable dialogical rationality. Let us take a natural right to be prejudiced in favor of our own case, or to pursue revenge. This leads to no human right. We may understand seeking revenge, but we cannot approve its success in a context of inquiry and human rights. What we approve is seeking revenge only in a situation that represses its success. We voluntarily institute a human right to neutral courts, as John Locke saw, to obstruct, not cancel, the pursuit of revenge.

7. Discussion vs. Conversation

A dialogical right to freedom of thought ideally includes the freedom to be a dialogue partner with anyone. It might someday even be a freedom to discuss with *everyone* if we included passive participation in universal consensus formation. Not objecting to a public target theory, we acquiesce in it. Modern human rights were compatible with mutual non-intervention and indifference.

They needed no lines of communication connecting all. Contemporary human rights require the internet, email, fax machines, travel, books, and mail.

Concern with truth in defining human rights may seem to fall under what Richard Rorty criticizes as a human rights foundationalism stemming from an Enlightenment faith in reason, on an assumption that we can progress toward objective truth.[12] Yet even to argue against this assumption is to suppose one objective truth, the point at issue. The dialogical pursuit of truth is one concept of the good life. Conversation conceived by Rorty is another.[13] He abandons the pursuit of objective truth to keep the great conversation of humankind going by the rhetoric of edifying, even dazzling disruptions of consensus. Unlike discussion, conversation works toward no universal consensus on truth. Discussion partners do not seek to keep discussion going at all costs. They aim at closure.

Habermas is close to Charles Sanders Peirce. The arrival of a new rational consensus is a step closer to objective truth, the object of a chimerical final consensus: "[A]ny man, if he have sufficient experience and reason enough about it, will be led to the one true conclusion. . . . [S]cientific investigation has had the most wonderful triumphs in the way of settling opinion."[14] Only dialogue leads us toward this conclusion. "Different minds set out with the most antagonistic views, but the progress of investigation carries them by a force outside themselves to one and the same conclusion. . . ."[15] Only rights-protected inquiry guarantees the rationality of its conclusion.

We cannot climb outside our consensus to compare the facts with it in order to see if they mirror each other. Yet, not content with mutual contradiction, we search for rational consensus, presupposing a non-contradictory fact of the matter. Inquiry cannot prove this presupposition of public inquiry. Without an anchor in presupposed consistent facts, discussion is provocative unending conversation producing solutions that provisionally work for different people. Peirce is not explicit that individuals fated to agree by reason and experience must enjoy human rights. Yet these rights are as much a presupposition of inquiry as objective fact. They do not merely reflect "sentimental stories" leading to empathy with sufferers across ethnic boundaries. We need to *convince* those who do not empathize that they should do so.[16]

8. United Nations Preferred Human Rights

Exercise of a human right to legally acquire or sell property is a way of exercising a natural right to seek to possess what we wish. The exercise of human rights remains an option. All may have human rights that only some exercise. Those who never practice homosexuality may have a human right to do so. If we opt to exercise freedom of thought at all, exercise of a right to property is not optional. Not placing our will in some property, we remain unrecognizable by others. A right to marry is a right whose exercise is optional. We have shaped a natural right to pursue sexual gratification into the civil right to marry. Yet ought there be a human right to seek gratification outside marriage? The Declaration neither affirms nor denies such a right. It affirms the human right to marry not as a duty, but only as a right (Article Sixteen). An implied right exists to opt for the non-exercise of the right. The natural right to seek gratification still exists, but we manage it in a different way.

The Declaration may fail to cite a right to divorce because in many nations the right to marry includes that right. If it featured a right to divorce instead of to marry, it might help break up an age-old institution of civilization. The Declaration promotes marriage by an explicit right, leaving incidental rights unspoken. As the modern view of rights gives way to the more contemporary view, to declare a right is to invite, not just tolerate, its exercise. The Declaration presents no exhaustive list of rights. Being selective, it promotes a way of life. It commends secondary rights that condition exercise of a primary right to participate in dialogical rationality through "the free development" of "personality" (Article Twenty-Two) endowed with "reason" (Article One) and able to "receive and impart information (Article Nineteen)."

The right to "housing," which is more than shelter, applies the primary right to sedentary populations (Article Twenty-Five). Australian aborigines or Central African pigmies have only a *counterfactual right* to housing. Selection of a right to housing, if taken literally, favors a non-universal sedentary way of life. Where the right to housing depends on a condition that does not universally obtain, the right to medical care depends on the universal human condition of being subject to illness. (The primary right is itself hypothetical, depending on a hypothetical ability to put forth a claim: we have a right to freedom of thought *if* we claim it, but not everyone may claim it, at least not always. Someone in an irreversible coma cannot, but someone else may claim it on behalf of the stricken individual.)

We may foolishly exercise a right to marry, to express opinion, or any other human right, in a way that does not empower inquiry. A human right is an opportunity but no guarantee of the development of one's personality (Article Twenty-Two). Exercising all rights in the Universal Declaration while being unexemplary in creative dialogue is possible. One who enjoys all human rights may be a complacent, spoiled non-achiever. Unlike such persons, who may take human rights for granted, those individuals who have achieved the most in the arts and sciences have not enjoyed a full range of human rights, and have struggled to gain recognition and respect for even some. Basing ourselves on the Declaration (the numbers in parentheses refer to articles in the Declaration), let us describe an individual merely insofar as she or he enjoys human rights. Suppose a human rights heaven in which everyone fits the following description of Ms. X. (Or Mr. X, abstracting from gender, sexual orientation, nationality, race, age, or other factors irrelevant to this person's humanity—Articles One-Two).

Ms. X is secure in the knowledge that others will not take her life, and she lives with a sense of being secure from attack (Article Three). She is confident she runs no risk of being in bondage or forced servitude to anyone else (Article Four). She is also confident that others will treat her respectfully, and that any punishments she receives will be fair and not cruel; she knows that no one will try to torture her without facing the most serious penalties (Article Five). She lives in a state where the laws recognize and protect her as a person with equal basic rights and obligations, and without discrimination based on factors irrelevant to her humanity (Articles Six-Seven). If others ever violate her human rights, she is sure that courts of the state in which she is a citizen will support her (Article Eight). She knows that the police will never come knocking to take her away without any reason. She falls asleep at night sure that she will never be forced to leave her country without just cause (Article Nine). If the state charges her with a crime, she is confident of a fair trial (Article Ten). She knows that others will presume her innocent until proven guilty, and that no punishments not on the books at the time of the crime will apply to her (Article Eleven). She feels secure that no one will invade her privacy and that no one will feel free to attack her honor and reputation maliciously (Article Twelve). She is sure that no one will stop her from traveling from one part of her country to another, and that she can leave her country without anyone preventing her from returning (Article Thirteen).

She knows that if her country were to persecute her for political reasons she would be able to seek refuge in another country (Article Fourteen). She has a nationality, but knows that no one could stop her from changing it (Article Fifteen). She may not marry, but she knows no one would stop her from doing so if she decided on marriage with a consenting adult (Article Sixteen). Someone might well rob her, but she is confident that the law would be hot on the thief's trail (Article Seventeen). No belief exists that others would prevent her from expressing (Articles Eighteen–Nineteen). Joining an association or attending a public meeting would not land her in trouble with anyone as long as the association does not oppose fundamental rights (Article Twenty).

She, like other adults in her country, enjoys one vote in determining who governs, and she knows that even she could be President (Article Twenty-One). Experience tells her that no discrimination will prevent her from obtaining a government job. She is appreciative of the social security and public services necessary to support creative interchanges with others (Article Twenty-Two, Twenty-Five). She is sure of a job or of unemployment benefits if she has no job. No discrimination exists to deny her a job for which she is qualified, or to deny her the wage that another equally qualified worker would earn. No matter what her job, she is confident of a minimal living standard consistent with human dignity. Even if she does not belong to a trade union, she knows that she could have recourse to one if needed (Article Twenty-Three). She counts on not only fair pay for her job, but also on adequate rest and leisure time, including holidays (Article Twenty-Four). She has had free school education. If she needs higher education, she knows that she can get it based on merit (Article Twenty-Six). She never feels excluded from enjoying what artistic, cultural, and scientific life has to offer (including the benefits of new technology), and if she were to contribute to this life she knows she would benefit from income for her contribution (Article Twenty-Seven). She is secure in the knowledge of all these things, in part, because she knows that no wars will arise to disrupt her life plans.

If you are envious of Ms. X, you are envious because she enjoys respect for human rights and you do not. If you are resentful, you are resentful because, assuming the above description is complete, she wastes the rights for which many far more creative human beings still struggle. She may leave her rights, like the right to vote of a non-voter, unexercised. For that very reason, she may be on the verge of losing them. Even when she exercises her rights, Ms. X may lead a dull life. She may accomplish little, though she cannot blame the rest of us. A world filled with people like Ms. X is all that universal morality can assure. The exercise of human rights at most assures public achievements of civilization like marriage and democracy, not the realization of sublime goals of truth and beauty. Are these achievements sufficient or necessary for exercise of the basic right of dialogue seen in the exchange of transcendent achievements between the great men and women of history, such as the dialogue which Aristotle instigated between himself and Plato, or which Einstein created between himself and Newton prior to a new consensus in physics?

Aristotle and Einstein lived in a world in which human rights did not exist. It was impossible to address the universal audience. Yet we believe that *more* Aristotles and Einsteins would have existed if human rights always existed, rights that some people—maybe famished children who never had a chance to go to school—never achieve because of deprivation. How many Aristotles and Einsteins have gone undiscovered? We do not protect human rights because of the hidden or manifest genius of every person, but because all have a role to play as we sift through humanity to discover talent. If you do not enjoy human rights, we cannot be sure that you lack talent.

A person's human rights are justifiable even if that person does not use them in superior achievement. We discover most preferred human rights in the victim's consciousness of their violation, in the the victim's awareness of being victimized. If we allow some to suffer oppression, no one's rights, even those of the most talented, are secure. We would like to uncover a complete list of human rights from social science research into universal ways of enabling persons to exercise dialogical rationality.

Three

NATURAL LAW-BASED HUMAN RIGHTS THEORIES

The last chapter distinguished three candidates for "natural rights": non-artificial Sophoclean rights based on family duty, Aristotelian species nature rights, and Hobbesian rights to do what we cannot help doing. Beyond natural rights, we now distinguish three concepts of "human rights." (1) Ancient theological human rights came from a supposed universal duty to live in community with all other rational beings. This view alleges that reason is a theological excellence in human beings regardless of what they do or could do, and regardless of their station in life. (2) Modern human rights are certain rights to do successfully what we cannot prevent ourselves from seeking to do by natural law. Human rights would then be rights to the successful exercise of Hobbesian natural rights, but only if we could assume such rights to be approximately and for the most part a universal convention.

(3) Contemporary human rights differ. They divorce human rights from natural law and theology. They suppose a universal self-assigned duty to secure conditions of dialogue for participation by all. They suppose no divine excellence in human nature. They offer no prospect for happy fulfillment of natural potential for its own sake. They imply no presumption in favor of satisfying natural strivings as such. The one link with nature is that fulfillment of the above self-assigned duty must be empirically and technically possible.

1. Duty Consciousness and Rights Consciousness

To some a human rights ethics based on duty consciousness can have only limited success because it cannot resolve conflicts between human rights.[1] Yet conflicts between types of rights, if not between holders of one right, is resolved if we recognize only one human duty grounding one basic right. The one duty recognized by Jürgen Habermas, Chaïm Perelman, Karl Popper, and Charles Sanders Peirce is to realize and preserve the ideal dialogue situation. The one right is the equal right to available support as one participates in that situation. Instead of the duty stemming from a self-evident right as in modern rights theory, we derive the right from a more nearly manifest duty.[2]

Jeremy Bentham and Auguste Comte cite an anarchical, ultra-individualistic facet of modern human rights. I am an island unto myself. I am most conscious of my rights against others when they exercise their rights against me. I exercise my right to defend what is mine in competition with your right to defend what is yours. The exercise of individual rights out of

37

mere consciousness of one's own rights exacerbates conflict. Yet if you are conscious of owing what you are to family or country, a duty of gratitude for their collaboration arises, and you cease to claim anything as the product of solely your labor. Duties to others then supersede rights against others.

Duty consciousness need not be a gnawing consciousness of unfulfilled duty. Empedocles fulfilled a duty of fellow feeling with the beasts by vegetarianism. In Confucianism, duty consciousness is a consciousness of bestowing, not just owing, blessings out of gratitude for blessings received. Duty consciousness, based on indebtedness, becomes a consciousness of a fulfilled duty to benefactors. This concept is the ancient one of rights as unspoken. Contemporary human rights are similar yet different. We respect them out of duty, viewing even our present rationality as a gift from merely potential interlocutors. Yet some interpersonal conflict and rights consciousness are present even in duty consciousness. Those accepting dialogical duties to us may not know all that our rights require, so rights consciousness still plays a subsidiary role.

2. Duty-Based Rights: Ancient and Contemporary

Ancient duty-based human rights advocates respected an implicit right of kindred rational beings to be treated with dignity.[3] "For all things were tame and gentle to man, both beasts and birds, and friendly feelings were kindled everywhere."[4] Reason was not an effective power of reply as in contemporary human rights, but was an inborn divine excellence that slaves could display even with no power of reply.

The right to realize the natural potential of our species, cited in the last chapter as an Aristotelian idea of natural moral rights, assumes that our potential is good. Our rational faculty is even divine, so Aristotelian "natural rights" turn out to be theological, based on human nature and its affinity with God. The task posed by such natural rights is to exercise this faculty successfully, not just to pursue its exercise. For nature assures no respect for it. Hobbesian natural laws of behavior enforce the pursuit of self-defense, but do not enforce success. Similarly, if a "natural right" exists to actualize reason, observance of it depends on something non-natural: recognition and respect by others. The right assumes natural faculties, but is not "natural," since recognition of its validity and observance of it depend on convention.

Aristotle never spoke of "human rights." Yet rights consciousness for Aristotelians can begin to eclipse duty consciousness if the duty to help another actualize herself is no longer evident but depends on her discovery of a potential she had never suspected. Rights consciousness begins to supersede duty consciousness when her rights become epistemologically prior as rights claimed upon such self-discovery. Yet if only the gods, not human beings generally, know the science of human potential, we cannot speak of "human rights," which exist through human recognition.

Contemporary non-theological, duty-based human rights depend on a self-imposed duty to seek truth through discussion open to participation by all. They are empowered by global economic, scientific, and moral institutions. Not everyone commits to the search for justification as the highest standard, and so human rights, though justifiable, are not justified to everyone. Contemporary duty-based human rights do not restore the beautiful ancient idea of a human duty to respect human dignity, with its divine excellence in quiet contemplative fellowship with all rational beings. Nor do they imply an Aristotelian duty to nurture the realization of such excellence in others. The contemporary duty is one of relentless investigation, social reconstruction, and active recruitment of dialogue partners drawn from all quarters. This duty has a material basis in contemporary civil society.

3. From Modern Natural Law to Human Rights Ethics

Intervening between ancient human rights based on a theological excellence of reason and of contemporary human rights are modern human rights. Modern Hobbesian natural law engenders modern human rights contracted to ensure the successful exercise of "natural rights." (Scare quotes, as explained, mean that what we refer to are not literally rights with conventional enforcement.) An inalienable self-evident "natural right" to seek property conditions a possible human right to unimpeded ownership as a successful completion of the quest. "Government is instituted to guarantee to man the enjoyment of his inalienable natural rights."[5] The right imposes the duty, not the duty the right.

The revolutionary National Assembly in Paris decided against basing "natural rights" on duty.[6] Self-evident "natural rights" grounded the irksome duty of others to refrain from encroachment. Natural and human rights defended the tolerance of individual belief from state interference. Today the problem is to find a creative way for people from different cultures to live in community. Diversity is something in which multiculturalists, without necessarily admitting relativism, today take pleasure.[7] The cause upheld by modern human rights was non-intervention in private lives or in the internal affairs of states. Today the cause of human rights continues even if we achieve tolerance and mutual non-intervention. We no longer merely endure diversity with shows of tolerance.

The Universal Declaration stresses peace as the purpose of human rights (Preamble, Paragraph 1). Yet if we attain peace, do we need any further realization of human rights? The Preamble proceeds to say that a world in which human beings have freedom of belief and speech by way of freedom from terror and poverty is the highest human aspiration. This aspiration continues unfulfilled if only peace is present. Tolerance is consistent with indifference toward others so long as they, too, refrain from encroaching. Human rights ethics arises from a freely embraced obligation to promote others in the exercise of freedom of thought, and of rights to subsistence and security as its two principal modes.

We cannot realize the right to freedom of thought if some interfere with the right to eat. If food fuels thought, we respect a right to real freedom of thought only when we are ready, if need be, to provide food. Since libertarians deny this, let us not be dogmatic. Let us compromise by making the right to food a contingent human right dependent on empirical research into the relation between thinking and eating. The universal freedom of thought needed for the full justification of anything is the only human right not requiring empirical social science and biological research.

Contemporary human rights ethics restores duty consciousness, which modern human rights had overturned. Self-evidence attaches more to the dialogically driven duty to respect rights than to the rights themselves. The duty to pursue truth is unfilled if we assert it without insistence on the universal right to witness and offer testimony. The United Nations Declaration of 1986 on the Right to Development calls for not only the "observance" of rights but also their "realization" or exercise. The Declaration promotes "free, active, and meaningful participation" by all in economic, social, cultural, and political developmental processes.

Yet human rights are not an invitation that you cannot refuse. Even the right to eat is not a universal moral obligation. Starvation or more generally the refusal to dialogue may be a statement. The right not to be enslaved is optional even if the alternative to enslavement is death. Human rights belong to a menu of what may promote dialogue. Each person responds to the invitation by exercising a selection of rights. The gift of freedom of thought and action is weighty, but the credibility of dialogue requires that it impose no obligation to use the freedom. Contemporary rights assume the positive value for inquiry of diverse freely adopted and practically enacted beliefs.

4. Theological and Non-Theological Human Rights Theories

Rights were first tacit. Yet Alasdair MacIntyre is misleading when he says, "there is no expression in any ancient or medieval language correctly translated by 'right' before 1400."[8] "Right" as a noun translates terms in the Justinian codes and the Magna Carta. Yet an idea does not require a dedicated term. Karl Popper traces the concept to the Periclean age.[9] So does Jacques Maritain.[10] Sophocles, Empedocles, the Cynics, Antisthenes, Diogenes, the Stoic Zeno of Critium, Cicero, Marcus Aurelius, Saint Thomas Aquinas, and John Locke upheld theological human rights theories. Some of these theories take the form of pagan panentheism based on the all-embracing divinity of Nature. Elsewhere they presuppose a creationism by which human beings, without being divine, exist in the divine image. In either case, they assert a *de jure* human right to respect in virtue of a *de facto* theological excellence of human nature. The right is "natural" only because we justify it by human nature, but not by what humans do or ought to do. A person has a right to life because human life embodies divine reason. Yet no human rights declarations circulated in the ancient Greek world.

A problem with theological human rights is that they are culture-bound, impeding universal recognition. If rights have non-procedural presuppositions, we would have to vindicate these presuppositions before the court of human reason to justify the rights. We would then have to justify theological rights by non-sectarian argumentation presupposing non-theological dialogical human rights. Yet rational theological and non-theological universal rights can co-exist. Theological rights depend on particular arguments, while public discussion presupposes dialogical rights.

We find non-theological "natural rights," with possible human rights supporting their successful exercise, in Thomas Hobbes, Hugo Grotius, and Samuel von Puffendorf. Unlike Hobbes, Grotius had a duty-based theory of "natural rights." The American and French Revolutions invoked rights-based non-theological "natural rights," though remnants of theology appear in revolutionary texts. Though modern natural and human rights theories divorce themselves from theology, their advocates need not be agnostic or atheist. They simply do not rely on natural or revealed theology in developing rights theories addressed to those of different faiths. Modern natural law theorists made non-procedural assumptions, but they were non-theological. They appealed to natural laws of behavior to establish "natural rights" like the right to pursue security. Grotius asserted a natural duty to pursue sociability.

5. Three Theological Human Rights Theories:
Sophocles, Cicero, Locke

Sophocles (496-406 BC). In the last chapter, we spoke of Sophoclean non-artificial "natural rights." A non-artificial right to life turned out not to be universal, since there was no duty to respect it in some natural family institutions. We now point to Sophoclean human rights. Beings are obliged to be rational if they are to live in accordance with their nature. Since Nature is intelligible and rational, to conform to our human nature is also to conform to Nature. Since Nature is divine, to conform to it is to partake of divinity. Nature shows intelligible natural law, and includes rational beings who can grasp it. Human nature thus leads us to conform to Nature, to the cosmos of which we are thinking microcosms. It also leads to fellowship with other microcosmic rational beings, and such fellowship assigns to each a right to dignity.

A right is a claim socially recognized to be valid. Since recognition depends on convention, "natural rights" are strictly impossible. Yet when we speak of "natural rights," we may mean something else: some inability of the species to act otherwise (Hobbes), or an ideal conventional right based on an optimistic view of human nature as embodying reason. A "natural right" may not be an actual right, but may be an ideal right that, by an ultimate standard of rationality whose adoption is inherent in human nature, we ought to universally claim and recognize as legitimate.

If human beings cannot help seeking fellowship with other rational beings, our fellows have an ideal human right to dignity, though perhaps not an actual one. Human beings, being rational, cannot help seeking to understand natural law and conforming to it, and cannot help sharing community with others who seek the same. If this ancient impetus to human rights had prevailed, human rights would have arisen of a very different sort from contemporary human rights. Our fellows would have a right to dignity because of their striving to internalize natural law in general, not because of their possibly precise replies to our precise questions.

A possibility exists of respecting a human right to be treated with dignity without recognizing a universal right to individualistic freedom of thought and choice. In China, individuals enjoy polite treatment without enjoying a right to freedom to dissent. In the Athenian abolitionist movement, fellowship with all others as miniature replicas of a rational universe was a form of universal citizenship. It implied a theologically based "natural right" to the freedom of being a thinking being. Yet it was not a universal right to freedom of criticism:

> All of you who are here present I reckon to be kinsmen and friends and fellow citizens, by nature and not by law; for by nature like is akin to like, whereas law is the tyrant of mankind, and often compels us to do many things which are against nature.[11]

The duty to live harmoniously with Nature is a duty to oneself, a condition of personal virtue. Respect for the rights of others included in this harmony requires nothing beyond this personal virtue. The rights of others go unmentioned and no single name for rights exists in the ancient world. Karl Popper says the open society began in Athens. "Our Western civilization originated with the Greeks. They were, it appears, the first to make the step from tribalism to humanitarianism."[12] He meant Sophocles, Antisthenes, and associates of Pericles like Herodotus. He also cites Protagoras and Democritus.[13] We find theologically based natural rights theory in Empedocles, who belonged to an Ionian mystery cult.[14] But Athens was not a Popperian open society. As Socrates' trial showed, criticism still came at a price. Universal human dignity came more from each human being mirroring and striving to reflect the cosmos. It did not come from the possible relevance of one's replies to another's questions.

Jacques Maritain cites Sophocles as a source of "natural rights" theory due to his distinction between natural and artificial conventional law in *Antigone*.[15] More significantly, he is a source of the ancient concept of human rights. His natural law was theological. The law of Zeus is higher than that of

Creon, divine justice higher than human law. Natural law is unwritten and unshakable. By this law, not just Polyneices, but also any human being, as a microcosm of natural law, has a tacit human right to the dignity of burial. In the particular situation of the tragedy, a sister brings the right to respect, but if there were no sister to do so, there would be a background duty of someone else to do so. Yet the noun "right" never appears in *Antigone*. What is explicit is that Antigone has a non-artificial natural duty.

Cicero (106-43 BC). Human rights were also tacit in Stoic natural law theory. We trace the contrast between convention and nature through the Cynics and Antisthenes back to Socrates. Non-theological natural law is that of a species, not of Nature as a whole. No one can help seeking to live in accordance with one's species nature, though conflicts inherent in the human species nature may impose choices between equally natural ways of life. A tacit and largely ideal right arose—ideally recognized and enforced by one's fellows—to exercise faculties we cannot help seeking to exercise. Living according to Nature meant, to Cynics and Stoics, not living as slaves. An ideal right existed to pursue freedom and equality as a rational being in a universal city. A human right to succeed in this pursuit ought, if possible, to exist.

The Stoics were under the sway of duty consciousness, with human rights remaining implicit. Cicero wrote a book on duties, none on rights. His question was: "What ought we to do?" The answer: we ought to live in accordance with our nature by conforming to Nature, and ought to love fellow rational beings who accept the same duty.[16] The ideal right to be loved remains tacit. We cannot extinguish the pursuit of conformity to natural law, but the pursuit may not go on to fruition. The law of the species or cosmos is subject to temporary violation. Such law differs in this respect from the law of gravity. We fail to live in accordance with our nature by pursuing mere pleasure and obstructing the rational tendency of the species. Yet, although success in the quest for a rational life may suffer interruption, the quest continues. No one can violate the natural law by which we pursue rationality. We may consciously seek immortality even though by natural law we are born to die. By our animal nature, we seek death ever more closely even as we seek to avoid it by our affinity with the gods. Reflection on failure in opposing natural law brings us acceptance of it:

> All things intertwine with one another in a holy bond. . . . Have you ever seen a dismembered hand? Such does man, so far as he can, make of himself when he refuses to accept what befalls. . . . You are cast out of the unity of nature. . . . But here is this beautiful provision, that it is in your power to re-enter the unity. No other part of the whole doth god privilege, when severed and dismembered, to reunite.[17]

Though Cicero retained the ancient view that Nature is divine, he is at a transition point between the ancient human rights ethics of quiet fellowship and an anticipation of contemporary human rights ethics. He cited a duty of universal beneficence. The Stoic passivity of accepting what we cannot change begins to pass into the active doing of things we can actually do. Duty began to be our contemporary duty to treat others as possible dialogue partners. Reason and language unite us all. To be beneficent is to assist humans in their inquiries: by reason we learn, teach, communicate, and discuss.[18] A universal society with slaves is imperfect. Yet, acting justly toward them, we pay fair wages, which is a step toward emancipation, creating property owners. We bring the polis closer to the cosmopolis. A duty to assist all in inquiry implies a universal right to be considered in the distribution of assistance, though perhaps in diminishing degrees as others become more remote.[19]

Utilitarian beneficence may be imperfect, since others may not have an equal right to one's beneficence.[20] Yet, if beneficence is not just the utilitarian promotion of well-being and reduction of suffering but is a duty to create and address the cosmopolitan audience, Cicero suggests that beneficence is a perfect duty aimed at realizing contemporary human rights. I ought to empower as many as possible to "learn, teach, communicate, and discuss," and I will then be the beneficiary of my beneficence. Contemporary human rights would actualize the Stoic ideal of human rights for all potential dialogue partners. Contemporary human rights would also perpetuate a form of ethical egoism, not the ethical egoism of seeking self-interest to the exclusion of the self-interest of others, but an *inclusive* ethical egoism based on the ego's inclusive self-identification with the cosmopolis.

John Locke (1632-1704). Lockeans, like other social contract theorists invoking natural law, distinguish civil and natural freedom, human and natural rights. Natural rights do not negate human rights. We could create human rights contractually, like citizen rights in a single state, only by a global contract. Natural rights would in part justify human rights. Contemporary human rights secure the success of pursuits inseparable from a person's nature. While a person has a "natural right" to seek to breathe and an inability not to do so, a human right to clean air is justifiable if dialogical inquiry requires clean air.

Natural law is evident to natural reason. Locke says natural law is natural reason.[21] Different species follow different natural laws. The law of human nature points to an inalienable natural right to pursue life, liberty, health, and property, insofar as assets leave resources for others. These rights exist in nature and are not lost in civil society. Yet one natural right is lost in society, the right to judge in our own case when others obstruct basic natural rights to the pursuit of life, liberty, health, and property.

An exercise of natural rights is morally permissible if nothing else is possible. Laws of human motivation enforce such rights. Natural rights are self-evident to natural reason if we merely "consult it."[22] All natural rights, except the right to try to be a judge in our own case, we protect better in civil society than in nature.[23] Individuals form states to secure such satisfaction.[24]

Some do not recognize that Locke had a theological theory of natural rights, and of humanly constructed rights assuring the success of inescapable human pursuits. Jack Donnelly holds that reason is primary for Locke, and that Locke calls on faith merely to confirm it.[25] However, the theological underpinning of moral rights for Locke is not window-dressing. Theology is necessary to the vindication of human rights. Only the assumption that natural law and rights are good, as part of God's creation, assures us that they are moral rights, and not just rights that we must tolerate.

The *Second Treatise* cites equality as support for human rights in a theological context, since the empirical warrant for equality is unclear. Theism is part of the case for human rights, though in the *Second Treatise* he assumes theism more than he argues for it. He defends equality theistically:

> [M]en being all the workmanship of one omnipotent and infinitely wise Maker . . . are His property, whose workmanship they are . . . ; and being furnished with like faculties, sharing all in one common nature, there cannot be supposed any such subordination among us, that may authorize us to destroy one another, as if we were made for one another's uses.[26]

The reason we should all consult is "the common rule and measure God hath given to mankind."[27]

Lacking instinctive survival skills, our nature is to labor. God, laboring in creation, created us in his image. Locke retains theological natural rights while rejecting the ancient and medieval primacy of duty over rights. As with William of Ockham, rights consciousness emerges from a victim's perspective. A natural right to be acquisitive and a humanly constructed right to products of labor shine most brightly in being violated, allowing a human right to revolution to restore the tranquil exercise of the natural right.

6. Saint Thomas, Hobbes, and Grotius:
Three Concepts of Non-Theological Natural Rights

Saint Thomas Aquinas (1225-1274). If an inability to act otherwise is a "natural right," our comments on Locke raise a difficulty in using non-theological natural law to prove natural rights as moral rights. The shark may exercise a natural right to bite, but if it could survive by not biting it would lack a moral right to bite. We may not blame compulsive murderers for their compulsion, but if prisons exist to prevent them they have no tolerable moral right to kill.

Saint Thomas asserts natural law by which mothers care for the young. That rats have a natural right to spread disease is more ominous. A universal moral right to actualize potentials of all species assumes divine providence harmonizing the happiness of different species, which returns us to theological natural rights. Yet the universality of reason independent of faith makes it possible for the theist, too, to conceive non-theological natural rights.

Saint Thomas used Stoic distinctions between *natural law, international law of nations,* and *civil law,* while adding eternal *divine law.* Holding natural law to be independent of theology, he did not follow Cicero in associating it with the divine law of Nature. We establish natural law non-theologically by noting universal human behavior. The essential equality of human beings we know by natural reason, by discovering, for example, universal human acquisitiveness. A natural right to be acquisitive exists if by natural law a person cannot be otherwise. This discovery may lead to a human right to own property. The human right is justifiable because it assures care for property more than communism, though reasonable exceptions would exist, as with someone who has lost his or her sanity and intends harm if property is returned.[28]

Thomas's claim of natural human equality is more Stoic than Aristotelian. Yet God for him is not Nature, but is supernatural. Beyond the natural law basis for equality, he suggests theologically-based human rights: in a division of divinely ordained human labor, some lead and others follow, but all are on the same plane. Kings are not *above* others as righteous Augustinian masters. God himself leads only to serve.[29] The divine image becomes one of service or Christ more than of the Father, and this points to a theologically-based right to the help of others. Still, he supposes that slavery is admissible where masters serve to punish the sins of slaves.[30] He does not say this on a philosophical basis, since sin violates only divine law. Natural reason cannot justify slavery. By our species essence, each is an end in him- or herself, not a natural tool of others. Thomas rejected Aristotle's justification of slavery by observed inequalities, e.g., between Greeks and barbarians. But observation without theological certainty is a fallible basis for establishing equality.

Human rights ethics asserts equality as a heuristic claim, not as an empirical one. Out of deference to our rationality, we ought to assume that each person's ability to discuss and enlighten, on some topic, by example or word, is equal to that of every other person's. We ought to make this assumption even in the case of a person who has failed to instruct or enlighten. In not fully known ways, individuals make unequal contributions on different issues. We do not know problems we will someday pose. Reducing anyone to his or her past record and entirely disconnecting with him or her is unfruitful.

Most duties imply unspoken if not spoken rights. A duty to rule respects the right of the governed to government for the common good. Thomas recognized a natural right to resist tyranny, since "tyrannical law, through not being according to reason . . . is a perversion of the law,"[31] aiming at the good of the tyrant, not of the people. An adult people has a right to defend itself in war against foreign aggression, and one people has a right to assist another in resisting internal or external aggression. If aggression is wrong against your land, it is wrong against others. Thomas anticipates humanitarian intervention.

A just war is wont to be described as one that avenges wrongs, when a nation or state has to be punished, for refusing to make amends for the wrongs inflicted by its subjects, or to restore what it has seized unjustly.[32]

Thomas Hobbes (1588-1679). We ought to leave one another in peace in the pursuit of survival and security, for the pursuit is inescapable. The case for a "natural right" to actualize essential potentials of all species presupposes, we have noted, divine providence harmonizing potentials between species. Yet no theological presupposition is present in a "natural right" merely to *seek* survival or happiness. Universal laws of motivation enforce such "rights." An unavoidable right to pursue security and a right to its *successful* exercise are distinct. Natural rights do not enforce their successful exercise. No naturally enforced "right" exists to the enjoyment of security. This fact points to possible conventionally enforced *human rights* to the successful exercise of "natural rights." Hobbes held that we can protect the successful exercise of rights deriving from passion by a social contract founding the state. This suggests a distinction between natural rights to do what we in any case will do and human rights requiring human protection.

State protection of a general right to successfully exercise a "natural right" to seek security represses the exercise of certain natural rights successfully exercised by some in the state of nature. The "natural right" to pursue security exists in the state of nature, which frustrates its successful exercise by all. Its successful exercise by all is protected by a state.[33] Some successfully exercise a "natural right" to pursue their interests by stealing and killing in nature, though the state represses this exercise. A state shows a preference for a human-made right of all to the successful exercise of the "natural right" to seek security over the same natural right in a war of all against all.

Hobbes held that, in nature, everyone rightfully pursued his or her own self-defense, but successful exercise of the right suffered from the exercise of the same right by others. Attack is sometimes the best defense:

> In all places [in the state of nature], where men have lived by small families, to rob and spoil one another, has been a trade, and so far from being reputed against the law of nature, that the greater spoils that they gained, the greater was their honor.[34]

We have a "natural right" to act if by nature we cannot do otherwise. "A law of nature . . . is . . . a general rule, found out by reason, by which a man is forbidden to do that, which is destructive of his life, or taketh away the means of preserving the same."[35] We cannot pursue insecurity, so we ought not. A natural right "is the liberty each man hath, to use his power, as he will himself, for the preservation of his own nature; that is to say, of his own life."[36] The state of nature allows us to rob, but the state bans this exercise of the right to pursue security. The right to pursue security in *general* is an inalienable "natural right," while the right to pursue it by robbing is the same "natural right" in a particular situation. A *particular* right implementing an inalienable natural right in one situation is an "alienable natural right." The right to steal is in general alienable, but is *inalienable* in the state of nature.

The state of nature is a predatory state from which the fear of death drives us away. Hobbes allows unsuccessfully exercised "natural rights." Since our "natural right" is to pursue self-preservation, not a right to self-preservation, no one in the state of nature violates the right if the pursuit is unsuccessful. Yet we exercise the natural right to seek safety by actions permissible not only by our general nature but also in our particular state. How we pursue our general right depends on the lawful or lawless state in which we live. A "natural right" to pillage exists if pillaging is the only means to security, but it ceases to be just if forbidden by a state. The state, making the pursuit of security without pillaging possible, cancels any moral right to pillage.

No one strictly has a "right" to a pursuit if the right needs no human enforcement, if we cannot evade the pursuit. If nothing can prevent us from seeking survival, no right to seek it exists. Inviolable rights are not rights. Bodies have no right to follow the law of gravity. Others can threaten your life but not your right to pursue survival. Exercise of a true "right" is at the right-holder's option. We use scare quotes in referring to "natural rights." Nature protects a "natural right," so it is not really a right. Others can torment us, but cannot prevent us from defending ourselves short of taking our lives.

No inalienable natural right exists to do *anything* merely because it is a pursuit of self-defense if the state commands gentler ways of pursuing self-defense. Yet human-made rights in Hobbes's state are not human rights if the state is not global. To have a human right today is to be able, with the complicity of all, to do something our nature does not necessitate, for example, to enjoy, and not just seek, fresh air. Even if the natural right to pursue security were strictly a right, if it were our sole natural right such rights would be meager. We would have no natural right to life, let alone to property, political participation, public works, welfare, fresh air, or freedom of thought.

Some actions falling under "natural rights" in nature, like the right to a preemptive strike against neighbors, cease after the social contract. A foreign policy premised on preemptive strikes models international relations on the Hobbesian war of all against all. Following Hobbes's argument, consciously or unconsciously, such a foreign policy models current international relations as a prelude to world government formed by a global social contract.

The successful general exercise of "natural rights" defines the sole positive rights that the sovereign protects. A new range of actions by which we exercise a natural right to self-preservation, actions the state of nature represses, emerges in the state. The range of neo-Hobbesian human-made rights can grow by making new rights depend on the right to security:

For the laws of nature, as *justice, equity, modesty, mercy*, and, in sum, *doing to others, as we would be done to*, of themselves, without the terror of some power, to cause them to be observed, are contrary to our natural passions, that carry us to partiality, pride, revenge, and the like.[37]

The right to security by any means possible is born of unavoidable human passion. The obligation to treat others justly is a genteel way of exercising the same right under the law. A right to mercy and equity are the new means of pursuing self-preservation in a state. Under a sovereign's threat, we successfully exercise the right to pursue security only by behaving justly.

Two stages appear in a developing "natural right" to pursue self-preservation: a passion-based pursuit by whatever means in nature, and a gentle pursuit under the law. We exercise a "natural right" to pursue survival involuntarily, but nature does not guarantee its civilized exercise. We can only try to defend ourselves, and in nature we have a right to do so unjustly: justice as known only in a state can never win in nature, but can win in a state as a way of avoiding legal punishment. A Hobbesian basis for contemporary human rights ethics is possible. But we now look at an alternative basis given by Grotius, whose logic still allows a return to Hobbesian methods in emergencies.

Hugo Grotius (1583-1645). Grotius was a non-theological natural law theorist like Hobbes, but he inferred natural rights from natural social duties. He denied the dependence of natural law on the divine will. Without denying God's existence, he held that God could alter nothing in natural law.[38] Even if God did not exist, natural law would follow from human nature. If God has created human nature, natural law bears the imprint of divinity. Yet we can develop natural law theory without even raising the question.

For Hobbes, inescapable, natural selfishness led to a right to be selfish that no one could reasonably deny. For Grotius, rights belonging to all others could not, consistent with our social nature, fail to be recognized. Natural law is the dictate of reason that shows whether an act is rightful, depending on whether it accords with our rational nature.[39] Our rational nature is at once social.[40] As rational social animals, we follow natural law by free choice. Bees follow the social law of their species with neither understanding nor consent. We are free to violate our natural sociability. Yet this sociability means that we ought not to take what is not ours, so that a natural right not to be robbed follows from the natural obligation. Natural law also creates an obligation to return property to owners, keep promises, and compensate for injuries.

Since self-interest is also a human motive, and since conflicts between self-interest and sociability arise, we may also steal by free will. We might expect Grotius to admit a law of natural human selfishness alongside the law of natural sociability, but he does not. After warning against "being led astray" by fear, pleasure or "rash impulse," he says that whatever is contrary to "well tempered judgment" is contrary to "the law of nature, that is, to the nature of men."[41] Others can encounter disrespect for their rights traceable to our natural sociability, though the natural law of our social impulse is inviolable. For Hobbes nature always "enforces" the right to pursue self-interest. For Grotius nature "enforces" a duty to respect rights, not actual respect. In both cases, what nature enforces is a propensity, though Grotius also recognizes a contrary propensity. A person may claim rights out of selfishness, but he or she wins respect only if the sociability of others outweighs their selfishness.

Grotius, like the Stoics, distinguished involuntary natural law based on human nature, the voluntary law of peoples based on customs of civilized nations, and voluntary domestic civil law. Though the laws of civilized nations derive largely from the natural law known by philosophers, we more easily discern natural law indirectly from the laws of civilized peoples. Legislated civil law, if just, applies natural law to particular conditions.

Natural law has no utilitarian justification for us. If following natural law is justified by consequences, this is due to God who created nature to reward those who follow natural law without their regard to consequences. Sociability preserves society. Yet we cannot deduce the utility of following natural law without introducing theology. Since sociability is a part of human nature that we do not legislate, for us it is simply an end in itself.

Like Hobbes, Grotius held states to exist by convention, not by nature. An obligation to a state comes from the natural social obligation to keep promises made in concrete situations. A promise of political loyalty based on consent commits us to the civil law of our country. As the consent creates domestic law, so the consent of states creates the law of peoples. Once we have made promises, we obligate ourselves to do what we promise regardless of the results, though we can consider consequences in deciding whether to promise. States may commit to particular international laws out of concern for the common or national welfare. Natural sociability promotes the common welfare. We act according to natural sociability in calculating the utility of humanly made laws for welfare, even if we do not deliberate upon the utility of sociability. We leave such deliberation to God, if God exists.

The purpose of just war is to punish a private or public party for violating natural law. Grotius classifies types of war. Wars between states are *public* wars. Between urban gangs, we have *private* wars. A civil war between a state and a rebellious private body desirous of state power is a *mixed* war. The state has a monopoly over public punishment. Only public state punishment can resolve private war. Civil wars, too, ought to end in public punishment, either in punishment of the guilty rebellious party or of the unjust state that provoked rebellion.

War is just if one state exercises a natural right of self-defense following from another state's violation of its natural duty not to injure. War is unworthy of human nature, a way of settling disputes more appropriate to brutes. Yet we ought to mitigate the evil of war, so long as it exists, by an internationally agreed upon law of peoples. International law should codify permissible wars. War always suffers from a rational prejudice against it, but may be legitimate if conducted to defend natural rights. International law helps protect the natural rights of individuals and conventional rights of states, rights that, due to free will, natural duty might not otherwise enforce.

Natural human sociality motivates international law. International law prohibits the sacking of cities, pollution of drinking waters, torture of prisoners, and poisonous arms. The taking of prisoners, conquest of territory, taking of hostages, private commerce with belligerent parties, reprisals, and the confiscation of enemy property fall under international and natural law. Given that nations do fight wars, some ways of fighting them agree with natural duties and rights more than others.

Natural law demands not any particular content of treaties, but procedures for determining such content. Natural law is determinable, not determinate, in its requirements. Most crucial is the natural right to have agreements kept. Natural duty binds us morally, not just legally, to our word. War can issue in peace because victors and vanquished are all human, subject to the same natural law of faithfulness, and because by natural law we may trust all who are subject to natural and international law.

Grotius holds we are sociable by nature. Others, appealing to our nature, have a "natural right" to our sociable behavior. They also would seem to have a right to have us behave meanly, and yet do not claim that right. Hobbes did not show that what follows from inescapable human nature is commendable, but that it is permissible or forgivable. Having selfish inclinations and acting on them is *permissible*. Grotius's sociable "human nature" is not inevitable, but it is *commendable*. We act commendably, not by acting inescapably from human nature, but by acting by what is highest in our nature, according to social inclinations, not as "beasts." This value judgment means that our right to commendable behavior by others (not to behavior we regret but tolerate) does not derive merely from matters of fact. It also means we can betray our social nature. Grotius's natural rights are less secure than Hobbes's.

Human rights enforcement by the United Nations follows Grotius by appealing to sociality, imploring states to keep promises, including promised respect for rights. Human rights ethics adds that we ought to respect, in the first place, a commitment to the public pursuit of truth. Yet Grotius's theory allows for Hobbesian enforcement if the appeal to sociality fails. As asocial international terror renders states insecure, the United Nations may evolve from non-interference in domestic affairs toward a sovereign agent of intervention, commandeering state contributions that states dare not refuse when palpably necessary for world security. Security conditions freedom of thought, and the social pursuit of truth is a gentle passion that states can help enforce. And so a Hobbesian contribution to human rights ethics is possible.

Four

PROCEDURAL HUMAN RIGHTS THEORIES

Human rights, unlike natural rights, arise from a procedure of making claims, and of struggling to win recognition and respect for those claims. Human rights ethics does not base rights on our species nature or laws of human behavior. Thomas Hobbes and Hugo Grotius provide usable methods for enforcing human rights, but their "natural rights" are not human rights as conventions justified by the requirements of justification itself. If rights are claims socially recognized as valid, they cannot be natural, but are historical constructions. Human rights ethics takes respect for such rights to follow from the cognitive point of new. We now examine selected moral philosophers to show that human rights ethics is not original, that it has precursors.

1. Herodotus

Herodotus (ca. 484-425 BC) was an early representative of the procedural view of human rights. He celebrated the Athenian democracy in his time. The advocacy of equal rights for all citizens to political participation does not exhaust human rights. Yet it implies the central right of self-mastery in dialogue. Democratic decisions come from discussion. Democracy is a training ground in discussion ethics. Thucydides has Pericles say:

> Here each individual is not only interested in his own affairs but in the affairs of the state. . . . We Athenians, in our own persons, take our decisions on policy or submit them to proper discussion. . . . [T]he worst thing is to rush into action before the consequences have been properly debated. . . . I declare that our city is an education to Greece, and I declare that . . . . each single one of our citizens . . . is able to show himself the rightful lord and owner of his person.[1]

In Herodotus's *Histories*, like Plato's dialogues, discussion unfolds without the pressure of democratic decision-making. A conversation Herodotus reports with a Persian shows that he viewed Greeks as only contingently superior. Nuances are present in Herodotus's critique of Persia. A king ruled Persia. Yet even Persians debated the virtues of democracy and aristocracy before deciding. Herodotus attributes the defense of democracy to a Persian, Otanes, so political rights can appeal to foreigners.[2] This international equality of dialogue partners makes Athens into a school for all humankind. Herodotus's *Histories* show a dialogical quest for truth with representatives of most known cultures of his time. If Otanes considered democracy, perhaps reflecting Persia's tribal roots, Herodotus had direct experience of democracy in Athens, the historical source of a worldwide human rights movement.

Herodotus praised the Athenian victories over Persia that inaugurated Western leadership in history as the story of freedom:

> Athens went from strength to strength and proved, if proof were needed, how noble a thing freedom is . . . . [S]o long as they [the Athenians] were held down by authority, they deliberately shirked their duty in the fields, as slaves shirk working for their masters, but when freedom was won, then every man amongst them was interested in his own cause.[3]. . . There is not so much gold in the world nor land so fair that we would take it for pay to join the company of the enemy and bring Greece into subjection.[4]

Yet the story of freedom was transnational. Speaking through Octane, who did not live in a free society, Herodotus says that in democracy "all questions are put up for open debate."[5] Slaves in Athens belonged to an ideal Athens of unrestricted dialogue that never came to fruition.

2. Democritus and Protagoras

The textual basis for including Democritus (460-370 BC) as a proponent of human rights rests on scant fragments: "Poverty under democracy is as much to be preferred to the so-called happiness under tyrants as freedom to slavery."[6] "Virtue is primarily respecting other men."[7] Such fragments show Democritus associating with the abolitionist movement Plato opposed. Democritus was drawn to Athens though still young and did not receive the recognition he expected.[8] As an atomist, Democritus rejected the gods, and did not view nature as divine. Natural law for him was universal causal necessity. Human law, based on convention, did not fall under natural law.

Protagoras (ca. 490-420 BC), belonging to the Great Generation that broke with aristocracy, may have agreed.[9] We might interpret him rationally as upholding unspoken human rights as presuppositions of reasonable discussion. One interpretation of his relativism is that the collective judgment of all, not just one person, is the measure of all things. A credible consensus making human beings collectively the measure requires respect for human rights in discussion. Universal agreement as the measure of things is agreement, not about what certainly is objectively true, but about the current target belief that discussants must get beyond if inquiry into objective truth is to continue. Einsteinian physics is by consensus a body of target beliefs, and Einsteinians invite us all to try our hand at target practice against it.

A credible agreement as to target beliefs supposes a human right to judge freely. The measure of all things is a test of what things are, but does not show what they are in themselves. A consensus can change, so no final test exists. What the current collective judgment of free persons holds to be objectively true will appear to be so. The idea of objective truth remains, but is unknowable by itself. No way of approaching it exists except finding a consensus of persons exercising a right to free inquiry. If no consensus regarding target beliefs exists concerning some issue, discussion aims to establish such beliefs.

3. Rousseau

The possibility of human rights by a contractual procedure between citizens becomes explicit in Jean-Jacques Rousseau (1712-1778). In John Locke's social contract individuals in civil society retain their natural self-wills directed to their respective interests. They retain the individual wills and "natural rights" enjoyed in the state of nature, but gain a human right to be less disturbed in their exercise.

In Rousseau's social contract, individuals capable of esteeming moral freedom abandon their diverse natural wills to identify with the general will of the state. Losing their "natural rights" (propensities), they are born again, and acquire more. In the state of nature, some have the natural wills of males, some of females, some of Africans, others of Caucasians, but we abstract as citizens from such natural differences. We contract a right as equal moral agents, self-determined by the rational will of our state. We get back our will as the general will, raised up and strengthened by union with the same will in others. The state is not a way to protect prior Afro-American rights or Muslim rights. Nor does it protect the greater or lesser product of labor. Like France, it replaces the unequal rights of rich and poor with the equal rights of citizens.

This announces the totalitarian side of Rousseau's state: even as black or white, a person is never more than a citizen. Women's rights dissolve into human rights, which belong to women as to everyone by the general will. Civil society outside the state does not exist. The problem is that people cannot so easily surrender natural and civil distinctions between them—their different histories and claims, and in that case the general will is fictitious. Some do not see how they get more in return by surrendering their particular will to a general will, or if they once thought they saw, they no longer do so.

By the social contract you agree to punishment should your selfish natural will return. Natural rights are alienable. Human rights do not depend on natural rights. Natural rights are inalienable only to the human animal, but human beings displace natural man. Reason supplants nature. In the state of nature as in the despotisms of history, we had a natural right to pursue property. After the social contract, we gained a human right to be freely self-determined through the state's determination of us, and to receive what private property the state recognizes should it choose not to be totalitarian.

Rousseau gives a systematic defense of institutionally constructed human rights independent of natural rights. The lost natural rights are the basic rights of Hobbes and Locke. Hobbes's or Locke's civil society protects a human right to property, allowing the natural right to pursue property in nature to flourish. For Rousseau, civil society is not a true state. It may protect particular human rights like property, but not the basic human right to rational freedom, to self-determination. The Hobbesian state is a despotic state in which the individual is subject to the alien will of the sovereign. The Lockean state is also alien. Locke is sufficiently suspicious of it that government is kept as limited as possible, even calling for a right to revolution.

Hobbesian and Lockean natural law survives as long as a psychology of individualism or exclusive egoism survives. Citizens of a true state leave such egoism behind and unite in the general will, gaining a right to democratic discussion in which everyone adopts, for the sake of argument, majority views. This right "is a right—a sacred right . . . as the basis of all other rights; *it does not . . . flow from force* [like despotic rights]. Yet it does not flow from nature, *either* [like the right to do what one must to survive]. It therefore rests upon agreements."[10]

This higher moral right, your human right, is not one of doing as you please. It comes from accepting determination solely by the general will to which you have consented. All agree with the majority, not because it is right, but because, in a state in which everyone's vote counts as one, the majority view is the one that we must refute if inquiry is not to be justifiably at an end.

The idea of target beliefs helps save the rational core of Rousseau's idea of citizens all rallying around majorities. Majority rights do not mean that individuals abdicate reason or bow to unintelligent majority votes. No tyranny of the majority exists. If in the Bible Belt the majority view is creationism, even atheists in public discussion need to grant creationism for the sake of argument, as an assumption facilitating inquiry rather than as an indisputable premise. Democratic discussion requires the acceptance of majority target beliefs over those of a self-designated elite. Some lead in finding a new majority view and others follow, but followers who consent are as necessary as leaders. Each citizen is reconciled with every other citizen. One target belief overturns another, which in free inquiry may be overturned again.

Can the elimination of conflict between majorities and minorities in favor of unanimous majorities be the aim of human rights? Rousseau allows short-term conflicts in assemblies prior to a binding majority vote creating a unanimous consensus. He prefers unanimous votes:

> The common good reveals itself plainly so that nobody with a little good sense can possibly fail to see it. *It offers, in a word, maximum guarantees against error on the part of the general will.* . . . The common interest, *in such a state* [in which the social bond has begun to wear thin] is clouded over, encounters opposition: votes cease to be unanimous."[11]

Unanimity is methodological in supporting the majority target belief, though some support it precisely as dissenters. Dissent occurs against a background unanimous agreement within the community as to how disagreement is to be resolved. Contracting individuals methodologically unite in adopting the majority view for the sake of argument. Not to do so is to unravel the community, the general will. Substantive agreement as to what beliefs are true may be more difficult than Rousseau supposed. Human rights enable universal participation in attempting to forge a rationally motivated universal consensus, so that the consensus, if established, becomes until further notice the best available criterion of truth.

Conflicting conjectures have a place in inquiry. If humankind is the measure of truth, when it does not speak with one voice, no measure exists. Discussion becomes necessary. An assumption of infallible majorities barring future discussion is hard to make, but Rousseaueans may not require it. Rousseauean majorities do not force a dissenting minority to abdicate to make a consensus universal. By the social contract, the minority has already agreed to side heuristically with the majority. The majority is always right only in that the path toward objective truth always passes through it.

Stoicism assigned natural rights because individuals bore a spark of divinity. Hobbes and Grotius based natural rights on human behavior, not theology. Procedural theories base human rights on what a universal will can rationally will. After Rousseau, we find proceduralism in positions as different as (1) Immanuel Kant's ethics based on universalizing maxims; (2) Georg Wilhelm Friedrich Hegel's method of obtaining mutual recognition in a rational state by salaried civil servants without particular interests stemming from occupations in civil society; (3) John Rawls's assumption of an original moral position by dropping a veil of ignorance over what we gain or lose in constitutional negotiations, attending only to our common humanity; and (4) Jürgen Habermas's grounding of human rights in universalizable interests that all accept procedurally in a dialogical quest for truth.

4. Kant

Contrary to Rousseau's view that we agree to punishment if we violate the general will, that our rational will consents to forcing our resurgent natural self to be free again, Immanuel Kant (1724-1804) excludes legal enforcement of the moral duty to respect persons in the *Critique of Practical Reason*. Legal protection of moral rights, putting fear in the minds of wrongdoers, blocks the rational motive of acting merely for duty's sake and not for consequences.

Moral *duty* impresses itself on the person who takes the moral viewpoint. From this viewpoint *ideal moral rights* are known indirectly as implied by duty. Moral duty is immediate from the moral viewpoint, while we infer moral rights. Because we ought to treat persons as ends, they have an ideal human right to act as ends in themselves that we ought if possible actualize.

That we ought not to treat persons *merely as means* is consistent, we know, with the permissibility of treating them as means. In exchanging products and services, we treat one another as means. We could never treat one another as ends unless we also treated one another as means. If we were in different worlds, each without exchange with the others, none could treat others as ends in themselves. The extension of moral relations between persons requires the rise of globalized economics and communications.

Kant came to see the role of non-moral institutions in promoting morality late. Reacting to the French Revolution, he modified his view that morality and legal institutions must be independent. He realized the possibility of promoting moral progress by domestic and international institutions protecting human rights and liberty through compelling respect. The *Metaphysics of Morals* (1797) commands legislators: "Act externally in such a manner that the free employment of your will may coexist with the freedom of everyone following a universal law" (Introduction). The principle gives moral content to the law. Universalization tests the morality of legislation. In heeding law we do not act from a moral motive, but if the laws are good we act in conformity with morality, a step toward acting out of morality.

Rousseau anticipated the French Revolution without predicting it. Kant was the first major philosopher to greet it despite reservations, to react to the beginning institutionalization of human rights in the modern world beyond philosophy. Morality was not the legal enforcement of human rights. Yet he saw emerging constitutional human rights as reflecting, in institutions and law, his concept of morality, of the right to be treated as an end.

In *Über den Gemeinspruch: Das mag in der Theorie richtig sein, taugt aber nicht für die Praxis* (1793), the first principle of civil society is a person's liberty as a human being. The principle is not legislated by the state, but is a moral principle by which we create a rational state. By the principle of liberty, we cannot force a person to be happy in a particular way. We have an ideal-moral right, protected from the moral point of view, to seek our own happiness. Paternal government, obliging subjects to seek happiness by another's idea, conflicts with autonomous persons assigning ends to themselves. For Kant, the ideal moral right to seek happiness by one's own idea is protected by the moral obligation of others.

In 1797, Kant adopted Rousseau's idea of the social contract and popular sovereignty, except that revolution came from above, from the duty of rulers, not from the rights consciousness of the people. Already in 1793, he wrote:

> [T]he legislator must issue his laws as being capable of emanating from the collective will of an entire people, and . . . must consider each subject, insofar as he the ruler wishes him to be a citizen, as if he had concurred by his vote in forming a will of this sort.[12]

Rulers act on behalf of subjects. Kant replaces discussion and majority votes with a monarch's consultation with himself and advisors. Revolution by the people errs by casting them as judges in their own case. Kant largely restricts "rights" to legal rights. When he mentions the "rights of man," he follows, but does not innovate, on usage. Yet his pre-Revolutionary essay "What is Enlightenment?" concerns an ideal moral right of adults to escape tutelage. As adults, we are each an end in ourselves by a moral right to assign an end to ourselves. Even members of unborn generations will be ends in themselves:

> An age cannot bind itself and ordain to put the succeeding one into a condition [such] that it cannot extend its (at best very occasional) knowledge, purify itself of errors, and progress in general enlightenment. That would be a crime against human nature.[13]

We comply with positive law from fear, we obey moral law by reason. Yet Kant saw a possibility of moralizing politics. The *Metaphysics of Morals* approves much of the French Declaration of the Rights of Man and the Citizen. Aspects of the Revolution that it rejects include recourse to violence.[14] It also rejects utilitarian justifications.[15] Moral legislation forbids utilitarian laws imposing ideas of happiness on others for their own good.[16] A mature person has a right to decide her future without imposition.[17] Kant believed that moral education could reduce intentional violation of the rights of man. Despite its deficiencies, Kant saw in the Revolution a surprising intersection of the external phenomenal and rational noumenal worlds:

> The Revolution of a gifted people which we have seen unfolding in our day may succeed or miscarry; it may be filled with misery and atrocities to the point that a sensible man, were he boldly to hope to execute it successfully the second time, would never resolve to make the same experiment at such cost—this revolution, I say, nonetheless finds in the hearts of all spectators (who are not engaged in this game themselves) a wishful participation that borders on enthusiasm, the very expression of which is fraught with danger; this sympathy, therefore, can have no other cause than a moral predisposition in the human race.[18] . . . [S]uch a phenomenon [as the Revolution] *is not to be forgotten,* because it has revealed a tendency and faculty in human nature for improvement such that no politician, affecting wisdom, might have conjured it out of the course of things hitherto existing, and one which nature and freedom alone, united in the human race in conformity with principles of right, could not . . . have promised. But insofar as time is concerned, it can promise this only indefinitely and as a contingent event.[19]

In *Perpetual Peace* (1795), Kant made the "rights of man"[20] depend on republican government with a separation between the executive and popular legislative powers.[21] All men are free, subject to the same laws, and equal as citizens.[22] Since the people suffer in war more than despots, republican governments favor peace. His position here is less paternalistic than the idea of revolution from above expressed later in the *Metaphysics of Morals.*

Grotius invoked natural rights to codify war into closer harmony with sociability. For Kant, the rights of man include a right to peace. War interrupts the best-laid life plans. Successful pursuit of self-assigned goals requires peace. The customary law of nations, authorizing war, is not moral. War coerces people by extra-legal force, by non-universalizable rules like "Declare war if you hold an advantage over a rival" which the weaker rival cannot will.

A "state consisting of [all] nations" is a rational way to emerge from the horror of war.[23] Yet, short of a world state, which Kant first approved but then rejected, only a universal alliance can prevent war and protect rights against violence. Here we should enforce compliance with morality, respecting each person's ideal but non-moral right to pursue his or her idea of happiness in conditions of peace, allowing talents to be developed in predictable environments. Progress, the universal development of talents, includes a history of legally protecting rights exercised in the pursuit of self-assigned ends.

If we are right to use international law to compel nations to refrain from war, we are at times right to enforce conformity with moral law non-morally by appealing to fear of consequences. To allow war is to allow lapses in the duty to treat persons as ends. It means the robbery of land, breaking promises in reversals of alliances, taking civilian and enemy lives as mere means to victory, and the knowing disruption of the life-plans of persons.

Horrors of war preclude leaving peace to conscience. We must go beyond endless striving to respect an *ideal* right to peace by enforcing an *actual* right. Treating persons as ends means achieving legal and customary respect for rights. It cannot stop with purely moral respect. This insight points beyond Kant's ethics of acting only out of reverence for the moral law, never out of a fear of punishment. It points to human rights ethics.

5. Hegel and Freedom of Thought

Georg Wilhelm Friedrich Hegel (1770-1831) is also a precursor of human rights ethics. This is not because his system justifies such rights. Rather, only dialogical human rights can justify his system. His *dialectical* method supposes a more general *dialogical* method. For Hegel personality is a "capacity for rights."[24] By "rights" he, like Johann Gottlieb Fichte, means claims recognized as valid even if not respected, enforced by volition and not by nature.[25] The process of establishing a mutual recognition of valid claims is the procedure creating them. I make my recognition of the validity of your claim to freedom of thought contingent on your recognition of the validity of my claim. If the claim you make is valid, so is my similar claim. The imperative of rights, viewed abstractly, is: "Be a person and respect others as persons."[26]

One universal right is the right to appropriate.[27] This right includes a valid claim to our bodies. We can recognize an individual only by recognition of his or her body.[28] Still, the morally basic right is to freedom of thought. Universal recognition of a universal claim to such freedom alone would establish human rights. Exercise of this right advances the quest for truth by the possibility of ever wider but provisional forms of consensus. Some fail to respect the basic right, but reason requires it:

> Since the man of common sense makes his appeal to feeling, an oracle within his breast, he is finished with anyone who does not agree. . . . In other words, he tramples under foot the roots of humanity. For it is the nature of humanity to press onward to agreement with others.[29]

This "nature of humanity" is not a natural propensity we cannot help having, but is a will to know by the exercise of a dialogical right to freedom of thought. If common sense neither claims nor recognizes such a right, a human right does not yet exist. The man of common sense is essentially or potentially rational, but not yet actually so. Actualization of what we are essentially requires a historical response to a moral imperative:

> Man, because he is mind, should and must deem himself worthy of the highest; he cannot think too highly of the greatness and the power of his mind, and, with this belief, nothing will be so difficult and hard that it will not reveal itself to him. The being of the universe, at first hidden and concealed, has no power which can offer resistance to the search for knowledge.[30]

Only by universal freedom of thought do we cease trampling humanity under foot. We do not validate this freedom by claiming it will lead to any particular truth, let alone all truth. Trust that the truth will come out we presuppose but never fully justify. By instituting such freedom and then inquiring, we demonstrate our hope that the truth will emerge without any certainty. Knowing that we cannot know all reality also presupposes freedom of thought. Through the dialectical method, truth may arise by the self-correction of past contradictions, but the self-correction may generate a new contradiction. We test the results of the dialectical method by a more general dialogical method.

Hegel held that absolute knowledge, the knowledge that God has of himself in and through our knowledge of God, enhances human dignity.[31] He considered such knowledge the highest achievement of the absolute itself.[32] This suggests a theological justification of human rights based on acceptance of a doctrine prior to adoption of human rights. Yet the vindication of all doctrines presupposes the acceptance of dialogical human rights. To find a non-theological procedural justification of such rights we must return to the Preface to the *Phenomenology*: "it is the nature of humanity to press on to agreement with others."[33]

Divine self-knowledge by human freedom thought therefore cannot justify dialogical rights, which we must justify prior to entering upon public inquiry. Yet Hegel himself has a procedural, non-doctrinal, justification of rights based on the natural impulse of human beings to press forward to agreement. Universal human rights center on the right to freedom of thought and opinion.[34] The French Revolution set out to realize this right around the globe.[35] Before the Revolution, the world of equal human rights was limited to heaven. The Revolution, seeking to bring this heaven down to earth, was not the end of the end of history, but was the beginning of the end. We are still in the middle of this end, and will stay here until we actualize human rights:

> I am about to be fifty years old, and I have spent thirty of these fifty years in these ever-unrestful times of hope and fear. I had hoped that for once we might be done with it. Now I must confess that things continue as ever. Indeed, in one's darker hours it seems they are getting ever worse.[36]

6. Hegel on Property

The French Declaration of the Rights of Man and the Citizen viewed property rights as "natural and inalienable." We need some property for freedom of thought. An inalienable natural right to pursue possessions becomes a human right to property. Absolutized abstract human rights in the Revolution negated the multi-tiered ethical life of the Old Regime, in which family, civil society and state all expressed feudal lordship. Persons, without being property, belonged to property. Abstract human rights fall under "abstract right" in Hegel's *Philosophy of Right.* "Abstract law"—commanding respect for human rights of appropriation, owning, and contracting—has its root in the "natural law" of inescapable human propensities.[37] Abstract rights are the human rights that channel an involuntary propensity to seek possessions. They channel it toward realization of the basic right to freedom of thought. They express the Rousseauean right to moral freedom in deliberations of the general will by distributing property as required by that one central right.

7. Hegel on Abstract Human Rights and Concrete Ethical Rights

By owning property, a person is externally embodied and recognizable by others.[38] You appropriate your body by investing labor in it. Except for slavery, the right to own is actual, not merely ideal like Stoic freedom of thought. Abstract rights abstract from the substantial duties of concrete ethical life. Ethical life is a sphere in which—in the family and state if not always in the marketplace—*duty consciousness eclipses rights consciousness.*[39]

For Hegel, morality internalizes the external abstract law to which we are subject in a society of emancipated persons. The principal example of such a society is Rome.[40] External law commands each to be a person, and to respect others as persons by respecting their property.[41] Duties sometimes go unfulfilled, but an internalized duty to respect property presupposes recognition of its validity. One internalizes the law of respecting persons due to a universal human criminal impulse to violate it followed by moral reconciliation with the community by the acceptance of deserved punishment.[42] Crime alienates individuals from one another, and from a legal system of respect for even their property. They emerge from this alienation by a will to confess and accept punishment, achieving moral reconciliation with others.

The family, before losing its sovereignty due to individual rights consciousness in civil society (the marketplace), knows only duty consciousness. The human rights recognized in civil society express the right to property. Hegel views emergency welfare as a concrete ethical right:

> [F]actors grounded in external circumstances may reduce men to poverty, and yet since society has withdrawn from them the natural means of acquisition . . . their poverty leaves them more or less deprived of all the advantages of society. . . . The public authority takes the place of the family where the poor are concerned. . . . Subjective aid [charity] . . . is dependent on contingency and consequently society struggles to make it less necessary, by discovering the general causes of penury and general means of its relief, and by organizing relief accordingly.[43]

Welfare applies the right to compensation for injury and damage. Populations suffer injury by the destruction of livelihoods. Global civil society has impersonally injured them by technological innovation. It subtracts from the value of the shoemaker's shoes. It produces a rabble of unemployed individuals with lost self-respect. Yet a concrete ethical right to compensation exists.

Rights fall into two groups. (1) Abstract rights occur when one person recognizes any other's body and property as embodying the other's claim to hold rights and obligations. The right to property and the associated rights to use or sell are the sole actual human rights cited in the *Philosophy of Right*. Freedom of opinion enters as a freedom to use your mind as property appropriated by personal labor. In the *Philosophy of Right*, we do not find the procedural justification of freedom of thought present in the Preface to the *Phenomenology*. In the *Philosophy of Right* universal human rights, including freedom of thought, are "abstract rights." (2) Concrete ethical rights are non-universal domestic, economic, welfare and political rights that implement abstract rights and that spring from history and exclusive commitments. In the family and state they are duty-based, based on duties others have accepted.

8. Rome and the French Revolution

In history, abstract rights have twice appeared apart from the concrete ethical life of family, civil society, and state: Rome and the French Revolution. The Revolution showed the realization of abstract human rights exhausting reality itself, negating feudal ethical life.[44] "Man's existence centers in his head, in thought, inspired by which he builds up the world of reality. . . ."[45] Here was a first institutional expression of Hegel's definition of the absolute by human personality, by self-knowing spirit. Roman abstract rights, by contrast, did not negate particular established ethical institutions: they provided a standard for judging and reforming them. In Rome abstract rights appeared in the cosmopolis of Stoic philosophy and in the law of persons, property, and contract. This law governed the gradual reform of civil and customary law, emancipating sons or protecting wives, aliens and even slaves.

9. Hegel on Lordship and Bondage

Hegel's philosophy of history concludes with a celebration of human rights as they began to descend to earth in the wake of centuries of struggle. The struggles of history are those of bondsmen against despots or lords, and of lordship against itself. They are struggles against domination in different guises, including theocratic domination by the Lord. God in truth is not Lord but Spirit, including the spirit of ethical life in the modern state protecting rights of freedom of thought, freedom from bondage, and freedom of appropriation. The struggle against lordship succeeds because lordship embodies a contradiction with which thought cannot rest. A thinking being pressing toward credible confirmation of him- or herself by others has a duty to overcome the contradictory depersonalization of those with whom he or she trades services, goods and thoughts. The lord *both* claims to possess an absolute exclusive selfhood never lost to other selves *and* commands free recognition of himself by bondsmen as other selves. The contradiction is resolved when the lord surrenders lordship and enters into dialogical relations of mutual recognition with erstwhile bondsmen who are instructively different from the lord.

In thought, mutual recognition emerges from lordship and bondage as the mutual recognition of thinking beings in a Stoic cosmopolis. Real mutual recognition arises only by owning one's body and mind.[46] Recognition of one another as propertied persons appears in the first section of the *Philosophy of Right* by itself, without the preceding dialectic of lordship and bondage. The section treats "rights which only concern abstract personality as such," not "rights which presuppose substantial ties, for example, those of family and political life."[47] We recognize persons in their personal property.[48] Our free existence through property is the sign of our common freedom from bondage.

In Chapter Five of the *Phenomenology*, we find Stoic mutual recognition between masters and slaves. Persons recognize one another as having freedom of thought, but some lack the ownership of their bodies by which others can recognize this freedom. Stoic mutual recognition allows slaves to remain. Such mutual recognition is imperfect compared with the *Philosophy of Right* in which slaves yield to persons. Stoic freedom of thought is only the *thought* of our mutual recognition as thinking beings.[49] Its *reality* emerges out of medieval lordship and bondage in modern civil society. Roman law in its Justinian form still expresses the mere Stoic thought of it, acknowledging the economic reality of slavery despite its illegitimacy by the standard of natural law.

History consists in variations on lordship and bondage. As we overcome the contradiction of lordship and bondage in one form, a new form arises. The Revolution overcame the contradiction as it appeared in sacred monarchy. The "master/slave" dialectic—eventuating at history's end in concretely realized human rights—appears without literal slavery in medieval lordship, in agrarian/pastoral patriarchy, in Oriental divine kingship, in Hebrew supernatural divine lordship, in capitalist lordship, and in colonial/imperial lordship. In communism, capitalism was to have yielded to mutual recognition between capitalists and proletarians in their common role as creative laborers.

Abstract human rights, everyone's recognition of everyone's valid claim to be a thinking being, emerge from historical forms of lordship and bondage, despotism, and patriarchy. These forms yield to mutual recognition of one another as emancipated by the ownership of property. The absolute abstract human right is the right to own.[50] This right implies a contract leading to the emergence of human rights. Neither human nature nor causal laws of motivation immediately provide for human rights without action on our part. The mutual recognition by which the abstract human right to appropriate emerges out of lordship and bondage is a voluntary agreement. Both sides give and receive. The agreement is initially voluntary, even if it becomes an ineluctable given, no contract at all, as society comes to presuppose universal ownership.

10. Hegel on the State

Abstract human rights emerge out of lordship and bondage, ending in free mutual recognition. Unlike a Lockean *external* state merely for the protection of life, liberty and property, a Hegelian *internal* state enforces mutual recognition between holders of the right to freedom of expression. This state is not an alien power. It is not an optional contractual means of protecting unhampered exercise of "natural rights." A constitutional embodiment of one's rational identity cannot depend on an ordinary contract in the marketplace.[51] Protection of the basic right requires a rational state with which we can identify. The right is insecure if left to conscience, public opinion, or custom. A legal right to the protection of human rights arises by disidentification with one's particular self and by construction of a state animated by a general will with which all identify:

> In the state, as something ethical, as the interpenetration of the substantive [the universal] and the particular [persons], my obligation to what is substantive is at the same time the embodiment of my particular freedom. This means that in the state duty [political obligation] and [individual] right are unified in one and the same relation.[52]

Rousseau said the individual can be forced to be free.[53] To violate rights is to violate the contract to which all have agreed, which protects each individual's rights. The state can force you to be free, to enjoy your rights coherently, by forcing you down a path leading to recommitment to the social contract. The higher self has agreed to applying force to the lower self should the lower self resurface. Hegel replied that to be free you must want to be so. An uncoerced conversion must occur in the criminal.[54] An unfree self cannot become suddenly free and self-determined by force. Yet the state can force you to start down a path of indictment, trial, conviction, and punishment that by rehabilitation may restore rational freedom.

If forcing someone to be free allows this indirect, uncertain undertaking, Rousseau may be right. In referring to target beliefs, we suggested modifying his claim that the majority is always right to make that claim true as well. Further, Hegel might also agree with Rousseau's claim that a rational state exists by contract for an immigrant like Rousseau himself. The contract remains optional for the individual, if not for a people. Hegel was no Romantic belonging to a land. His land belonged to him, and he changed it four times. In the course of employment as a civil servant he changed allegiance by contract from Württemberg to Weimar, Bavaria, Baden, and Prussia. Each such contract was optional. Only a relation to some rational state was necessary.

11. Freedom of Thought Again

We place our will in personal property by which our will is recognizable by others.[55] Assertion of a claim to be a person and recognition of one's claim begin the construction of human rights, which have never existed. They did not exist in life and death struggle or in lordship and bondage. Yet the right to be recognized as a person capable of appropriating things is not the basic human right, but is only a necessary mode of it. The basic right is freedom of thought, appropriating your brain and mind in possible dialogue. This is the right we saw Hegel asserting without theology in the *Phenomenology*:

> Since the man of common sense makes his appeal to feeling, an oracle within his breast, he is finished and done with anyone who does not agree. . . . In other words, he tramples under foot the roots of humanity. For it is the nature of humanity to press onward to agreement with others.[56]

12. Rawls

Fairness as the adoption of the *original position* implies, for John Rawls (1921-2002), detachment from all we know about ourselves and about others in particular, of what we stand to gain or lose in negotiation. The position is one from which we deliberate just constitutional arrangements. This position is the same for all. All we can know about individuals in that position is that they are human, which is why rights arising from the original position are human rights. The original position ought to generate the general will of a just state, but constitutional assemblies often fail to take that position. They are unfair. Delegates to the American constitutional convention initially knew they came from big or small states. From Rawls' perspective, they did not get it right at first. Bicameralism may in the end have expressed the original position for some, but for others America may have remained a matter of horse-trading.

Adoption of the original position supposes that all who set out to negotiate already share fairness. Only if negotiators are fair will they drop the veil of ignorance over self-interest. If they lack the will to do so, or if this will is not allied with some material interest, the original position will remain a pure "ought." The institutions negotiated may establish particular human rights beyond a general human right merely to be treated as human. Once we renounce, out of fairness, the desire to know what each stands to win in negotiation, we will be ready to assign more specific rights to all. These are likely to be traditional civil, political, legal, public service, and welfare rights. Satisfaction of the needs of different groups comes by a just distribution addressing risks run by humans who are, for example, ignorant of being rich or poor.

Property rights will satisfy middle class needs, welfare rights will satisfy those of the poor. Without privileged information about our situation, we attend to both types of rights. Everyone agrees to have as much freedom as is possible without obstructing the freedom of others, and everyone agrees, in helping any group, to assist those who are worst off. Those who do not adopt the original position but negotiate out of self-interest exploit what information and power they have to obtain privileges. Yet all agree to the protection of property and welfare from the original position. We all prefer to respect property in case we turn out to be propertied and prefer welfare in case we are poor, but without anyone knowing where anyone's particular self-interest will lie.

We contractually construct a intersubjective or public world in which diverse subjective human pursuits are then regulated by cognitive claims about the objective world.[57] Constructing moral principles through shared intuitions and preferences in bargaining from the original position, we do not justify moral principles from the cognitive standpoint. They result from discussion in the original position, from the moral standpoint. The Rawlsian contract differs from the Hobbesian social contract inspired by self-interest.

In 1985, Rawls regretted not distinguishing Hobbesian and Kantian positions in *On Justice*. He rallied to a Kantian view of the contract negotiated from the moral point of view.[58] He evolved away from a procedural morality that takes all norms to be set up contractually. Trying to bring people to adopt the original position, he came to place value on the virtues of those entering negotiation. He came to locate the source of fair negotiation in the prior moral competence of persons to understand justice, form a concept of the good, view themselves as subjects of moral obligations, and undertake just collaboration. Morality begins to make metaphysical assumptions about those who negotiate. He is less ready to rely on a contract based only on itself. It must express the moral will of rational persons.

He also admitted that his original concept of justice was based on intuitions in modern Western countries.[59] The egalitarian West contrasts with the hierarchical East, though both can accept a list of human rights:

> Though in hierarchical societies persons are not regarded as free and equal citizens, as . . . in liberal societies, they are seen as responsible members of society . . . [A] hierarchical society . . . secures for all persons at least certain minimum rights to means of subsistence and security (right to life), to liberty (freedom from slavery, serfdom, forced occupations), and (personal) property, as well as formal equality as expressed by the rules of natural justice (for example that similar cases be treated similarly). This shows that a well-ordered hierarchical society . . . respects basic rights.[60]

This list of rights excludes the basic right, freedom of thought, and political rights. If an established religion exists, it excludes freedom of worship.[61] Without democratic control of the state, we lose the political protection of civil rights as we know them in the West. Without experience of egalitarianism in the family or in national life, without having known the original position of fairness on the domestic level, leaders of hierarchical societies have difficulty adopting the original position in international negotiations. They negotiate internationally to protect the non-egalitarian domestic arrangements, hence not from the original position. Just how officials in hierarchical states can voluntarily enter into egalitarian relations with other states, unless their weakness internationally leads them to see a Nietzschean advantage in such equality, is hard to see. Yet then they would have lifted the veil of ignorance over what they have to gain and lose in bargaining.

If hierarchical states contemplated dropping the veil of ignorance domestically, those in high position could not be sure to retain their positions. Unfairly, they will not opt for domestic egalitarianism. Yet fairness is a potentially universal virtue. If we refrain from insulting non-Westerners by declining to call on their sense of equal justice, we must insist on negotiating constitutions from the original position domestically and internationally.

Yet Rawls does not withdraw from such insult. He holds that, in a stable hierarchical state, those in high position need not drop the veil of ignorance domestically, though they may do so internationally. The supposition is questionable in the case of great powers. How could China, without domestic experience of the original position, adopt that position internationally? What moral motive could China muster, in negotiating an international social contract, to drop a veil over its being the most populous country? The Chinese government, not having taken the original position domestically, has not been a strong voice for human rights internationally.

The problem Rawls's position faces domestically even in Western society, that of motivating powerful actors to drop the veil of ignorance, recurs internationally. Adopting the original position is perhaps an obligation if we are to be fair, but bringing self-interested parties to be fair is difficult except for the least well off, who may adopt it out of egoism, realizing that they have nowhere to go but up. Retaining knowledge that the only way to go in bargaining is up (or down) is itself a failure to take the original position.

Rawls is right that only an international order, no nation by itself, can realize human rights. Human rights in but one land are a contradiction. All a nation can do is to make a local contribution to global rights. Hierarchical states limit human rights in the West. Limitations on free exchanges among and with Cubans curtail freedom of thought even in the United States. If the nations dropped the veil of ignorance internationally, none would know if it was hierarchical or egalitarian. Yet Rawls's international social contract supposes that hierarchical nations carry knowledge of being hierarchical into negotiations—knowledge that they have not practiced fairness at home. If this knowledge keeps them from practicing fairness internationally, the international consensus that arises is far from Rawls's initial understanding of justice. He thought he needed his more recent position to avoid Western chauvinism. The human rights idea arose in the West, but it suffers dilution for the more hierarchical East.

13. Gewirth

A recent theorist who seeks to base human rights on necessary universalizable conditions of rational agency is Alan Gewirth (1912-2004). He has sought to justify rights from the standpoint of rational prudential action. No one can take this standpoint without claiming conditions of minimal welfare and personal freedom—subsistence and security—as conditions of the possibility of rational agency. If we treat similar cases similarly, one agent cannot claim such conditions of rational agency without granting all a like claim to these conditions. The only thing a rational agent cannot justifiably do is to deny like claims by all such agents.

> [E]very actual or prospective agent logically must . . . hold or accept that freedom and well-being are necessary goods for him because they are necessary conditions of his acting for any of his purposes; hence, he holds that he *must* have them . . . he logically must therefore hold that he has rights to freedom and well-being; for, if he were to deny this, he would have to accept that other persons may remove or interfere with his freedom and well-being, so that he *may not* have them; but this would contradict his belief that he *must* have them . . . the sufficient reason on the basis of which each agent must claim these rights is that he is a prospective purposive agent, so that he logically must accept the conclusion

that all prospective purposive agents, equally and as such, have rights to freedom and well-being.[62]

This argument establishes only that every rational goal-directed agent must agree that all such agents must claim rights to freedom of action and well-being. However, the fact that they all claim such a right is no proof that the claim is a genuine right, that it is a claim socially recognized to be valid. Nor does it give any reason to believe that the claim, however universal, is actually valid, that it would be a moral right if it were socially recognized as valid. Gewirth fails to cite universal freedom of thought as a condition of maximal justification, or any other good reason, to respect the claim to freedom of action and well-being of prudentially rational goal-directed agents. He thus fails to justify human rights. The fact that an agent must claim liberty and well-being no matter what his or her purpose is does not justify the claim. We cannot issue blank checks to purposive agents without knowing that their purpose, like freedom of thought as the condition of maximal justification, has some merit.

14. Habermas and Principle U

For Jürgen Habermas (1929-), presuppositions about human rights underlie inquiry, refutation, and justification. I want to highlight the merits of this view, reserving criticism for the next chapter. Morality and inquiry, for Habermas, are two sides of the same coin:

> [A]nyone who seriously undertakes to participate in argumentation implicitly accepts by that very undertaking general pragmatic presuppositions that have a normative content. The moral principle can then be derived from the content of these presuppositions of argumentation if one knows at least what it means to justify a norm of action.[63]

> [I]n rational discourse, where the speaker seeks to convince his audience by the force of the better argument, we presuppose a dialogical situation that satisfies ideal conditions in a number of respects: . . . freedom of access, equal rights to participants, truthfulness on the part of participants, absence of coercion in taking positions, and so forth.[64]

The ideal speech situation in public argumentation, in everyday discussion as in the formal scientific method, recognizes "the force of the better argument" alone. This situation presupposes human rights: universal freedom to access information, the empowerment of equal participation without constraint by all those affected by the issue, and protection for vulnerable groups.

For Hobbes, by laws of human behavior we can do nothing else than seek security and so we have a natural right to do so. For Grotius, at our best we are naturally capable of reason and sociability, and others have a natural right to expect our best. Habermas does not hold that nature obliges us to take the cognitive/moral point of view of respect for rights. Yet if we do take up unrestricted inquiry as enlightened contemporary institutions lead us to do, we necessarily adopt the moral viewpoint from which we pursue ideal human rights. Once we have taken the moral point of view, Grotius's appeal to promise keeping helps preserve it. If necessary, a Hobbesian world state might train us to respect human rights by making the non-observance of them illegal. Habermas clearly tells us what the rational moral point of view is.

Habermas has revived duty-based deontological ethics based on the "pragmatic presuppositions" of discussion understood as a cooperative search for truth."[65] We do not accept human rights because of good consequences such as knowledge. Nothing guarantees such a result. Even if we could guarantee a resulting increased chance of knowledge, we accept human rights as presuppositions of inquiry for inquiry's sake. For even knowledge of this chance depends on inquiry. What is morally right is what rational inquirers can all will with the interests of all in mind. To take the moral point of view is to take a rational point of view from which all will the same thing. They all share a general will to inquire into truth:

> The procedure of rationally motivated discussion presupposes that only those maxims *may* be accepted as valid whose universalization *could* be accepted as satisfying the interests of all by all persons affected more than any alternative maxim.[66]

Habermas refers to diverse *interests* of all. His general will does not abstract from interpersonal differences as Rousseau's general will does. Habermas's general will does not necessarily will to satisfy the diverse particular wills *of all*, but initially of all those who feel concerned, and finally of all those who actually are concerned by the issue. A particular will is valid if it survives rationally motivated discussion of the issue by all affected. If some want same-sex marriage, the question is not "Why?" but "Why not?" If we negotiate satisfaction only of a general will that abstracts from our different particular wills, we will emerge from negotiation to find our particular wills left unsatisfied. We will be unsatisfied by the negotiation, which will lack concrete rationality.

We *could* accept the above-noted "universalization" to the satisfaction of all affected even if no discussion occurred. Yet we actually show something to be so acceptable to all concerned only by showing its actual acceptance, in discussion by all concerned, of what all concerned can will. We actually justify a maxim in discussion, at once showing it to be capable of justification, if by discussion we find universal observation of the maxim, undertaken in the interests of all concerned, to be acceptable, even in its secondary effects, to all concerned more than any alternative maxim, without coercing anyone:

> [E]very valid [intersubjectively validated] norm has to fulfill the following condition: ([Principle] U) *All* affected can [and do] accept [without constraint] the consequences and side effects which its *general* observance can be anticipated [by them] to have for the satisfaction of everybody's interests (and the consequences are preferred [by them] to those of known alternative possibilities for regulation).[67]

Kant *tests* maxims by the consistency of universalizing them. Habermas, in his version of the moral imperative, *would have them tested* by the actual acceptability in discussion of the results of the universalization to all concerned. This retains something of Kant's categorical imperative based on respect for persons more than on his universalizability principle. Habermas's concern is with morally good results of universalization, in the first instance the actual acceptability of universalization to those concerned. Yet once a maxim's universalization to all affected is acceptable, nothing obstructs its acceptability without qualification to all. He cites human rights as maxims that could satisfy his Principle U: "Human rights . . . manifestly embody universalizable interests and can be justified from the point of view of what we all could will."[68]

Discussion between all can lead to agreement on rules of respect for human rights as satisfying the interests of all. Yet has a discussion including all ever occurred? We might suppose that a universal consensus exists if we broadcast a belief globally to a rights-empowered audience without anyone denying it. The ideal discussion situation has an egalitarian dimension. All concerned have an equal say. The authority of experts does not extend beyond their ability to convince the lay public. Is not a physician *a priori* more authoritative prior to entering health discussions than an untutored nonprofessional or glib charlatan? What we say in discussion we must interpret in context. The context may show the physician to be an authority and the charlatan a charlatan. Yet prior reputation does not alone establish the credibility of contributions. The discussion itself must show who has the better argument. Authorities must convince others that they are authorities. Yet the force of the better argument may remain unrecognizable if not supported by the force of material resources such as education.

If interest in truth is universal, discussion ethics has an advantage. It has been a problem for Rawlsians to get players to adopt the original position. Habermas would have the same problem if the acceptance of human rights rested, not on an existing interest in truth acceptable to all, but merely on a desirable virtue such as fairness. Little difficulty exists in getting others to avow interest in truth. Everyone pursues truth about something.

Hedonists pursue not just pleasure, but also the truth about pleasure, about its value and how to get it. Yet the pursuit of truth is rational only if we are alert to non-chosen alternative pursuits. Interest in a particular truth is interest in truth in general, and in the truth of alternatives to the pursuit of truth. Respect for human rights enables all to contribute to maximally rational inquiry on any topic. The standpoint from which we ought to respect human rights we already adopt in countless diverse inquiries into objective truth:

> Practical discourse [the practice of discourse without coercion] . . . is a warrant of the rightness (or fairness) of any conceivable agreement that is reached under these conditions [of non-coercion]. Discourse can play this role because its idealized, partly counterfactual presuppositions [concerning the existence of the ideal speech situation, concerning each and everyone's right to obtain satisfaction, and concerning the speaker's ability to keep his/her promise that, if all could investigate, a rational consensus would emerge supporting his/her belief] are precisely those which [unlike the Rawlsian presupposition that discussants ignore their respective particular interests in adopting the original position] participants in discussion do in fact make.[69]

15. Conclusion

Procedural theories of human rights do not make them depend on controversial substantive claims. They are compatible with such claims, but these claims cannot justify them. Procedural theories claim that human rights, as rights, merit winning social recognition of their validity. Such recognition belongs to a rational procedure of making and arbitrating claims. Human rights are a historical construct still under construction.

For Rawls and Rousseau, recognition of human rights arises from a *moral* procedure. The mutual recognition of rights arises from adoption of an original position, yielding our individual wills to the general will. For Habermas, the recognition of rights arises from a *cognitive* procedure presupposing that all who feel or ought to feel concerned have a right to participate in discussion. Hegel maintains that human rights emerge from the reciprocal recognition of all by all at the end of historical struggle surrounding lordship and bondage. Human rights would result if lordship and bondage yielded to a cosmopolitan community of dialogue partners made possible, in part, by general property ownership. This community, at first purely ideal, we can realize insofar as the material and geographical conditions of history permit.

What I call human rights ethics draws on Habermas and Hegel. We presuppose human rights by a procedure of inquiry whose institutionalization results from historical struggle against domination. An obligation to respect rights and to assure their respect by others is an obligation to convince maximally a universal audience. Until this audience fully exists, only partial rationality is possible, and we have an obligation to work for fuller rationality.

Habermas's universalizability principle shows the truth of saying that everyone has an ideal human right to freedom of choice. We ought to act without compelling or preventing decisions by others, without hiding the full range of options or the direct and indirect consequences of action, and without excluding from a discussion any who feel or ought to feel concerned. If humanity becomes the discussion circle, Habermas's principle becomes the moral law.

Part Two

THE JUSTIFICATION OF HUMAN RIGHTS

Five

Habermas's Procedural Justification of
Human Rights

1. Habermasian Dialogical Rights vs. the
Self-Righteous Definition of Rights

We have distinguished *ancient* and *modern* rights, rights to fellowship and to security.[1] Jürgen Habermas upholds a third concept of the basic right as a right to address a potentially universal audience, based on a self-imposed duty to discuss in the public sphere: "the public use of one's reason must always be free, and it alone can bring about enlightenment among men."[2] The third concept links human rights with democracy, with discussion steering toward majority decisions. Democratic discussion, like rational discussion, generally requires us to equalize upward the rhetorical and socio-economic power of discussion partners, so that only the force of the stronger argument prevails, not that of money, or even that of superior intelligence.

In the polis, discussion is the prerogative of citizens. The Stoic cosmopolis implies ideal universal citizenship. Its earthly realization leads to contemporary human rights. Stoic discussion is exclusive to a republic of thinkers floating abstractly above material concerns until the cosmopolis descends to earth in a real global polis.

Exercise of the other's human right of dialogue, unlike that of modern human rights, is an object of avid general interest. The other's exercise of the modern right to free choice is not an end in itself. Rather, we tolerate it for the sake of our own unperturbed freedom of choice. We invite the exercise of contemporary dialogical human rights, neither compelling nor merely tolerating their exercise. Public inquiry requires communication with discussion partners whom nobody intimidates. Modern human rights preserve mutually insulated atomic individuals from interference with one another. The exercise of contemporary human rights realizes shifting divisions of labor between individuals in countless discussions. Peace is indispensable. Yet it no longer exists for the sake of undisturbed individual action, but also for the sake of undisturbed channels of communication.

Can the truth-directed duty consciousness behind dialogical human rights secure individual rights? A right to something seems to be a right to demand it.[3] Yet if my right depends on your self-imposed obligation to me, I owe my right to you. Instead of demanding it, I must thank you for it. I cannot demand respect for my right, since you may always suspend the duty you have freely assumed. A demand that you respect my right supposes that I can take for granted your self-imposed duty to seek truth by discussion.

Dialogical rights thus show some contingency. They are not self-evident or inalienable. This follows from viewing rights as claims that others recognize to be legitimate. We may decline the view of John Hospers who, among others, holds self-righteously that moral rights require no social recognition of their validity, that they are justified claims which we each justify by individual insight without generating a social consensus.[4]

No right is a moral right merely because we socially recognize it as valid. Yet we may provisionally entertain the hypothesis of the justifiability of a socially recognized right for the sake of testing its validity. A social and legal right to physician-assisted suicide in Oregon is a hypothetical moral right, allowing us to test the idea of a moral right to physician-assisted suicide.

The self-righteous view of moral rights rejects Charles Sanders Peirce's view of truth as what inquirers universally agree on at the end of the history of inquiry. This self-righteousness holds that you can definitively justify claims today by your own insight without seeking the agreement of others, even in facing a wall of social non-recognition. On this view slave societies do not prevent a runaway from having a socially unrecognized but actual moral right to freedom. Libertarians deny that a moral right to the product of labor must await conversion of a welfare society to the free market. For them the insight of one individual can disqualify the judgment of the mass. Such a non-social definition of moral rights encourages a demand that others respect claims that they do not recognize as valid. This procedure fails to respect their right to freedom of thought. Self-righteousness ultimately encourages contempt for others, justifying non-dialogical and even violent opposition to save others from error.

The universal audience may be wrong, but the dialogical road to truth would lead through its views and their correction. Dialogical critics heuristically respect a social right for the sake of argument in order to oppose it dialogically. Moral rights are actual and not merely ideal rights only if they exist socially. Without social recognition of the validity of claims, we have only claims, not rights. Our successful effort to obtain recognition of the legitimacy of our claims ought to precede our insistence that others respect them as our rights. Without such social recognition, rights activists must work for recognition of their claims not self-righteously but with a respectful admission to others that all claims are open to refutation.

The commander of a prisoner-of-war camp may obtain the *compliance* of his prisoners with his orders, but he cannot demand respect for his rights on unwilling individuals. Respect goes beyond compliance. Without social recognition of the claim's validity, the most we can say is that a right to respect by others ought to exist. Dialogical rights are at risk, for they do not depend merely on one's own self-evident claim.

We justify human rights by showing the irrationality of denying rights to any who might test our belief. If we exclude their testimony, our rights claims are less falsifiable. Those who deny the right to freedom of expression can justify themselves only non-dialogically by appeals to private intuition. Terrorism eliminates dialogue partners who should be a part of any discussion putting a right to terrorism to the test. Osama bin Laden in videos made a pretense of sweet reason convincing the universal audience that terror was valid, but did so by eliminating a vitally concerned portion of that very audience. Such a justification of a right is contradictory, presupposing a universal right of reply to justify the very denial of such a right.

Acting on a denial of human rights hobbles those whose rights we deny in the discussion circle of concerned parties. Only a purely academic denial of rights that we do not act upon except in imagination is consistent with a free universal consensus justifying such a denial. Yet such an academic exercise shows acting on a justifiable denial of rights to be contradictory: by indirect proof, rationally denying rights affirms them.

Human rights ethics assigns a large role to indirect justification. Direct justification even of the claim that maximal justification presupposes universal rights consists in submitting it before ever more members of a rights-empowered audience. Some in this audience might approve slavery. Yet if slaves are not convinced of this right, or lack any dialogical freedom to disagree, the right is not universally recognized and is not a human right. A quest for informed consent by slaves tests the assumptions of slavery for possible falsification more than praises of slavery by everyone else. Rather than seeking out those who agree with a claim, we must seek out those who disagree. Yet informed consent by slaves to slavery would end slavery.

Human rights ethics is close to Habermas's discourse ethics, diverging in two respects. The first concerns the relation of human rights to politics. Habermas writes: "[W]henever existing conditions make a mockery of the . . . demands of universal morality, moral issues turn into issues of political ethics."[5] Yet whether he remains faithful to this claim is unclear. The second concerns the ineffectiveness of his procedural justification of refraining from human rights violations in the case of persons who have not adopted any procedure of rational argumentation presupposing human rights norms.

2. International Human Rights Law vs. National Human Rights Foreign Policy

(1) *Moral Human Rights.* For Habermas human rights exist on two levels. First, they are presuppositions of rationally motivated discussion. Here they are potentially universal customary rights flowing from participation in the ideal discussion situation, largely dispensing with legal enforcement:

Anyone who seriously engages in argumentation must presuppose that the context of discussion guarantees in principle freedom of access [right of access to discussion], equal rights to participate, truthfulness on the part of the participants [right to be told the truth], absence of coercion in adopting positions [right not to be compelled to adopt a belief], and so on.[6]

If these rights are dialogically ideal, no classical philosopher ever fully engaged in ideal argumentation! Fully rational argumentation is absent if human rights do not exist. Such rights "embody universalizable interests" and are "the moral substance of our legal system."[7] Some human rights ought also be legal rights, but even they are not essentially legal. The moral substance of legality is not legality, even if we come to enforce some rights by positive law, not just by custom and conscience.

(2) *Legal Human Rights*. As legal rights, human rights are moral rights that are protected through the courts, whether by national constitutions or by international treaty. Because the world judicial system is still incomplete, politicized enforcement sometimes occurs through the human rights-based foreign policies of major sovereign states rather than through courts. Yet enforcement in the courtroom is morally preferable. Such enforcement of human rights calls for fine points of procedure and analytic detachment. Nations should not take justice into their hands internationally, dishing out punishment moralistically to adversaries. We justify human rights morally, but we ought not to enforce them self-righteously from an alleged moral point of view.[8] Here is one rationale for the International Criminal Court.

To distinguish legal and non-legal moral human rights, imagine the ideal speech situation. What happens if one discussion partner tries to exclude another partner? If discussants called the police to fine the wayward discussant, we already would partially lose the ideal speech situation. That situation presupposes virtues on the part of participants, enforcement by conscience, not by the fear of punishment. The legal enforcement of human rights against criminal violation is justified only as part of moral education leading to the ideal speech situation, not as part of that situation.

Human rights disconnected from the ideal speech situation can become a fetish. Robespierre enacted a tyranny of virtue against enemies of the Revolution and of its legally declared human rights.[9] Yet it is difficult to object to the Allied pursuit in World War II as a struggle against demonized evil. For Habermas, moral human rights are conditions of the ideal speech situation. He objects to human rights politics and crusades against vilified adversaries, especially when they mask economic interests.[10] Politicized pursuits of human rights unfold with less than clean hands. Still, if no other way exists, genocide ought to stop even at the price of nationalistic self-congratulation by those who stop it, even at the price of the economic advantage the United States gained in World War II. Human rights must sometimes ride piggyback on other interests if they are to advance at all.

Best of all is an enforcement of rights by conscience, but Habermas rightly prefers enforcement by the law to military intervention or foreign policy human rights fetishism. Yet a legal human rights world order is but in its infancy. Legal human rights are justifiable by moral human rights. They would police a playing field in which moral human rights can one day emerge without the need for as much enforcement by litigation.

Even now we refrain from defending some human rights by litigation. No international law declares a human right to be treated politely, or even an unqualified right to be spoken to truthfully. When a moral human right becomes legal, its defense passes through a cumbersome machinery of the state. Few wish a right to polite treatment to pass through such machinery, even if politeness helps optimize the exercise of public freedom of thought.

3. Human Rights as Moral in Nature

Legal human rights, though justifiable morally, originated in the political struggle of the eighteenth century for a new legal order. Constitutional law enforces them.[11] Today international law protects them without full enforcement.[12] While human rights law attends to procedure, we see its failure in the zealous righting of wrongs by sovereign states. World War II, the Vietnam War, the Gulf War, the Balkans, Afghanistan, and Iraq show human rights rhetoric moralizing conflicts to the detriment of exact justice. To avoid the self-righteous demonization of enemies in human rights foreign policies, the public face of the human rights struggle should be legal, not moralistic—even though we justify legal human rights morally.[13] The private practice of human rights ethics between individuals empowering one another's right of reply invokes moral norms. Yet the public pursuit of human rights by the same persons often may selectively excerpt slogans from international human rights law and turns them into moral absolutes.

Habermas's Principle U asserts the basic right of his "discourse ethics" as a moral right. Valid maxims require that all affected freely agree. Everyone has a moral right to participate in discussion of any *maxim*—and more generally any propositional *claim*—without being either constrained to agree or disagree or restrained, including constraints and restraints stemming from withheld information on consequences or alternatives.

This right may or may not be legal by state enforcement. But it is essentially moral. It expresses a dialogical rationality enforced by conscience and only then by custom and law. Yet human rights ethics today has an immediate source in international human rights law, starting with the Universal Declaration. Reflection on United Nations human rights helps us recover human rights ethics. This ethics was the original inspiration of current human rights law, which stores that ethics away for us when conscience dims. We recover human rights ethics, the rational core of the international human rights law heaven, by decoding that law and seeking to bring it down to earth in all human encounters. Current international human rights law does not cover all applications of human rights ethics, but in correctly covering some applications it reveals something of what human rights ethics requires. To practice human rights ethics is to know such law.

The high visibility of human rights in domestic and foreign policy tends to transfer individual responsibility for respect for human rights to the state. In this respect human rights culture today diverges from human rights ethics. Because modern human rights emerged in eighteenth century political struggle to protect individuals from despotic states, many wrongly hold that respect for human rights is still chiefly a political function of liberal states and not a responsibility of individuals.

4. From Insight to Conscience

For Georg Wilhelm Friedrich Hegel, the political and legal human rights struggle in the eighteenth century was driven by enlightened insight recollected as the voice of conscience.[14] Moral human rights have a pre-legal, cognitive origin, nature, and justification:

> The various forms of the negative attitude of consciousness . . . are inferior shapes compared with that *of pure insight* and its diffusion, of the *Enlightenment*; for pure insight is born of the substance [of Spirit], knows the pure *self* of consciousness [the human subject] to be absolute, and enters into dispute with the pure consciousness of the [despotic, transcendent divine] absolute essence of all reality. . . . [B]y the negative movement towards what is negative to *it*, it [pure insight] will realize itself and give itself content. It knows that faith [the church] is opposite to pure insight . . . it sees faith in general to be a tissue of superstitions, prejudices, and errors [for example, Jean Calas, *Ecrasez l'infame*]. . . . The masses are the victims of the deception of a *priesthood* which, in its envious conceit, holds itself to be the sole possessor of insight and pursues its other selfish ends as well. At the same time it conspires with *despotism* [arch enemy of individual freedom of thought] which . . . stands above the bad insight of the multitude and bad intentions of the priests.[15]

Insight is distinct from the recollection of it by conscience. Conscience recollects the voice of a person's more enlightened, insightful self. Human rights in the ideal speech situation rest on the insight that we presuppose such rights in any maximal testing of knowledge claims. We cognitively motivate respect for human rights, and conscience then enforces them as moral. They are moral before they are legal. Legal enforcement introduces a non-moral motive, the fear of punishment. The moral motive, not being the fear of punishment, is not even a fear of the pangs of conscience. Motivation by the fear the agent's pain in any form is narrowly egoistic. The moral motive is insight, conscience carrying with it the enlightened insight that a person's action conduces to reason and truth.

5. The Development of Habermas's Discourse
Ethics as Human Rights Ethics

Ideally speech implies a promise that the speaker makes and can then redeem in an ideal speech situation in which all enjoy a right to validate what is said. Speech in pre-cosmopolitan culture did not presuppose this right, and, even today, some speak the same words promising only provincial redemption. Chaïm Perelman clarifies Habermas's ideal speech situation by reference to the "universal audience." Habermas does not use the phrase, but the ideal discussion situation implies the underlying idea. This situation excludes none *a priori*. Everyone must be able to address the universal audience at the onset of a discussion, and then freely agree to withdraw from the discussion depending on its course.

I first came upon the present idea of human rights in Perelman.[16] I concluded that human rights are a historically constructed condition of the possibility of full truth-directed inquiry. Building on Peirce's idea that such inquiry, in integral or abortive forms, is a permanent pole of human experience, I inferred that ethics, universal morality, is the gradual construction of and eventual respect for human rights. Only then did I discover that Habermas had greatly developed the same idea.

If human rights ethics is the ethics of maximal intersubjective inquiry, this ethics is procedurally justifiable to anyone undertaking such inquiry.[17] Defending slavery is a "practical," "pragmatic" or "performative" contradiction. We deny a right to freedom of thought to some by a performative contradiction if we nonetheless intend vindication of our belief through a rational consensus of all.

Human rights ethics is a discourse ethics in which the presuppositions of rationally motivated public discourse include nothing but human rights. Yet human rights ethics is itself fallible if our formulation of just how rights condition dialogue is itself fallible.[18]

Habermas has charted a new deontological position in normative ethics alongside both teleological theories and the Kantian position which it in some ways resembles. He has reformulated one-rule deontological ethics with a new version of the principle of universalization as the rule of rules:

> [E]very valid norm has to fulfill the following condition: (U) All affected can accept the consequences and the side effects its *general* observance can be anticipated to have for the satisfaction of *everybody*'s

interests (and these consequences are preferred to those of known possibilities for regulation).[19]

To put it otherwise:

A norm is valid if, and only if, all those who feel concerned or who ought to feel concerned—acting without constraint or restraint (including constaints or restraints stemming from concealed consequences or alternatives)—enter a rationally motivated consensus to accept the norm as one whose universal observance they expect to result in an indirect and direct satisfaction of everybody's interests superior to that obtainable by any known rival norm in the situation. (U)

For Habermas, valid norms are a subject of discussion that can end in agreement, but that lack the propositional truth of declarative statements.[20] Yet a norm is propositionally valid by the above formula. A statement that a norm is valid is propositionally true or false even if the norm itself is not. Consequently, a discussion of norms can yield propositional truths. Here is a criterion for the maximal rational credibility of propositions:

A proposition is maximally credible if, and only if, all who could inquire into its truth effectively form—with neither constraint nor restraint, with neither concealed consequences nor alternatives—a rationally motivated consensus to accept it as more likely true than any known rival proposition.

Applying this criterion for maximal rational credibility to the case of propositions asserting the validity of moral norms, we get:

A proposition to the effect that a particular norm is valid is maximally credible if, and only if, all those who could inquire into its truth effectively form—without constraint or restraint, without concealment of consequences or alternatives—a free and rationally motivated consensus to accept it as more likely true than any known rival proposition.

Rational discussion, a historical achievement, is not an eternal norm. For us dialogical public reason has a proximate source in the Enlightenment ideal of freedom of expression. Critical reflection on the contradiction of assuming both rights-based dialogical norms and the validity of repressive measures belongs to an enlightened consensus free of such contradiction.[21] By such a consensus of all who inquire, the universal observance of human rights norms works, in its indirect and direct consequences, to the satisfaction of everyone's interests (including an interest in truth capable of validating interests in subsistence and security) more than any known alternative norms. Human rights are reducible in principle to a single *conglomerate right* implied by the above principle of maximum rational credibility:

> Everyone has an ideal human right, which may not be actual, to inclusion in a discussion partnership concerning all topics which concern him or her (or even which seem to him or her to be of concern), exploring the indirect as well as direct consequences of any proposed belief, while other partners in dialogue obligate themselves to inform him or her of any known alternative beliefs or known remote consequences of belief, and to refrain from compelling or preventing him or her in the adoption of any belief.

Universalizable ethical norms become the norms we presuppose in all truth-directed discussion. Habermas's discussion of declarative statements or "constative" speech acts shows this. Drawing on John L. Austin, Habermas concludes that we presuppose ideal human rights norms—norms requiring submission of statements to all concerned persons viewed as having an ideal human right to judge—when we make factual claims understood as *illocutionary* speech acts of promising.[22] Contemporary students of philosophy know how Austin showed "I promise" to be a non-declarative performative speech act.[23] To say "I promise" is to act by speech, *is* to promise. On Habermas's showing following Austin, even declarative speech acts contain a performative use of language and are promises.[24] To make a factual claim is to promise that, were all to inquire, all would agree. Yet those promised can fully redeem this promise only if we actually enable them all to exercise the human rights with which to inquire. (Human rights without their possible exercise are not true human rights. However, if some who are enabled to inquire do not do so, the one who has promised is blameless for not having maximally redeemed the promise.)

Habermas cites Michael Dummett's fallibilist confession regarding the dialogical redemption of validity claims: "An assertion is a kind of gamble that the speaker will not be proved wrong."[25] The further step we need to make this gamble a sincere contribution to inquiry is to assure that the range of those whom we enable to attempt falsification of the speaker is one we never avoidably restrict. *The realization of the ideal speech situation is the realization of human rights.* A passage from Habermas shows his proximity to "human rights ethics:"

> It is part of understanding a sentence that we are capable of recognizing *grounds* through which the *claim* that its truth conditions are satisfied *could be redeemed* [by rights-empowered public inquiry]. This theory explains the meaning of a sentence not only mediately through knowing the conditions of its validity, but immediately through knowing the grounds that are objectively available to a speaker for redeem-

ing a validity claim. Now a speaker might still produce such grounds according to a procedure that can be applied monologically; then an explanation of truth conditions in terms of grounding validity claims would not make it necessary to move from the semantic level of sentences to the pragmatic level of using sentences communicatively. Dummett stresses, however, that the speaker is by no means able to undertake the required verifications in a deductively compelling manner, relying exclusively on rules of inference. The set of grounds available in any given instance is circumscribed by internal relations of a universe of language that can be explored only in and through [dialogical] argumentation. . . . This I understand as indicative of the fallibilistic character of the discursive [intersubjective] redemption of validity claims. What is important is only that the illocutionary claim the speaker raises for the validity of a sentence be criticizable in principle. . . . In any case, truth-conditional semantics in its revised form takes into consideration the fact that truth conditions cannot be explicated apart from knowing how to redeem a corresponding truth claim.[26]

To make a factual claim is to promise that all interested parties could agree if they had human rights. However, no one is yet fully able to redeem such a promise today. To make a factual claim is ideally not to ask listeners to accept on authority a counterfactual claim that if all *could* inquire all *would* agree, but is to make a redeemable promise that the claim will prove capable of justification through future public inquiry. It is to promise that the claim will prove justifiable through redemption in public inquiry by a range of inquirers that none have limited, whether intentionally or by a lack of conscientiousness. If respect for the enjoyment of human rights enjoy is doubtful, the redeemability and hence credibility of claims is also doubtful. In a contemporary discussion within a provisional human rights ethics that does not yet presuppose existing human rights, saying "The grass is green" commits speakers to collaborate in realizing the human rights which we must presuppose in a ideal speech situation of the claim's full redeemability. If anywhere concerned listeners are not free to inquire, no factual speech act is fully redeemable.

Habermas's justification of human rights norms is that they are assumed by the procedure of fully justifying any claim. The maximum possible justification of any claim depends on the maximal possible realization of such rights. The procedure of rationally defending a claim in the public domain presupposes human rights norms already in part institutionalized in the contemporary world. These norms are justified as belonging to the procedure of justifying a claim. Some persons may have had private insight into the truth that public freedom of thought is required for the justification of claims before that insight was established as the presupposition of existing institutions. Today many who contradict that insight may be reminded of public rights assuming the insight to which he or she is party. We have less need *argue* that access to a discussion and to uncoerced dialogical freedom of thought is justified in order to gain acceptance of the point. We can now simply point to the fact that discussion partners take that insight for granted in their adopted procedure of discussion. We participate in procedures, practices or institutions presupposing that insofar as possible we ought to realize ideal human rights in order to maximally justify any claim. Invoking presupposed shared procedures no longer requires us to take time out to repeat how human rights are justified and not just presupposed.

A renewed obligation to justify dialogically human rights norms conditioning inquiry would again put them at risk. Habermas's procedural justification of the non-violation of basic rights presupposes justification of the procedure of testing beliefs by the promotion of human rights. It is only a reminder to the person who is party to established normative presuppositions, but who has acted in contradiction to them, that these presuppositions are in place.[27] Procedural justification of course cannot invoke an established normative procedure to persons who are not party to it. A true justification of the procedure is needed to convince those who are not yet converted to it or who become disaffiliated, who cannot just be reminded like those who already implicitly agree.

If justification of the human rights norms of rationally motivated discussion falls under such discussion, it is circular. Karl Otto Apel holds that such norms are justified because no other norms of dialogical inquiry are possible.[28] Habermas says that as far as we know no others are possible.[29] Circularity is avoided if we validate addressing a human rights-empowered global audience before a more restricted audience. Limited audiences, correcting the conclusions of even more limited audiences and corrected by wider audiences, may conclude inductively that any limited audience ought to yield to less a limited one, and so ought ultimately to yield to the least limited one. We do not say that a restricted circle of Copernican astronomers ought to yield to a wider consensus of flat earthers. Rather, it ought to scan the wider audience for motivated inquirers capable of criticizing Copernican astronomy. That we ought address the universal audience in human rights ethics is a heuristic dogma held without inductive tentativeness, maximizing possible reply from different quarters. We do not do all we can to locate such inquirers unless we heuristically assume their existence as a working assumption and then search.

The imperative of justification in a world of competing hypotheses escalates into a requirement of maximal justification, imposing the logic of human rights whether we are Easterners or Westerners, members of hierarchical or non-hierarchical societies. A prosperous world society with a universal distribution of individual freedom, without populations which some states hold in an informational quarantine, is an epistemological necessity. If we deny the normative function of human rights in the treatment of a minority, we can validate this denial only by inconsistently submitting it to the universal audience including this minority, an audience in which we nowhere restrict the rights of willing disputants.

6. Modern versus Contemporary Human Rights

We are born with inalienable "natural rights" to the pursuit of life, liberty, and property. Nature, not human beings, enforces inalienable "rights," so such rights are technically not even rights. Laws of biology and of psychology enforce these propensities even if we do not recognize them. Modern Lockean human rights theorists base human rights on natural rights. A "natural right" to do what is necessary in a situation to defend yourself may ground a modern human right to have others restrained from interfering with your successful pursuit of self-defense. This "natural right" is inalienable, but a corresponding human right is alienated if addressees of the claim do not recognize it as valid. Thus the "natural right" to seek revenge has led to no human right to do so successfully. A "modern" human right is a negative right to exercise natural rights without interference. A "contemporary" human right is a positive right to do so with success.

Contemporary dialogical human rights, unlike ancient and modern human rights, give positive assistance supporting freedom of thought and choice. Modern human rights need not exist for nature to enforce Hobbesian or Lockean "natural rights." We need modern human rights only to protect the inalienable pursuit of freedom from being avoidably set off course by the state or by individuals. One can exercise even in prison the "natural right" to pursue freedom, though with a limitation on an right to do so successfully. Modern human rights would be universal rights to a humanly unperturbed pursuit of self-defense, food, or free movement. Such negative rights to freedom from disturbance are not worthless, but dialogical human rights absorb and surpass them.

All rights are alienable, but ideal positive dialogical rights are inalienable in the ideal speech situation that is normative for discussants addressing the widest audience. We must recognize claims as valid for them to be rights, but we may fail to respect them without annulling them. Recognized human rights claims may exist as rights which we are incapable of respecting. Cosmopolitan defenders of any target theory promise that if everyone enjoyed the respect for human rights with which to credibly judge—if repressive conditions disappeared—a rational consensus would support the theory. This promise has limited weight if no time limit exists for attaining universal rights. Yet we attach some weight to the promise of redemption by striving to realize human rights, and to show total trust in them.

Since dialogical human rights have not yet existed, human knowledge may show progress if we succeed in creating them. Statements we make today without dialogical human rights we do not make in the ideal speech situation. In making maximally credible statements we must strive to assure that they will be human rights-tested. Many have not viewed the ideal speech situation as ideal. Yet today—as communication lines arise in all directions between cultures, nations, races, religions, and ideologies—some in the *real speech situation* see the validity of a universal claim to freedom of thought, though they may not yet be able to respect such a right. Elitist, sectarian or provincial speech acts that we can redeem only by addressing restricted audiences still abound.

When did dialogical human rights claims begin to pass as valid? The ideal of addressing a cosmopolitan audience was present in Roman Stoicism. Yet the Stoic cosmopolis, due to a resignation to chains, could not realize human rights. Voltaire's Enlightenment audience recognized the validity of human rights when he wrote on behalf of persons still incapable of speaking for themselves. Human rights violations silence voices, reducing the redeemability of promissory notes issued in speech acts. Human rights can be *putative* rights of all defended by a few speaking for all, so long as the many in time take up the cause, and so long as the few hold the cause in trust for them. Franklin Delano Roosevelt's Four Freedoms Speech and the Universal Declaration mark a second coming of human rights after the Enlightenment: "Whereas the peoples of the United Nations have in the Charter reaffirmed their faith in fundamental human rights. . . ."

7. A Procedural Justification of Human Rights

A strong argument can be built, without presupposing either existing human rights or even a global human rights movement, for the thesis that the ideal of rational discussion would presuppose human rights. Yet however strong this argument may be, it is even stronger if it passes the test of being promulgated without being refuted in the global community. A settled consensus that the thesis is well tested and not falsified may then begin to find expression in the emergence of a worldwide procedure institutionalizing recognition of the validity of human rights claims.

Today such a worldwide procedure still does not exist. It is difficult to defend the view that human beings everywhere so widely realize human rights that any participant in a discussion falls into a performative contradiction by not respecting the freedom of expression of another individual. A procedural justification of a true human right through condemning its violation could only operate within an existing global procedure establishing respect for the right as a public rule of practice. The justification would show that any individual's failure to respect the right is in contradiction with a presupposed shared worldwide procedure to which he or she is party. Not respecting the right in a particular instance would then be to fall into a pragmatic/practical/performative/procedural contradiction with a presupposition of an already adopted practice.[30] If human rights do not yet exist, what exists instead is a non-universal procedure of human rights activism presupposing an obligation to work for the creation of such rights.

The fact that any procedure presupposes certain norms does not mean that these norms are justified in themselves as the well-tested conclusion of an argument promulgated globally for possible falsification. Yet we adopt a norm as commendable *to us* as long as we are caught up in the procedure. Yet Robert Pippin reminds us that procedures are of many kinds:

> Habermas has always had trouble convincing his critics that these communicative norms [for example, human rights] are "presupposed" in so much human activity, that we simply *cannot*, under pain of "performative contradiction," engage in such activity without a commitment to such norms."[31]

Practicing any procedure implies presupposed norms that that are commendable to those who participate in the procedure. Contract killings in the Mafia are contrary to respect for human rights, but a Mafia member may be called to order by being reminded of a practical contradiction due to a background code of conduct to which he has committed. Avoiding a practical contradiction is necessary only to be consistent in following the procedure. It does not imply that anyone ought ultimately to commit to it. Final justification of fidelity to a procedure is possible only if we in the first place ought to commit to it. Justification of the presupposition depends on justification of the procedure. Yet even consistency with a procedure contrary to respect for basic human rights may sometimes tragically be justified as a stage in the course of moral education leading beyond the procedure. The holocaust was horrendous, but would the Universal Declaration of Human Right have had the form and influence it has had without it?

The existence of a social right of participation in a discussion without coercion means that we can elicit habitual respect for the right without repeatedly having to justify at length the ideal conditions of rationally motivated discussion. It means that tacit recognition of these conditions is a secure acquisition within a given community. They can largely be taken for granted and invoked as compelling should anyone lapse into challenging them. A person violating them normally need only be called to account by a reminder. Since a human right is a shared rule of practice rule, human rights ethics is by definition a rule-based ethics based on publicly adopted rules. Such a right, unlike any private rule of practice, defines a rule of respect that is socially recognized to be obligatory.

Some procedures are procedures of oppression and exclusion. Some enact racist presuppositions. Speech is no single morally univocal procedure. Many speech situations do not invoke the normative authority of the ideal speech situation. One speech act intends the truth and presupposes the ideal right of all listeners to inquire, but another intends domination. Even if Habermas shows that we presuppose human rights norms in some speech acts and practices, many speech acts fail to realize the ideal speech situation. Promissory notes assigning positive rights of investigation are not conveyed by linguistic activity as such.[32]

We must justify the validity of justification by universal rights if we are to justify anything else by it validity. Habermas's justification is that so far we have not found any better justification than justification by human rights norms. That human rights exist actually must, until further notice, be a *true* presupposition of any *fully* rational procedure of intersubjective justification. If we falsely presuppose the existence of human rights, fully rational discussion is an illusion. However, that we ought to maximize progress in the creation of ideal human rights may be a *true* presupposition of a *maximally* rational existing procedure, though not a universal procedure.

Although the imperative of maximum justification is entrenched in part of the contemporary world, some individuals like Slobodan Milosevic vindicate themselves before a much more limited, e.g., merely national, audience. Still others may opt to simply live without justification. But if you try to maximally justify any claim, even one that denies human rights norms, you address as many as possible for maximum confirmation. We may not rationally ask the question as to whether such rights ought to be normative, but if we do raise the question with full seriousness, we then presuppose the moral right to freedom of thought of any who can respond. Maximally justifying a denial of human rights against a backdrop of globally instituted freedom of thought presupposes their normative function as a condition of fully justifying anything. If we may assume that Plato released the *Republic* outside his Academy, he sought to justify a denial of human rights to a general public. Different people, he held, ought to keep to their different businesses, and truth is the business of philosopher kings. Yet if he allowed his arguments to be made public, he subjected them to testing, if not by all, then by any who could read or even hear. This act contradictorily assigned freedom of thought, a matter of concern only to some, to many whose business it was not, if not to all. It was a practical contradiction.

The imperative of maximally rational justification is hypothetical, and not even essentially tied to human beings. *If* you value truth seeking by open discussion, then you ought to value a universal right to freedom of thought. If we are committed to truth seeking, we must also value any species capable of it. Procedural justification invokes *human nature* only to know whether we can justify freedom of speech *to* human beings and perhaps not *to* cats. We do not justify human rights merely by human nature. Yet the justification of universal rights, assuming the value of truth seeking, ratifies of whatever in human nature allows us to seek truth. It justifies reflective confirmation of what Hegel calls the impulse rooted in human nature to press forward toward agreement.

The need for oxygen creates only a "natural right" or propensity to seek it, not a human right. The impulse to press on toward agreement is also such a natural right. The propensity may exist unratified within any procedure to which one commits oneself. Yet if human nature does harbor a cognitive interest to which we procedurally consent, satisfaction of the desire to know by pressing on toward agreement is adopted as the purpose of much else that we do. If human beings actually commit to maximize a cooperative search for truth, then an otherwise hypothetical command to progress toward justification by universal human rights may end as an actual command issued to actual humans beings. The ideal cognitive point of view presupposing ideal human rights was not within the reach of ancient Stoics. Yet the potential increase of wealth in a globalized economy, in which fewer romote populations exist whose lives do not touch ours, means that the ideal is beginning to be within human reach. Yet "human rights" might also be justifiable to Martians if they harbored our cognitive interests.[33]

Not everyone in the post-1945 world under the auspices of the United Nations norms commits to human rights-protected dialogue. An Adolf Eichmann may continue to disengage from any procedure of justification by an obligation to press toward agreement with others by dialogue, thus violating dialogical rights without a bad conscience. We condemn torture even if it does not result in a practical contradiction by the standard of a scrupulously consistent torturer. The maintenance of human rights norms by all is not the only way to avoid practical contradictions in violating rights either historically or even today. A practice of torture may exist in which torturers, in practical contradiction with their background commitment to respect human dignity, act with a bad conscience. They may feel that they ought to be able to justify their dehumanization of others before a universal audience including the tortured. Yet, seeing the practical contradiction, they may circumvent a bad conscience by assigning different presuppositions to their practice of torture. They may base their practice on a narrowly nationalistic premise. Or they may decide to live and torture merely by impulse without presuppositions, and so avoid all possibility of a practical contradiction.

Because what we condemn as the violation of human rights is even commendable by some standards, getting the violator to condemn him- or herself by the procedure of respect for basic rights is not always easy. If someone does not refrain from torture merely by being reminded of a rights-based procedure to which he or she is party, we will need to convince the person to respect human dignity non-procedurally, by an indirect argument that first leads the violator to consider such a procedure.

8. Justification by Indirect Proof

Habermas may agree that no practical contradiction exists between denying human rights and the presuppositions of many procedures that have existed and do exist. He only needs to suppose a contradiction between fully rational public argumentation and action implying a denial of human rights, not between all human activities and their denial. A practical contradiction exists if we take a denial of human rights to be rationally justifiable in the court of human reason with a procedure assuming an ideal universal right of reply. A theoretical contradiction occurs where our argument contains premises and assumptions implying a contradiction. A practical contradiction occurs where our premises and assumptions, without being internally contradictory, contradict presuppositions of our rhetorical procedure in addressing our argument to a universal audience. Correcting the assumptions of our argument then occurs by a practical rather than theoretical version of indirect proof. But Habermas must grant that the conversion of individuals to human rights norms they initially do not accept must operate by a different method than procedural justification.

Unlike ethical nationalists, human rights ethicists believe that we maximally justify a thesis if it wins the agreement of all concerned discussion partners whom we can access. The thesis is then a target thesis for further inquiry. If we exclude some whom we could access, human rights ethicists hold that we have not justified the thesis as fully as possible. If saying that human rights are not justifiable is ever justifiable, we must inconsistently presuppose that their normative function is justifiable, doing so precisely to assure a maximum audience capable of a consensus that they are not justifiable. If any belief is justifiable, the belief is also justifiable that we ought to respect human rights to the maximum. This belief alone assures the audience and jury necessary for maximum justification.

We cannot maximally justify violating basic rights without a practical contradiction. You might justify the violation merely to fellow citizens, but a justification excluding *a priori* the testimony of aliens could not be maximal. But indirect proof in which torturers are moved to heed a human impulse to press on to agreement with external voices beyond their initial audience can begin a process of moral education that in the end may result in conversion to human rights norms. In this way, human rights stand a chance of being saved from being an under-justified culture simply accepted or not accepted.

9. Human Rights and Peircean Pragmatism

In the case of those who, unlike rigorously consistent torturers, recognize a human rights-based discussion procedure, a practical indirect proof reminder of procedure is possible. There is no circularity here if this reminder assumes but does not argue for the procedure. Pragmatists hold that we engage in theory to solve problems, not for the sake of theory. Yet, since theoretical inquiry remains essential to solving problems, problem solving means a commitment to human rights discussion norms. Peirce tacitly assumed human rights in upholding objective truth in problem solving. Objective truth is what all inquirers will agree on at the end of history.[33] We must assume that this agreement will arise from a universal right to consent freely to one's belief. Otherwise their agreement would fail as a criterion of truth. If some investigators were cowed into agreement, the history of inquiry could not really be at an end. If not all can freely pursue inquiry, universal agreement can never be a credible witness to truth.

On any particular issue, for Peirce and John Dewey, experience, if it proceeds reasonably, alternates between poles of *belief* with a confident readiness to act in the world and *doubt* inducing inquiry into a credible restoration belief. Those who do not immobilize themselves in the pole of belief, who can inquire with openness to the range of discussion partners, respect human rights. Respect for human rights is present in the method of resolving doubt into belief that we learn to be most successful.

Taken at first by surprise by the arguments of others, we learn by experience the advantage of seeking them out. Respect for rights is necessary if we are to establish beliefs that, unlike ones established by appeal to authority, others are less likely to falsify. *Once you resolve to practice human rights-protected discussion of whatever target theory concerns you, proceed to do as you wish!* In the idiom of human rights, that is the moral law.

Peircean inquiry contemplates a consensus of all inquirers as we approach the end of history: "There is a general *drift* in the history of human thought which will lead to one general agreement, one catholic consent."[34] Inquiry fails when someone prevents an individual from inquiring into any subject of concern, and from publicizing findings. We prevent individuals from inquiring when we deny them available means of doing so. When a neo-Peircean like Habermas takes the consensus of all who practically could inquire as the criterion of truth, we widely follow him today. Only those who seek no objective truth lack any reason to respect human rights.

The pursuit of such truth rejects foundationalist tyranny over those who lack our intuitions of self-evidence. Confidence in the infallibility of one's private intuition which others allegedly lack contains the seeds of tyranny. A fallibilist pursuit of objective truth is the opposite. A consensus in which some concerned inquirers are disabled is not a criterion of truth. Restricted inquiry before a limited number of discussants increases the risk of aborting in falsehood. Human rights are epistemologically imperative.

Rationally motivated universal consensus is the criterion of truth, not its definition. Though a consensus restricted to inquirers accessed thus far is never fully reliable, it is today the only applicable criterion. We rightly doubt the real possibility of a universal consensus on an issue if we stipulate that the consensus prove stable into the future.[35] Our statements, correctible by new statements more closely approximating what would be fully correct, correct past approximations. A public error-correcting process is in progress, sometimes falling two steps behind to take a step forward.

In pre-contemporary philosophy and science, the presupposition that modern human rights ought to exist presupposed procedures of inquiry and justification alleging self-evident knowledge. Freedom of thought was often the right to profess that of which one is certain, with the obligation of tolerance toward the presumed false professions of others. Today the belief that human rights ought to exist is a presupposition of a new ideal procedure of inquiry. The existence of the ideal inquiry situation supposes that universal rights actually exist. The attempt to realize that situation supposes that they ought to exist. Yet ideal inquiry is not a non-moral good resulting externally from the existence of human rights. The existence of human rights is rather the other side of the coin from valid inquiry. Existing human rights are a logical implication of ideal inquiry. Less than ideal public inquiry implies an obligation to approach human rights.

As two sides of the same coin, fully rational inquiry is the cognitive side and the verifiable presupposition of publicly instituted human rights is the moral side. They are one procedure under different descriptions. Respect for rights is not a means to ideal inquiry, but is an integral part of it. Yet public inquiry is the more encompassing description, implying rights and motivating their maintenance. For Plato, to know the good was to do the good. For human rights ethics, to seek truth is to do the good. An imperative of inquiry emerges. (1) Accept definitively all and only factual hypotheses to all potential inquirers agree at the end of history. (2) Accept provisionally all and only those hypotheses to which present inquirers agree. (3) Accept for the sake of argument, should present inquirers disagree, the belief of most present inquirers as the target belief to be refuted if inquiry is to continue. (4) If no majority belief exists, provisionally create two mutually respectful communities of inquiry. (5) Raise as many as possible potentially concerned inquirers to the level of willing actual inquirers.

The cognitive imperative commands us to measure our confidence in our beliefs in proportion to the agreement we win in the widest possible circle of discussion partners. The moral imperative commands a *rhetorical* choice to address a maximally universal audience. A reasonable consensus between inquirers on any thesis requires a consensus on ethical rules governing discussion. If some dominate others, whether by superior ability or circumstances, all inquirers with a prevailing interest in truth will find rules tending to equalize the playing field upwardly to be acceptable.

Those who do not obligate themselves to inquire will not find themselves moved to recognize the human rights of others. Yet inquiry takes forms beyond its purely academic form. In economic life, sports, the arts, and politics it takes the form of rivalry laying down the challenge "Top this if you can!" As rivalry, inquiry extends to a greater number of people than we supposed. Many inquirers are quite distant from academic inquiry, but want wide public recognition when they claim they have achieved something. Nationalism as an "ism" is a theory, not just a pursuit of a nation's self-interest.

National*ists* dearly wish nationals of other counties to recognize the evidence of their nation's superior achievement.

Our argument is hopeful, since we base human rights on a prior duty consciousness, consciousness of the self-imposed duty to seek to vindicate oneself in the court of human reason. In view of our need for legitimacy, we become more forthcoming in recognizing the validity of the right of others to dialogical freedom of thought. Others will claim their rights with less litigation, grieving, striking, complaint, and self-assertion on their part. They will do so with some confidence that we will predispose ourselves to help reverse violations of their rights. They become able to obtain respect for their rights merely by reminding us of our general duty should we fall into a practical contradiction. Often informing us of their particular plight will be sufficient to obtain respect for their rights, with less need to fight for rights. Yet anyone's chance of being credibly affirmed by others is at once a chance of being corrected by them, as one identifies more deeply with the quest for truth than with vindicating our present belief:

Even if learning from some people seems improbable, to justify raising the issues we raise we must know the range of issues which we could have but do not raise. You ought to respect those who address issues that you could but have not raised. For you could always change your mind. Respecting the choices of others recalls your freedom to choose otherwise. It keeps options open. A rational decision requires knowledge of the alternatives. Justified interest in one issue requires maximal knowledge of all issues. The human right to freedom of thought is the other's equal right to be different. The right does not rest on a question-begging appeal to the dignity of persons. If we ask why persons are worthy, the answer is that they are potential discussants, even if only rarely actual discussion partners.

Distinguishing interim and definitive human rights ethics, we ask whether ideal inquiry situation is attainable. Some cite the Universal Declaration as evidence of a consensus behind human rights after World War II. Yet some nations abstractly approving international human rights have slavery. For example, domestic slavery has existed in Ghana.[36] Granted, we know this because human rights organizations in Ghana and outside denounce it. Existing human rights do not mean that we never violate them, but only that efforts exist to bring violations to justice. Many believe that the interim situation, the continued construction of inexistent human rights, is definitive. The ideal, the regulative idea, is just that: a benchmark, a standard of progress. This sounds Kantian, but we may give Hegel have the last word. Let us not get lost in what Kant calls *the bad infinite*. By the progress we make, we already participate in the kingdom of the end.

10. Rights: *Prima Facie* and *de Facto*, Subjective and Objective

If the right to life, subsistence, and security is the *instrumentally* basic right, the *teleologically* basic right is the right to think freely in a context of discussion. More exactly, the right to life is a necessary mode of the right to freedom of thought: an individual exercises the right to think freely only *by* remaining alive. No reasonably based obligation exists to respect any human right, such as the right to life or the right to food, if such respect would not be a condition of maximal inquiry. Yet compassion, as a *motive*, may move us to respect rights regardless of potential inquiry, which is the only good *reason* for doing so. Compassion is a laudable motive and virtue, but there are cases of unfair and irrational compassion. Compassion for those who are closer to home, but who are less needy than distant populations for which we have less compassion, is sometimes unfair.

If the right to life is a necessary mode of the right to freedom of thought, the right to life is substantively the same human right. Yet one individual's right to life is only a *prima facie* right. We could learn something from anyone, even a serial killer. We may learn nothing from him, but that does not mean that we *could* learn nothing from him. Yet the conflicting *prima facie* rights of the great many who are not serial killers are the actual *de facto* rights that we ought to respect. Your right to life is subjectively different from mine, though objectively it the same. An *objective right* is a right to something (some freedom, good, or service) that remains the same regardless of whether one person holds it or another. A *subjective right* is just such an objective right as held by one person and not another. One objective right may be held by different subjective right-holders, yielding many subjective rights corresponding to a single objective right.

Your respect for others as potential discussion partners requires that you respect their *prima facie* subjective rights to life. This holds true unless—in interim human rights ethics—a greater obligation exists to respect subjective rights to life of a greater number, or the subjective rights to life of persons more likely to bring the world closer to human rights for all. Cost-benefit analysis of what we stand to lose and gain from maintaining particular individuals in life becomes necessary.

Two types of conflict between human rights exist: those between *prima facie* subjective rights falling under the same objective right, such as your right to eat and mine, and those between objective human rights, such as the right to eat in general and the right to the product of labor in general.

In competition with a different objective right, the right to freedom of thought always wins, demoting the other right to being less than a human right if it does not support freedom of thought. A right to food that does not support freedom of thought is not a human right to food. Freedom of thought is never merely a *prima facie* type of right. It wins as the sole objective human right necessitated by the Habermasian categorical imperative directing us to embrace the maxim most acceptable upon discussion open to all concerned parties, without constraint in its direct and indirect effects upon all. Yet as a subjective right, the right to discuss is only a *prima facie* right. In a conflict between my right to discuss in a particular situation and yours, my right may not be actual if you have not finished your reply to me.

Note that the above categorical imperative is only heuristic. As we look to see where duty lies, the imperative regulates our search but does not guarantee we will discover anything. Several maxims of conduct commanding respect for different particular human rights may equally satisfy the imperative, in which case conflicts between *prima facie* maxims are possible despite the categorical imperative. Conflicts between welfare and property rights provide classical examples. Sometimes no maxim may satisfy all affected. Other times we may discover no maxim satisfying all affected. Or, human rights ethics may justify a maxim under one description (for example, providing health care), but under another description (for example, taxing income producers) we may condemn the maxim.

We must weigh a serious infraction of a minor right (for example, the right to polite treatment) against a minor infraction of a serious right (such as the right to freedom of thought). So human rights ethics does not solve all ethical problems.[37] What ethical theory does solve all problems? Human rights ethics only promises guidance in the search.

We distinguish between the subjective/objective classification and the *prima facie/de facto* classification of rights. Most moral philosophers hold that we cannot arrange different objective types of moral obligation in a hierarchy in which one type always takes precedence. The duty of non-injury, as an objective obligation regardless of who has it or in what situation, does not always preempt that of truth telling. Each of these rights is only a *prima facie* right. Yet, among objective human rights, one objective right, the right to contribute without constraint or restraint to any discussion by which we are affected, is hierarchically supreme: it is always the *de facto* objective human right. It is highest since only it is a necessary condition of maximal dialogical justification—though this is true only if our fallible reconstruction of such conditions is correct.[38] Objective rights other than the highest one are at most *prima facie* human rights. The right to life, the right to food and many other rights are at most empirically necessary modes of freedom of thought. Yet the highest objective right is not just one person's right to discuss or not, but is, as much as possible, the right of all.

The highest objective human right to discuss or not then always prevails over other objective rights—such as the right to a public defender—that are *prima facie*. Yet, my subjective right to discuss will not always take precedence over your subjective right, or over your subjective right to sleep. Further, since human rights imply human duties, the duty to respect the actual right to discuss or not is also actual. The obligation to solicit participation by as many as possible in overlapping discussion circles, including circles that do not concern us, is no mere *prima facie* obligation. You never know what issues will concern you, directly, vicariously, or in the future.

If objective human rights arrange themselves in a hierarchy in which a single right always wins, contrary to what many assume moral duties, as to respect the exercise of human rights, also arrange themselves hierarchically. Respect for the right to discuss is primary, and the weight of other duties will vary according to the varying importance of their contribution to carrying out the primary duty. We have a one-rule deontological ethics in which duties other than respect of freedom of thought are more hypothetical. Preserve life, tell the truth, or be beneficent *only if* doing so helps as many as possible exercise the right to inquire about issues of concern.

In interim human rights ethics, rights that would be human rights if they were universal extend to as many as possible. As they extend to more, they grow ever closer to human rights. As they become rights of almost all, they become quasi-human rights. Approximately and for the most part, we may recognize human rights to exist even if they never exist in the strict universal sense. Here the job of interim human rights ethics approaches its end. Interpersonal relations become, for the most part, indistinguishable from those of definitive human rights ethics. No one's rights endure sacrifice on the altar of the future rights of all.

Falling short of quasi-human rights are "nation-specific human rights," rights enforced within a nation that are often incorrectly called "human rights," but which, were they enforced in all nations, would be actual human rights. Interim human rights ethics, as an extension of nation-specific "human rights" ethics, we see in the exportation of "human rights" to another nation, as in the United States' dealings with Germany and Japan, and perhaps with Afghanistan and Iraq. Yet if we almost but not fully actualize the ideal speech situation, its current actualization represents a quasi rationality presupposing quasi-human rights. Ideal human rights make possible ideal inquiry. Purely local rights enable only local inquiry. Quasi-human rights empower quasi-rational inquiry. Acting only *as if* human rights existed makes it possible to act only *as if* we pursued full inquiry.

11. Human Rights as Empirically Testable

We test for the existence of human rights by data on recognition of their validity and on enforcement. If most recognize and respect rights as valid, we can enforce compliance if a few do not. Good enforcement would then suggest that all generally recognize them as valid and respect them. United Nations reporting mechanisms assessing the compliance of ratifying states with United Nations rights covenants, along with reports by non-governmental organizations, empirically help test for the existence of rights. Some states (for example, Singapore, Malaysia, Saudi Arabia, the United States) have rejected parts of the Universal Declaration, but direct interviews with their most vulnerable citizens may show wide public recognition of officially rejected rights.

Immanuel Kant called presuppositions of the moral life "postulates of practical reason." They were theoretically improvable though the moral life took them for granted. Yet we cannot allow the existence of human rights to be a possibly false presupposition of the cognitive-moral standpoint of dialogue. Inquiry without really existing human rights cannot be fully successful. Kant's postulates, neither self-evident nor provable, are necessarily presupposed within moral practice. We perform our duty only by postulating that free will allows us to act otherwise than we do, that God exists to make possible the justice not possible in this world, and that immortal souls exist to make possible our moral perfectibility. If these postulates prove non-demonstrable to theoretical reason, the Kantian moral life remains possible because it is divorced from the theoretical point of view.

Kant felt no compulsion to prove in theory what we must presuppose practically. Yet the human rights ethics here is only the practical side of theoretical inquiry. The moral standpoint *is* the cognitive standpoint, but under a different description. The moral requirements of theoretical reason are themselves subject to theoretical inquiry, as it reflects on the rights allowing inquiry fully to exist. Instead of the existence of human rights being non-demonstrable Kantian postulates of practical reason, they are presuppositions of theoretical reason whose truth is empirically disconfirmable by the United Nations and data collection by non-governmental agencies. If the data disconfirm them, theoretical reason does not fully exist.

12. Restriction of Human Rights by Restrictions on Discussion Topics

To promote freedom of thought is to progressively eliminate both constraints making individuals think and do what they do not want to think or do and restraints preventing them from thinking and doing what they want to think or do. Some constraints and restraints are beyond our control. Others are within our control, yet we commonly leave them in place. One restraint lies in restrictions that we impose on discussion of particular subject matters. When a topic becomes sacred, we place limits on rights. Kantian ethics sacralizes only persons. To expand freedom of thought is to desacralize sacred realms beyond persons. The secularization of objective events, processes, narratives, institutions, things, and laws means moral progress for any capable of exploiting its potential for dialogue.

Some seek universal consensus in solving problems of natural science, while seeking consensus only within a restricted realm of fellow believers in issues of ideology or theology. We must decide whether ideology or theology is a subject in which objective truth is possible by inquiry, or in which non-rational faith must decide. In a totalitarian state imposing ideology on private and public life, the state may respect human rights in natural science but not in other areas. Yet to have rights depending on the subject one investigates is to operate under serious limitations in their exercise.

Respecting human rights on scientific issues but not on political issues means a conflict of cultures. Once we know rationality in one area we may be restless if forced into dogmatic belief in other areas. Subject-specific human rights force those who achieve maturity in some areas to withdraw from it elsewhere. States that restrict human rights to only some issues risk unpredictable behavior. The conflict in the individual between submission to authoritarian limits and emancipation from them resolves itself in different ways and by different compromises, depending on issue and the person.

13. Human Rights Restricted by Restricting Dialogue to Specialized Audiences

Dialogue is limited in validity and extent if it addresses a limited audience, and this is so even in the case of an audience of experts. Dialogue has full validity in identifying target theories for further discussion when it engages a universal audience including non-specialists. Specialists select fellow specialists. Given rival specialists, non-specialists judge what specialists we should heed. This blurs the distinction between limited expert discussion and dialogue with unrestricted participation. Recognition by the universal audience of rationally motivated inquirers ideally identifies the experts.

The "universal audience" is not simply the entire human population.[39] An audience has interests and skills with which to respond to a speaker lacking in a mere population. The universal audience judges according to universal rules of argumentation capable of general agreement. It will not exist until humankind organizes itself to at least informally be receptive to speakers according to universally recognized canons of interpretation, data collection, and logic. We address a universal audience by remaining sensitive to these canons even if we fail to win its agreement or response.

Specialist speakers in a closed session exclude others from their immediate audience without necessarily excluding them from a more universal audience to which they will later appeal. Such speakers know that non-specialist hearers can become specialists, and that as they address the universal audience some members of that audience will train to be specialists to judge specialists. Specialists must argue by rules of logic and hypothesis testing that may convince non-specialists in the universal audience. Only then can the universal audience test the consensus of a specialized audience. If a limited consensus becomes a universal consensus, most members of the universal audience judge specialists by reputation and other indirect means, without becoming specialists themselves. Yet rational discussion within a limited audience aspires to vindication by a universal audience.

Actual universal dialogue on a given theme does not exist until all concerned individuals participate directly, by representatives, or by passive acquiescence. If we truly publicize a theory universally and no one criticizes it, until further notice it has the approval of the universal audience.

The participation of all in the universal audience means reducing the distortion imposed on rationally motivated discussion by the unequal distribution of power. Everyone merits direct or indirect access to an unrestricted range of willing rights-empowered discussants on every issue about which he or she is concerned. A person needs to hear and filter as many voices as possible on an issue. A redistribution of resources to those whose voices are the least audible is a resource for many discussions. Edward Allen Kent writes that "while human rights are presumed to be universal, the important test for particular societies lies in their treatment of the worst off."[40]

Those who are less deprived need less assistance to become contributors to discussion. Here bargains become possible in the creation of new discussion partners at the other end of the economic scale. Human rights ethics seeks to generalize audibility among voices. If some voices on some issues deserve to be intimidated into silence, this we cannot do *a priori* by the initial conditions of dialogue, but only by the process of dialogue itself, by demonstration of the strength of the stronger argument.

14. Human Rights Restricted by Addressing Only the Present Generation

Maximally rational inquiry requires that, if possible, unborn individuals enjoy human rights. Collaboration in the creation of future persons is collaboration in establishing of new subjective human rights—new voices. Speaking of the rights of future generations, we cannot translate this concept into rights of particular countable individuals. Generations do not have human rights. As many as possible who are alive should be able to inquire, and yet we ought to favor those who are most capable of extending this ability to more people now and in the next generations.

Exclusive obligations exist to our children, and to our children's children if they actually exist. Yet if we of the first-generation have an obligation to individuals of the second generation, and if individuals of the second generation have an obligation to members of the third generation, it does not follow that we have an obligation to persons of the third generation. We have none if individuals of the third generation are not yet born. Our obligations to respect human rights are only to individuals who exist in particular, not merely in general. We may still have a self-imposed obligation to help bring as many competent new dialogue partners as possible into being.

15. Restriction of Human Rights by an External Duty to Dialogue

Discussion is a right, not a duty. The right to discuss is a right to discuss or not. Though non-ideal discussion may impose an external duty to dialogue, ideally no such duty exists, whether on any particular issue or with any particular person. Ideally, others do not violate your human rights by preferring not to talk with you. As a moral duty, the duty to discuss can only be self-imposed. Yet a decision not to discuss may itself be a contribution to the dialogue, and may be more instructive than dialogue under duress. A self-imposed duty to dialogue imposes no such duty on others. Participation in genuine dialogue is sincere, not servile. Yet when the behavior of persons not inclined to dialogue serves to test hypotheses, interpretation of such behavior integrates them into the dialogue despite their disinclination.

The basic human right is not simply a right to dialogue, but is a right to respect as a merely potential partner in dialogue. Perelman has asserted a duty to dialogue, but this must be understood as a *self-imposed* duty to enter a cooperative search for truth.[41] Where dialogue is an externally imposed duty, participation in it loses credibility. Jean-François Lyotard clearly sees that the right to address another is basic while asserting neither any duty to speak, nor any right to have active dialogue partners in reply.[42]

16. Restriction of Human Rights by the Assumed Validity of Market Dialogue

Realization of the ideal speech situation between individuals in different life situations is the emergence of a point of view that is at once moral and cognitive. Realization of this ideal would cancel any society based on domination. Your emancipation is essential to my recognition of your status as a potential respondent, capable of uncoerced vindication or falsification of my belief. I must grant others proprietorship over their opinions, over their bodies as a vehicle of speech, and over available personal property necessary to the unconstrained expression of their beliefs.

Dialogue, not limited to academic exchanges, may unfold through behavior instead of words. Can it occur through market behavior? If an individual is relevantly similar to others in transportation needs but cannot afford a car, we lose his or her dollar vote for or against the choice of a particular car meeting particular needs. To vote in the market requires purchasing power. We may be producing more meat in the world than we would with greater economic equality. A world with equal purchasing power might prefer more grain, less famine.

A morally ideal speech situation for discussion partners could exist in the world market only if we could construe this market as a series of overlapping credible dialogues *via* purchasing behavior—only if the voices of no group as expressed in purchases are louder by disproportionate wealth independently of the merit of their arguments. Market dialogues would be fully credible only if market participants voted with equal dollar votes, and only if consumer satisfaction consisted in finding a rationally motivated consensus as to what goods and services in truth we ought to produce.

If the reply is that some individuals are less perceptive players in the market, so that their participation with equal dollars contributes less to a rationally motivated consensus, their participation may require the assistance of advocates. Today's market consensus may evolve as market participants gain in experience, or as they find more effective consumer advocates. Advocates who speak on behalf of players who lack purchasing power may putatively defend the rights of those players.

Market dialogue with equally well-represented dialogue partners fails unless equal means give them equal market votes. Given these preconditions of rational market dialogue, we conclude that such dialogue does not fully exist. However, development strategies might bring it closer to existence. This development is also important because the market conditions even non-market dialogue. Goods and services actually purchased today give only a limited basis for inferring what individuals around the world should purchase. They distort non-market dialogue.

As noted in Chapter One, critics like Barbara Hernstein Smith hold that Habermas is naive to hold that the force of the better argument can determine the course of public inquiry. Discussion transpires in a marketplace in which players have differing native abilities, investments in education, and degrees of political weight.[43] Such critics hold that efforts to realize human rights are an impossible attempt to force the marketplace to yield to the demands of an ideal exchange of ideas on merit.

We replied that the marketplace can, to some degree, accommodate rationally motivated discussion by consumer education and advocates. Granted, a single vast seminar conducted under cognitively ideal conditions will never swallow the informal adversarial pursuit of truth in the marketplace of products and services, in politics, or in the arts. Yet the non-academic dialogical pursuit of truth by rival achievements throughout civil society realizes dialogue in the world, however raggedly, on a far larger scale than is possible in academia. A free global civil society compromises dialogue by academically ideal standards, but also makes dialogue a much greater power in the world than ivory tower academic purism ever will achieve. It projects the power of dialogue on a global playing field. Purely academic discussion is *in* but not *of* the world. Dialogue projected upon the stage of free global civil society, though imperfect, is not only in the world but thoroughly of it. It degrades dialogue, but not entirely, since it upgrades civil society. If Shakespeare could say metaphorically that all the world is a stage and that we are its actors, we can use a related metaphor. All civil society is a forum and—as buyers, sellers and traders of goods, services and information—we all participate in its tacit and not so tacit discussions.

Six

HUMAN RIGHTS IN THE OPEN SOCIETY

Human rights ethics, not unique to this book, has advanced through recent thinkers other than Jürgen Habermas. We now highlight one of them, Karl Popper. We assume human rights in any broadly public procedure of rational falsification. The falsifiability principle says that scientific conjectures are conceivably falsifiable, and that well tested conjectures have survived falsification attempts. It also asserts that we can test conjectures *well* only in an open society in which all potential critics enjoy rights. We find an inner identity between Popper's philosophy of science and his social philosophy. The *open society*, deriving from one basic impulse while the *closed society* derives from another, realizes human rights by maximizing chances for falsification.

In justifying the *public* falsifiability principle of science, Popper did not test the principle circularly by itself. My proposal is to test the falsifiability principle by a prior private, *non-public* falsifiability principle that tests conjectures by dialogue with inner voices. I also reject the "comprehensive rationalism" Popper rejected as circular because it required reason to justify itself. Yet I at once reject Popper's own "critical rationalism," a moral rationalism in which rationality is justified by a *decision* to respect others.

Private inquiry, first seeing that it can learn from internal voices, eventually converts to private dialogue. Private inquiry can engage in private discussion with internal voices, and on occasion stands corrected by them. It admits a principle of testing by private falsifiability (or criticizability), seeing that such voices could again falsify it. If the private principle justifies the public one without circularity, what non-circularly justifies the private principle? Initial self-correction by an internal voice does not occur by a *principle* of testing by private falsifiability. It occurs by a sudden unexpected taking of the standpoint of the other, by the embarrassment of seeing yourself as the other sees you. Initial self-correction has this *cause*, but not a *justification*. The mechanism causes adoption of the private principle to avoid future embarrassment by seeing that the very first error is the fear of error itself. Accumulated corrections and practical success then pragmatically justify self-correction by internal voices after its initial adoption.

1. Historical Fatalism and the Story of Freedom

Street curbs for the handicapped and homosexual domestic partners mark an age of human rights struggle. Legitimate minority rights are applied *human* rights. The human rights struggle is, like struggles for power, pleasure, or wealth, one view of history's meaning.[1] World history is not what Popper calls "History." When he says that "History" has no meaning, he does not mean the histories that individuals make.[2] "History" is an abstraction apart from particular struggles. Jean-François Lyotard called it a meta-narrative, a master story. Either you accept the invincible march of History or you reject it in frustration. Popper holds that such "History" refers to nothing. Railroad tracks of "History," delivering us to our destiny, are a myth.

Yet human beings can still make meaningful history by the struggle for rights. "History" can refer to countless individuals who oppress, acquiesce in oppression, or resist.[3] In trying to conceive this history, we fail to take in all individual stories. Yet a correct concept does not mean knowing all applications. Astronomical knowledge dispenses with knowing all stars. We have a concept of human beings without knowing all. We have a concept of history without listing all its players. Meta-historical struggle for rights is concrete in open-ended micro-struggles that the meta-level story in large part omits.[4] Yet these micro-struggles may still express the larger story. Meta-history may exclude micro-history, as in Popper's "History," although we can also conceive it more concretely to include some micro-history.

"History" as an irresistible force is not the one we make. Actual history has the meaning we give it. Yet such meaning is the very meaning Popper's nemesis Hegel finds! Hegel did not find us on Historical tracks independent of our choice. We choose to oppress, to acquiesce, to resist, laying our tracks before us, determining the immobility or forward movement of the train. Universal freedom is the solution to the problem of history, but, depending on human choices, we may not attain it. "It is we," Popper says, "who introduce purpose and meaning into nature and into history. Men are not equal, but we can decide to fight for equal rights."[5]

2. Open and Closed Societies

"The open society" is a society that does not restrict freedom of thought in the range of addressable persons and in the range of issues it can take up.[6] This society is the moral public good realized by general respect for rights. No society is fully open unless all are. Closed societies anywhere restrict freedom of thought everywhere, restricting the range of addressees. Since potential addressees exist in any closed society, no open society can be content to coexist with closed societies. If it were content, it would not yet be fully open.

Habermas suspects that the moral pursuit of this public good would ground discourse ethics teleologically in the pursuit of a higher end, not in duty for duty's sake:

[Karl Otto] Apel's auxiliary principle [the duty to strive for moral progress] introduces a teleological perspective into deontological moral theory, as he himself remarks: the realization of morality itself is elevated to the highest good. But Apel's goal thereby explodes the conceptual framework of deontological ethics.[7]

Since the goal itself, unlike general happiness, is intrinsically moral, the principle of interim human rights ethics that Apel suggests here remains deontological. The interim ethics is a second-best ethics that would collapse into definitive human rights ethics. Morality, not striving to realize it, is the highest moral good. Realizing morality is only the highest interim good.

Closed societies burden the exercise of human rights with restrictions on the range of discussion partners, of allowable topics, of known implications of a choice, and of known alternatives to a choice. You may have a right without always exercising it, but rights never exercised are abandoned property. No particular exercise of a right is obligatory, but an open society invites regular exercise.

Totalitarianism has seduced masses. Some supposed that after the Cold War it would be obsolete. Yet totalitarianism is the ideology of the closed society—partially closed to discussion and diversity. It precedes and postdates Marxist-Leninist and Fascist varieties. It continues to exist in atavistic fundamentalisms—whether Christian, Muslim, Amish, or others. These fundamentalisms are more typically "totalitarian" than the dictatorship of the proletariat. They invoke the authority, not of a future society that never existed, but of a past closed society to which we inevitably return at History's end.

The choice of an open society is justified by a decision not to insulate ourselves against the painful discovery of error, to view error as a chance to learn by discussion and experiment. For Popper, who credits Henri Bergson with distinguishing closed and open societies, the open society ideally coincides with humanity.[8] For Bergson, the open society is open to a charismatic "mystical" influence of individual genius breaking down traditional barriers.[9] Popper sees it as open to rational criticism in general, without restriction on the source. A role for genius exists as long as it can eventually express itself in rational terms.

The gap between the two diminishes if we distinguish between the reactionary mysticism that Popper criticized and the progressive mysticism Bergson praised. Reactionary mysticism marks the decline of a closed society as an attempt to idealize and restore a golden age. Progressive mysticism decompartmentalizes theories and groups, anticipating a universal open society. Neither philosopher states the connection between the open society and human rights by name, but the connection exists. Both are fallibilists. A closed society's presumption of infallibility implies it has nothing to learn from any other's exercise of freedom of thought. Ossified dogmas and rituals repress a right to be different. Yet Bergson has trouble showing why closed societies should become open. He describes the transition as a conversion without rational checks.

Popper could cite the Third Reich as a closed society. Based on Popper's idea of a "comprehensive rationalism" that circularly justifies the falsifiability principle by falsifying the principle's denial (see next section), Nazism was the refutation of a conjectured denial of the principle. Hitler falsified the closed society which rejected the principle. Assuming that his unscientific dogmatism prevented him from adopting the falsifiability principle, he did not falsify it for himself, but he did so for us. He showed how a closed society avoids an immediate painful awakening to error by unfalsifiable delusions that only postpone the awakening and make it ruder. In a fallibilist open society, we acknowledge error without threats to our identity.

A person's rational identity lies not in current beliefs, but in possible error correction. National Socialists, finding their identity in racist ideology, provided a trial of the closed society's rejection of trial and error. The Communists, with different dogmas, equally refuted the closed society's general principle. Germany's painful realization of the error led to a more open society. Yet we can only fallibly know that we should approach some open society. No particular open society stands before us with definite contours.

3. The Circularity of Rationally Arguing for Rationality

If we assume individuals not already committed to reason, to rational argumentation, converting them to it by direct rational argument is impossible. No one can depend on direct rational argument to convince persons not already committed to reason, to rational argumentation. A master who converts by dialogical reason to abolitionism must have already wanted the rational assent of the slave. Those who have chosen the open society and its morality must lure those who have not, since they cannot debate with them. We may dispense, to those not committed to the open society, a moral education by example, which at once may be an aesthetic education to entice.

We may get those who reject reason to agree that they do so, but this will not change their minds. To prefer the open society is to prefer survival, adaptation, and the adventure of further evolution informed by falsifiable knowledge claims. We cannot convince those who prefer something else. Bergson held that the two societies reflect two temperaments. Both will always be with us. The open society presupposes historical closed societies, since it is the opening of what is closed. Only retrospectively, from within the open society, does a closed society appear closed.

A vigilant open society requires an idea of the closed society as a foil. A right to freedom of thought in potential partnership with anyone else in a search for truth is a polemical right to oppose dogmatic fidelity to existing belief. The quest for the open society weaves itself into the polemical fabric of life from the beginning:

We can find individual foragers who believe that certain magical rituals will attract game, but we can also find businessmen on Wall Street who link their achievements to praying the rosary. Both forager and business executive will likely have taken all the technological and pragmatic steps necessary to assure success. . . . We can also find foragers and business executives who reject magico-religious techniques or who have sophisticated understandings of the role of ritual in human life.[10]

Dialogue with internal voices, the precursor to rational dialogue, is as ancient as human nature. A justification of human rights does not convert individuals to this very first form of dialogue. Rather, it motivates expanding the audiences addressed both in proto-rational dialogue with internal voices and in dialogue with a restricted range of external voices. Commitment to an unlimited dialogical pursuit of truth obligates us to validate and respect, if possible, everyone's claim to freedom of thought. Because you commit to unrestricted dialogue, others have rights you ought to respect.

This inference passes from *is* to *ought*. I promise to respect the private space in which others conduct thought experiments, and so I ought to respect it. This is no naturalistic fallacy, but, following John Searle, an inference to a specific *ought*, a promissory *ought*.[11] To make a promise is to place an obligation upon yourself to yourself to keep it. If possible, we ought to keep a promise to respect human rights. A cognitive *promissory obligation* to oneself becomes a *moral obligation*. We discover that we can keep the cognitive promise to justify or correct our belief only morally by dialogue. The cognitive obligation is to yourself, while the moral obligation is to others. *The* cognitive *promise founding this promissory obligation constitutes the moral life, and so does not fall under it.* Promissory obligations arising in the family, civil society or the state are moral only by presupposing a prior cognitive commitment which can be kept only by respect for others.

By a nationalistic promissory obligation, we ought to reinforce solidarity with compatriots in a closed ethnic community giving us a discernible identity in the human mass. This obligation conflicts with one to construct human rights, and at times weighs more heavily. Given such a conflict, the obligation to seek truth dialogically prevails if we ask all obligations to be cognitively justifiable. *Ought* implies *can*. Only dialogically do we know that solidarity in a closed ethnic community provides identity in mass society. Yet you can place an obligation on yourself without any commitment to its cognitive justification. Conflicts then emerge between a commitment to human rights and other commitments. Moral education instills a commitment to human rights and reduces the intensity of other commitments.

Popper has asked whether the principle of falsifiability, of the possible falsification of conjectures underlying all discussion, is justifiable by that principle itself, as a well-tested but falsifiable conjecture, or whether it issues from a theoretically unjustified moral decision.[12] He distinguishes between comprehensive and critical rationalism. *Comprehensive rationalism* applies the falsifiability principle of science to itself. His own *critical rationalism* holds that the falsifiability principle is not self-justifying. Such justification would circularly assume the principle's validity prior to its justification. He concludes that we should embrace the rationalism of conjecture and refutation based on a moral law commanding positive respect for the freedom of expression of others. Critical rationalism is *critical* in a Kantian sense. Science has ethical conditions of its very possibility:

> [R]ationalism is an attitude of readiness to listen to critical arguments and to learn from experience. It is fundamentally an attitude of admitting that "I may be wrong and you may be right, and by an effort, we may get nearer to the truth."[13]

Yet this statement makes the morality of listening depend, if not circularly on the falsifiability principle in the open society, at least on the discovery by private inquiry of its self-correction by a single external voice. This leads to what we may call *developmental rationalism.* Popper gives a moral justification of the falsifiability principle. Yet what justifies the initial conversion to the ethics of listening? We first ground this resolve in private inquiry, in a theoretical search for truth in a very general sense which does not yet presuppose respecting universal freedom of thought and expression.

A theoretical justification of rights by the falsification principle in the open society fails because it presupposes a theoretically unargued assertion of human rights on which we cannot without circularity rely. Yet a commitment to universal rights is justifiable beginning with private inquiry, which does not circularly presuppose these rights, but still anchors them in truth seeking. Private inquiry exhibits two stages. It begins with claims of self-evidence and then passes on to self-corrections through private reflection. Public science invites falsification by external voices, but private inquiry has its own falsification principle before public inquiry begins, inviting refutation by inner private voices. By a higher-level reflection, private inquiry discovers that external persons sometimes, to its surprise, correct its internal voices.

Discussion with other persons optimizes falsification more than discussions with friendly internal voices offering an insufficient range of counterexamples. As soon as one other person falsifies results of private inquiry, the inquirer recognizes that its falsification by still others is possible. This conclusion is reasonable, though reason forces no one to follow it. A seed of rationality exists in private inquiry, and it can develop into rights-based public inquiry unless it faces stronger contrary winds. Assuming that the claim that you cannot learn from others who *seemed* to have nothing to teach has refuted itself in the case of one other person, the assumption has collapsed in the case of all. Foundationalist epistemology appealing to private self-evidence has collapsed. Private inquiry can convert itself first to the ethics of listening and then to a universal extension of that ethics in science.

No human right ought to exist to have others listen to you, and listening to everybody is impossible. Yet the dialogical right to freedom of thought is a right to try to create thought worth listening to, and which is available for listening by as many as possible. This implies a theoretical grounding of moral practice ultimately in private inquiry. The circularity that seems to arise when reason vindicates itself disappears if we distinguish two tribunals of reason. Private monological reason indicts itself, transforming itself into public dialogical reason. Yet private reason indicts itself only because it already contains the seed of intersubjectivity. Even in appealing explicitly to private self-evidence, we discover after unexpectedly learning from others that we were already implicitly ready to learn from them.

I now sketch a possible scenario for the development of reason. Private reason typically establishes itself in its pursuit of self-evidence by negating instruction from superior significant others within the family. The child initially constitutes itself by internalizing dialogue with these significant others. The child is initially for itself what it is for the other, for the parent. When the burden of the other's criticism, to which the child cannot begin to reply, becomes too heavy, the child denies the possibility of falsification by the other person. It reinforces its repression of the other's criticism by tacitly claiming that particular beliefs are self-evident.

If this is correct (child psychologists must decide), by the assertion of self-evident knowledge, the child detaches itself from its original dialogical context in the family. The child has constituted itself as a self through dialogical relations that it now comes to disown. The denial of self-evident knowledge that comes with the eventual recognition of universal human rights and the possibility of falsification by anyone (and not just by internal voices) reinstates the primitive sociality of the child on a level where the child's ego, new strength, and maturity permit it to accept that sociality.

The pursuit of science is inherently moral. The lamp that it holds up to human faces rigorously distinguishes between moral and immoral. The scientific point of view exists in the world as a power with which to contend. Other powers limit it, such as nationalism, but its advance and retreat are the advance and retreat of morality. The Enlightenment was not wrong about this. Respect for persons, if advanced independently of the search for knowledge, has little compelling about it. Such respect may appear sentimental and impossibly idealistic in the face of the brutal forces opposing it in the world. Yet modern science makes itself a force in the world. The scientific point of view always existed in true courts of law. Today vast programs of corporate research and development aspire to be science, though their scientific character diminishes when competitive advantage excludes the publication of results to a universal audience before placing them on the market. Research and development cannot assure maximal reliability for its results without, through divulging secret information, making the sponsoring company less competitive. Submission to the universal audience takes instead the form of exposure to the market, with the risk of casting customers as experimental research subjects.

The scientific point of view gives training in honesty by multiplying chances for either upholding or falsifying claims. You do not achieve confirmation in discussion by dishonestly stating something you do not believe. Without the support lent to honesty by inquiry the temptation is to say whatever serves immediate interests. Honesty is not necessary to respect for human rights, but is present wherever respect for rights serves inquiry.

The Enlightenment allegedly overrated the influence of the scientific point of view, and catastrophic nationalistic wars in the twentieth century allegedly show this. Yet we assume, not that the scientific point of view is all-powerful, but only that it is a power, a cosmopolitan power that has begun to check nationalistic or sectarian claims since 1945. International human rights courts introduce the cognitive point of view in national contexts where it had been absent. The advance of human rights in the world will depend on the extent to which the scientific point of view progressively institutionalizes itself as a force in the world. We understand "science" to include interpretive human sciences and the natural sciences. According to the German usage, "science" exists wherever you pursue objective truth systematically. In a court of law, you pursue truth by the methods of the human sciences. Documents, testimony, and exhibits become evidence for an objectively correct interpretation of texts or understanding of individual actions and motives.

The reason for justifying moral practice by theory lies in the nature of theory, which is to correct and justify practice. We are confident that we ought to pursue truth before we see that we ought to do so by respecting rights. No obligation to pursue truth follows from human nature. Yet nature allows us to place an obligation on ourselves to seek it. Once truth seeking becomes a commitment, the conclusion of private inquiry will be that inquiry must go public. In fact, we will seek truth only if we have made no contrary promise of greater weight to ourselves. The commitment to truth seeking usually ranks high because it has survival value. Acting on true belief is not always more successful, but it tends to be. True beliefs identify means that tend not to be effective merely by accident. This reflection points to an explanation, not a justification, of the commitment to human rights.

The promise that carries more weight than any other promise becomes foundational to personal identity. It constitutes your highest chosen standard of commendation. Not all persons experience the same promise as carrying the greatest weight. Yet the rights of all, in a sense falling short of the human rights of all over and against all, do not demand that *everyone* commit primarily to truth seeking. They demand only that *some* make this commitment. These individuals will recognize the legitimate rights of those who claim human rights, and at once the legitimate natural pursuits of others as long as they fall within limits compliant with respect for human rights. Even those who never commit themselves maximally to the pursuit of truth may enter the pursuit. They may enter as dialogue partners capable, if only by our observation of the result of their action, of providing a wider testing ground for the conjectures of those maximally committed to public truth seeking.

4. The Emergence of Human Rights
Culture in Classical Athens

The open and closed societies are not historical, but are ideal types, permanent poles. Without underestimating the persistence of slavery, Popper sees in Athens the emergence of the idea of universal rights in the West, an idea that he attributes in large part to the city's maritime exposure to other cultures. Athens' naval imperialism revealed claims to validity for the traditional beliefs and customs of every city. Yet the historical success of Plato's aristocratic reversion to the idea of the closed society overshadowed the human rights and abolitionist movement in Athens.[14] Ultimately the movement did not create the idea of human rights, it only recalled it. Trying to open closed societies is as ancient as the closed society it seeks to open:

> [I]n each culture great diversity exists among individuals in their faith and beliefs. Just as in industrial societies, people everywhere range from atheists to true believers, with all degrees of commitment to the belief system exhibited between these two extremes. It is an error to assume that members of other cultures are uniform in their beliefs and outlook on religion. Even among contemporary foragers, some people take religious beliefs as symbols for abstract processes and concepts of the supernatural, while others hold literal, fundamentalist beliefs. Analysts must distinguish socially shared assumptions about the supernatural from individual commitment to and understanding of these assumptions.[15]

Foragers isolated from an enforcing agent enjoy no human rights. Yet as individuals, some reflect on customs and conventional beliefs and inquire privately into them. Freedom of thought also exists in some historical civilizations without a guarantee of rights. No serious promissory note to the effect that compatriots or inquiring human beings would agree may accompany one's assertions. Yet we know that some freedom of thought exists among foragers only because some communicate their reflection on customary beliefs and practices to one another or to anthropologists. Such communication implies an intention to express criticism which the forager believes will not be unwelcome to the anthropologist. With such freedom of thought in pre-patriarchal society comes the seed of human rights, a concern of some for freedom from provincial oppressiveness. The emergence of the human rights idea in Athens was a recollection because hierarchical patriarchal historical society had interposed itself between Athens's abolitionists and foragers, creating despotic barriers, of which foragers knew little, to the human rights ideal.

Seven

A DIALECTICAL JUSTIFICATION OF HUMAN RIGHTS

1. The Distortion of Rationally Motivated Discussion by Domination

For Habermas, to pursue the stronger argument is to renounce the domination to which distortions of communicative praxis are due. We ought equalize the power of discussion partners upward by universal rights. Those in positions of power have a motive to concede rights, not merely as Richard Rorty holds by sympathy for the weak, but by their need to legitimate their own authority.[1]

Discussion in the American Congress rarely pursues the stronger argument. Partisan politics, the political balance of power, makes a victory of such an argument a coincidence. Discussion between labor and management depends on uneven balances of power, as do negotiations between nations. The winning argument between attorneys can depend on which side buys the more expensive legal team. In such situations, discussion fails to weigh arguments by merit alone, and manipulates those who enter with less power.

We may wonder where rationally motivated discussion between equally empowered partners does occur. Unaffiliated academics survive by exploiting the stronger argument regardless of where it goes. Vital questions depend on how public discussion declares its independence of influences irrelevant to the evidence. Even in distorted discussion, discussants seek agreement. Republicans and Democrats aim at bipartisan policies. Labor and management seek wage and benefit packages acceptable to both sides. Diplomats seek durable peace accords. Yet the disproportionate power of one side imposes inauthentic agreements. If the weak can only assent, the dominant remain with an uneasy truce, not trusting agreements to stick with shifting balances of power. Agreements are dependable only if power is relatively equal. *Human rights help establish conditions of genuine and lasting accords in the place of imposed solutions.*

2. Priority of Respect for Persons in Kantian Ethics

Respect for persons as ends in themselves may appear as the least problematic form of Immanuel Kant's categorical imperative. A. J. M. Milne defends human rights as moral rights to be treated as a person with self-chosen ends, not merely as a means.[2] We can easily criticize Kant's universalization of the maxim of one's actions as a test of their morality. We can universalize both morally irrelevant maxims ("Tie your left shoe string first!") and immoral maxims ("Cheat if you have a particular social security number").[3] Clever individuals find applicable maxims they can universalize without incoherence. The universalization principle appears purely formal.

If we reply that morally irrelevant or immoral maxims do not arise from the moral point of view, we admit that universalization of a maxim fails to capture morality fully. We must formulate maxims offered for universalization from a moral point of view that excludes clever egoistic maxims. The reason for respecting others is not that we cannot universalize rules of non-respect. We capture morality by respecting them for lack of a good reason to limit the range of respected persons. All should be audible since all are potential sources of instruction.[4] Using others for your instruction is never *merely* using them. *We use the other for our instruction only by respecting his or her right to pursue and test presuppositions of his or her self-assigned projects.*

All persons have an ideal right to act as agents with self-assigned ends which are socially respected, not merely respected by a few Kantians. Why this is so is not evident merely from the right itself. This right is not a rights-based right finding its basis in itself alone. The reason for social respect of persons is that intersubjective inquiry requires others to successfully act as ends in themselves, with self-assigned ends possibly giving instruction by rights-protected pursuits. The good will of one Kantian cannot create a right.

Kant did not place respect for persons as ends in the context of inquiry. Kantians hold that the duty of such respect is evident outside such a context:

> Man, in his individuality, possesses a value which confers a certain dignity upon him; he is a value in himself, simply because he is human. If this principle seems naive, it cannot be avoided, however. It has an axiomatic status insofar as it represents the *sine qua non* condition of any further theoretical developments. There is no other way, at the ethical level, to justify human rights.[5]

Yet if no other way exists, the justification of respect for persons is question begging in the face of Nietzschean critiques it was supposed to lay to rest.[6]

Respect for autonomy, the third version of the categorical imperative, is respect for self-determined rational freedom. Yet for Kant the autonomous self is not the whole person, since we can act heteronomously from inclination. Respect for the whole person is more indulgent than respect for autonomy. Respect for persons is respect for agents capable of autonomy who do not always demonstrate it. Respect for the autonomy of persons comes with disrespect for some of their actions. Yet the freedom of the whole person, including persons who consent to inclination, is essential to inquiry. Human rights norms justify this freedom. Inclination and passion can lead to instructive experiments. They and their self-correction are integral to the larger form of reason in which nothing great occurs without passion.[7]

Habermas does not use Hegel's philosophy of history to vindicate human rights. He opts for a procedural justification by a universalization principle. His universalizability principle ("Act so that universal observance of your maxim is acceptable in its direct and indirect consequences, without constraint or restraint, as satisfying the interests of all whom the maxim affects—not just all that feel themselves concerned—more than any known alternative maxim") is a new version less of Kant's universalizability principle than of his second version of the categorical imperative, commanding respect for persons. It differs from Kant by placing respect for persons in a context of inquiry into the acceptability of maxims and beliefs. You respect persons when you seek the acceptability of universalized maxims or beliefs to all persons who are or feel concerned as a condition of its acceptability to you.

3. Back to Hegel

Can a dialectical justification of human rights norms in the case of those who do not presuppose them complement Jürgen Habermas's procedural justification of not violating human rights to avoid a practical contradiction in the case of those who do presuppose them?

Hegelian dialectical triumphs over institutionalized contradictions of the limited rationality of the past, over the incoherence of historical lordship, are not invoked in Habermas's dialogical morality. The Hegelian theological and metaphysical apparatus, which Habermas disowns, can be retained only at the cost of sacrificing a procedural justification of rights for doctrinal justification before a limited Hegelian audience.[8] Secularized remnants of Hegelian world history as a struggle for rights working through forms of lordship remain in Habermasian history as a struggle against forms of "domination." Yet Habermas suspects Hegel of telling an ethnocentric story of Western freedom reflecting "prejudices of adult, white, well-educated Western males of today."[9] He also finds it theology-laden, hence unusable in a post-metaphysical age: "[T]he gradual embodiment of moral principles into concrete forms of life is not something that can be safely left to Hegel's absolute spirit."[10]

A dialectical self-transformation of a contradictory monological reason of the past into contemporary dialogical reason does not concern Habermas. His concern is with pragmatic contradictions into which we fall in diverging from contemporary dialogical reason. Cosmopolitan discussion supposes human rights. Yet why should others not practice ethnocentric discussion presupposing no such rights, recognizing merely a duty to seek local assent? Ethnocentric discussion contains no background commitment to convince a universal audience. No performative contradiction exists in such discussion by excluding from discussion all but our tribe. It may not violate human rights, but it lacks maximum safeguards. Is there a valid logical transition from ethnocentric to cosmopolitan discussion? Without one, we have but a causal process of cultural dissemination. Cosmopolitan discussion catches on or does not.

Habermas finds dialogical reason beginning to eclipse monological reason in institutions of the contemporary world. Dialectically, however, we can show monological reason—which historically has left the impulse of human nature pressing forward toward agreement unappropriated—converting to dialogical reason. I wish explore Robert Pippin's suggestion that we go back to a version of the Hegelian dialectic.[11] I do not mean that we should go back exegetically to any particular text, but that we should return to Hegel's dialectical method of reconstructing how, in embracing inquiry before a merely private or limited audience, we in the end validate the opposite.

In rethinking the gradual emergence of dialogical rationality, Habermas appeals, not to a historical dialectic, but only to Lawrence Kohlberg's developmental psychology, reconstructing the development of individual moral autonomy.[12] For Hegel, individual development (ontogenesis) repeats intersubjective historical development (phylogenesis).[13] The open society generalizes respect for personality. We did not fully inquire when we did not welcome insights from all quarters. Avoidable exclusion of Africans from discussion is now inconsistent with our procedure of inquiry in mathematics, natural science, law, social science, the courts, and education. The presupposition that all should have a right of reply implies that none with something to say should be inaudible. *Morality is not obsequiousness, but is solicitude toward all.*

4. Justification of Human Rights through the
Dialectic of History to the French Revolution

The commendability of actions within a practice by an accepted standard may occur by a non-rational standard. Torture may be quite consistently commendable to torturers by their own standard. An exclusively nationalistic standard is possible by which it is commendable. Yet the commendability of torture in maximally rational discussion would be an irrational suspension of the rights of the tortured as potential discussants. Their unconstrained testimony would be missing, while by dialogical rationality all affected should be free to participate without constraint. None can suffer more than the victims do. They are indispensable witnesses.

Habermas's justification of not violating rights takes the form of a reminder to those already committed to rational discussion before a universal public. They fall into a practical contradiction by violating human rights. But this justification of not lapsing fails before *consistent* practitioners of ethnic cleansing. As Pippin notes, the establishment of universal discussion is a tenuous creation of the sort of world-historical story of freedom Hegel recounts.[14]

For Hegel human rights on earth are the end game of philosophical world-history proceeding from the freedom of only one, through some, to all. History would have a meaning even if it unfolded by the standard of pleasure or mere power instead of dialogical freedom. Yet by realizing dialogical reason globally we would vindicate history at its end and do not just cut if off. But for Hegel freedom of thought at the end of history does not belong merely to human beings. The unfolding of dialogical freedom of thought on earth also actualizes the highest potential of reality. Human rights come to define reality by its highest achievement of coming to think and know itself in and through human inquiry. Hegel writes:

> A constitution . . . was established in harmony with the conception of Rights, and on this foundation, all future legislation was to be based. Never since the sun had stood in the firmament and the planets revolved around him had it been perceived that man's existence centers in his head, i.e., in Thought, inspired by which he builds up the world of reality.[15]

Asserting "rights of personality" along with the French Revolution, Hegel held that "absolute freedom" is "conscious of its pure personality and therein of all spiritual reality. . . . [T]he world is for it simply its own will, and this is a general will."[16] Such metaphysics, expressed in the ultimate concept of the absolute in the *Science of Logic*, dismays Habermas.[17] Taking human rights to be metaphysically the highest achievement of the absolute, showing its essence to lie its potential for rationality, goes quite beyond the purely procedural justification of human rights to which Habermas is committed.

In Hegel's *Phenomenology of Spirit* the downside of Revolutionary human rights is that they are anarchical. They end in the "absolute hard rigidity and self-willed atomisms" of individuals who are mutually exclusive precisely by their common identity.[18] A web of affiliations and communal bonds distinguishing persons no longer exists. "In this absolute freedom . . . all social groups or classes, which are the spiritual spheres into which the whole is articulated, are abolished."[19] Universal objective human rights pass into subjective rights by their exercise. We share the same universal "objective right" to own or join, but not the same exercised subjective right to own this house, or to belong to this church.

A web of affiliations and historical bonds must return in the exercise of rights. The Terror was not an accident befalling universal abstract rights in the Revolution, for the Revolution severed abstract rights from the concrete ethical rights that would realize them. "Universal freedom . . . can produce neither a positive work nor a deed; there is left for it only *negative* action; it is merely the fury of destruction."[20] Rights in the Revolution were abstract objective rights. Making them absolute apart from different exercised subjective rights in different communities is a *totalitarian human rights fetish*. In the name of abstract equality, the Revolution negated the subjective communitarian rights by which our identities differ. Absolute freedom is "*in itself* . . . just this *abstract self-consciousness*, which effaces all distinction."[21]

The possibility of torture, terrorism, or ethnic cleansing without any pragmatic contradiction through an established background commitment to enlightenment leads us to a Hegelian justification of human rights norms as the historical resolution of the contradiction of domination maintained along with the emergence of enlightened insight.

> It certainly might be the case that there are or were forms of social life and linguistic activity, and assumptions about acceptable claims-making, which involve no . . . "ideal speech situation" norm, and such societies functioned. . . . For Habermas to claim what he does about "universality" and "rationality" and the like, he shall have to show, for example, that such alternate activities created (or would create) some sort of crisis or failure that in some way "led" (or would lead) to the realization of these modern [rational] differentiated spheres. . . . And with this sort of justification we are getting much closer to Hegel.[22]

By the dialectical justification of human rights norms, those in dominant positions first come to adopt such norms. They do not correct practical contradictions by a background commitment to an already acquired set of consistent human rights norms. Without yet ceasing to deny the humanity of others, they inconsistently raise the natural human impulse to press on to agreement from being an impulse which we alone attach to them into one which they affirm for themselves.

5. Dialectical Coversion to a Consistent Commitment to Human Rights Norms

Habermas shows human rights violators finding a pragmatic contradiction between the violation and their own contrary commitment. By a practical version of indirect proof, they contradict themselves in the violation. But a certain dialectic of lordship and bondage shows a conversion to reason by persons still caught up in contrary institutions of domination. The impulse to press on by human nature toward agreement passes into a will to do so. They inconsistently both dominate others and seek to justify themselves by the free judgment of others.

The dialectical justification begins by showing how masters still try to compel others to agree even while beginning to seek their free assent. They discover that they cannot trust others if they compel agreement. They adopt human rights norms to make genuine consent by the weak possible. This insight may be possible even today. It is not excluded that unrepetent agents of domination today—e.g., scrupulously consistent torturers—may fall into a similar internal conflict between old norms and new insight.

6. The Dialogical Surrender of Domination

Someone in a position of domination may be led to consistent adoption of human rights norms by being moved to vindicate him- or herself through appropriating and then acting on the natural human impulse to press on to rationally motivated agreement. Either procedures not based on such norms remain consistent by not heeding that impulse or they become self-annulling and self-transcending. As long as torturers have no contradictory working assumptions, they are not open to self-refutation by reflection on a pragmatic contradiction.

In a dialectical justification of human rights norms one first takes the standpoint of one who does not assume such norms and thus who falls into no practical contradiction by their violation. The dialectical justification of human rights corrects no contradiction between a violation and a consistent dialogical procedure. Rather, it corrects an inconsistent dialogical procedure, the contradictory assumption *both* of domination asserted without needing free confirmation by others *and* of a subjective will to win confirmation by pressing forward toward agreement with others.

A simple example is the man who clings to the dogmatism of common sense as cited in the Preface to the *Phenomenology of Spirit*. Such a person, exerting domination through the weight of common opinion, tramples humanity under foot. Yet at first the man of common sense does not do so self-consciously, in what Hegel calls his being for himself. He does not have a bad conscience. Unlike Habermas's reminder to someone violating rights in contradiction with his or her own background presupposition, a dialectical justification depends on the man of common sense for the first time consenting to the human impulse to press on toward agreement. He does this by surprising himself in the discovery and correction of error despite himself with the help of another's criticism. After he admits having learned something from another, he contradicts himself in his own mind by maintaining the dogmatism of common sense. It then becomes possible for him to resolve the contradiction, whether by retreating into a consistent trampling of humanity under foot or by abandoning the dogmatism of common sense and consistently pressing on toward agreement.

An agreement is genuine only if both sides are free not to agree. A lord who wishes an agreement with a bondsman must free the bondsmen, empowering them to think differently than he. Contracts between lords and bondsmen are not genuine. The usual justification of human rights as a struggle against oppression suggests that only victims have a direct interest in rights. The interest of masters is less evident. Yet lords discover an interest in recognizing the human right to be instructively different. The duty to be open to difference is universal in the open society. No longer conceding this right begrudgingly, the erstwhile lord positively solicits its exercise.

The feudal dress of "lordship and bondage" should not fool us. The issue is pre-enlightenment domination in any form. Dialectical justification of human rights norms uncovers a rational motive for accepting them by those who exercise institutionalized domination. They may find domination unstable due to possibly shifting balances of power. Yet they do not merely realize that domination threatens to return to *life and death struggle*. They now also realize that it limits their ability to correct error and advance toward truth in promoting their success in any venture. They want affirmation by others, and see that for this affirmation to be credible they must recognize the other's right to disagree.

This rational motive for surmounting domination may have been historically active in the minds of some lords or masters. Yet to say that this motive has been sufficient for abolishing historical forms of lordship and bondage would be untrue. In actual processes of emancipation material factors enter as well as insight. Without favorable material forces, criticism showing domination vacillating with insight to be contradictory will more likely succumb to consistent domination rather than abolish it. Bondsmen of course also have an interest in emancipation. Yet the dialectical justification of rights takes up the lord's standpoint and accompanies him on a rational path to emancipating bondsmen in resolving his own self-contradiction.

By human rights norms, the quest for truth proceeds neither by infallible private judgment, nor by privately corrected fallible judgments. The quest is interpersonal. The need for other persons in inquiry, though not at first evident, is an elementary lesson of experience. We abandon the method of infallible private intuition or purely private self-correction when others refute results of the method. From a non-dialogical point of view, adoption of the dialogical method of justification cannot be dialogically justified. We must justify surrender of the monological standpoint to the dialogical standpoint monologically.

We do not establish the belief that all have an initially equal right to contribute to public discussion by our experience in all discussion. Much experience more likely shows that many persons have little to contribute. Yet a single counter example of being surprised by such a person is enough to make one reflect. The presupposition of an equal right of reply can then arise from a point of departure within monological inquiry, as the conversion to dialogue before a limited public audience gives way, through the same motive of avoiding error, by conversion to dialogue before a global audience. The result shows a one-time lord that maximum confidence in himself depends on confidence that no testimony is left out.

Since bondsmen are not free, emancipation cannot result from negotiation but only from a proclamation by the master. The master lays down the universal right to partake in discussion in a unilateral emancipation proclamation. This proclamation conditions any subsequent bilateral contract by which bondsmen, not just the lords, agree to end lordship. Intrapersonal dialogue occurs within a monological rationality including conversation with inner voices. Yet human rights cannot protect inner voices as distinct from flesh and blood persons.

The monologically rational motive to inquire is that thinking cannot rest with an internal contradiction between two statements. Dialogical rationality adds that thinking cannot rest with a contradiction between its statement and that of another person. A rational monological transition to dialogical rationality starts by noting that interpersonal inquiry inspires more confidence by correcting more error than intrapersonal inquiry. Unrestricted inquiry, giving error correction its best chance by including a maximum number of potential participants, presupposes human rights norms.

Cosmopolitan Stoic discussion resolves the contradiction of lordship in the *Phenomenology*. The lord is lord only by his relationship to a bondsman on whose consent the lord depends to be a lord. Yet a lord who has become a cosmopolitan dialogue partner no longer wishes agreement with the bondsman merely as to who is lord. If the bondsman is intelligent, a nominal lord who is a cosmopolitan discussion partner knows many matters on which he would like confirmation, and this motivates a move to Stoicism, to ideal human rights, and beyond Stoicism toward their realization. The lord then depends on liberated bondsmen for confidence in a vast array of his beliefs in cosmopolitan dialogue. The truth of lordship is that it requires the bondsman's free assent to serve. It requires emancipation of the bondsman if service is to be more than the fear of death.

7. The Self-Critique of Private Inquiry as the Seed of Human Rights Norms

For Habermas, a reminder of human rights norms presupposed by existing cosmopolitan procedures of justification arises by reflection on pragmatic contradictions. Dialectical justification of such norms, of the claim that all ought to have a right of reply, arises when we adopt the norm of maximal justification beyond the more error-prone norm of justification discovered in merely addressing a restricted public audience. Yet this argument requires a prior argument showing that private inquiry, in consultation merely with one's own internal voices, ought first to yield to interpersonal discussion even of the most restricted sort.

We justify ourselves within a restricted dialogue circle more fully by going beyond it, by reflection on the act of discovering individuals outside the circle to uphold or surprisingly correct us. Maintaining a shrunken discussion circle reflects domination by still excluding some. Any master who does not participate in procedures of unrestricted intersubjective inquiry including bondsmen renounces full legitimacy, condemning himself to ruling in and by fear. Such rule cannot even qualify as stable lordship and bondage. It arises against the backdrop of a Hobbesian war of all against all in which a lord has the upper hand only insecurely.

Habermas attends to a practical contradiction between violating universal public freedom of thought and nonetheless still presupposing this freedom as a norm institutionalized in the contemporary world. He justifies suspending violation by making the practical contradiction explicit, leading the violator to conclude that consistency by ceasing the violation is easier than by withdrawing from a now widely entrenched norm. Eliminating violations occurs in part because human rights norms, intersubjectively adopted by participation in contemporary institutions, come to be more stubbornly presupposed than their violation.

The example of trying to recall committed Nazis to respect for human dignity by reminding them of modern eighteenth century Enlightenment cosmopolitanism, to which they already have a background commitment as twentieth century Germans, illustrates the uncertain outcome of invoking a practical contradiction. The failure of invoking existing human rights norms leads us to hope for their establishment or reestablishment. Nazis who identify solely with a human propensity to the dogmatic fixation of belief absolutize an abstract, one-sided concept of their humanity in negation of the equally human propensity to seek agreement. Repression of this second dimension of one's humanity by the exclusive assertion of the first results in a contradictory self-concept. Propositions that imply a contradiction do not imply that anyone will infer the contradiction, or correct it assuming that it is inferred. Yet fallibly justified discussion merely among Nazis creates an opening and opportunity for possible wider discussion. The more experience they have with discussion with those outside their circle, the more reason they have to follow such discussion more widely. Nazis who do not even implicitly presuppose human rights must be lured into justifying them non-circularly, by a self-critique of monological or restricted dialogical inquiry leading them to join a wider circle of discussants.

Inquiry before less limited audiences, correcting inquiry before ones that are more limited, can inductively support the hypothesis that human rights-based inquiry before an unlimited audience optimizes truth seeking. Experience with purely private insight at length inductively supports the likelihood that the range of those from which we can learn is unrestricted. At length more evidence supports this insight. Yet there is no guarantee that Nazis, even if they resolve to correct the above contradiction, will choose to do so by drawing the inductive conclusion and opting for truth seeking in an open society over a retreat into a rigorously consistent unconditional dogmatism. Even we cannot know such a conclusion to be true with certainty. Yet by acting as if it were surely true we construe it as a practical postulate of theoretical reason, a heuristically adopted dogma maximizing the prospects for learning.

There is no audience beyond the universal audience to correct it, though this audience continues to grow and correct itself. That you *have* learned from a particular other person may be unsupported by past experience with that person. Yet that you *could* learn from a person on some issue or other does not meet with falsification no matter how many unfruitful encounters you have. Cognitively, and hence ethically as we adopt the above postulate of practical reason, we act as if it were always unsafe to write anyone off. Once consultation with one's private voices has proven fallible by listening to a single external voice, dependence on such consultation as a source of certain knowledge has failed. Listening to that external voice is likewise fallible. Yet it is shown to be fallible by the less fallible method of listening to an ever increasing list of external voices, not by claiming self-evident intuition again. Human rights norms emerge as an empirically supported but non-falsifiable (hence non-scientific) practical postulate of theoretical reason or science. (Yet, though they are empirically non-falsifiable, the possibility remains of their being logically falsifiable by conceptual analysis.)

Behind the dialectical justification of universal rights is justification by monological inquiry's own self-critique: listening to some outside our circle can be instructive. Since this is a *self-critique* of monological inquiry, a latent, unappropriated dialogical impulse accompanies such inquiry. A readiness to listen to other flesh and blood persons avoids error more than the avoidance listening. Here is the rock-bottom beginning of a justification of universal rights. Here an opening emerges for moral education in respecting human rights. This justification eventually justifies human rights norms from a standpoint that does not presuppose them. The justification initially motivates an adoption of limited intersubjective inquiry. It warrants at first only conversion from a monological standard to one embracing intersubjective freedom of thought with some. The further conversion to human rights norms, asserting the protected judgment of all as the sole standard, can come later.

Converting from appeals to self-evidence to confessing readiness to dialogue with some, and then finally with all, is not circular. This beginning of an argument for human rights norms is pre-scientific because it presupposes a readiness to discuss with merely some, not with all as in science. It presupposes a limited version of the method of conjecture and refutation, but not yet the validity of human rights in scientific conjecture and refutation before a universal audience in the open society.

8. Human Rights as Implied by Knowledge

We justify human rights as a condition of inquiry. Those who deny universal rights come to accept them to legitimate themselves. We conclude with an argument for rights based on the very nature of knowledge. If knowledge actually exists, rights are necessary to protect it, assuring discussion of alternative hypotheses. Inquiry and human rights can exist without knowledge, but knowledge cannot exist without rights. *If knowledge is true belief with the maximum available evidence, part of the evidence is that so far no one has refuted the knower in a universal free society.* The fullest evidence for knowledge claims includes the existence of rights. To want to know is to commit to human rights. *The criterion of knowledge is a consensus that is credible in part due to the human rights protecting the freedom of all to share in its formation.*

Part Three

HUMAN RIGHTS ETHICS

Eight

THE ETHICS OF RESPECT FOR HUMAN RIGHTS

Human rights ethics is a position in normative ethics, alongside traditional positions like utilitarianism and Kantianism. To justify human rights ethics is to go beyond the justification of human rights norms discussed in the last chapter. It is to argue that such norms are the sole standard of normative ethics. So far, we have justified the norms by indirect proof: to justify maximally a denial of human rights is to fall into a contradiction, since to justify anything maximally is to win the free, rights-protected assent of all.

A lord, who for maximum confirmation of his position needs affirmation by bondsmen, concedes human rights because only then can he tell whether a bondsman's affirmation is sincere. To argue for human rights from within lordship and bondage is to suppose a lord already converted from private to public inquiry including erstwhile bondsmen. The lord erred compelling confirmation that must be free in order to be credible. In this chapter I seek to justify human rights ethics by showing how the rule of creating and respecting rights subordinates the traditional rules of normative rules. I want to show that rules other than those of creating and respecting human rights are either invalid or can be rationally reconstructed as applications of that rule.

1. On the Moral Point of View:
Human Rights Ethics vs. Kant

Alasdair MacIntyre notes a lack of argumentation by the United Nations on behalf of human rights.[1] Michael Freeman, reviewing attempts to ground human rights, surveys Jack Donnelly, Ronald Dworkin, Alasdair MacIntyre, Richard Rorty, and Alan Gewirth, concluding that no agreed theoretical foundation of rights exists.[2] Yet he sees the importance of the missing foundation both to individual conduct and to institutions. The positivist rejection of objective ethics contributed to the ease with which totalitarianism won in 1933.[3]

The lack of a consensus may not mean there is no foundation. It may only mean it has not been identified. I have sought out that missing foundation with the help of Jürgen Habermas, Karl Popper, Georg Wilhelm Friedrich Hegel, and now in the next pages with Immanual Kant. The reluctance of the United Nations to endorse openly a particular justification either of human rights norms or of a full-blown human rights ethics reflects a desire for a broad verbal consensus. Yet to be fully committed to these norms is to uphold this ethics. It is to hold that the norms in question cannot be defeated by any higher norms. Any theoretical foundation of this ethics remains in the realm of controversy unless we create a universal consensus around it. What I argue still belongs in the realm of controversy. Readers will judge whether it helps in working toward a general consensus.

Human rights ethics is close to Kant. The duty to respect human rights is positive, at times requiring interventionist respect for the freedom of persons. Respecting other persons as ends does not exclude using them as means. If we did not interact globally, exchanging goods, services, and information, we would have no chance to treat each other universally as ends; our lives would not touch. Yet economic globalization, though necessary for practicing human rights ethics, is not sufficient. Treating others as ends ought to go beyond merely showing sympathy for their plight as we proceed to use them. It means helping them to pursue any self-chosen ends that are consistent with those of others.[4] To say that we ought to respect, if possible, the freedom of all is to say that each person has an ideal moral right to such respect. Yet only an actual right recognized as valid by more than a few Kantians can establish others as credible dialogue partners. An actual right exists as a claim actually recognized as legitimate throughout some community.

While Kant wrote under the sway of duty consciousness, Westerners often think much the same by rights consciousness. By the categorical imperative we ought to treat persons as ends. By implication, they have an ideal right to be treated as ends, but the right exists only if a consensus exists to so treat them. Kant held that if human rights existed, respect for them would be required if we were to treat one another as an end: "[H]e who transgresses the rights of men intends to use the person of others merely as means."[5] Yet, since human rights do not strictly exist, he does not say that treating persons as ends *is* to respect universal rights. Human rights ethics, unlike Kant's *Critique of Practical Reason*, posits protection of human rights by law and not just by custom and conscience as the aim of moral striving.

Contrary to Kant's belief that definitive morality is always possible whether on earth or in the afterlife, human rights ethics holds that, before human rights, only the *provisional* morality of striving for full morality is possible. Kant greeted the French Revolution and Declaration of the Rights of Man and the Citizen with astonishment. Provisional human rights ethics makes the duty to foster rights central, but we do not find ourselves in the Kantian predicament of taking definitive morality to lie only in commending ideal rights that have no prospect of ever existing even after endless striving.

An ideal right with enforcement restricted to conscience is not actual in societies whose members do not chiefly act by conscience. Since a society based solely on conscience does not exist, we define a right as an enforced claim socially recognized to be valid. Most societies enforce a moral right only if their members exert customary or legal authority on one another to heed conscience. A right enforced only by conscience is an ideal right whose actualization is only desirable. Yet legal enforcement does not preclude respecting the right by conscience. Legal enforcement of morality has a positive effect on it, but no effect on those who already act from conscience. It protects rights against those who lack conscience, and serves their moral education.

Some say we ought not enforce moral rights by fear of punishment. For Kant conscience is the moral motive. Yet we ought to protect moral rights even at the price of inducing some to compliance them, not out of reverence for the moral law, but for morally irrelevant reasons. We ought to enforce the duty to respect some moral rights. Observance of the right to life, even if by a morally less worthy motive, is better than not observing it at all. Exacting compliance from individuals sometimes matters more than the state of their souls. Conscience does not always motivate action conforming to morality. One assimilates oneself to life as a moral agent by following the customs and laws of a good state that constitutionally protects human rights.

Ethics embraces customary and legal implementation of moral education for respecting human rights. Since due to rampant non-compliance these rights do not exist as hard law and so are not yet be open to respect, ethics provisionally is the construction of human rights, an endeavor already underway. The construction of universal rights extends, and progressively cancels, the privilege of enjoying freedom to the exclusion of others. Since the motive, in human rights ethics, is cognitive—consultants whose free thought we respect are more reliable—we may seem to be reducing the moral to the cognitive standpoint. Is it not objectionable to explain one region of life by a region foreign to it? Yet neither point of view is identical in sense with the other, any more than the evening and morning stars are reducible to each other in sense.

Each point of view is identical to the other under a different description. To take the cognitive point of view is under a different description to take the moral point of view from which we seek to respect persons. The cognitive point of view is one from which we respect persons by respecting their rights. Combining both descriptions, a single cognitive-moral point of view exists from which we seek knowledge by respecting persons and respect persons in pursuing knowledge. Yet the cognitive point of view is more comprehensive, requiring the moral point of view as we approach truth dialogically.

Do we respect human rights for non-morally good results (knowledge)? Such respect, without any guarantee, yields the best chance for finite minds to achieve knowledge. Is this a teleological justification of respecting rights by knowledge as a non-moral result? We first find that maximizing respect for rights is an external means to a non-moral good, knowledge conceived generally. Pursuing knowledge once did not mean respecting rights, which is more specific. It did not mean respecting rights even as late as Kant. Yet, upon discovering that knowledge best comes by respect for rights, we reconstruct pursuing knowledge to include such respect. That we pursue knowledge by respecting rights begins as a substantive discovery. But we then reconstruct the cognitive point of view by including the moral point of view of respect within it. Moral achievement is no longer an external means to truth seeking, but is an integral part of if. The imperative from the cognitive point of view now becomes deontological morality: seek knowledge by respecting rights!

Morality for Kant is respect for persons. If human rights existed, such respect, for Kant, would be respect for those rights:

> [H]e who transgresses the right of men intends to use the person of others merely as means, without considering that as rational beings they ought always to be esteemed also as ends, that is, as beings who must be capable of containing in themselves the end of the very same action.[6]

Yet Kant does not make the eternal voice of conscience depend on the contingent human rights, or even on the contingent world movement to construct rights. Respect for persons lies only in assisting others, even if inadequately, in exercising their non-moral (not immoral) right to pursue self-assigned ends consistent with their own moral respect for other persons. The alliance for peace in Kant's *Perpetual Peace* illustrates such assistance. War disrupts the best-laid life-plans of all. Yet the alliance for peace remains historically contingent. It is not an eternal structure of the moral world order.

In human rights ethics, we ideally commit to helping all by active respect for human rights, without privileging some agents over others. If, in the contingencies of provisional human rights ethics, we suspend respect for the prospective rights of some in the name of the rights of the greatest number, this must be a matter of rational preference, not arbitrary privilege. Privilege has its place in the exclusive rights enjoyed by family and friends. Within inclusive human rights, we still privilege our children or spouse. The limitation on these exclusive rights is that even they must constitute the exercise of and respect for inclusive for human rights. In marrying, acquiring a morally permissible exclusive obligation, we exercise a universal freedom of choice and ought not to violate anyone else's freedom of choice.

For Kant, practical reason is independent of theoretical reason. For Habermas, a command to respect persons is a practical condition of inquiry, of theoretical reason. Since this command is a condition of inquiry, persons are not external means to discussion or knowledge: treating others as a means to truth in inquiry at once coincides with treating them as ends in themselves. We cannot imagine inquiry as we know it without discussion between persons. Inquiry between purely intrapersonal voices does not assure those voices of the protection and equal amplification assured by human rights. Yet discussion between intrapersonal voices replays past public discussion and rehearses future discussion. A consensus reached among internal voices requires submission of the result to an audience of physical persons.

No one will ever fully convince the maximal universal audience, as distinct from addressing it. Many of its members are unborn, dead, unreachable, or will never fully return to life, even by scholarship. Some skepticism is always in order. Yet the standpoint of public discussion protected by rights, unlike the Kantian moral point of view or John Rawls's original position, is already in the course of institutionalization. We need not exclude the possibility of creating institutions by adopting Rawls's the original position. Yet the standpoint of public discussion that we in fact take, not escaping institutionalized practices of inquiry, is not merely one that we ought take.[7] Many already commit to the method of settling belief that is most successful in problem solving, scientific research, progressive education, civil and criminal justice, and the everyday process of forming and testing hypotheses.

2. The Rules of Ethics Rationally Reconstructed

Having seen how we can reconstruct the Kantian imperative of respect for persons as a rule of human rights ethics, we will now consider how we might do the same for classical rules of *prima facie* moral obligation. We first recall that seeking knowledge without maximum respect for others confuses knowledge with untested subjective or provincial opinion. Intersubjective inquiry in ordinary life, as in science, is the school of morality. The practice of morality is the pathway of inquiry. Today we can more closely realize the cosmopolis than ever seemed possible to ancient Stoics. We approach it as we place ourselves under an obligation to seek truth in collaboration with as many as are today possible. We must exercise this obligation by *prima facie* obligations of non-injury, compensation, fairness, truth telling, and beneficence.

Can we order these obligations hierarchically? Some hierarchy exists. A duty of compensation derives from that of non-injury. Compensation is a form of non-injury, reversing injury done to another. A duty of non-injury follows from that of beneficence. Refraining from distributing evil is a condition of the maximum distribution of good.

Respect for human rights requires *beneficence* where a lack of it would amount to disrespect. Natural disasters by themselves do not violate rights, which only persons can violate. Yet not to show beneficence in the face of such disaster may violate them. Indifference may fail to do everything possible to prevent natural disaster from undermining universal freedom of thought. Further beneficence is superfluous within the minimal ethics of respect for human rights, though it might not be superfluous within some fuller local ethics consistent with human rights ethics.

An obligation to seek truth also exists, and all other obligations turn out to be subordinate to it. We acquire obligations by promising, and their justification depends on what we promise. We promise tacitly, incurring institutional obligations, as we buy into linguistic and other practices. We acquire a social obligation to others by placing ourselves, through gesture or speech, under a promise to abide by it. Promising implies, within the institution of promise making, the act of placing upon oneself an obligation to keep the promise. If, by contracting, you promise to pay a mortgage, you place upon yourself an obligation to do so. That you ought to be beneficent or fair is not analytic, but that we ought *prima facie* to keep promises is analytic.

The gesture of extending a hand to one in need implies an institutional promise to help, to be beneficent and non-injurious. The social obligation of truth telling derives from a promise in dialogue to tell the truth as we see it, as a condition of learning from the replies of others. Finally, different criteria of just distribution—free birth, being human, friend or foe—arise from further tacit promises made to ourselves and to others by gestures and speech. To display an equal employment opportunity emblem is to promise not to hire by race. Promise keeping is the universal *constitutive* obligation. Truth telling is an obligation thereby *constituted* for all who commit to exposing their claims to criticism. Promise keeping is the obligation by which we subscribe to the other obligations in Sir David Ross's list of *prima facie* obligations: non-injury, compensation, beneficence, gratitude , and fairness.[8]

Promising yourself is the source of any obligation not externally imposed, but it does not justify the obligation. For promises exist that morally you ought not to make. The obligation of promise keeping constituting further obligations is *prima facie*, but this is not because it competes with non-injury, compensation, beneficence, or any other *prima facie* obligation. These obligations presuppose the obligation of promise keeping as their source. Promise keeping is a *prima facie* obligation because morally only some promises ought to be made.

We ought to make and keep a promise to seek truth by respecting rights, and ought only to make and keep this promise, with all it implies. The promise to be beneficent, fair, or non-injurious is justified if it helps in the construction and exercise of human rights. Otherwise, the obligations we have or promises we make have no moral force. Promising, which establishes a *prima facie* obligation to keep whatever promise we make, means for utilitarians a *de facto* obligation to promote only the greatest non-moral good (or least injury). According to human rights ethics, promising results in a *de facto* obligation to advance rights. Ross's *prima facie* obligations, viewed as expressions of a single obligation to keep promises to yourself and others, express respect for human rights only if understood as obligations to everyone.

A rule of non-injury only to compatriots applies no universal human right. Injury in human rights ethics means the annulment, derogation, or violation of anyone's freedom of thought, not just pain inflicted on a restricted number. We do not injure a student who deserves to fail by giving a failing grade. The cognitive-moral good of expanded freedom of thought, in assessing a maximum range of alternatives and their implications, means that the student has no human right to pass without achieving. Passing would not maximize his or her exercise of the basic human right.

Global civil society knows varying degrees of depth along the path leading from society (*Gesellschaft*) to community (*Gemeinschaft*). A society that limits beneficence to reciprocal non-injury is shallower than a community that extends it to a fair distribution of positive good. In human rights ethics, rules promote the widest participation in quality discussion. What this norm requires is morally obligatory, while what is consistent with it is morally permissible. Deepening human community by mutual beneficence is obligatory not as an end in itself, but to implement rights. A shallow community of beneficence limited merely to universal non-injury protects universal participation in discussion less than a deeper community of positive mutual beneficence beyond non-injury. Application of the basic human right to discussion in the family, market, and state leads to apparent secondary rights, civil rights, legal-access rights, political rights, public service rights, public works rights, and welfare rights.

The exercise of human rights leads to exclusive rights, to special rights held exclusively by some against some. Unlike universal human rights, special rights arise out of particular transactions or relationships.[9] Different people acquire different special rights implementing one universal right. We exercise a universal right to marry or work by acquiring and exercising the special rights of this spouse or that employee. We exercise the general right to participate in discussion by exercising special legal, political, public service, public works, and welfare rights over and against the state and other individuals.

Many believe that primary responsibility for respecting human rights lies with the state, since legal, political, public service, public works, and welfare rights address in the first instance the state. Yet this impression is deceptive if citizens delegate responsibilities to the state. Human rights ethics, like all normative ethics, is an ethics of primary individual responsibility.

Reconstructing ethics as creating and respecting human rights remains controversial. Hugo Adam Bedau writes: "We live at a time that some writers have described (and deplored) as a 'rights explosion,' an overemphasis on rights to the exclusion of other moral considerations."[10] Ronald Dworkin in *Taking Rights Seriously* does not take them so seriously as to say they exhaust ethics: "Claims of political right must be understood as functional, as claims to trump some background collective justification that is normally decisive."[11] I merely argue as a dedicated attorney for my case that the controversy ought to yield to a consensus.

Judith Jarvis Thomson would limit the rights explosion, holding that "claims [rights against others] do of course have significance . . . but they are not the only things that do."[12] She adds: "I suggest that we should take the stringency of a claim to vary with how bad its infringement would be for the right holder."[13] We may also infringe on an individual's just claim if the good we thereby do to others sufficiently outweighs the evil suffered by the individual.[14] Dworkin and Thomson develop theories of rights against a utilitarian backdrop. Thomson holds that moral intuitions may show that it may be permissible, if not obligatory, to act for the good of others in violation of the rights of some.

Quite correct. Yet this does not show the realm of rights to be morally limited. Doing what is good for adult rational agents can only mean doing what assists them in their rightful voluntary pursuit of their goals, in the exercise of their rights. It does not mean deciding paternalistically what is good for them independently of these goals or rights. If doing what is good for others means only active respect for their right to freedom of choice (by removing obstacles to such freedom), it does not lie beyond the realm of rights.

3. Just Distribution and Beneficence

Suppose, then, that the obligation to keep our promises is the source of other obligations not externally imposed. Self-imposed obligations are obligations of promise keeping to ourselves. Yet such obligations are only *prima facie* moral. The obligation of promise keeping is actually moral if the promised action advances human rights. We test whether the realm of human rights is morally limited by reviewing the usual rules of ethics to see if any valid rules are independent of justice understood as maximally equal active respect for everyone's right to participate in discussion.

In building a case for human rights ethics I assume any necessary presuppositions of dialogical reason, though as we have seen in the last chapter assuming them is not justifying them. We have sought to justify them indirectly. What remains, in order to justify human rights ethics, is to exclude moral obligations outweighing the obligation of respect for human rights underlying ideal inquiry. If we justify claims in normative ethics by public inquiry, the imperative of respect for human rights is a practical presupposition of our inquiry. We may view this imperative as categorical, but it retains a hypothetical element. We cannot show categorically that we ought morally to uphold human rights, but only that—*if* we seek maximal justification of claims—we so far find no viable alternative to holding we ought do so. We all seek truth, though not always maximally. Human rights ethics is a falsifiable yet unfalsified hypothesis as to the ethics of justification, as to the rules of conduct and virtues needed if human justification is to succeed. It would be falsified if infallibility were established, or perhaps if the super-intelligent were to mutate into a species needing no dialogue with the rest of us.

In application, the basic right to freedom of thought in a context of possible dialogue is, as much as possible, a right of respect for universal and non-universal secondary rights by which we implement, in a proportionately equal fashion, the basic right for people in different situations. Without the support of such secondary rights, freedom of thought lapses into the ancient Stoic right to freedom of thought that Hegel called the mere thought of freedom.[15]

William K. Frankena and others have recognized an independent obligation of beneficence equal in rank with the obligation of justice.[16] They do this because they understand justice as an obligation to give proportionately equal consideration to all in distributing non-moral good—not as an obligation to produce non-moral good for the maximum proportionately equal distribution of dialogical rationality. Yet no obligation to maximize non-moral good exists if we do not need it to advance universal dialogue. We cannot distribute out of respect for the equal opportunity to exercise human rights if nothing exists to distribute, but this does not argue for beneficence as an independent rule. We ought to produce enough non-moral good (pleasure, need satisfaction) so that we can distribute to all what they need for rational agency in a proportionately equal manner. Yet we are uneasy with producing more than what we need for this end, or as much as might be possible. A non-moral good like pleasure is not morally good if not used for the most extensive distribution of rational agency. Extra sweetener tastes good, but if it is not good for empowering rational agency its distribution is not morally good.

Utilitarianism claims that maximizing non-moral good is always morally obligatory, thus adding to the non-moral good enjoyed by an individual so long as doing so agrees with maximizing non-moral good for as many as possible. Human rights ethics offers a reasoned justification for promoting limited non-moral good as a means to the universal rational agency necessary for the fullest justification of claims. A moral duty to be fair exists only when what is distributed is a moral good. It may appear that this claim defines teleological ethics out of existence. Yet a teleological ethics is itself reductionistic, defining itself out of existence as ethics by defining moral obligation exclusively by non-moral concepts like pleasure.

Pleasure in itself is morally indifferent, but justice is not. The only thing that makes the equitable distribution of pleasure a moral good is that some might have reason to complain unless we distribute pleasure justly. As much pleasure as possible is not the pleasure we morally ought to have. Yet I am defending ethical rationalism, not Puritanism. We ought to have pleasure as is necessary and sufficient for exercising rational agency, a moral good. Too much pleasure is an obstacle to rational agency. If we cannot realize rational agency due to some missing satisfaction that is otherwise non-moral, the satisfaction indirectly becomes a moral good. A justified rule of beneficence obligates us, not to maximize satisfaction, but to supply, if possible, the missing satisfaction.

Just beneficence is not distributing ice cream for the pure pleasure of as many as possible. No moral obligation exists simply to distribute non-moral good. Yet, though in itself it is non-morally good, pleasure is morally good as a means. The intrinsic moral good lies in exercising and respecting rights. Advancing respect is an instrumental moral good. We must give more assistance to some if all are to attain rational agency. In equalizing rational agency, we must distribute resources in, absolutely speaking, an unequal fashion. We need not be equal in ability to have equal human rights. Unequal by birth or environment, we need different levels of support to become more nearly equal in discussions. Those born with less, or who have received less from the environment, deserve more if it can help equalize upward ability in discussions.

How can we exclude beneficence as an independent rule of ethics, re-taining justice, enabling equal dialogical agency, as alone basic? We illustrate denial of the most extensive possible actual dialogical rationality, distribution of non-moral good for a purpose other than rationality for as many as possi-ble, by voluntary distribution of more than sufficient food to some and less to others when enough exists for all to exercise basic rights. Yet full justification of this denial must appeal to a consensus of all affected discussants, including all who must enjoy further non-moral goods to participate equally in discus-sions. A rational denial of rationality restores and reconfirms rationality.

We have no moral obligation to produce as much pleasure as possible. Beyond a point, pleasure is morally counterproductive and even obscene. Morally excessive happiness conflicts with an earnest effort required to per-form moral duty. Yet many require additional need satisfaction to exercise freedom of thought in areas of their talents. Beneficence in meeting need is then an application of justice, of the obligation to promote the equal enjoy-ment of rights by all without privileging our interests at the expense of the rights of others. The rule of beneficence applies justice to situations in which agents are tempted to put their interests ahead of the moral rights of others and of the needs associated with those rights. Beneficence is not a teleological moral duty, since it pursues an obligatory intrinsic moral value: justice, or egalitarian human rights. We can still promote human rights without any immediate possibility of their exercise, like those of concentration camp in-mates. However, until we not only recognize but respect universal human rights claims, the duty of justice, and of beneficence, is interventionist.

In intervention, difficult choices arise. A battlefield surgeon may face a choice between saving one person's life or another's. Active respect for the right of one person conflicts with active respect for that of another. If "ought" implies "can," and if we cannot actively assist all, we have no actual moral obligation to do so. Assisting some is better than assisting none if it promotes the rights of as many as possible, but the choice as to whom we should assist contains an element of arbitrariness. Why Kosovo and not Rwanda? Greater resources, knowledge, and determination may eliminate some arbitrariness.

4. Human Rights Ethics and Habermas

Habermasian discourse ethics, if we ground it dialectically and limit it to human rights maxims, becomes human rights ethics. Yet human rights ethics still owes much to Habermas. A Habermasian joining human rights ethics would hold not only that human rights norms are valid, but also that they are the only valid norms. Upon justifying human rights indirectly, a human rights ethicist wills human rights maxims and only such maxims, without concealing either their consequences or any alternative maxims, without compelling their acceptance, and without excluding any who feel or who ought to feel con-cerned by discussion of their validity.

The challenge is to show that universalization of the lone rule "Create and respect the human right to freedom of thought!" enables rational procedures of justification, that the alternatives to the above imperative are not as fully rational, that we can freely adopt such universalization without coercion. The one rule in human rights ethics, that of respecting freedom of thought and action in all potential discussions, is higher than any utilitarian or other rule. But it subdivides into four sub-rules. (1) We ought not to mentally or physically coerce others to consent, nor to restrain them. Each has a right to think and act without being compelled or prevented. This is a right to freedom from domination—including domination arising from the control of information, of institutions, or property. An ideal right exists to freedom from the external authority of any who would make us think or do what we do not wish to think or do, or who would prevent us from thinking or doing what we wish. These two negative freedoms, freedom from constraint and from restraint, make up freedom of choice, the positive freedom to do what we choose to do. This right holds even if others find our choice unenlightened.

(2) The second sub-rule directs us not to exclude others from discussion. We should include all who feel concerned by it, excluding none because others believe the issue does not concern the individual. Those who ought to be concerned but who do not feel concerned we ought also to include, bringing them to feel concerned. That an issue does not concern an individual should emerge to the satisfaction of that individual only in the discussion itself. A competent discussion circle on any issue is not limited to credentialed experts.

(3) The third necessary sub-rule directs us to inform discussion partners of the consequences of any choice. Everyone has a right to full disclosure by discussants of known indirect and direct consequences of any proposed belief or decision. We have a right to understand the fine print. Violation of this right to informed consent is domination by the control of information.

(4) The fourth sub-rule requires that we disclose to discussion partners all known alternatives to any contemplated position or option, increasing both their confidence in the correctness of the position they ultimately take, and in the rationality of whatever consensus we reach. We do not respect the basic human right of individuals unless they are maximally aware of what they might do or conclude but do not do or conclude. Concealment of the alternatives available to individuals is also a form of domination by the control of information.

The imperative to create and respect the basic human right replaces Kant's categorical imperative to respect persons with self-assigned ends without necessarily succeeding to create universal rights. Yet both imperatives are in a sense still hypothetical for the person who must choose. They depend on an optional commitment *either* to follow conscience rather than inclination *or* to seek truth in as unrestricted a discussion circle as possible. Yet respecting freedom of thought is an option we cannot refuse without risking success in all our endeavors. Only those who fix belief by inquiry aiming at an eventual consensus of inquirers make this optional commitment. The commitment enjoys support by universities, by research and development, by courts of law, by the human rights culture, and by the redeemability, through universal inquiry, of promissory notes implied by non-provincial statements of alleged fact. Currently human rights are only ideal rights of all. Not all obligate themselves to justify their beliefs as far as possible before all, much as for Kant not all renounce inclination. The greater the number of those who do so, the closer the world comes to the existence of universal human rights. Yet human rights, if really possible, are obligatory for those who commit to them.

5. Rule Human Rights Ethics and Utilitarianism Compared

"I may ascribe a predicate to an object if and only if every other person who could enter into a dialogue with me would ascribe the same predicate to the same object."[22] We speak with full confidence only if the universal audience would agree. The implications of Habermas's claim for human rights are great. No avoidable limitation on the range of potential dialogue partners is rational. You are never right to willingly limit your discussions to family or neighbors. An obligation exists to bring foreign cultures to life, even dead cultures.

Creating the universal audience includes retrieving voices from the past and the present. Barring determinism, what future persons will exist is not determined. Yet definite persons existed before history. Prehistoric human beings had no human rights, and probably did not claim them. Yet we may retrospectively assign human rights to prehistoric persons. Prehistory did not presuppose the state as the public works rights, legal-access rights, or welfare rights in our time do.[17] The conscience, custom, and state law of our time may enforce the human rights of prehistoric persons. We pursue claims on behalf of the deceased by respecting prehistoric sites, which the state may directly protect. We make the voices of the deceased audible by interpreting artifacts. Prehistoric persons acquire a putative right to be audible with archeological help for which we may assume responsibility.

You cannot fruitfully address an audience that is denied food, access to information, or freedom of dissent. To reject human rights ethics is to prefer less justification, a narrowed audience harboring fewer discussants, which is not rational. Inquiry into what maximizes realization of a person's capacities as a participant in dialogue with all others is an infinite task. We must commit to it, not out of sentimentalism, but out of respect for truth. Lamenting people ravaged by war, whose ability to advance a common quest for truth needlessly suffers, is not merely sentimental but rationally grounded.

We admit we ought sometimes to suspend respect for the *prima facie* human rights of some for the sake of human rights for as many as possible. Moral justice consists in respecting the basic human right of all as equally as possible, if need be by distributing non-moral goods unequally. Justice is the general rule, but this rule by itself cannot decide between particular rules. We must invent particular rules and institutional applications upon research.

Instituting rights for as many as possible that would be human rights if they were universal might still exclude many. We must address the issue of sacrificing respect for the prospective rights of some in favor of those of a greater number. Many have invoked human rights to block sacrifice of an individual or minority to the good of the majority. "One major objection to act utilitarianism is that we should not sacrifice some persons for the good of others."[23] This also counts against rule utilitarianism. Yet interim human rights ethics itself says that the duty to respect rights universally is only *prima facie.*

Human rights ethics and utilitarianism face a similar problem. Does not an organ-carving human rights moralist have as much reason as a utilitarian to sacrifice the life of one person to save the lives of as many as possible? We sometimes say that respect for *prima facie* human rights of one ought to yield to respect for the similar rights of a greater number. The difference between utilitarianism and human rights ethics is between saving as many as possible maximally happy people consistent with the greatest overall happiness and saving as many capable dialogue participants as possible who are sufficiently happy to conduct dialogue if they choose.

No utilitarian reason exists to distribute happiness to enable inquiry for as many as possible. Even if the happiness of one person is to count for no more than the same happiness of another, maximum overall happiness might belong to only a few if they are more capable of happiness. Yet utilitarianism offers no basis for adjusting happiness to optimize rational agency.

Human rights moralists do well to concentrate effort on transferring those close to the threshold of human rights enjoyment into the class of those actually enjoying such rights. Not all resources should be concentrated on helping individuals who are so far from human rights enjoyment that they are poor candidates for such transfer until those with better prospects enjoy human rights (or those rights that would be human rights if held by all).

Yet we should still always help the worst off. Their children may benefit from human rights if they do not. The justification of assistance for those enjoying the least security and subsistence need not be to give them adequate support for optimal freedom of thought now, but to keep them alive until their prospects become brighter. Other individuals who lack rights may be closer to having enough to enjoy them in the line of candidates for the enjoyment of rights. The line starts with those who already have enough, and ends with those with the least. Once those who have enough to enjoy rights in fact enjoy them, those with fewer resources become first in line, until we have admitted all in some utopian future. Yet the first in line need not be the most gifted in any particular discussion that we might single out prior to the discussion of discussions.

Those solving difficult problems enjoy no preference over those who do not. The value of truth is not proportional to its difficulty. The truth about how to beat a chess master is more difficult, but it need not be more significant than the truth about preserving geraniums in the winter. Yet the economic fortune of some groups, regardless of the difficulty or alleged importance of the problems they master, makes their inclusion in the circle of rights-protected discussants easier without assistance. We have evoked the question of whom to first grant rights protection. We may also consider whom to exclude from the enjoyment of rights. Someone may be a more promising organ donor than the rest. Supposing that taking the life of one healthy inquirer has a unique ability to save the lives of fifty contributors, should not that individual be the donor according to human rights ethics itself, on analogy with utilitarianism?

One solution to this problem is to prefer *rule* human rights ethics to *act* human rights ethics. Suppose we institute rules of practice promoting the exercise of rights for more and more. We can follow such rules in a society in which all do not equally enjoy human rights, and even in a society in retrogression, since the possibility of reversing the retrogression always exists.[24] Sacrifice of respect for an individual's rights on the altar of the more extensive rights of others may at times be justified. Even the one sacrificed, if he or she is reasonable, may agree with such sacrifice, since the same rule tends under favorable circumstances to its own elimination, and since in a world with limited resources sacrifices are unavoidable. Yet provisional human rights ethics can at times, based on conscientious inquiry, mandate suspension of an individual's right not to be sacrificed without informed consent.

We privilege inquiry by inquiring, and hence by inquiring into the justification of inquiry, inviting replies from all quarters. We also privilege eating by eating, exercising by exercising. Yet we inquire into both eating and exercising. All these other goal-directed activities leave a place for possible inquiry. Human rights keep this possibility open even if we are not inquiring. Human rights ethics is more egalitarian than utilitarianism. It seeks the minimum satisfaction needed to enable inquiry for as many as possible, ideally for all. Inquiry is dialogical, and the extension of some happiness over a greater number offers greater chances of advancing inquiry than its intensive concentration in a few. When we reach a plateau of minimal satisfaction necessary for inquiry, human rights ethics ceases to increase satisfaction limited to those who have reached the plateau. Yet we cannot strictly respect human rights because they do not strictly yet exist. No moral point of view yet exists for human rights ethics to adopt as a condition of full rational inquiry. Ethics is under construction. What exists instead is interim human rights ethics obliging all who take and promote the moral point of view to work to create human rights, without unnecessarily violating prospective human rights of others in doing so.

6. From Human Rights to Personal Rights

Sanctifying anything but persons restricts open inquiry. Do human organisms all have basic rights? And what about persons who are not human organisms? Should human rights yield to personal rights? Not all human organisms are actual persons (take Karen Quinlan, or ostensibly a fetus in its early stages), and not all persons are human organisms (perhaps Martians, or even dogs).[25] The justification of human rights is the justification of the rights only of persons who seek and test for truth, not of all human organisms, and not only of human beings. Moral relations are interpersonal. Human beings in the last stage of Alzheimer's may be worthy of respect as monuments to their former selves, much as a zygote may enjoy respect as a potential person. Indeed, since the persons emerging from evolution are potential at the start of evolution, and even in the inanimate matter from which life evolved, it would seem that the universe as a whole merits respect. Hegel's definition of the absolute as personality at the end of the *Science of Logic* implies such respect.[26]

Yet neither the single-celled organism, nor the zygote, nor a terminal Alzheimer's patient, nor an individual in a coma, is an actual person with actual personal rights. The danger of a slippery slope of course exists where, once we deny the actual personal rights of some human beings, we never know where this denial will stop. Proceeding on the inexact assumption that all human beings have the personal rights of inquirers is safer. Many Alzheimer's patients are still such persons in their daily inquiry as to how best to cope with a situation many of us will face at their age.

Alan Gewirth criticizes Douglas Husak for defining "person" by a moral criterion.[27] Husak allegedly does so without specifying what criterion is involved, and without explaining what, other than human rights, makes a criterion moral. The best definition of a person by a non-moral criterion appears to be neo-Kantian and Kierkegaardian. A person is conscious of his or her identity over time (1) by making commitments (including the staking out of beliefs) with the possibility of changing them, (2) by possibly returning to commitments from which he or she has strayed, and (3) by possibly recommitting himself or herself to the future realization of past commitments.[28] The commitments that we make to ourselves, and that define our personal identity, may be morally good, evil, or indifferent. A right-holder is a person who has staked out claims seen by others to be valid. This concept of a person is psycho-social, not a concept of anything necessarily moral or praiseworthy. What we must add to complete this psycho-social concept, to conceive persons capable of holding human rights, is a capacity to engage in dialogical inquiry, whether self-consciously or by contributing to such inquiry by publicly acting on and hence testing beliefs. This concept helps avoid circularity in the imperative of respect for persons.

An individual merits human rights because the exercise of his or her freedom is potentially heuristic. If the exercise of freedom by Martians has heuristic value, we should grant them "human rights" in a sense arrived at by generalization from the human case. Martians discovering us might attribute Martian rights to us by generalization from their case. Martian and human rights would be identical under genetically different descriptions.

Nine

THE STANDARD OF
DIALOGICAL RATIONALITY

1. How a Final Unchosen Standard of Commendation
Tests a Person's Final Chosen Standard

Human rights are commendable in light of intersubjective truth seeking as a final *chosen* standard of action. We signal a final standard by replying to the question "Why do you do *x*?" If you do it for the sake of *y*, why do you do *y*? By a familiar regress, we arrive at a standard justified by no higher standard. Yet, because we may delude ourselves about our motives, behavior more clearly determines our final standard than consciousness.

If we make truth seeking our sole final chosen standard, conditions making the search possible are objectively justifiable to us. Whatever helps close the gap between the known situation and the final chosen standard is justifiable by the standard. We thus ought to pursue knowledge by public inquiry. We proceed validly here, without any naturalistic fallacy, *from* facts about (1) the final chosen standard adopted by an agent, (2) the actual situation and (3) the agent's range of available behaviors, *to* conclusions about what is objectively obligatory to the agent by that standard.

We universally accept realizability, the possible conformity between whatever final standard we choose and the existing situation, an *unchosen* standard superseding any ultimate chosen standards about which we disagree. This unchosen standard prevails no matter what our chosen final standard is. No matter what standard we choose, we choose it in part by the standard of its realizability. A chosen standard of action is uncommendable if we cannot realize it or at least progress towards its realization. A chosen standard of making a perpetual motion machine is not commendable by the unchosen standard of possible conformity between the standard and actual situation. Realizing a standard tests both standard and reality.[1]

2. Can People Be Converted to the Final Chosen
Human Rights Standard?

Let us return briefly to the foundation of human rights. When we view human rights norms as presuppositions of intersubjective inquiry, they remain unfounded in any direct fashion. For such rights are directly justifiable only circularly to those who already accept them. We must presuppose and privilege them if we are to defend any position at all in the court of reason. Circularity apart, we must reject such a foundation for human rights if what we mean is the justifiability of human rights dialogue to all. For those who have not given up private intuition or consensus within a tribalistic group as the standard of correct belief, human rights will not be directly justifiable.

Yet we should not reject human rights-protected dialogue simply because it is not rationally commendable by every final chosen standard of commendation. For it provides a final standard that some recognize, while others may come to recognize it dialectically by finding alternative standards to be incoherent. The final chosen standard of trust in private intuition, or in a restricted ethnic consensus, results less reliably in conformity between the situation and standard than the final chosen standard of cosmopolitan consensus. This is so even though any contemporary cosmopolitan consensus will appear provincial from the standpoint of future. Such a consensus is not capable of fully assured congruence between the existing situation and the standard.

3. The Human Rights Standard Emerging out of the Incoherence of Lordship and Bondage

Preceding chapters have argued that no chosen standard of commendation exists normatively higher than the one human rights ethics supposes. The error-prone standard of private inquiry, from which standard we convert to public inquiry and human rights ethics, is lower than that of this ethics. For human rights ethics, private intuition is no longer final, but is the ladder that we discard upon reaching the standard. Sincere affirmation of our views received from those whom we dominate is also incoherent. We see the incoherence of this standard as it leads beyond lordship to truth-directed cosmopolitan dialogue. Suspicion that those whom we dominate affirm us outwardly only because they have no choice may infuriate us. The deflating suspicion arises that we are not as admirable as they say, not as close to the truth.

Since the standard of receiving sincere assent from those whom we dominate is incoherent, an unavoidable choice exists between sincere assent by others and domination of them. Domination over others accompanied by their insincere assent is not safe. Insincere assent is not reliable, lasting only as long as a favorable balance of power. Domination without sincere assent by the dominated fails to get beyond life and death struggle, a war of all against all. Such domination is an unstable truce in the course of struggle. Unless we choose life and death struggle as the final standard, we must opt for the standard of sincere assent. Human rights ethics argues that this standard is minimally sufficient for normative ethics. The standard of seeking consensus with the support of human rights implies the possibility of others sincerely affirming us by their exercise of freedom of thought.

A consensus about human rights, as a condition of seeking a maximally credible consensus about anything, we justify by the final non-chosen standard of conformity between a final chosen standard and reality. Domination over freely assenting persons is contradictory. War to the death by all is not a coherent standard because the death of all, or of all but one, annuls even war. We can realize the standard of agreement on human rights as a condition of seeking credible agreement on everything else without internal incoherence.

4. The Normative Relativism of Final Chosen Standards and the Problem of Moral Education

Justifying an action *in itself* as realizing an ideal is not justifying it *to* an agent as advice. Justification to an agent commends an action by a standard. A standard is a benchmark by which an agent compares achievement with the known situation, and tries to close any detected gap. To commend action is to give an agent a reason to act. The *prima facie* reason is that the commended action follows from, or conforms to, a final standard accepted by the agent. An actual reason exists if only *one* final standard exists that the agent accepts. We act by different final chosen standards. Advisors at times choose whether to recommend at all. Recommendation by a standard we do not accept is justifiable if it advances moral education substituting a more coherent for a less coherent standard. Acting by different chosen final standards illustrates what William K. Frankena calls normative relativism, not relativism as to truth.[2]

Gilbert Harman justifies human rights by normative relativism.[3] Let us suppose that the rich act by the standard of non-infringement on property rights, and that the poor act by that of assistance to the needy. By negotiation from different standards, Harman holds that rich and poor have an interest in agreeing with the ultimacy of a compromise standard that includes non-infringement on property rights as a primary duty and some assistance as secondary. We see the superior power of the rich in the priority of respect for property rights and the threat of revolt by the poor in the agreement of the rich not to ignore claims of the poor. Harman justifies a simplified version of the human rights standard adopted by the international community today.

The position I espouse is different. I do not justify property protection and beneficence as human rights because they serve the interests of different classes. I justify them because they conform to a coherent standard of truth seeking. Property protection is the final standard of some, and beneficence of others. Yet discussion between the groups, not negotiation based on relations of power, may show that the defense of some property motivates inquiring entrepreneurship and is heuristic. It may also show that some beneficence enables the deprived to engage in deeper, more extensive inquiry. Property and beneficence, without either being a universal right, may help protect a universal right to freedom of thought and action.

Human rights are a valid ideal even if no truth seeking beings capable of adopting them as a standard exist. We should not use normative relativism to acquiesce in the current norms of our discussion partners. It should define a point of departure for moral education in which the adoption of more coherent norms is possible. The justification of human rights as an epistemological ideal of inquiry calls for moral education creating persons capable of respect for human rights as their actual standard of choice.

Human rights are not a compromise between the self-interest of one group and that of another. Compromise is never a satisfactory end to a discussion. That the rich want property protected while the poor want needs met does not imply that we ought to realize these two goals by any rational standard. The two respective interests exist and may be justifiable, but their existence is not what justifies adopting human right standards. What Harman provides is a motive explaining the origin of human rights, not a justification.

5. How Moral Education Exploits a Dialogical Impulse in Human Nature

Respect for human rights would be justifiable by truth seeking even if we humans were not truth seekers. Yet we share in truth seeking, which makes moral education possible. Initial inquiry is monological inquiry with intrapersonal voices, or interpersonal inquiry with some external discussion voices but not others. Neither form of inquiry proceeds by the standard of commendation adopted in human rights ethics. Moral educators justify human rights by adopting either form as a point of insertion and engagement with the individual as we accompany him or her toward the human rights standard.

If human rights ethics is to be justifiable *to* us in moral education, by monological or restricted dialogical inquiry we must conclude that persons outside the charmed but restricted discussion circle may have something to say. Without initially assuming the human rights norm, inquiry concludes that we recruit valid discussion partners by assuming that we ought to exclude no one *a priori*. Monological or restricted dialogical inquiry, though neither is justifiable, indirectly concludes in favor of human rights ethics. Human rights ethics is the enlightened destination of any more limited ethics of inquiry.

What grounds the more general ethics of inquiry that issues in human rights ethics? Inquiry prior to human rights ethics is open to self-criticism by its own standard of truth seeking and self-correction. Such inquiry is the seed from which human rights ethics can develop. The pursuit of dialogue in some form needs no justification, being an non-chosen standard inscribed in human consciousness. A question of justification arises if an option exists, and, in the pursuit of dialogue in one form or another, none does. As George Herbert Mead showed in *Mind, Self, and Society*, consciousness is reflective and dialogical, whether intersubjectively or in the intrasubjective internalization of intersubjectivity. To think creatively is to conduct dialogues with yourself, with your internal voices. Such conversations we originally model on intersubjective discussions. In these internalized discussions, real or imaginary discussion partners say things that no one ever openly said. Thinking is social, consisting in imaginary dialogue.

The human rights ethics of inquiry is subject to justification to human beings by starting with a procedure of inquiry without human rights. If we cannot justify this procedure, we can justify nothing by means of it. Inquiry without human rights becomes self-correcting as its error-prone nature emerges. We morally oblige no one to privilege truth seeking over other life projects. Yet if we commit to this search as the sole highest standard, we ought to seek truth as best we can. Whatever we decide to do as the aim of our lives, we ought to do as well as possible or not at all. The goal of human rights ethics is not casual truth seeking, which we can pursue by appeals to self-evidence or by agreement before restricted audiences. The aim of rationality, openness to error correction, is truth facing all possible criticism, even if the solicited criticism is not forthcoming or is unusable.

6. From Commendation by an Actual Standard to Commendation by a More Coherent Standard

The standard of universally open discussion directed to truth emerges from less coherent standards passing through lordship and bondage. Bondage for Georg Wilhelm Friedrich Hegel yields to Stoicism, which ideally implies cosmopolitan discussion between slaves and lords as equals in thought. Yet Hegel makes no direct mention of discussion in analyzing Stoicism. Stoic discussions suffer from real disproportionate relations of power between lord and bondsman. Stoics do not discuss in an ideal speech situation. Hegel's most prominent mention of post-Stoic discussion is at the end of the Preface to the *Phenomenology*, where he states that our destiny is to work toward agreement. Yet doing so depends on eliminating lordship from discussion, not in preserving it as in Stoicism.

The attempt to realize a standard presupposes a critique of reality, but the failure to realize or progress toward a standard may reveal a critique of the standard.[4] If the standard is pleasure, we learn that pleasure is not a fully realizable standard since pleasure is parasitic on regulations of civilization which hamper it, on what Hegel calls "necessity."[5] Similarly, full domination by a lord over a bondsman is not a realizable standard. Free recognition of the lord's legitimacy, which the lord wants through domination, contradicts domination.

Declarative statements promise to all concerned that they would, if empowered by basic rights, agree that the statement is justifiable.[6] Let us suppose that for your audience to redeem the promissory note human rights must exist. Robert Pippin doubts that mutual recognition has any grounding in much actual discussion and language.[7] Jürgen Habermas admits that domination has historically distorted discussion, preventing the realization of rights. "Discourse cannot by itself insure that the conditions necessary for the actual participation of all concerned are met."[8]

Discussion notoriously suffers from an unbalanced distribution of wealth between the industrial North and the Third World.[9] Dialogical rationality presupposing human rights is an ultimate chosen standard of justification, and no more ultimate chosen standard exists by which these rights can be justified. Such a justification would circularly make claims that would have to be human rights-tested. Full dialogical rationality arises as a less fallible alternative to monological or restricted dialogical inquiry. Human rights do not yet exist despite local practices of discourse that, if universalized, would amount to such rights. Yet by these practices, the human rights ideal already has a toehold in the world. Moral education, accompanying agents in their passage to more coherent norms, must work with material forces in the world. It must work within distorted practices that we can subvert.

7. Human Rights: Existing but Non-Respected or Purely Ideal?

A fully rational denial of human rights contradictorily assumes their inclusion in our final chosen standard. Opponents of human rights must abandon opposition or accept less than fully rational justification. Assume that non-respect for a right to political asylum is justifiable. A contradiction results if justification means testing the assumption by discussion with a maximum of concerned persons, including those whose testimony requires a right to political asylum. Human rights are a moral ideal. If we exclude those who might contribute, we cannot maximally ground any conclusion.

Do human rights exist? Their existence depends on a global consensus, proven by, action that human rights claims are valid. They truly exist even if the world fails to respect them if all discussants work to include a maximum of concerned discussion partners. Non-respected human rights are rights that exist without fully realizing the concept of what they ought to be. In a state that is not fully true or rational, rights exist without being true. Maximal respect for them is missing. For example, until Cuba chooses to embrace free dissent, human rights will remain purely ideal and non-existent.

8. From Mere Commendability to an Agent to Rational Commendability to an Agent

Ideal justifiability is distinct from justifiability to an agent. If agents have different final chosen standards, an action justifiable to one agent may not be justifiable to another. If an action is commendable to an agent, he or she ought to do it. To say that a person "ought to perform an action" means that the person's final chosen standard requires the action. Whether a person is committed to a particular standard is a matter of behavior. Whether the agent narrows perceived gaps between the standard and existing situation is observable. To test commitment to a final standard we create a perceived gap, learn the agent's behavioral capabilities, and observe behavior.

So saying an agent "ought to do something" is a factual claim. A form of ethical naturalism is true: a possibility exists of deducing "ought" from "is." If an agent, by promising, places an obligation on him- or herself to act by a final chosen standard, he or she has a promissory obligation to him- or herself to so act. He or she may make a non-moral or immoral promise. "Obligatory" means only "conforms to the final standard of action which the agent adopts over any alternative available standard." A *morally* obligatory action conforms to the final chosen standard of dialogical rationality adopted by the agent more than any alternative available action. Yet action that, objectively, is morally obligatory is not subjectively obligatory if the agent has not committed to dialogical rationality as the final chosen standard of decision. We solve the problem dialectically. Let the agent pursue his or her subjective obligation until the impossibility of realizing the standard implied by that obligation so impresses itself upon him or her that the standard yields under self-critique to a new obligation and standard, and eventually to an objectively moral obligation and standard. This is the dialectic of moral education.

We ought not to deprive ourselves of a discussion partner on a particular issue until a grounded but fallible consensus emerges that the person no longer has something to say. If this time arrives before the person draws the same conclusion, we still ought to reserve some space for his or her participation. We ought to avoid retreat within closed discussion circles. If discussants are not open to responses by all, discussion is not fully rational. If a person is not ready for open discussion, we need to reach that person. To such a person, human rights ethics is not yet subjectively commendable. We must take recourse to moral education. We must help the other person discover and adopt the standard of full dialogical rationality without feeling externally obligated.

9. The Judeo-Christian vs. Hellenistic
Prehistory of Human Rights Ethics

We ought to teach ethics as the theory and application of human rights in truth-directed discussion. Diverse final chosen standards of commendation are consistent with normative relativism, but dialogical rationality is the one chosen standard concluding moral education. The idea of human rights is recent, though it has roots in Stoicism. Something of it appeared theologically in Eastern religious traditions. It also appeared in the Judeo-Christian-Islamic belief that each human person enjoys the dignity of the divine image in which God has created him or her, as also in Biblical and Islamic ideas of tolerance and hospitality to the stranger and minorities.

Yet human rights in merely one theological tradition fail to address a universal audience. Such human rights are not those which some, beginning in the ancient Greek world, presupposed by their procedures for testing beliefs in open discussion. These procedures arose with the thought of addressing others as members of a still largely inaccessible cosmopolitan audience. The *cosmopolis* on earth cannot be a *cosmocratic* city resulting from conquest of other cities. It would include citizens of all cities, making possible discussions that exclude no discussants, in which we assist all to participate.

Stoics, unlike the Hebrews, did not respect minority rights because they had been strangers in the land of Egypt. Stoics were only accidentally members of a nation. They were disaffiliated intellectuals. Imaginary discussions floated above diverse ethnic identities. Before Stoicism and Periclean antecedents, egalitarianism was not strong enough in slave societies for a wide understanding of human rights. Agricultural and pastoral revolutions removed society further from an understanding of universal rights than did hunter and gatherer societies. Stoic freedom was but the thought of freedom, not the abolition of bondage. Inner freedom of thought could exist without protection of rights by state or custom. In time, Christian compassion for the vulnerable overcame Stoic resignation to a world that seemed to defy change. If conscience is too weak to respect freedom of thought, institutions must support respect. We must bring dry moral law in human rights declarations to life in discussing individual and public policy, and in the reform of institutions.

10. United Nations Canonical Texts of
Human Rights Ethics and the Discovery of New Rights

The United Nations promotes human rights education. It fosters study of human rights documents, and the introduction of such study throughout education.[10] Its teaching of human rights ethics applies such rights to situations unknown in 1948, in imaginary scenarios, and in historical case studies.

Imagine a Roman Stoic slave owner believing he can have a reasonable discussion with a slave, an unemancipated Epictetus, because the slave enjoys freedom of thought though his limbs are in bondage. How should the slave owner behave? Could he have understood the incoherence of slavery as we do? Did such an understanding move Romans to free slaves? Were the insights of human rights ethics intermittently present before contemporary rights declarations and institutions? The record only says that Epictetus achieved emancipation when Domitian exiled philosophers from Rome.

Human rights are universal, belonging to all capable of inquiry. The Universal Declaration addresses all. The Declaration is not legislation but publicity, so that we may avoid violating rights from ignorance. Yet the Declaration does not list all human rights, but only those with a history of violation occasioning human rights struggle. The world may declare new rights upon blatant violation. A right not to be sexually harassed or to enter same-sex marriage has attracted attention only since the 1948 Declaration. The Declaration is complete in general, asserting the universal right of freedom of expression and action, but is not a complete list of applications of the primary right. If sexual orientation pervades behavior, the right to same-sex marriage supports freedom of thought, lifting arbitrary restrictions on its expression.

11. Discussion Ethics beyond the Human Species

By human rights ethics, the possibility exists of being ethical without inquiring. Yet inquiry, if coherently pursued, results in moral conduct. Full inquiry is ethical, presupposing human rights. The ethics of universal dialogue, in direct justification of it, presupposes itself. Yet, as a postulate of public reason, it conditions the fullest justification of any belief. Interim human rights ethics is already a widespread practice, but one into which many do not participate on a full range of public issues. Significant topics exist that some have not desacralized.

Practicing human rights ethics is exercising and respecting any existing human rights. Doing so without inquiry before the universal audience is possible. Yet such inquiry *guarantees* respect for human rights. Human rights ethics can only benefit from inquiry. Human nature does not justify inquiry. Such justification would be a naturalistic fallacy. That the highest potential of human nature is reason does not imply that reason is good. Sharks potentially bite, but that gives their bites no moral value. Nor is inquiry good because it respects human rights. Private inquiry must see whether inquiry by respect for rights solves problems more than other types of inquiry. Moral education starts with appeals to self-evidence by private inquiry. We surmise that it ends with private inquiry preferring discussion before a universal audience over a restricted audience. Public reason does not mean the coercive authority of the public domain, but means private inquiry freely appreciating public reason.

Human nature makes an encounter with the impulse of reason difficult if not impossible to avoid. Other species may favor reason as much as or more than we do. *Human* rights ethics may yield in authority to discussion ethics more generally, as an ethics of the rights of all inquiring persons. If other species can include us in their discussions insofar as they concern us, we ought to join such discussions for the possible cognitive benefit of both species. We include species in our discussions if their behavior tests beliefs we suppose they have, such as a dog's belief that a visitor is dangerous.

When discussions within another species are beyond us, our commitment to truth seeking must lead us to admire it. If its inquiries address its problems and not ours, we continue with our inquiries. If we share problems with a higher species that only it can solve, we are consoled, for someone is solving these problems somewhere. If the higher species adopts us as pets, we may even find our subordination to it justifiable. The reducibility of discussion ethics to narrowly *human* rights ethics depends on the contingent fact that we have not yet discovered such circumstances to hold.

Ten

HUMAN RIGHTS ETHICS VS. THE CLASSICAL NORMATIVE THEORIES

1. Human Rights Ethics among the Classical Positions of Normative Ethics

Should those who deny human rights still enjoy recognition of their human rights by others? One answer is that, if they did not, universal human rights could not exist. Further, they ought to enjoy respect for their human rights to be able to attempt a justification of the denial of rights dialogically, even in order to discover that such a justification is after all rooted in an acceptance of those very rights. A similar case exists for defending the human rights of convicts who have violated such rights. A murderer who has violated the right to life may have such a right, assuming that he or she is capable of inquiry. (The prosecution took such a position in declining to seek the death penalty for Gary Ridgway because he could help resolve unsolved murder inquiries.)

Interim human rights ethics may condone capital punishment in the name of the rights of as many as possible, but such punishment has no place in any definitive ethics of respect for such rights. If the criminal is not committed to inquiry, we ourselves may inquire by observing the success or failure of his/her pursuits, and he/she might merit personal human rights as a goal-seeker even if not as an actually inquiring person.

The claim that there can be nothing worth learning from an individual convicted of a heinous crime may be emotionally compelling, but the claim is not self-evident. If we argue against rights-protected inquiry as the highest standard, we can do so only by right-protected inquiry. Because of the horror of some crimes, many will view such an argument against capital punishment as purely academic. Yet when academic points are wrong, they should be refutable on their own academic terrain. The sense of horror should not overwhelm academic argument.

In arguing against capital punishment, Hugo Adam Bedau comes closest to my argument when he writes:

> In 1992, Roger Keith Coleman was executed in Virginia despite widely publicized doubts surrounding his guilt. . . . Were Coleman still incarcerated, his friends and attorneys would have a strong incentive to resolve these questions. But because Coleman is dead, further inquiry into the crime that resulted in his conviction is unlikely.[1]

155

Continued life means the continued possibility of inquiry on countless matters beyond the guilt of the convict. The case against capital punishment does not stop at showing that retributivist or utilitarian arguments for ending life are wrong. We ground the human rights-based case for perpetuating life with possible inquiry (even if in prison) in an ethical perspective independent of utilitarianism or retributivism. This perspective may be cogent even if public emotions are not ready to embrace it. Consistency requires the human rights ethics to take this position on capital punishment.

Ascending to a more theoretical level, a vicious circle not only invalidates those who argue for capital punishment by breaking off the dialogue with the parties who are clearly the most concerned, but also invalidates those who would argue for any of the familiar positions in normative ethics other than human rights ethics. This array of positions includes utilitarianism along with numerous others. The thesis is that human rights ethics ends the history of normative ethics.

If we base human rights ethics on none of the traditional doctrines of normative ethics, but take it to be the autonomous ethics of all truth-directed discussion and inquiry, it will emerge as the ineluctable destiny of all traditional normative ethical theories when pushed to vindicate themselves. Utilitarians, ethical egoists, Kantian deontologists, practitioners of religious ethics, and others do not sufficiently realize that they share a background ethics of dialogical inquiry transcending their differences.

In light of continuing disagreements in normative ethics, human rights ethics, reflecting upon itself, must subject itself to the most inclusive dialogue possible. Acting out of moral, social and legal respect for human rights is rationally commendable because it addresses a universal range of discussion partners. This range includes proponents of the different theories of normative ethics. A normative position of positions with teeth emerges from a rights-governed procedure for discussing first-order positions, including traditional normative theories of ethics.

2. Act Utilitarianism and Human Rights

Consider utilitarianism. Two differences between human rights ethics and utilitarianism appear. First, human rights ethics is more egalitarian. In the utilitarian heaven, an unequal distribution of non-moral good may result from maximum overall happiness. So long as we attain the greatest good for the greatest number, some individuals may receive little or nothing. In the human rights heaven, all individuals equally enjoy a human right to freedom of thought and choice. Yet some today may need to exercise more secondary rights than others do. Greater investment in them may be necessary if they are to exercise such freedom, such as more medical care or more security.

A second difference between utilitarianism and human rights ethics is that human rights ethics—including the interim human rights morality of sacrificing the empowerment of some to that of the greater number—does not view morality as the pursuit of a non-moral good. It is deontological, not teleological. The practice of definitive human rights ethics is simply the practice of dialogical rationality; in the worst case, it is the practice of a rationality limited by the number of voices unavoidably silenced.

The practice of interim human rights ethics is the pursuit of a goal, but the goal is the moral one of greater dialogical rationality. Silenced voices limiting such rationality include voices of the deceased whom scholarship has not resurrected. We should not maximize pleasure or other non-moral goods dear to utilitarians for their own sake, but should distribute them to enable the equal exercise of human rights. The social sentiment of benevolence belongs to our nature, but beneficence is morally obligatory only by helping others exercise the right of free self-expression in the quest for truth.

We single out human rights ethics in relation to utilitarianism only as an example of the more general relation between human rights ethics and other classical positions in ethics. There was a time, not too long ago, when utilitarianism seemed destined to remain the orthodox position in normative ethics. Today we increasingly see respect for individual rights as an essential part, if not the totality, of any valid normative theory. Writers in recent decades show utilitarianism on the defensive. Some, like Alan Gibbard, hold that human rights, if formulated in simple unqualified rules which readily appeal to most people and which most often are justifiable by the greatest good for the greatest number, are justifiable by utilitarianism.[2]

Richard Palmer and Kenneth Lucey concur, but hold that in some situations act utilitarianism can justify not respecting human rights.[3] They suggest that human rights theories snatch an all-too-easy victory by restricting consideration to favorable examples in which utilitarianism does not support respect for human rights. Suppose, for example, that the choice is between (1) torture justified by act utilitarianism as the least costly effective means to maximum happiness of the greatest number (exceeding the minimal happiness necessary for the exercise of human rights) and (2) refraining from torture without any such resulting happiness. Human rights ethics appears to say we ought not to torture. It would seem that we recognize here a *prima facie* non-utilitarian human right not to be tortured.

Yet the sort of choice that human rights theorists consider less often, Palmer and Lucey hold, is one between torturing an individual as the only way to save forty innocent children and never torturing anyone while sacrificing forty innocent children. Utilitarians suggest that our intuitions may favor torture in such a case: "[I]n extreme situations individual human rights may *sometimes* be defeated by the overriding interests of the community as a whole, say in times of war or other imminent crisis."[4] Yet we do not base human ethics on our ethical intuitions formed in a world in which human rights did not exist or were not even the object of active pursuit. In the court of reason, only basic human rights for a greater number, such as the right to life and liberty for forty children, can defeat the human rights of some.

In human rights ethics, a right not to be tortured is a *prima facie* universal right. Torturing is *prima facie* wrong: it compels us to say or do what we do not wish to say or do. It undermines freedom of choice, and at once the credibility of what we say or do. No one who speaks or acts under the coercive influence of torture acts as a free partner in discussion. Yet interim human rights ethics itself might justify torture if it were an inescapable means of preserving forty future voices in discussion, as distinct from forty happy individuals. If refraining from torture would completely silence forty children, a justification for this particular act of torture might exist. Torture might be a person's actual duty, though it is always *prima facie* wrong. We do not always select our real duty from a list of apparent duties. We at times may select it from a list of apparent wrongs. We see that human rights ethics can accommodate Palmer's counter example following act utilitarianism.

3. Rule Utilitarianism and Human Rights

Some think rule utilitarianism to be more capable than act utilitarianism of preserving human rights. James Rachels writes:

> Suppose two societies, one in which the rule "Don't bear false witness against the innocent" is faithfully adhered to, and one in which the rule is not followed. In which society are people likely to be better off? Clearly, from the point of view of utility, the first society is preferable. . . . Analogous arguments can be used to establish rules against violating people's rights. [5]

Yet can similar arguments give us utilitarian rules against the violation of human rights in all imaginable or even real situations? According to Confucius, a good emperor had knowledge sufficient to obtain the welfare of the people. Whenever the people began to freely discuss public policy a sure sign existed that good government had failed.[6] A paternalistic theory of government, combined with utilitarianism, would require violations of the fundamental right, freedom of dissent and thought. Utilitarianism is incompatible with the existence of human rights even if the above paternalistic argument is false, so long as the paternalistic theory could be true. Human rights ethics cannot justify the sacrifice of human rights for the sake of maximum public happiness. The human rights norm requires that all hypotheses be subject to examination by free thought, even if this examination causes conflict between discussion partners and reduces overall happiness. Given the commitment to truth, the non-discussed life is not worth living, however happy it may be. Rule utilitarianism cannot secure human rights.

4. Ideal Rule Human Rights Ethics

Like utilitarianism, human rights ethics comes in act or rule versions. We have tacitly advocated rule human rights ethics by distinguishing between the primary right and the secondary rights which the primary right serves to justify. A rule of practice, such as "Do not torture," corresponds to each secondary right. If the practice of torture were widespread, the rule against torture would only be an ideal rule. If we do not practice an ideal rule, a further rule directs us to work for its application. Rule human rights ethics calls for the choice of *prima facie* rules of practice. These rules lay down right-making considerations in the ideal universal moral game of life that we seek to actualize. The rules are *prima facie* because they can conflict, in which case only the primary right and rule can decide.

Examples of ideal *prima facie* rules are: we ought to respect property rights, ought not to torture, ought to hold democratic elections, ought to provide education to children regardless of ability to pay, ought to provide work for the jobless, and ought to prevent starvation. Each secondary human right defines a distinct *prima facie* rule. An ideal moral institution of life, according to the United Nations, includes rules of civil, political, legal, welfare, and public work, and public service rights, with corresponding virtues. These rules define a life form that may contain little consciousness of the basic human right and of the corresponding virtue of humanity.

Rule human rights ethics has advantages similar to those of rule utilitarianism. It compensates for the inability to calculate the consequences of each individual act for the prospective human rights of as many as possible. The rule of not torturing has morally good results in promoting a universal community of potential inquirers, and we should follow it even when in an individual case it does not have a positive result— so long as the consequences of not torturing are not too costly by human rights norms. Yet a place for act human rights ethics remains within rule human rights ethics. The choice of rules in rule human rights ethics occurs by the rationale of act human rights ethics: each choice advances the basic human right for as many as possible. Act human rights ethics operates in the choice of rules, in deciding conflicts between rules, but not in the choice of particular actions under such rules.

5. Human Rights Ethics as Presupposed by the Maximal Justification of Any Claim at All

Any process of maximum justification presupposes human rights ethics, with its procedure of unrestricted dialogical inquiry, as the final standard that we must accept to justify any position at all. This is also true of any position in normative ethics other than human rights ethics. No standard other than human rights ethics can be final. Normative ethics has notoriously generated age-old discussion barren of any consensus. Religious ethicists, for example, do not find utilitarians or ethical egoists to be convincing. Yet human rights ethics should convince all people if anything at all convinces them. If we justify utilitarianism, religious ethics, or any other position as fully as possible, we must have justified practice of the ethics of discussion. Either we cannot justify religious ethics or we justify it by yielding to dialogical ethics. All theories that come up for justification presuppose a self-imposed obligation to justify beliefs before criticism from all quarters.

Human rights ethics cannot appeal to itself to justify itself. Yet the justification of any belief implies, without circularity, the belief that human rights are the final normative standard. If we ought to maximally justify any belief, human rights do or ought to exist. If we have a commitment to justifying any belief as fully as possible, we have a commitment to realizing human rights as fully as possible, to enabling as many as possible to show reasons for contradicting the belief.

An individual recognizes human rights norms as valid once he or she commits to full truth seeking. By denying such rights, we contradict ourselves in professing to continue with public truth seeking. Those who contradict themselves by implicitly recognizing others as potential discussants while instituting violations of their rights will, if rational, wish to reverse their violations. Justifying anything requires maximum realization of human rights: if justification is preferred, so are these rights.

Justification is in turn more likely to result in adaptive knowledge on which policies can rely for success. Yet the hypothesis that human rights favor success is itself a subject of the public discussion presupposing these rights, so that recourse to it to justify rights would again be circular. We can use human rights to justify anything directly but those rights themselves. They are justifiable indirectly by the irrationality that emerges from denying them.

In upholding a belief suppose we face a choice between a (1) society in which we violate human rights of members of our audience while lending merely verbal support to such rights and (2) a society without such violations but also without assured support for our views. Preference for the first society would evidence little confidence in the justifiability of our views or desire to correct our errors.

We have seen that utilitarianism countenances acts or rules of action violating individual human rights in the name of general welfare. This may be a good criticism of utilitarianism. Yet my point is general: no theory can justifiably contradict human rights ethics. The ethics of dialogue giving space to potential partners in dialogue is the ethics of all full justification. Any theory up for full justification other than the human rights ethics of justification must yield to that ethics. Indeed, it yields even if we vindicate it by particular arguments arising in the exercise of such rights. When rational discussion apparently vindicates any theory, the assumptions of rational discussion supersede it once we admit that it may later succumb to rational discussion. Though we cannot directly justify human rights ethics without circularity, we uphold it in justifying any belief. If you ask "Why?" in the ideal speech situation, you oblige yourself to respect any reply that the empowered liberty of as many as possible test and approve, ideally the free judgment of all. You may disagree with a current consensus, but your normative commitment prevents you from repudiating the quest for some rationally motivated consensus. You vindicate yourself only by re-appealing to the same universal court of inquirers that previously pronounced against you.

When the defenders of a position limit the audience to be convinced, they show diminished confidence that the defense is rational. Some limitations may have little importance. If we exclude children from the audience of those challenged to refute a mathematical theorem, the theorem probably will remain well tested. When we exclude much of Africa, it will have failed to pass the test of proper testing. The remediable poverty and disease of Africa, for which Africans and non-Africans are co-responsible, means that all science is quite seriously under-performing.

Institutionalization of the public quest for truth is rational in a privileged sense. Utilitarian choices satisfy a utilitarian standard, but utilitarianism is justifiable only if it emerges from universal discussion by motivated truth seekers all protected by rights. Though a grain of rationality exists in most human beings, not all endorse reason as the final standard of moral progress. Utilitarians heed a non-rational grain in human nature, sympathetically seeking the non-moral good of all who suffer uselessly.

The problem with utilitarianism, as with any rival to human rights ethics, is that unless utilitarians open evaluation of utilitarianism to a universal audience, or to the most universal audience possible, they have not done everything to vindicate utilitarianism. Yet if they do cultivate the consensus of such an audience, utilitarianism tacitly yields in ascendancy to human rights ethics.

The ethics of justification by dialogue preempts any contrary ethics proposed for justification. If the court of inquirers ever vindicates utilitarianism, rights associated with uncoerced participation in that court will enjoy an even higher moral and rational authority than utilitarianism. We can justify utilitarianism as a secondary normative standard only by a human rights ethics incompatible with utilitarianism as a final standard.

6. Concluding Critique of Utilitarianism

Utilitarianism is possibly justifiable to the universal audience only as a subordinate ethics. A maximum justification of belief respects the basic human right as the final standard of normative ethics, a standard higher than utilitarian or other normative standards. The ethics of justification by dialogue, to use Ronald Dworkin's term with a different twist, "trumps" any contrary ethics.[7] Egoists, practitioners of religious ethics, utilitarians, and other normative ethical theorists pursue wide-ranging discussions in search of maximal justification without often realizing, we have noted, that human rights ethics is their common ground. No right exists to dictate the course of discussion. Yet we may trust that discussion will someday discover, by a consensus of its own, that human rights ethics is the enabling presupposition of all discussants, a presupposition justified by the disappointments of discussion merely with ourselves or with a restricted audience.

So, unless utilitarians open the evaluation of utilitarianism to a universal audience of free inquirers, or to the most universal audience possible, they are not sure to have done everything to vindicate utilitarianism; yet if they do cultivate such an audience, utilitarianism yields to human rights ethics. The ethics of justification by unrestricted dialogue preempts any contrary ethics proposed for justification. An objection to the very idea of one true ethical theory has been that many theories remain in contention. They remain in competition today as ever, and no representative of any theory admits the legitimacy of any other.[8] The reply is that, at the point where a theory most insists on its own legitimacy, it must admit the greater legitimacy of the human rights ethics of justification which establishes all maximum legitimacy.

7. Human Rights Ethics Eclipses Other Theories of Normative Ethics

If direct justification of reason is circular, reason is an unjustified practice or is justified indirectly. If reason is an unjustified practice, the crucial point is that, though we cannot directly justify dialogical rationality as a final standard without circularity, neither can we directly justify any other standard justified as final. We could justify it as final only contradictorily by the *more* authoritative standard of dialogical rationality!

People criticize utilitarianism because it allows violation of individual rights, such as scapegoating for the greatest happiness for the greatest number. Utilitarianism might justify a *secret rule* of scapegoating, allowing citizens to retain a public sense of security as a part of happiness for the greatest number. Even human rights ethics might allow a *secret exception* to the public rule of treating individuals as innocent until proven guilty, but only for the sake of human rights for the greatest number, not for maximum happiness of the greatest number. Human rights ethics might justify a secret act of scapegoating that preserved a sense of public security needed for optimal freedom of thought, but never for a non-moral good. Yet, even if utilitarianism contained a contingently true utilitarian justification of respect for human rights, the necessary truth would remain that no justifiable theory, not even utilitarianism, could possibly contradict human rights ethics. For this ethics, we have seen, is the ethics of dialogue, of the ethics of justification itself.

Any theory, if maximally justified, yields to the ethics of justification no matter how contrary to that ethics it may initially appear. The ethics of justification may seem to fall within *metaethics*, not *normative ethics*, since it appears to be a method of justifying or refuting one or another theory of normative ethics. Yet human rights ethics is not merely a metaethical ethics justifying a choice between traditional theories of normative ethics. For, as the Universal Declaration of Human Rights shows, it directly justifies choices between actions and rules of social life, and so goes beyond meta-level criticism of traditional normative theories to become a normative ethical theory with its own cutting edge. One argument against other normative theories is that the ethics of justification has no need of them for rationally motivated justifications of individual actions and rules. Indeed, any other theory of normative ethics yields to human rights ethics precisely when dialogical ethics apparently vindicates it. The assistance lent by dialogue to any assertion of an alleged final norm is a double-edged sword, indeed a poisonous dagger: the needed assistance demotes the alleged final standard to a secondary standard.

We cannot justify human rights ethics directly without circularity, but that is not the end of the matter. We always indirectly justify this ethics in the process of maximally justifying any other theory, including any theory of normative ethics that would challenge human rights ethics. No theory justified by the ethics of justification, or proposed for justification, can contradict the claim to priority made by that ethics. Yet the denial of human rights ethics cannot survive maximal justification. Procedurally, to discuss is to accept an ethics of discussion, unrestricted or not. Either we merely assert an appeal to the common good (to the divine will, or to pleasure, or to serenity) to be final without maximal justification, or it receives maximum justification through rights-based dialogical ethics and we sacrifice its finality.

We may illustrate the priority of the ethics of justification by the contemporary justification of *diversity* at the highest judicial levels in the United States. Diversity consists in maximally diverse people exercising, in maximally diverse ways, the basic right to freedom of expression itself described in the most diverse ways. Since the serial killers that excite support for the death penalty show diversity of a perverse kind, diversity is not a stand-alone concept whose legitimacy we can divorce from that of human rights. Respect for human rights sets moral limits on acceptable diversity. Paramount is diversity in freedom of thought. Other diversity—diversity that we can change such as religion and that we cannot change such as race—may be ends in themselves for individuals who inherit or embrace some form of such diversity. Yet the Supreme Court has supported other types of diversity as means to diversity in thought, to protection of freedom of speech:

> Justice [Lewis S.] Powell approved the university's use of race to further only one interest: "the attainment of a diverse student body." *Id.*, at 311. With the important proviso that "constitutional limitations protecting individual rights may not be disregarded," Justice Powell grounded his analysis in the academic freedom that "long has been viewed as a special concern of the First Amendment." *Id.*, at 312, 314. Justice Powell emphasized that nothing less than the "nation's future depends upon leaders

trained through wide exposure" to the ideas and mores of students as diverse as this Nation of many peoples. *Id.*, at 313 (quoting *Keyishian* v. *Board of Regents of Univ. of State of N. Y.*, 385 U.S. 590, 603 (1967)). In seeking the "right to select those students who will contribute the most to the robust exchange of ideas," a university seeks "to achieve a goal that is of paramount importance in the fulfillment of its mission." 438 U.S., at 313. Both "tradition and experience lend support to the view that the contribution of diversity is substantial." *Ibid.* Justice Powell was, however, careful to emphasize that in his view race "is only one element in a range of factors a university properly may consider in attaining the goal of a heterogeneous student body."[9]

Justice Sandra Day O'Connor's June 2003 ruling here shows that diversity is not ultimate. Whether a kind of diversity promotes the First Amendment is an empirical question, no matter how compelling the case may seem. The recent concept of diversity in American life has value only if tied to the time-honored concept of human rights.

Eleven

GETTING AROUND THE
CONFLICT OF RIGHTS

1. Secondary Human Rights in Relation
to the Basic Human Right

The argument of this book has rested on one basic human right, but the usual plural of "human rights" implies other human rights. The next chapter will call the plurality of different types of human rights into question, and this will cancel the possibility of conflicts between such types. In this chapter we will retain the use of "human rights" in the plural, which is enshrined in ordinary speech and is likely to remain so. Yet we will distinguish between primary and state-guaranteed secondary rights while addressing apparent conflicts.

A distinction between the primary right and secondary rights promises a resolution of conflicts between types of human rights, which we may call objective human rights. Such rights are rights to some freedom of action, thing, or service which functions as their *object*, regardless of the individual person or *subject* to whom the right belongs. A right viewed as belonging to a person we call subjective right. The main argument will be that objective types of human rights cannot conflict. Yet subjective rights can and do conflict. The main hope for solving conflicts between them lies with new technology, the facilitation of immigration to countries with local rights regimes that are more congenial to a given individual, or both.

One way to view the relation between the primary and secondary rights is to view secondary rights as a *means* to exercising the primary right. Freedom of thought if empirically situated requires secondary rights. Yet the means color the end. Subsistence on a high-fat diet is different from subsistence on a low-fat diet. Freedom of thought by means of welfare is, for better or worse, different from such freedom attained by a person's own labor. Freedom of thought is always limited, and limitation by the desire to please the government is different from its limitation by the desire to please one's customer base.

Truth-directed discussion might proceed successfully within some non-human species, endowed with a more robust physiology than our own, without any right to annual paid vacations or even to medical care. Yet it could not proceed successfully without the right to freedom of thought. Only infallible private intuition throughout the species, by dispensing with public inquiry, could deprive something like our human rights of their purpose.

165

In calling the right to freedom of thought primary, we do not insist on respect for it in the case of all persons in all situations. As a subjective right belonging to one person or another, it is a *prima facie* right, conditioned by equal respect for the similar right of as many as possible. A restriction on one individual's freedom may be justifiable by the more extensive liberty of all.

2. Civil Rights

While distinguishing six types of secondary human rights, we may acknowledge, subject to discussion, other possible secondary human rights beyond this litany of six. We need research to show whether all six are universally necessary to support the primary right. The first type is civil rights, which include rights of appropriation and rights to the appropriated product of our labor. The absolute right of appropriation, for Georg Wilhelm Friedrich Hegel, rests on the nature of *things* that, unlike *persons*, have no end in themselves, and so do not merit the respect owed to persons. The right to appropriate things in the pursuit of ends complements the right of persons to be treated as ends in themselves, with self-assigned ends. The two rights are equally absolute.[1]

Positive law and custom protect these rights. They are, to begin with, rights to your body and brain conceived as the product of invested intellectual and physical labor. No right exists to own anything in particular beyond your body, leaving only a right to appropriate what the freedom of thought of one person requires consistently with the appropriation by as many as possible of what their freedom requires. A right to a particular object is not a human right since we do not universally have such a right. Your right to own your house is not my right to own my house.

Parents, physicians, and others have mixed their labor with the physiological basis of every person, but this does not cast doubt on ownership of one's body and mind. At some point, others cease to have a recognized claim to own or co-own a fetus. Discussion may conclude that this moment occurs when a fetus tacitly claims a right to appropriate its body by defending itself against interference. We then recognize the fetus as existing for itself, not merely for the parents or for the teachers who may later intervene.

Slave societies suppose that masters have appropriated slaves in mind and body, so that the slave cannot appropriate by their subsequent labor. Whether we can justify slavery depends on whether it supports the primary right in the context of dialogue, on whether slavery or ownership of another's body and mind has greater heuristic value. If free individuals in discussion find that every individual's ownership of his or her body and mind advances credible discussion more than domination by a master, the primary right justifies the civil right to appropriate physical and intangible property in his/her name, despite the contrary claims of masters. In any case, since human slaves have self-assigned ends in themselves, slavery in fact rests on the false assumption that some human beings are things.

Stoic slaves show freedom of thought can exist, though feebly, even without civil rights. External domination does not totally suppress inner freedom of thought. The pursuit of freedom of thought is a "natural right" that in normal health and wakefulness we cannot avoid exercising, even when it is not a socially or legally protected civil right. Yet successful exercise of the "natural right" requires real civil rights protecting the external expression of thought—something the ancient Stoics lacked.

3. Political and Legal-Access Rights

Beyond civil rights, we find political rights. They are universal ideal rights to participation in a state—the right to vote, to run for office, to assemble, or to publicize. The Lockean function of political rights is to exercise a degree of control over the state that we commission to protect our civil rights, so that we may in part prevent the state from abusing the citizens it was to protect. Political human rights are subordinate to civil rights:

> The only way whereby anyone divests himself of his natural liberty and puts on the bonds of civil society is by agreeing with other men to join and unite into a community for their comfortable, safe and peaceable living one among another, in a secure enjoyment of their properties and a greater security against any who are not of it.[2]

A third type of secondary rights is legal-access rights. Individuals use these rights to access the legal system in defense of all legally protected human rights. They include the right to be judged innocent until proven guilty, the right to legal representation for those who cannot afford to pay, the right of appeal, the right not to be subject to retroactive laws, the right to a fair trial pursued with all deliberate speed, and so forth.

"Legal rights" in one sense contrast to moral rights and purely social rights. Custom minimally enforces social rights. Moral rights are justified social rights, while legal rights are social rights enforced by the state. Such legal rights need not be human rights at all: even slave owners have their legal rights. Yet we may also mean by "legal rights" a type of human right in contrast to other types such as civil or political rights. Such legal human rights are universal moral rights, justified by dialogical rationality, to initiate legal procedures protecting universal human rights generally, and protecting all the exclusive rights by which we exercise human rights. The exclusive right to be a citizen of Monaco, which excludes most of us, is one way to exercise the universal right to a nationality.

4. Public Service and Public Works Rights

Secondary rights also include public works and public service human rights supporting freedom of thought. Examples are freedom of thought procured in part *by* roads and *by* hiring teachers. The state necessarily secures any *public* service and *public* works rights. They are entitlements to services and goods. Does a legally enforced right to day care centers or recreational facilities enhance the freedom of thought to which we have a primary right? To the extent that voluntary associations and individual charity spontaneously provide libraries or roads, the state need not act. Yet the state's readiness to act can provide background guarantees in support of freedom of thought.

5. Welfare Human Rights

The final class of secondary rights covers emergency assistance rights. Rights to public services and public works are not welfare rights. If you are not receiving emergency assistance thereby, the use of a public park bench or attendance at a publicly funded university does not make you a welfare recipient. Yet those currently assisted by welfare distributions are not the only ones to exercise welfare rights. Compulsory state-guaranteed insurance policies enforce such rights, and we have the insurance even if we never draw on it. If we suppose that only persons receiving benefits held welfare rights, such rights would not be universal and so would not be human rights. If welfare rights are human rights, we are all on welfare, and we all enjoy the peace of mind of knowing that our government will protect us should the actual need for welfare assistance arise.

Few can be so confident of their ability to rely on themselves as to despise those who actually need welfare benefits. "There, but for the grace of God, go I" seems the more reasonable attitude. Only individuals or species not exposed to the rude shocks of life would not run the risk of becoming candidates for welfare receipts.

Even if not all of us needed welfare rights, for most of us they may be a significant application of the primary right. Most individuals exercise freedom of thought with more independence and less worry by enjoying welfare rights. Yet we speak of ideal welfare rights, not of the existing abuses with which so many people confuse such rights. Whether a right to welfare is ideally a human right depends on whether emergency insurance would universally support freedom of thought. The matter is subject to empirical inquiry. The amount and kind of welfare provided by a given society depends on a political judgment, not on a judgment of political philosophy. It depends on the character of the people, the resources of the society, and the tendency of different types of welfare to promote or frustrate truth-directed discussions. Kenneth Minogue holds that social and economic rights are not genuine universal rights to anything that anyone can demand. Instead, we may propose them as "statements of ideal conditions of life for every human being."[3] They are currently only ideal human rights, not actual ones.

We must not suppose that, if human rights exist, all six types of secondary human rights also exist. For welfare human rights to exist, humans must universally claim them, whether directly or indirectly through advocates. We cannot force rights on those who eventually do not claim them. Even if everyone ought rationally to claim them, libertarians want neither themselves nor others to have them: "[T]hose who are handicapped or disabled or somehow unable to work . . . cannot claim a portion of my income as their right."[4] Yet to assert this categorically would be to anticipate the result of a dialogue including all concerned parties. If freedom of thought does not require universal welfare rights, one type of hypothetical human right in the Universal Declaration ought not to exist even if human rights ought to exist. We might still justify welfare rights as *regional rights* which implement the basic human right in particular regions. Possibly the extent of welfare rights that reduces insecurity and increases creative freedom of thought in France discourages initiative by eating into the product of labor in the United States.

6. First- and Second-Generation Human Rights

One established usage considers "civil rights" to the product of labor and democratic "political rights" to be "first-generation rights," since people already defended them in the eighteenth century. Rights to public works and public services, along with welfare rights, we call "second-generation rights," in that their worldwide general proclamation as human rights awaited the 1948 Universal Declaration, even though public works are as old as history.

Respect for second-generation rights is not necessary for our enjoyment of *negative* first-generation rights, for avoiding external interference in the exercise of those rights. Yet respect for second-generation rights is necessary for the enjoyment of *positive* civil and political rights. Those who do not exercise a right to work (a second-generation welfare right) cannot exercise a right to appropriate the product of labor (a first-generation civil right). We hold a right to the product of labor without the possibility of exercising it in the absence of any labor. To cite a second example, without universal public or private education (a public service right), we may never intelligently exercise political rights of citizenship (first-generation rights).

We secure the universal exercise of political or civil rights for most by a minimal plateau of public service and welfare rights permanently enjoyed with the real possibility of benefits. We may justify permanently held second-generation human rights without justifying permanently drawing upon them. We justify drawing upon them only as needed in support of first-generation rights, ultimately in support of equal freedom of thought.

Universal human rights are a moral ideal. Due to limited resources, state guarantees for drawing upon second-generation human rights by all may not be obligatory. Yet to the extent that the inability of some to exercise these rights is due to avoidably inefficient allocation, correction of this failure is obligatory. We often suppose the moral ideal to be more nearly realizable, and more often obligatory, in the case of civil rights. Respect by self-restraint and non-intervention we often think to be sufficient for civil rights to exist—rights to the product of intellectual labor, to freedom of opinion, and to expression. Yet positive civil rights benefit from public works and services.

A right is an option. Not to exercise a right that we still hold is to have an option not taken. If a right requires resources that are absent, no option exists, no actual right. Even the option to exercise the right to freedom of opinion sometimes requires survival resources that may depend on others. Exercise of the right to freedom of opinion requires health, and, often, medical care. Respect for this civil right as a positive right that we can effectively exercise, and not just passively hold, requires active intervention even if it does not require a universal welfare right as a human right.

For all who would justify themselves, an obligation exists to establish, if possible, conditions necessary for the option of freedom of thought to exist universally. We currently debate whether welfare rights or universal health protection rights are among these conditions in a spirit of political partisanship. This partisan politicization of the discussion remains a major impediment to judging the matter intelligently by dispassionate empirical inquiry. While the right to freedom of thought is more nearly categorical, social scientists and ethicists should seriously study the right to welfare as a hypothesis.

7. The Primary Right as Supported by Debatable Secondary Rights

Implementation of the right to freedom of thought requires resources. In slavery the master *implicitly* recognizes the slave's right to freedom of thought in recognizing the slave as a person instead of a mere thing, though the master *explicitly* and legally denies this right. Since the slave has no enforceable civil rights, the master recognizes his or her freedom of thought only very incompletely, in unspoken rituals of complicity between master and slave. Whatever freedom of thought the slave has is due to the master's graciousness. A human right to freedom of thought does not exist if civil rights and other possible secondary rights do not implement it. We greatly suppress in range and quality a right to freedom of thought without a civil right to freedom of expression, of freedom of assembly, and of freedom of association.

An ideal human right to freedom of thought is a right to the maximum range of freedom consistent with a similar range in that freedom belonging to others. A political and legal decision not to interfere with the exercise of negative civil rights assures negative respect for them. Assuring positive rights by providing resources needed for their exercise is more difficult, but perhaps necessary to the widest exercise of freedom of thought. Support by some secondary human rights, with varying resources depending on varying needs, would probably have to exist if we were to exercise the basic human right universally. The freedom of thought of a slave rarely matches in range and quality that of freeborn individuals. We cannot invoke such freedom as evidence of a universal right to freedom of thought. We resolve most apparent conflicts between secondary rights by shifting prioritizations in support of the primary right depending on the community and available global resources.

In different communities we justify different trade-offs. Greater investments in democratic political rights empower inquiry in a first community more than in a second community which (like Hong Kong under the British) benefits from a benevolent colonial administration. The protection of property rights may be more crucial in motivating members of a second community to undertake entrepreneurial inquiry, so that its members are confident of receiving rewards according to the fruit of their labors. A third community may enjoy such abundant wealth and security that its members inquire for the pure joy of inquiry without little regard to profit. *Equal enjoyment of the basic right requires inequality in the administration of secondary human rights, including legal-access rights, civil rights, political rights, welfare rights, and public services/public works rights.*

Secondary human rights are human rights only by promoting, in their different mixes, equal enjoyment of the primary right. If intelligence is not humanly controllable, those of different intelligence may equally enjoy the same basic human right to maximally equalized freedom of inquiry even if they never benefit from full equalization, so that the intelligent always achieve more than those who are less intelligent. Yet we cannot exclude the possibility that some allegedly retarded individuals lack some nutrient naturally produced in the bodies of others, to the provision of which they, but not others, have a right in application of the right to food.

We justify unequal distribution of any secondary human right to promote, insofar as possible, equal enjoyment of the basic human right. Assuring equal discussion rights for inhabitants of the sparsely populated artic would require far greater public works/public service investments than inhabitants of world class cities need—cities in which we have already made such investments. The only practical solution may be the right to immigration to a city for those who wish to participate in cosmopolitan dialogues.

8. Conflicts between Secondary Human Rights not Solved by a Fixed Hierarchy of Rights

A human rights declaration may list many freedoms, but conflicts will arise if they are all basic. Such conflicts pose no serious threat to human rights ethics only because the conflicting secondary rights are not primary. We resolve a conflict between two types of secondary human rights in any particular situation by seeing what conflicting secondary right most supports the primary right. When we see this, the conflict disappears. A classical conflict is between the right to the product of labor and welfare rights funded by taxing the product of labor.[6] No self-evidence or inalienability attaches to any secondary rights, which we can never justify beyond their support of the basic right.

The heart cries out to those who lack life necessities. Yet, if libertarians ask why we ought to guarantee necessities, no answer is evident. Why you should enjoy the product of your labor we rarely ask. When others ask, we see no evident answer, despite Locke and the Declaration of Independence. We ought to argue the merit of a particular property or welfare right on a case-by-case basis, maximally empowering each individual's publicly valued freedom.

Uniting within one country the conditions supporting the primary right for all people is probably not possible. Remaining within the institutions of one country, individuals cannot, for example, be maximally motivated by having the product of their labor and remain maximally secure in face of the risk of failure. Each individual must decide which of these two competing *prima facie* rights is more motivating. If individuals differ in what motivates them, support that is effective for some will not be effective for others, and the rights providing support for only some ought not to exist as universal human rights. In that case, a relatively unlimited right to the fruit of our labor ought not to exist everywhere, and the same would be true of a relatively unlimited right to social protection. This arrangement allows for freedom of choice by immigration. This is an argument against construing libertarian rights or welfare rights as human rights.

The conflict between welfare rights and civil rights equally calls to mind potential conflicts between legal-access rights and civil rights, and between political participation rights and civil rights. If we cannot justify these secondary rights as universal, the solution is similar. Providing more and better trained public defenders, or more and better resources to prospective candidates for public office would cost tax money and so restrict ownership of the product of labor. Cost-benefit analysis must identify the different trade-offs and determine where the greatest dialogical benefit lies from situation to situation. It determines whether an alleged secondary human right, in light of the universal primary right, is a real human right at all.

We must empower dialogue, for it to be maximally universal, by a set of universal secondary human rights with a shifting mix of non-universal local human rights applications adapted to each situation. We have raised the question as to whether property rights or welfare rights are universal secondary human rights, or whether we should view them as local applications of the one universal human right. The right to freedom as a potential contributor to dialogue alone determines whether any proposed secondary civil, legal, political, public works, or welfare right is a mandatory human right.

No list of secondary human rights is self-evident. Such a list results only from empirical inquiry into the shifting conditions necessary to realize universal freedom of thought. The just mix of universal secondary human rights and non-universal human rights applications varies not only between individuals but also between societies and generations. Selecting non-universal human rights applications for a population, instead of for an individual, fails to recognize the needs of each individual as a holder of the basic human right in the total population. Populations are not human beings, nor bearers of human rights. We may best serve human rights by maintaining as much ethnic, cultural, and institutional diversity as possible between nations and regions in a world protected by a small number of uniform human rights. In principle, we can then meet individual needs for non-universal applications of secondary human rights by immigration. A valid argument for world government can never be an argument for cultural and institutional uniformity.

The state, which ought to enforce secondary human rights more uniformly than custom, can also violate them. Non-enforcement is itself a violation. Yet the violation or non-enforcement of civil and political rights is not solely due to state oppression. Local populations can infringe on voting rights, and private theft violates civil rights. Political rights may require instituting publicly financed electoral campaigns, and civil rights require police. If some do not voluntarily respect rights by conscience, we hold custom, and finally law, in reserve in order to oblige. Sometimes individuals and voluntary associations enforce respect for human rights. Yet, lacking such individuals and associations, the state is the guarantor of last resort, whether by legally mandated redistribution in the case of welfare and public works/public service rights, or by court protection in the case of civil, legal, and political rights.

9. The Basic Human Right
Protected by the State as a Civil Right

Human rights ethics holds the right to freedom of inquiry to be the final right. Stoic masters and slaves have shown that such a right can exist locally without being legally enforced. Unenforced custom recognized even by masters may protect it. The essential privacy of thought, which leaves it sometimes unexposed to external control by custom or the state, also partially protects it. Logically freedom of thought can exist merely by customary respect, without legal protection by the state. Yet the state re-enforces it by secondary rights, including by the *civil right to freedom of thought*. Highest priority among secondary rights goes to the civil right of freedom of thought. We justify the other secondary human rights only as supporting that one secondary right, which is the primary right itself in legal form.

If individuals can violate human rights, they can also respect them. A right to freedom of thought can exist before it becomes a state-enforced civil right. All civil rights, public service rights, public works rights, welfare rights, political rights, and legal-access rights that serve to protect the basic human right by definition enjoy state protection. For an individual to respect a right is minimally not to violate it. For a society or state to enforce a right is to stand ready to punish violation. By protecting human rights, a good state helps individuals respect them. It offers rudimentary moral education, until individuals are able to respect rights simply because they are right.

Viewed as a secondary civil right, freedom of thought is a right to the fruit of your intellectual labor. We can justify such a right because ownership of the fruit of your mental labor has heuristic value for the inquiring public. This ownership gives you a stake, a motivating vested interest, in your past: individuals inquire in part because they take responsibility for the implications and mistakes of their past inquiries.

Civil rights are, first, rights to appropriate without expropriating. Once appropriation occurs, civil rights become property rights, which contain a right to use property within the limits of respect for the universal human rights and exclusive contractual rights of others. Though human rights are not *special* contractual rights, they are *general* contractual rights that include the right to acquire special rights and obligations.

Exercising freedom of thought adds further labor to the present product of the past labor of your mind. The Stoics understood this to be a fundamental natural right, since nothing could alienate it from us. Even if others enslave you, your mind remains free, never becoming the property of a slave owner who would vainly struggle to appropriate it. The Stoic right to pursue freedom of thought is an inalienable "natural right" or propensity, not a human right, since regardless of our situation we cannot help somehow exercising it.

Most of us are not as optimistic as the Stoics were. Torture, brainwashing, advertising, and ideology can coerce the mind into subservience. Saying, as Stoics must, that such subservience is merely due to a lack of Stoic self-discipline for which the individual is responsible is difficult. Stoics are right that you might be free to discuss even though others have expropriated much of your property, even including your body. Participation in discussion would be difficult, and the range of topics you might effectively discuss limited, but intrapersonal discussion could still occur. Yet if, in other situations, people can alienate from you your primary right to think what you wish (whether by intimidation, torture, or brainwashing) a *civil human right to freedom of thought* is necessary. At least this universal legally enforceable secondary human right ought to exist in correspondence with the basic human right.

10. Abortion and the Possibility of Intractable Moral Conflicts between Individuals

Ideally, a successful theory of normative ethics would resolve all ethical decisions, and in particular all ethical conflicts.[5] Yet let us not burden ourselves with the belief that human rights ethics, or any theory of normative ethics, must resolve all conflicts of duty to be true and illuminating. Even the best theory of normative ethics may not be fully decidable, telling us whether every moral claim is true or false. If, based on human rights ethics, the reasons weighing for and against an act (including the act of choosing a rule) weigh equally, such ethics will not be able to decide. A human rights ethicist might then say that the decision is ethically indifferent. Human rights ethics is not a magic wand guaranteed to abolish all moral dilemmas. Yet a normative theory surely would be deficient if it left us without guidance in most decision-making situations.

Let us briefly consider, for example, the implications of human rights ethics for moral conflicts surrounding abortion. The main conflict is not between types of objective human rights, but between the subjective rights of different persons. In particular, we consider the conflict between the rights of the fetus and the rights of the mother.

Johann Gottlieb Fichte, following Jean-Jacques Rousseau, was one of the first thinkers to see that human rights lie beyond natural rights, that they depend on historical acts of construction and recognition. "I limit myself in my appropriation of freedom by the fact that I also recognize the freedom of others."[6] He burst the confines of the traditional course on natural rights in the German university curriculum. If we agree with Fichte that we should restrict freedom when and only when doing so creates more extensive freedom for all, the survival of added subjective dialogical voices resulting from restrictions on abortion argues against abortion. Yet, in favor of abortion, we see that the subjective survival rights of the fetus do not guarantee eventual exercise by the fetus of the primary adult right to opt for partnership in dialogue. Resources to foster dialogue may be insufficient for all who survive. And a fetus' use of the womb as a means of survival and growth, with little respect for the mother's distinct voice and goals, indeed with slim knowledge of what respect is, argues for abortion in some situations, such as rape.

Even if the fetus is an actual person, it is a morally immature person, lacking conscience. Society may sometimes claim a right to step in to protect the woman's subjective rights from unconscionable treading on the rights of the mother by the fetus. Yet other adults may affirm and defend the fetus's *putative right to life* on behalf of the fetus itself. The price of the fetus's putative right to life appears to be the fetus's *putative obligation* not to irreparably injure the woman who carries it, not to irreparably violate her subjective positive right to her freedom of thought. Those who, acting on behalf of the fetus, defend this putative right must also accept the putative obligation. Still, the duty of a fetus close to becoming an actual person often falls short of sacrificing its life to forestall a temporary setback in the goal pursuits of the mother.

A conflict is inevitable in cases where new dialogical voices emerge only by violating the life space of women who do not wish to be mothers. Even if the fetus is not a person, we must weigh the *probable survival rights of a probable future inquiring person* against *actual non-survival rights* (like the right to take this job or the right to explore that line of thought) of an actual person. The fetus itself may well grow into an actual person who exercises non-survival rights, namely, the right to freedom of thought. Because the imperative of dialogue requires as many healthy voices as possible distributing themselves among discussion circles, we may accept use of the woman by the fetus as a means to its survival in the birth of new voices. The principal hope for saving the woman from victimization by the fetus lies in the action of the fetus's trustees. Such trustees, acting on behalf of the fetus in its obligations and rights, may protect the woman from treatment *merely* as a means without respecting her right to freedom of thought and choice. Those acting in the name of the fetus may also show regard for the mother's life plans, seeking to reconcile conflicting interests through the primary obligation to respect freedom of thought for as many as possible.

Human rights ethics encourages the hope that someday all conflicts between the subjective human rights of some and those of others may disappear, so that a definitive *moral world order* of universal human rights might actually arise. Yet the conflict between the non-survival rights of unwilling mothers and the survival rights of unborn fetuses will never vanish as long as mothers are necessary for the birth of new human beings, which is as long as artificial incubation or other technologies are not adequate.

New technologies and policies sometimes overcome economically- or sociologically-based ethical conflicts between the subjective human rights of individuals. The United States proposes solving the conflict between (1) the subjective rights of people in the industrial world to more economic growth as the fruit of their labor and (2) the subjective rights of people in the Third World to economic development by introducing new technologies. Such technologies would allow economic growth to take place simultaneously in the West and the Third World without conflict, due to reduced carbon dioxide emissions. New technologies and policies might also help solve the biologically based ethical conflict presented by abortion. If such technologies are not forthcoming, the interim human rights ethics of searching for ways to overcome ethical conflicts risks becoming non-interim or definitive.

11. Objective Individual Hierarchies of Ideal Rights

The secondary rights most enabling dialogue vary from one situation to another. We must discover them empirically. We must constantly reevaluate conflicting *prima facie* secondary rights in order to find what secondary or applied human rights ought to exist relative to the social and ecological environment, and to the needs of each population. Yet, since individuals, not populations, are the beneficiaries of human rights, the prioritization of *prima facie* human rights best adapted to a community may not meet the needs of an individual. An advantage resulting from a single primary right is that the *prioritization of secondary rights* in a particular situation becomes objective, and that most conflicts between human rights obligations do have solutions.

Yet we need to distinguish between universal human rights and the *ideal individual rights* that most support a particular individual in inquiry. A person's ideal individual rights may not be justifiable as universal human rights.

A society respecting one individual's right to be honored as superior in every way to all others might most empower that individual's exercise of freedom of thought, but such a non-egalitarian right could not be a human right, and would likely violate human rights. Logically, nothing prevents some individuals from going from society to society until they find a society that gives the honors they crave. No society may ever fully implement universal human rights to the equal opportunity of reply. Maximal support for the creative thought of but one individual is incompatible with human rights.

In a city with good mass transportation, a local right to use a private vehicle, applying a human right to work, ranks lower than in a city without mass transportation. Different rankings exist for an applied human right falling under a single secondary human right. In more broadly distinguishing between secondary legal, civil, political, welfare, public service rights, and public works rights, no universally *fixed hierarchy* can be justified. Situations vary and emergencies shift attention from one right to another. Only temporary local hierarchies exist as we pass from one crying need to the next.

Individuals vary, too. Non-intellectual property rights do not rank more highly than welfare rights for all individuals, nor welfare rights more highly than civil rights. Once we identify a stable hierarchy of secondary civil, welfare, or public service rights that most promote one's freedom of thought in a certain stage of life, finding another society that institutes these rights is often easier than institutionalizing them in one's original home. If immigration is crucial in matching each individual to a ranking of secondary human rights and to the local applications that most empower him or her, we must grant a human right implementing the secondary civil right to freedom of thought, namely, an ideal positive *right to immigrate*.

We would then have a duty to remove national borders as barriers. Yet individuals who choose the individually ideal society in which to live, according to the rights instituted in that society, do not merely consider human rights. One society may grant a right to greater honors to those who excel in sports than another society. In pursuing human rights as a *universal minimum of rights*, we do not seek to institute all rights morally justified by the support they lend to the dialogical rationality of a given individual. Different societies institute different *special rights* which are not human rights, but which promote inquiry by giving different incentives matching different individuals.

12. Secondary Human Rights and the State

Human rights are universal only if they are abstract, as in the single primary right. To have a universal human right to freedom in discussion implies only those further universal human rights which are not deducible from the primary right, but which apply the primary right to the general human situation. If a species existed whose members were capable of dialogical inquiry, but who required only the family and not the state to exercise that right, it would not need secondary human rights enforced by the state. Exercise of the human right to freedom in discussion requires institutions beyond the family.

The six types of secondary human rights we have considered all presuppose the state as the guarantor of last resort. Some kind of state counts among the underlying conditions for securing the basic human right. If human rights require states and legal enforcement, no such rights exist in prehistory or in para-historical stateless societies. Human rights are rights to freedoms, services, and goods secured with the help of a state, indeed of a state that has never yet really existed.

If the state is not a universal institution, we somewhere will fail to find the secondary rights that presuppose a state. Without state institutions, any legal, political, welfare, and public service/public works rights are unrealized ideals. Yet to say that they are ideals is to say that we ought to institute states if possible wherever they do not exist, meaning that states have a moral purpose. Stateless aborigines and Somalians in the early 1990s can only have ideal secondary human rights. The right to the protection of human rights by a state is itself a human right. It is a meta-right, a right to have state-protected rights. Bad states that do not protect human rights currently exist out of conformity with what, by its very concept, a state should be, but their very existence and concept hold the promise of something that we may improve. Even bad states have something good about them. They are better than no states. They give us institutions upon which we can go to work.

Part Four

HUMAN RIGHTS ETHICS
AND INTERNATIONAL LAW

Twelve

THE RIGHT TO FREEDOM OF THOUGHT AND ITS INTERNATIONALLY DECLARED CONDITIONS

1. International Human Rights Law and Case Studies in Human Rights Ethics

We may violate rights, but when we do so some agency must work to enforce them if they are to survive. The enforcement of rights is social, but may also be legal or moral so long as social enforcement through custom or public opinion remains. Human rights do not exist if no agents of enforcement exist in the above ways against violations, though enforcement need not be perfect. Today we hear more of *international human rights law* than *human rights ethics*, which emphasizes individual responsibility. Yet international human rights law, falling under the umbrella of the United Nations, fails to enforce rights. It has not even pretended to provide legal enforcement, but has sought only to assist sovereign member nations in their quest for enforcement.[1]

United Nations "human rights law" is the most authoritative statement of universal moral law today. If the basic right is freedom of thought and action, other so-called human rights eliminate restrictions on freedom of thought and action. In this way, they are modes of freedom of thought. Much as the Ten Commandments were authoritative in a pre-modern era that appealed to a divine will beyond human assessment, the articles of the Universal Declaration have become the center of a contemporary neo-Kantian morality, a moral consensus to the effect that the dignity of the human person as proclaimed by conscience is alone sacrosanct. We have now raised a fundamental law of Kant's moral teaching, the categorical imperative in its least controversial form, to the level of a universal creed. Human dignity lies in the capacity for reason, for the rational pursuit of goals that each individual assigns to him- or herself, thus becoming an end in him- or herself. Human rights ethics, as we have explained it, differs from Kant chiefly in grounding the moral point of view in the cognitive point of view.

The *Preamble* of the Declaration states that respect for human dignity is, first, respect for *freedom of speech and belief*, but this respect is at once also respect for *freedom from fear and want*. Fear and want impede freedom of speech and belief. Freedom from them is the chief empirical condition of the possibility of the basic human right. Since speech is relative to the possibility of others in a position to hear, the reference to speech in the Preamble places belief in the context of communication and action. Every other person represents intersubjective rationality in the form of a possible test for our beliefs. Reason is public criticism, not monological assent autonomously determined by private insight.

The Universal Declaration arose in the aftermath of World War II. That the Preamble should motivate respect for human rights by claiming their indispensability to *peace* was understandable in a war-weary world. People wanted to put their lives together without fear that they would again suffer intolerance of religious belief, race, ethnic identity, and of other expressions of freedom of thought. We say human rights promote peace by promoting tolerance, but tolerance may mean not caring and lapsing into indifference. Yet it can also be solicitous. Economic rights, in the Declaration, show active caring. Even civil rights like the right not to be tortured require more than refraining from violation. They require intervention when others show no restraint. When intervention goes as far as wars of humanitarian intervention, the pursuit of human rights does not always result in peace.

We must recognize the priority of individual over state responsibility in interpreting international human rights law. This recognition prevents the delegation to international organizations of individual responsibility for enforcing human rights from becoming a loss of such responsibility. Yet it also helps us understand the ethical content of international human rights law.

If the Universal Declaration with dozens of declared rights expresses the moral consensus of humankind, and if we agree that only one basic human right ought to exist, we may start with the Declaration when inquiring into expanding universal and non-universal *applications* of the basic right. We need not limit universal applications to those in the Declaration. They ultimately result from taking, not the legal point of view of establishing the implications of treaties, but the moral/cognitive point of view of inquiring into the requirements of maximally equal freedom of thought. The analysis of historical or imaginary case studies assists us in this inquiry. Such analysis informs the creation of new international human rights law.[2] New special rights movements since 1948—movements promoting gay rights, aboriginal rights, environmental rights, the rights of non-smokers exposed to indoor smoke, or the rights of human rights workers themselves—apply human rights to situations not explicitly foreseen in the Universal Declaration:

> It is the right of any individual to protect and promote the human rights enshrined in the Universal Declaration of Human Rights. . . . We deplore the fact that the increase in the number and influence of human rights defenders in the world has been accompanied by a development and systematization of repressive measures and practices used against them.[3]

2. Human Rights as Freedoms

Every distinct human right is a right to think as you choose, to express your thought, act, or avail yourself of a service or good. The freedom *to* choose is both a freedom *from* the coercion that would force you to do what you do not wish and freedom *from* the restraint that would prevent you from doing what you wish. A further freedom, freedom of rational choice, is present where insight, whether enlightened or unenlightened, causes the choice that in turn causes the overt action. Some consider this freedom to be of a higher sort than freedom of choice. For something other than insight—such as propaganda, advertising, or peer pressure—may determine non-rational freedom of choice.

Yet we should not limit the exercise of human rights to the use of rational freedom. First, saying when another's freedom ceases to be rational is difficult. If we rely on our personal intuitions about what is rational and restrict freedom of choice to what we deem rational, we will repress a considerable range of free choice. We often ought to allow freedom of choice even where we find it unenlightened, for, despite appearances, it may turn out to be actually enlightened, enlightening, and even true. Yet even if a choice is unenlightened, the right to make that choice is essential, as John Stuart Mill held, to the public demonstration of the fact.[4] Mill held that "all silencing of discussion is an assumption of infallibility." Yet he gives a utilitarian justification of freedom of thought and discussion:

> [T]he peculiar evil of silencing the expression of an opinion is, that it is robbing the human race; posterity as well as the existing generation; those who dissent from the opinion, still more than those who hold it. If the opinion is right, they are deprived of the opportunity of exchanging error for truth: if wrong, they lose, what is almost as great a benefit, the clearer perception and livelier perception of truth, produced by its collision with error.[5]

Mill is close to human rights ethics. However, his utilitarian justification of discussion and the right to freedom of thought by their consequences in the quest for truth ("The truth of an opinion is part of its utility," *Ibid.*) is itself open to free discussion. "The usefulness of an opinion is itself a matter of opinion," he grants.[6] Yet he does not fully see that the truth of the utilitarianism by which he evaluates free discussion is a matter of opinion open to discussion regulated solely by a trans-utilitarian ethics of truth-directed discussion. We must finally evaluate human rights, not by their usefulness for general happiness, but by their indispensability to public inquiry into truth.

3. Freedom in Human Rights Documents

Maximally equal freedom of choice in thought and action (along with all that is implied in the way of subsistence and security rights) is the primary right in existing declarations and conventions. Most notable in its influence is the United Nations Universal Declaration that, in its Preamble, makes "freedom of speech and belief" paramount. The basic right of freedom of thought appears in Articles 3, 5, 12, 18, and 19—on liberty, torture, privacy, freedom of thought, freedom of expression, and freedom of religious belief.

The United Nations Covenant on Economic, Social and Cultural Rights makes freedom of choice basic in its Preamble. It declares a right to freedom of choice in the labor market, a right not to be compelled to choose without alternatives. The United Nations Covenant on Civil and Political Rights holds that no right to equality exists except as equal enjoyment of the right to free choice. No one ought to prevent us from holding a religious belief, nor feel obliged to choose only one belief. Much the same is true of the European Convention for the Protection of Human Rights and Fundamental Freedoms. The American Declaration of the Rights and Duties of Man in its Preamble holds that "rights exalt individual liberty," while "duties express the dignity of that liberty." Duty consciousness rises to parity with rights consciousness.

4. The Human Right and Its Different Modes

A moral law that asserts only that we have a right to respect for our freedom of thought is too abstract to be very useful. Universal and local applications of the abstract human right clarify its relevance in different situations. The Universal Declaration makes no claim to have created the human rights standard. It declares, beyond a general right to freedom of thought, particular rights that give content to the general right. The conscience of civilized humanity allegedly already recognizes these rights as valid, even though we do not find them universally respected.

Civil, welfare, public service, and public works rights as recognized in family life appear in Articles 16, 25, and 26—on marriage, living standards, and education. Rights in *socio-economic life* we find in Articles 4, 13, 17, 22, 23, 25, and 26 on slavery, travel, property, social security, welfare, public cultural works and services, work, living standards, public services, public works, and education. *Political rights* appear in Articles 14, 20, 21, and 28—on persecution, assembly, political participation, and international law. *Legal-access rights* appear in Articles 6–11 and 14 on the rights of persons in the theatre of law, judicial appeal, arbitrary detention, fair trials, the presumption of innocence, and *ex post facto* laws and punishment. Still further *civil and public service and public works rights in cultural life* we find in Articles 15, 19, 20, 22, 24, 26, and 27—on nationality, freedom of worship, freedom of expression in the media, freedom of association, the right to cultural self-expression, rest (leisure, paid vacation), education, the peaceful tolerance of other cultures, and participation in cultural life.

If all human rights ostensibly distinct from the right to freedom of thought are only its universal applications, that right is the sole independent human right. *The justification of human rights no longer requires separate justification of dozens of different rights.* Justification of *the* human right suffices. Other "human rights" are justifiable as modes of the one right. "Multiple freedoms" are the one freedom to think *by* not being tortured, *by* not starving, *by* being empowered to vote, and so forth. They are that one right referred to under different descriptions. The "right to property" and the "right to health" differ in sense, but not in reference. Much as, according to Friedrich Ludwig Gottlob Frege, the evening star is identical under a different description with the morning star, the right to vote in free elections is identical under a different description with the right to the presumption of innocence until proof of guilt.

Human rights are *identical in substance* even when they are *modally distinct*. All universal rights except the basic one are modal human rights. They are rights *by* the exercise of which we are always still exercising the basic right. A modal right is similar to a modal action. For example, you get married *by* saying "I do." The two actions are identical. The right to food is itself identical with the right to freedom of thought. It is a universal mode of exercising the right to freedom of thought. Your right to a nationality is a right to think and act without inhibiting expression of your national identity. It is a modal human right because its exercise is a near universal mode of exercising freedom of thought. You exercise freedom of thought, for example, *by* having a right not to be prevented by others from expressing yourself in your native accent. The "by" locution introduces a modal right.

The right to work is a universal mode in civil society of the right to freedom of thought so long as we exercise this basic right only by exercising a right to an independent livelihood. You exercise the right to freedom of thought and action by exercising a modal right to express your sexual orientation. This modal right is not just a right to engage in particular sexual acts, but is a right to express your sexual orientation in the full range of thought and action. If others prevent you from expressing your sexual orientation throughout your speech or body language, you experience repression of your freedom of thought and action. If you must study your speech or action to avoid betraying your sexual orientation, you have less time to think.

Modally distinct but substantively identical human rights reflect ways in which freedom of thought may suffer different restrictions. "Freedom of thought *by* a right to freedom of worship" is, under a different description, "freedom of thought *by* a right to freedom of assembly." This account of human rights following Frege's sense-reference distinction radically simplifies the subject. Applying Ockham's Razor, it eliminates rights inflation. The justification of human rights is that of a single right. It focuses human rights research on the modes of one right. It allows only a multiplication of the descriptions under which we refer to one right.

In classifying applications of the general right to freedom within different institutions of life, we have used the six-fold typology from the last chapter: civil, legal, political, welfare, public works, and public services. The Universal Declaration gives expression to some of these rights as *freedoms*, as in the expression "freedom from persecution," but this is shorthand for a *right*. Freedom from persecution is the right not to be persecuted, freedom from slavery is the right not to be enslaved. Such universal rights have not come even close to existing in most of past history. Yet they are universally justifiable modes of the one right valid for all times and places. Ideally, ancient Romans and pre-Columbian Americans ought to have shared rights-protected freedom of thought, supported by transcontinental communication. Yet ancient Romans and pre-Columbians had no knowledge of one another.

Human rights embracing all human beings are not possible without universal civil society. If they are to embrace all human beings, the technical possibility of their creation must exist, and this depends on the *globalization* already underway since the mercantile and industrial revolutions. Some "human rights," unlike the right to own property, are permanent applications of the primary right. Article Thirteen of the Declaration declares a right of movement within and without a country, presupposing the borders of sovereign nations that might not always exist.

The universal right to freedom of choice in potential dialogue will never fully appear until we eliminate all forms of domination. Yet domination is not all or nothing. We can approach freedom of thought by eliminating some forms of domination to some degree, without eliminating all forms.

Strictly speaking, *slavery* has never existed. For to be a slave, a person owned as a thing, is contradictory. Yet we successfully use the contradictory description of being a slave, hence a thing, to refer to some individuals, and slave societies have institutionalized this usage. The trafficking in human cargo, especially women and children, that still exists with impunity in several countries shows that slavery still exists, and that no human right not to be enslaved exists. We may now be able to exercise the dialogical right to freedom of thought more fully than ever, with fewer restrictions, through media such as email and the internet. Yet masses of largely invisible individuals suffer from economic bondage preventing them from joining the great information highway.

To illustrate non-universal modal rights, if women need special protection against the threat of rape, some women's rights ought to exist that would not be human rights because males would not claim them. Yet a woman's right not to be raped is an application to the situation of women of a modal right that ought to be universal, the right not to be physically attacked, ultimately based on the right to freedom of thought and choice exercisable only *by* a right not to be attacked.

THE BASIC IDEAL HUMAN RIGHT AND ITS MODES

(1) The Basic Human Right to Freedom of Thought and Choice.

(2) Ideal Modes of the Basic Human Right Necessary within the History of States:

   a. Civil Rights: freedom of association, of worship, of assembly, right to choose sexual orientation, right to national identity, freedom from persecution, freedom from torture, right to privacy.

   b. Political rights: right to be free of abuse of human rights by citizen control of the state through democratic elections.

   c. Legal-access rights: right to a public defender, right to services, of an ombudsman, right to initiate legal proceedings, to judicial appeal, freedom from arbitrary detention, right to a fair trial, right to be presumed innocent until proven guilty, freedom from *ex post facto* laws and punishments.

   d. Universal welfare rights: right to participate in obligatory subsistence insurance guaranteed by the state.

   f. Universal public works rights/service rights: rights to infrastructure and staffing in support of other human rights.

(3) Ideal Modes of the Basic Human Right Not Necessary within the History of States:

   a. Civil rights: right to freedom of domestic and international travel, right to International rule of law, right to a national passport, right to peace or freedom from war. (All such rights presuppose multiple sovereign states.)

   b. Political rights: right to freedom of *press* presupposing a technology that once did not exist.

   c. Legal-access rights: right to televised legislative and court proceedings, presupposing a contingent technology.

   d. Welfare rights: right to work, right to rest (leisure, paid vacation), presupposing economic scarcity with survival by the sweat of the brow.

   e. Public works rights: rights to infrastructures subject to becoming outdated, such as trolley tracks in a city in which dependence on the automobile is not a form of domination by manufacturers.

   f. Public service rights: right to a traditional postal service subject to being replaced by electronic mail.

(4) Ideal Individual or Sub-Group Applications of the Basic the Human Right. These applied rights are not human rights because they are not ideally universal. Minority rights, such as women's rights, are an example.

5. Human Rights Texts Interpreted through Their
Contemporary Non-Universal Contemporary Applications

The moral/cognitive point of view is one from which we grasp human rights as a moral ideal and, insofar as possible, realize it. Yet not all have grasped human rights as a moral ideal. It makes little sense to speak of the human rights ethics or policy of a purely local community existing without any idea of the cosmopolis. Only intermediaries can bring members of different tribal communities into dialogue with one another. If they do not recognize the moral ideal of cosmopolitan dialogue, they will feel no obligation to realize it. Their human right of dialogue is still a putative right claimed on their behalf by anthropologists but left hanging unless tribe members take up the claim.

Cherishing the *privacy* of sacred rituals, tribe members may oppose enlightened attempts by others to exercise their dialogical rights on their behalf by bringing them into dialogue with the rest of humanity. Members of the tribe may view such attempts as a violation of a trust. The right to dialogue is consistent with a *right not to dialogue*, to protect what is private from the public inspection that would sap its energy. The recognition of a sacred domain restricts dialogical inquiry, but we ought not to constrain others to discuss any topic. We ought to respect the secrecy of another's life if he or she wishes, unless such secrecy is a cover for human rights abuse.

If some tribes do not practice human rights ethics, the same is true of historical societies held captive to the logic of *despotism*. An individual who is comfortable as a bondsman has no conscious aspiration to dialogical independence and equality. Far from being an actual right, such independence is not even an ideal. The sphere of human rights ethics is the contemporary world, a sphere of revolt against *bondage*. Yet we may exaggerate the range of persons subject to the logic of despotism, since despotism itself may have repressed evidence of genuine revolt against bondage throughout history.

If human rights are rights of all over and against all, we do not easily include deceased persons who cannot take possession of rights claimed on their behalf by historians. Nor can we mean merely rights today. The rights of all as recognized by all today are inexistent prospective rights. They include prospective rights of the living whom we hope will have rights tomorrow. They also include prospective rights of the unborn, rights to which we, in solidarity with future generations after our death, look forward. We respect the prospective human rights of the living, and of the unborn, by preserving life conditions for them. We recognize the validity of ideal prospective rights by present-day statements accompanied by a tacit promise that—if all living and unborn individuals enabled by human rights were to inquire freely—they would all agree. The validation of such statements depends on future acts of exercising human rights. A prehistoric statement within the closed circle of a tribe makes no appeal to a prospective consensus of a universal audience. Nor does a feudal statement appealing to the judgment of a lord make such an appeal. The act of stating a belief is different in each historical setting.

Each modal right applies the basic human right in different situations. The basic right is a *determinable right* that we make determinate only by applications not deducible from the basic right itself. The right to work applies freedom of thought in a world in which scarcity makes independence of thought dependent on an ability to earn a living. Application of the basic right in different situations shows its meaning in those situations. By unburdening freedom of thought of one or another restraint or constraint, each modal human right reveals freedom of thought in part. The right to dialogical freedom is a right not to undergo torture, to assemble, and not to have your future choices curtailed by the deprivation of life necessities or of a primary education. In some cities, it is a right to the use of an automobile.

One individual's subjective right to freedom of thought is only a *prima facie* right. Some Americans may lose a right to dialogical freedom by use of private vehicles to go to work if, by limiting sustainable development, they impede a far greater number of individuals elsewhere from exercising such freedom. Only discussion of the particular situation can determine whether a *prima facie* right is a *de facto* actual right. Human rights discussion ethics is a procedural ethics that cannot itself dictate any substantive conclusion beyond the conclusion that an obligation exists to build respect for persons *qua* potential discussion partners. Only the discussion itself can determine whether we can justify a more particular right. An account of the procedure of rationally motivated discussion requires no position on abortion, capital punishment, physician-assisted suicide, or cloning. We may conjecture a number of ideal modal human rights, but no conjecture about the outcome of rational discussion before the universal audience can replace the discussion itself.

Human rights ethics itself is not for or against abortion, for or against capital punishment. Yet a particular practitioner of discussion ethics may defend abortion or capital punishment as an action or rule fostering dialogical freedom for as many as possible. We may also guess on incomplete evidence that a consensus favoring abortion or capital punishment will emerge at the end of a discussion of finite duration.

The 1948 Declaration and later covenants cite many *prima facie* universal human rights applications. We may try to interpret the Declaration as canonical by returning to and entering empathetically into the voices of the text, by identifying intentions of their authors, and by carrying these intentions forward by asking what universal applications the authors would specify in response to our situation. But the historical intentions of delegates negotiating the Declaration varied. Our interpretation in the next chapter will be in the light of human rights ethics viewed, until further notice, as rationally inescapable. Such interpretation also results in applications not cited in the text.

Itemized applications of one human right help define the right imaginatively by seeing how it applies in varying situations. The nature of the right to freedom of thought and action would become fully determinate only in its application in all possible situations. Yet the meaning of the right becomes most poignant in application to our situation. Inhabitants of a country may at a given time understand freedom of thought most acutely as the right to unemployment benefits and at another time as freedom from press censorship.

We test judgments as to the different modes of the one human right by historical case studies and imaginary scenarios. Such studies identify new ways of reducing the external restraint and constraint in which freedom of thought operates. Private housing falls under freedom of thought, but without being deducible from it. We know empirically whether and how a lack of housing, with the rest and privacy it brings, restricts freedom of thought.

6. Freedom from Terror as a Mode of Freedom of Thought

A right not to be terrorized appears under no separate article in the Universal Declaration. Yet it is, like the right not to be tortured that the Declaration includes, a universal application of the basic right to dialogical freedom. Terror intimidates those who would act on their insight. It attempts to control individuals by striking fear into their hearts. It restricts the freedom of choice. The right to freedom of thought comes in degrees, and as we reduce restrictions on its exercise one after another the alternatives between which we choose expand. This is fortunate, since it makes progress toward human rights possible in an incremental fashion. Human rights do not exist, but we partake of them more or less fully—and more fully without private terrorism than with it. The existing nuclear powers claim the moral legitimacy of a form of state terrorism.

Can the evil of terrorism—killing the innocent to strike fear into the hearts of others, destabilizing an unjust society and loosening its habitual loyalties—ever be the least costly way to extend the secure enjoyment of freedom of thought to the many? Are the many more important than the victims of terrorism? If so, terrorism might occasionally be justifiable by the standard of human rights. We are not honest if we do not ask the question. Some say that the violation of the right of merely one is as morally condemnable as the violation of the right of many, since what counts is the principle, which throughout remains the same. Yet what is wrong is not the abstract concept of violating a principle. What is wrong is each violation of the right of an individual person, and *two individual violations are greater than one.*

Thirteen

THE UNITED NATIONS
UNIVERSAL DECLARATION

1. The Universal Declaration

Can we understand the 1948 Universal Declaration as expressing an ethics based solely on respect for human rights?[1] The United Nations endorses no particular ethical theory. The Declaration invites us to fill a gap that the United Nations, seeking the broadest possible consensus of atheists and believers, capitalists and communists, leaves unfilled.

What follows is not a full commentary, but a brief sketch of a rational interpretation of the Declaration as a canonical text. Since 1948, the document has gained such authority as an island of sanity in the international community that many would prefer not to interpret as false. Its authority arises from its gradually acquired position as a source of legitimacy for national and international institutions. This is especially apparent in the European Union.

The canonical status of the Declaration need not mean that we have fixed its meaning for all time, any more than we would imply this for the Koran, the Bible, or the American Constitution. Interpretation may apply the text to new situations unforeseen by the original authors. It may also take the form of going beyond the literal syntactical and semantic meaning to make the text consistent with a rational theoretical consensus prevailing today, but that did not exist at the text's inception. Yet, in the era of the Declaration, Karl Popper's *The Open Society and its Enemies* (1945) is one candidate for a theory capable of generating a rational interpretation of the Declaration.

Rational interpretation of a canonical text implies that we can find it, without violence to its semantics and syntax, to be true at a depth level. Such an interpretation of the Declaration would reinforce international institutions by reinforcing authority of their most basic legitimating document.

Is an ethics of respect for human rights the deep meaning of the Declaration? Though René Cassin called the Declaration the first international document of ethical value,[2] its authors shared no ethical theory. We may explore different ethical theories in justification of the Declaration. Yet (1) *if* we can independently justify some human rights ethics, (2) *if* that ethics implies the canonical claims of the Declaration, and (3) *if* no other ethical theory meets these two conditions, that ethics is the rational interpretation of the Declaration. An ethics of respect for human rights meets this third condition only if it contains a refutation of all competing ethical theories.

The Declaration does not lend specific support to the ethical theory of this book. Declarations declare, they do not argue. Yet human rights ethics, if used to interpret the Declaration, necessarily supports it. Its Preamble asserts freedom of thought and belief to be the final standard of moral progress, which we can realize only by freedom from want and fear. The Declaration contains basic claims of human rights ethics without the argumentation. Yet, despite this apparent convergence between human rights ethics and the Declaration, external justifications of the Declaration by religious ethics, ethical egoism, utilitarianism, ethical relativism, Kantianism, and natural law theory all remain possible. We can justify human rights ethics as the rational interpretation of the Declaration only if it prevails in argumentation over these rivals.

Taking up the Preamble and Articles, we interpret them from the *moral standpoint* of a *rational will-to-seek-truth-by-discussion.* Is there any right that rational agents cannot universally will, whose universal recognition would not express a universal will to seek truth by mutual respect?

2. Preamble to the Universal Declaration

> *Whereas* recognition of the inherent dignity and of the equal and inalienable rights of all members of the human family is the foundation of freedom, justice and peace in the world. . . .

Though the fabric of communication assigns dignity to each potentially participating member, some members of the species are not capable of participation, and some who are capable may not belong to the species. Yet the number of human beings who are not capable, ultimately who are not persons, is small if we understand dialogue broadly, and if we do not rank dialogues by their importance or difficulty. Still the possibility of a human organism without the human rights of an inquiring person exists, though such an organism may have other rights and forms of dignity.

Once we direct inquiry to truth without qualification, no higher or lower truth exists. Objectively, truth is truth. The truth about a better mousetrap might, in some situations, be as crucial as the truth about the destiny of the universe. If all truth pursued in inquiry were not equal, persons limited to discovering less valuable truth would not enjoy full equality with those capable of discovering valuable truth. The freedom of thought of different persons would not always have the same weight. Yet the question as to what is lower or higher truth must itself be the subject of egalitarian discussion. We cannot enter this debate with *a priori* assumptions as to its conclusion.

A human rights culture cannot exist if statements of belief fail to promise confirmation by future universal free inquiry. For this promise to be credible, we must show human rights advancing toward existence today. Dialogical truth seeking today depends more on the existence of rights-holders tomorrow than today. Human rights today hold value because they give promise of such rights tomorrow. Universal freedom of speech, even if it existed to-day, would be hollow if we saw it yielding to an authoritarian consensus that restricts the search for truth to self-validating messages of some elite.

Because the public pursuit of truth requires undisrupted communication, human rights imply a right to peace. They also imply justice. Justice is a pro-portionately equal distribution of rights and resources for discussion, at times requiring in absolute terms unequal distribution of resources.

Whereas disregard and contempt for human rights have resulted in bar-barous acts which have outraged the conscience of mankind, and the ad-vent of a world in which human beings shall enjoy freedom of speech and belief and freedom from fear and want has been proclaimed as the highest aspiration of the common people. . . .

The Preamble itself makes freedom of thought and speech first among human rights, but they depend on freedom from fear and want. Yet, rationally interpreted, the outrage was chiefly European and only potentially universal.

Whereas it is essential if man is not to be compelled to have recourse, as a last resort, to rebellion against tyranny and oppression, that human rights should be protected by the rule of law. . . .

Violent responses to tyranny may be legitimate but are never desirable. We ought to exercise the right to revolt against tyranny only in the greatest emergency. To assure that revolt remains a last resort, we can best ensure the protection of human rights through constitutional and international law along with custom. International human rights law seeks to lend support to each state's obligation to respect rights, though the obligation of states derives from the self-imposed moral obligation of individuals.

Whereas it is essential to promote the development of friendly relations between nations. . . .

Friendship implies taking pleasure in one another's intentions. It is a necessary condition of a secure peace. It encourages cooperation and mutual assistance. Dislike of neighbors or suspicion of their intentions makes the avoidance of hostilities more difficult. The purpose of human rights is, mini-mally, to maintain peace by the tolerance of actions that do not violate human rights, including actions that many people historically have not tolerated due to ethnic or cultural prejudice. This is the chief function of modern human rights since the seventeenth century.

Whereas the peoples of the United Nations have in the Charter reaf-firmed their faith in fundamental human rights, in the dignity and worth of the human person and in the equal rights of men and women and have determined to promote social progress and better standards of life in larger freedom. . . .

Member states of the United Nations, claiming to represent their peoples, have expressed faith in the future realization of human rights. They have committed themselves to realizing equal rights between the sexes, to expanding human rights by a reform of social attitudes and customs, and by advancing higher material standards of living. We need to make this progress if we are to enhance freedom of thought by exercising social, economic and cultural rights, not just by civil and political rights. The construction of rights has begun, we partake of them, but their construction is far from ending.

Whereas Member States have pledged themselves to achieve, in cooperation with the United Nations, the promotion of universal respect for and observance of human rights and fundamental freedoms. . . .

The members of the United Nations have promised to work to respect human rights in action and speech. This promise we can and ought to keep. To promise to realize human rights fully by a deadline, as distinct from a promise to strive for their realization, is unrealistic. The nations of the world have obligated themselves to strive. They might not have done so, and then morality would not have the foothold in the world it has. Human rights ideals would still exist, but without any recognized obligation to realize them.

Whereas a common understanding of these rights and freedoms is of the greatest importance for the full realization of this pledge.

We need universal knowledge of human rights if we are to work effectively for them. Knowing the good is necessary, if not sufficient, for consistently doing the good. The knowledge is not innate. We learn it by the moral education to which the Declaration contributes. All nations ought to teach the Declaration. Incorporating purely national documents and sources in public moral education is inconsistent with the Declaration. If all claim human rights and all recognize these claims, purely national declarations of human rights contribute less to human rights than the Universal Declaration, which is a declaration by all, not just on behalf of all by merely some.

Now, therefore, the General Assembly *proclaims this universal declaration of human rights* as a common standard of achievement for all peoples and all nations, to the end that every individual and every organ of society, keeping this Declaration constantly in mind, shall strive by teaching and education to promote respect for these rights and freedoms and by progressive measures, national and international, to secure their universal and effective recognition and observance, both among the peoples of Member States themselves and among the peoples of territories under their jurisdiction.

Human rights are the standard of moral progress. Every person and nation is responsible for knowing this Declaration and for teaching others to respect the rights it proclaims, so that gradually we do not just recognize the validity of these rights but also respect them. We have not yet achieved observance of human rights, and cannot do so merely by declaring them or by any other immediately available means such as national proclamations. We need moral education. Yet we have not nullified the standard of moral achievement merely because we have not yet universally achieved human rights and are not able to practice them customarily.

A historical consciousness of violations surrounds each right cited in the Declaration. The violation of each declared right has resulted in its public defense in solidarity with victims. Human rights consciousness arises from an awareness of wrongs committed. Human rights not in the Declaration, such as the right to eat ice cream, have not resulted in a public sense of oppression.

3. Equal Human Rights

Article One: All human beings are born free and equal in dignity and rights. They are endowed with reason and conscience and should act towards one another in a spirit of brotherhood.

This Article, like the ethics of respect for human rights presented in previous chapters, couples reason and conscience, the search for truth and respect for rights. Reason, as the quest for truth, proceeds through heeding the voice of conscience commanding respect for rights. Yet Article One raises difficult questions. Most importantly, does it imply that human rights really exist? If we could agree that human rights exist for all living adult human beings, we might then ask if such rights have existed since birth. We might then also ask if "all human beings" includes all human beings past, present and future. We would also want to know what "dignity" is if it is distinct from human rights?

The weight of the evidence is that human rights do not exist for many living adults today, so that human rights—which must be universal to exist at all—strictly do not exist. The question as to whether human rights have existed since birth, or as to whether they include those not now living, therefore does not even arise. We may at most say that all potential dialogue partners are deserving of the right to freedom of thought and expression, and that this merit assigns them a dignity falling short of actually existing rights.

In this book we have defended a definite criterion for the existence of rights: members of a society must agree that claiming the right is valid. Rights then exist even if the society is unable to respect the claim despite its best efforts. Human rights do not appear to exist by this criterion. To cite just a few examples, neither the European Union on the matter of farm subsidies causing Third World poverty, nor the United States and Israel in the matter of scrupulously avoiding civilian casualties, nor Russia in the matter of press censorship, nor the Muslim world punishing those who use freedom of thought to convert to another religion, nor China in obstructing free use of the internet has made the best effort it can to respect human rights claims.

We conclude that a rational interpretation of Article one, preserving the moral authority of the Universal Declaration, requires us to take it as asserting human rights as unrealized moral ideals, not actually existing rights. Human rights are moral ideals. They also become moral obligations insofar as their realization in the existing world becomes possible.

In large part due to the Declaration, states claiming to represent the nations of the world have nominally recognized unenforced basic rights as valid, but without ever making a full effort to enforce them in any time span. Because the world as a whole does not enforce rights declared in the Universal Declaration, it is a chiefly a moral declaration, not a legal code. Neither the Declaration nor the covenants that it has inspired are true enforceable law. This is true even though the European Court of Human Rights has seriously sought to enforce civil and political human rights as law within its region.

A non-Stoical moral conscience supporting efforts to realize the right to freedom of thought emerged in the Age of Enlightenment, outraged as it was by the execution of Jean Calas for his religious beliefs. Barbarous acts of World War II so outraged the conscience of many, especially in the Western world, that recognition of the validity of human rights became widespread, eventually even outside the Western world. National liberation struggles, struggles against Communist totalitarianism, and special rights movements (for example, anti-racist struggles, the feminist movement, and the gay rights movement) came to share in the conscience of human rights ethics. Sometimes recognition of the legitimacy of human rights has been purely rhetorical or even cynical. Yet a felt obligation to give lip service to human rights counts as a step towards universal recognition.

Individual spokespersons for humanity like Voltaire have long proclaimed the rights of all on behalf of all. Yet humanity as a whole never began to recognize these rights as legitimate prior to the nominal consensus created by the Universal Declaration. This Declaration was the first declaration by a true world organization, by the legal representatives of peoples of the world.

All adult dialogue partners are free and equal on entering any rational discussion as to whether we can justify a form of inequality. (See Chapter One.) Non-circular discussion as to who deserves rank must itself presuppose the authority of no ranking elite. The greater respect that some enjoy for their freedom of thought they need to have earned in prior discussion, which others can always reopen.

Jean-Jacques Rousseau deplored that human beings, born free and equal, have ended everywhere in chains. Starting out free and equal in a discussion and ending up with unequal rankings after the discussion is not deplorable. It would be deplorable only if we could not reopen discussion of the ranking of individuals, or if a person's ranking were due to physiological or environmental handicaps for which he or she is not responsible, or if the rules of discussion were not "fair" as defined, for example, by Jürgen Habermas. (See Chapter Five.) We promote discussion before a universal audience by democratizing hierarchical societies, redistributing some resources if we cannot increase them, and using technology and medicine to augment the abilities of the less able. We should do none of this out of pity, but out of respect for our rationality, requiring us all to ferret out valid discussion partners.

So what are "human rights" in Article One? They are not the existing legal rights in Western Europe protected by the European Court of Human Rights, a limited region of the world's living population. This interpretation would leave countless human beings unprotected by human rights, whereas the United Nations exists especially to serve vulnerable populations. The human rights of the Declaration are first ideal moral rights accompanied by local and regional efforts to realize their existence. These ideal human rights constitute moral obligations wherever progress toward bringing them into existence is possible. Yet we have not yet made a maximum effort worldwide to realize human rights ideals. This effort depends on a still unborn world human rights culture in the name of the rational legitimacy of all dialogue partners, uniting Oriental duty consciousness with Western freedom of dissent.

4. Minority Rights

Article Two: Everyone is entitled to all the rights and freedoms set forth in this Declaration, without distinction of any kind, such as race, color, sex, language, religion, political or other opinion, national or social origin, property, birth, or other status. Furthermore, no distinction shall be made on the basis of the political, jurisdictional or international status of the country or territory to which the person belongs, whether it be independent, trust, non-self-governing or under any other limitation of sovereignty.

The equal enjoyment of human rights requires that no one enjoy fewer or more rights, or rights supported by fewer or more resources, due to race, sex, language, religion, opinions held, national origin, wealth, place of birth, or other minority status. Discrimination either for or against a minority is justifiable only by non-discrimination in support of the basic human right. All ought to be as equal as possible in freedom of thought, if not in the particular rights implementing the general right. Rights that everyone has only as a member of a particular minority, and that all should if possible respect, are not universal human rights. Yet they show how human rights apply to the situation of that minority. Women's rights, like a right to maternity leave, are not human rights, but are applications of human rights to the situation of women. To have morally compelling women's rights is to have human rights that women can exercise only by exercising those minority rights.

5. Subsistence and Security as Modes of the Basic Right

Article Three: Everyone has the right of life, liberty, and the security of person.

Article Three asserts an ideal right to life in two dimensions, *subsistence* and *security*. These rights seem, empirically, to be universal. We can trade a steak dinner for a fish dinner. Yet we cannot trade nutrition in general for anything else. Since no one eats food in general, a right to nutrition is a right to some particular form of nutrition or other, but is not a right to any one form in particular. Subsistence is not an external means to freedom of choice that we can exchange for other means. Given an organism's subjection to precarious conditions, we can justify proportionately equal rights to subsistence and security as universal modes of the right to freedom of thought. The right to freedom of thought is a right to such freedom *by* subsistence and security.

A human right to security depends on the right to freedom of thought. It cannot be a right to absolute security, which is impossible for mortal persons. Utilitarian or other arguments may support an independent right to life, but all argument presupposes the ethics of argumentation itself. Compassion for those who suffer without dialogical potential is in varying degrees instinctive, but a universal morality responsible at the bar of reason does not require it. Compassion for some may even conflict with this morality.

Human rights are *indivisible*, all expressing one right. The right to subsistence is a welfare right, while the right to security is a civil right. Both are justified by their identity with the right to freedom of thought under one or another description. If we distinguish the right to subsistence from the right to freedom of thought, the right to subsist can exist without freedom of thought, as in totalitarian regimes. A right to subsistence in such a regime is not a human right, though it may be an animal right. A universal right to subsistence could exist without being a human right, but a right to freedom of thought is a human right only by also being a right to subsistence. Freedom of choice includes subsistence and security, but not the other way around.

The European Convention for the Protection of Human Rights and Fundamental Freedoms (Protocol 11) views the right to life in the Universal Declaration as excluding the death penalty even for the greatest crimes. If the death penalty violates a human right to life, the right is lost if efforts to reinstate respect for the right in lands imposing the penalty are absent. Yet if, in emergencies, we suspend respect for the right to protect freedom of thought the universal right survives. Derogation suspends the right without annulling it. Derogation may prove more widespread in societies that are more violent. In some societies, a state of emergency becomes the rule. People say that the principle is what counts, but the derogation of a moral principle ten times over is worse than its derogation once.

Even if someone contributes to discussion by surviving, human rights ethics implies a right *not* to contribute. But what of a right *not* to live? An argument for the duty to live still exists. No duty to dialogue exists, but a duty to protect and respect those who can discuss does exist. Every human rights ethicist ought to survive, not necessarily as long as possible, but as long as she can still be effective in the struggle to win respect for human rights.

6. Freedom from Bondage and Degrading Treatment

Article Four: No one shall be held in slavery or servitude; slavery and the slave trade shall be prohibited in all its forms.

Article Four concerns emancipation rights. Slavery, servitude, and forms of despotism in which the despot uses bondsmen as quasi-property for the satisfaction of his ends have existed in most of history. They contradict the right of liberty in Article Three. Being a mere means to another's ends undermines free experimentation in realizing a person's self-given ends in open discussion. The right to emancipation is a civil right following from ownership of one's body in which one has invested labor since the womb.

Free choice is limited when the motive of action is compliance with external demands which a despot or master imposes. The agent then ceases to be a credible, autonomous voice in dialogue. Creativity is rarely forthcoming by the *immediate* pressure of external obligation. Creativity requires privacy. A master can give a bondsman a long leash. Yet if you know that a representative of external authority is closely viewing your experience, you will suffer a loss of power in the development of autonomous thought.

We became able to recognize a right to be free of bondage only after the onset of world history with its different forms of patriarchy: pastoral, agrarian, domestic, military, and so forth. Members of prehistoric tribal groupings could not have laid claim to such a right. Tribes that lack cosmopolitan communication with other tribal groupings can neither claim nor recognize universal rights. Members of such groups can have universal rights and obligations only putatively, by the claims we make on their behalf.

No despots oppressed pre-patriarchal communities living in nomadic foraging and hunting communities. We sometimes press claims to liberty on behalf of persons innocently on the verge of succumbing to a despotism they have never known. Yet if they never assume these claims for themselves, holding them in reserve for them flounders. Individuals claim human rights for themselves only to counter forms of oppression that they consciously recognize. Article Four asserts a right that, unlike the rights to subsistence and security, not all claim directly or through advocates.

Several "human rights" in the Declaration are not universal rights, but are applications of such rights to non-universal situations. The secondary rights distinguished in Chapter Twelve apply only to individuals inhabiting states. The civil right in Article Thirteen to freedom of movement in state borders presupposes the existence of states, and so belonged to no one in prehistory except hypothetically. A forager has no categorical right to housing, but has a hypothetical counterfactual right to housing that the person would in fact have *if* he or she inhabited a sedentary society. Yet the Declaration itself does not state that some of its declared rights are universal only if they are hypothetical and counterfactual.

Political and legal human rights presuppose states that offer political participation. Welfare rights suppose the situation of modern states: a free market economy with human costs in global competition and with overtaxed charitable organizations that the state backs up as the provider of last resort. The public service and public works rights of human beings by definition call for respect by the state. Yet, ultimately, human rights depend on respect for them by the citizens who fund the state, delegating power to it. Ultimate state responsibility for respecting rights would take the matter out of the realm of normative ethics governing individual conduct.

The non-universality of some rights is not simply because states do not always exist. The particular technologies of public works are not universal. Different rights to different public works projects exist at different levels of technological development. An applied human right to an automobile can replace a right to a horse. Yet to say that a right to an automobile is universal, but hypothetical and counterfactual in most cases, would license an endless proliferation of modal human rights. A categorical right to health care is most economically interpreted as not including a right of some Romans to heart transplants *if* the technology and other resources had existed.

> *Article Five*: No one shall be subjected to torture or to cruel, inhuman or degrading treatment or punishment.

Respect for a right to be free of servitude has not always been possible. Entrenched institutions sometimes make slavery in the short or middle term inevitable. The Stoics knew that even universal enlightenment would not abolish slavery. Despite such enlightenment, people had to resign themselves to a division of labor in which some were slaves and others masters.

The right not to be subjected to torture or degrading treatment we sometimes suppose to differ from the right to freedom from servitude, in that we can respect it at all times and places. Yet this reasoning takes no notice of the possible institutionalization of torture. The hazing practices of university fraternities verge on a form of torture, while torture organizes itself around the world in intricate social practices, sometimes using dedicated equipment for torture. If a person participates in such a practice, a decision not to torture is no simple decision of self-restraint. For some a decision about torture is a difficult decision about a way of life.

Torture, like any degrading treatment, shows disrespect for the victim's dignity. No morally admissible code gives a right to torture. Can an isolated act of torture, severed from any code or practice, serve a moral end? Immoral means corrupt moral ends if the ends do not come about, but if a good end comes about can it purify the means as the least costly means available?

A right not to be subjected to cruel or unusual punishment or torture is a right to ownership of one's body and to its protection from injury. The presumption is against torture. A heavy burden of proof falls on any who would propose torture, capital punishment, or other action violating the basic *prima facie* subjective right to freedom of thought. Proponents of capital punishment face the same burden of proof. How can an intrinsically evil restriction on individual freedom ever be actually right?

Because interim human rights ethics cannot yet extend human rights to all, it strictly extends them to none. For human rights are either universal or non-existent. Human rights ethics extends prospective human rights to as many as possible. Prospective human rights, which would be human rights if all enjoyed them, are rights enjoyed only by some. Might we occasionally justify torture in building a world that will uniformly disallow torture? If we always could refrain from torture, morally would we always want to? This question has become poignant since September 11, 2001. Is the right not to be tortured a *prima facie* prospective human right that can benefit from derogation to save many lives? Torture, an intrinsic moral evil, has always existed. Instead of merely declaring that nations ought not to go to war, the Geneva Conventions provide rules for mitigating evils of war. Are parallel conventions on the practice of torture discussable?

International human rights documents disallow torture even in times of life-threatening public emergency or war threatening the life of the state. Yet suppose that a new world war would set back the cause of human rights for a century. Suppose that the Soviet government knows that a small group of Russian Maoists is intent on initiating such a war by simulating an attack by the Soviet Union on the United States through gaining access to Soviet missiles. Suppose further that the Soviets hold a member of this small group, and that the only known way of stopping the group is by torturing the individual in custody. Is such a situation impossible?

For the end to justify the means (1) the means must achieve the end, (2) no cheaper means to achieve the end must exist, and (3) the value realized by the end must outweigh any disvalue in the means. If we cannot realize the end more cheaply by other means, and if the end represents a net gain in moral good despite the means, the end morally justifies the means. If the moral good is human rights, progress toward human rights by an act of torture is not *a priori* impossible, however repugnant the question may be. We maintain a universal rule not subject to derogation against torture in international human rights law, but this may be is consistent with justifying an act of torture to realize subjective human rights to freedom of thought of as many as possible in an exceptional case of extra-legal ethical reflection. Such a justification would be most rare. Dams against a slippery slope are necessary. Never allow a decision on torture at the platoon level. Interim human rights ethics would relentlessly pursue alternatives to torture, and would have to assume heuristically until the last moment that an alternative exists.

Article Five does not make the ban torture non-derogable. Human rights norms except for dialogical freedom for as many as possible are *prima facie*. Article Three contains a *prima facie* right to life that an exceptional case of capital punishment we might override. The European Union prohibits legally capital punishment. Yet the rule against capital punishment is not deduced from freedom of thought for as many as possible. The issue is ethically discussable even if in the abstract we think of no exception. Article Five states a *prima facie* universal right not to be tortured that might conflict with freedom of thought for as many as possible. Johann Gottlieb Fichte's rule is that we justify restricting the freedom of one only by a net gain in freedom for all.

The presumption of an absolute moral prohibition of torture exists in part because terrorists and terrorist states have shockingly practiced torture. We feel the need to combat reprehensible acts of torture by banning torture without exception. A strong *prima facie* right not to be tortured exists, since torture radically restricts a victim's freedom of thought and choice: it reduces the victim's range of options to but one option, determined by the will of the torturer. Yet, in the cost-benefit analysis of human rights ethics, we cannot guarantee *a priori* that a *prima facie* will in all cases be an actual right.

7. Legal-Access Rights

Article Six: Everyone has the right to recognition everywhere as a person before the law.

Other Articles—such as One and Three—declare the universal moral rights of persons. Article Six asserts that the state should recognize persons having such moral rights. This recognition gives us access to the machinery of legal protection. We can directly respect human rights that are not *legal-access rights*, like freedom of thought, without state intervention. Yet, by definition, only the state can directly respect legal-access human rights.

Because law presupposes states, we can assert a legal-access right in prehistorical or para-historical communities only hypothetically and contra-factually. Legal-access rights assign a moral purpose to states. The world widely recognizes them as valid even if not respected. United Nations Covenants implementing the Declaration call for pledging and repledging state commitment to recognized rights. Given non-respected rights, lip service may eventually pay off, creating embarrassment for those who are willing to pay such service to enjoy the ideological cover of the Declaration.

The minimal moral aim of the state is to assure legal recognition of residents as ends in themselves, with self-assigned ends. A person has a legal right to make claims upon the state, for others to hear him or her if they wish, without anyone dispatching him or her as an object or obstacle to be overcome, a commodity, or statistic. Everyone has a right to be recognized as legally capable of assigning ends to him- or herself, and of invoking a *prima facie* right to pursue those ends without others reducing him or her to a mere means to another's ends.

In Article Six, the Kantian categorical imperative becomes visible. If everyone ought to recognize persons as ends in themselves, citizens acting through their state ought similarly to recognize all persons under the jurisdiction of that state. We derive the right to legal recognition as a person by any state from the purely moral right to be treated as an end. Everyone has a recognized right to invoke his or her status as a person to obtain consideration from the state that would not be given to an object.

Merely ideal human rights do not exist. They are not yet generally recognized as valid, and so are not yet candidates for respect. Non-respected human rights exist in disconformity with what such a right ought to be, and so are not yet fully genuine. Merely ideal human rights lack general recognition of their validity, though they ought to exist, if possible. Human rights today are *either* existent but not fully true *or* merely ideal. Ideal human rights, like the right to same-sex marriage, might be justifiable by existing human rights without yet being generally recognized as justifiable. Yet the very existence of human rights depends on a world human rights culture currently blocked by Chinese, Muslim, and other regional cultures, including some in the West.

Everyone has an ideal right of access to laws enforcing all the ideal rights enumerated in the Declaration. Promotion of such moral rights follows from recognition of persons as ends in themselves. We should recognize anyone's claim to these rights as legitimate and, if possible, should respect that claim due to every person's capacity for *reason* (Article One). Yet reason is dialogical. To enjoy full respect as a potential partner in dialogue is to enjoy all the rights of the Declaration. To be justifiable, rights to food, to education, and to voting in free elections must help empower freedom of thought.

Few states respect all rights that could be human rights if we recognized their validity universally, but if no state existed, no human rights could exist. The right to dialogical freedom we enjoy only by the support of state-protected rights—civil, legal-access, public works, public service, and welfare. Pre-political tribal life and the rivalry of clans provide no guarantee that proto-human rights will enjoy universal recognition. Sovereign nations make such a guarantee possible but unlikely. Would a world federal state protect individual rights? A question that Article Six raises is: how can a world state guarantee a universal right of persons to recognition and respect before the law, and if a universal state cannot guarantee this right how can we guarantee it without such a state?

> *Article Seven*: All are equal before the law and are entitled without any discrimination to equal protection of the law. All are entitled to equal protection against any discrimination in violation of this Declaration and against any incitement to such discrimination.

We understand this Article best in conjunction with Article Two. The right in Article Seven is one by which we access the police and courts of a state to protect human rights in general. Generally, human rights violations discriminate against victims, nullifying equal respect for all. Since the grounds for unfounded discrimination are very broad, including the unequal distribution of wealth, the responsibility of states to apply the law in a non-discriminatory way is potentially revolutionary. If laws result in poor education for the poor, we face a violation of a recognized right to equal protection against arbitrary discrimination.

A law legislating discrimination disqualifies itself. No way exists of applying it without discrimination unless the law is broken. Yet the revolutionary potential of this Article diminishes as long as enforcement of the Declaration lies with the sovereign states now responsible for the non-respect of declared rights, and as long as we call upon these states only to do what they judge possible.

Prejudice based on race, nationality, political belief, religion, sex, age, wealth, state of health, or other such factors ought not to avoidably restrict a person's freedom of thought. Those with more wealth do not deserve a better legal defense. Those who are elderly, who are children, who are disabled, or who are otherwise vulnerable have a right to what special assistance is available and necessary for them to be equally empowered in present and future discussions. They also have a right to live in a society protected by *anti-hate laws* against racist or other discriminatory propaganda encouraging violation of their rights. Yet if freedom of thought and speech is the sole objective human right, freedom of thought for as many a possible may still restrict the subjective individual rights to freedom of thought belonging to members of a minority. Article Seven may also allow special protection for the rights of human rights workers who promote the creation of and respect for rights.

> *Article Eight*: Everyone has the right to an effective remedy by the competent national tribunals for acts violating the fundamental rights granted him by the constitution or by law.

This legal-access right is second-order, presupposing first-order rights declared in Articles Three through Five, among others. In case of criminal, civil, or state violations, all have an ideal legal-access right to procedures enforcing their human rights in courts. By implication, all persons have a right to laws that guarantee enforcement of human rights. We more widely recognize this right as valid than actually respect it. The political effort of human rights ethicists aims at extending legal enforcement to human rights. We accomplish this, in part, by international tribunals as courts of appeal when national tribunals are incompetent to enforce rights. The possibility of recourse to international tribunals induces compliance by national tribunals.

Article Nine: No one shall be subjected to arbitrary arrest, detention or exile.

Citizens can violate rights, but this Article concerns crimes by the state. Everyone has an ideal right to legal-access to constitutional law to protect herself from the state's violation of civil rights. Arrest, detention, and exile ought never to occur without the safeguard of constitutional protection against arbitrariness. Anyone who is arrested, detained or exiled has a right to know the preliminary evidence and the law applying to the case. We should force no one to act out of a fear of arbitrary arrest or exile inhibiting freedom of thought and of choice. Respect for this right removes a particular range of restrictions on exercise of the basic human right, since everyone exercises freedom of thought in part by not facing the threat of unpredictable arrest or exile. Declared laws should publicize actions subjecting anyone to justifiable arrest, detention, or exile.

Article Ten: Everyone is entitled in full equality to a fair and public hearing by an independent and impartial tribunal, in the determination of his rights and obligations and of any criminal charge against him.

This legal-access right is to a hearing open to public scrutiny prior to a trial. The aim is to inform the accused of his or her situation, the law under which he or she is charged, the preliminary basis for the charge, the obligations of the accused during the trial, and the rights of the accused in his or her defense. A prior public hearing is necessary for the accused to prepare a defense without manipulation by the court or prosecutor.

The right to a fair hearing and trial is a modal right, presupposing a right to freedom of thought presupposing no further right. We are talking about a right to freedom of thought and choice as a right to exercise such freedom *by* knowing the limits to which speech and action can go without prosecution, and by confidence in a fair hearing and trial in case of prosecution.

A right to libraries is a right to freedom of thought by enjoying libraries. Ideally, a right to welfare or public services is a right to freedom of thought by knowing one will not have to alter one's beliefs to satisfy private providers. (Realistically a right to receive private charity is a right to such freedom by knowing one will not have to satisfy some existing public providers.) Studying and teaching at a public university ought to increase protection of freedom of thought. Welfare rights are the right to freedom of thought by not facing the threat of a loss of subsistence. A right to welfare that does not enhance freedom of thought is not a part of the universal moral minimum.

> *Article Eleven*: (1) Everyone charged with a penal offence has the right to be presumed innocent until proven guilty according to law in a public trial at which he has all the guarantees necessary for his defense. (2) No one shall be held guilty of any penal offence on account of any act or commission which did not constitute a penal offence, under national or international law, at the time when it was committed. Nor shall a heavier penalty be imposed than the one that was applicable at the time the penal offence was committed.

All have an ideal right to a human rights-based constitution. Under such a constitution, the burden of proof is on the state, not the accused. Further, no one has a right to be judged or sentenced by *ex post facto* laws. Neither of these legal-access rights requires any special initiative by the individual in defense of first-level rights. A right, a claim socially recognized to be valid and not just a valid claim, relieves the right holder of the need to press his or her claims arduously to gain recognition or even respect. If an individual has to press a special claim to be recognized as innocent until proven guilty, the right to be recognized as such does not yet exist. An individual has a right to freedom of thought by having such constitutional rights. They expand the range of permissible thoughts and actions. They extend an individual's right of freedom, since the individual can act without fear of arbitrary arrest, detainment and judgment by the courts.

8. Civil Rights

> *Article Twelve*: No one shall be subjected to arbitrary interference with his privacy, family, home, or correspondence, nor to attacks upon his honour and reputation. Everyone has the right to the protection of the law against such interference and attacks.

The right to privacy is a civil right to one's own thoughts, actions, or experiences—without sharing them through uninvited observation of them, of their expression, or of records preserving them. A right to privacy in home life and correspondence affords a form of rest supporting the right to freedom of thought. In privacy, a person reviews past public outings in discussion and rehearses future outings. In privacy, a person edits his or her future public self. The right to privacy complements the right to public expression in Article 19. Privacy promotes inquiry by enhancing the individual's contributions. The courts are directly responsible for enforcing this right even if state responsibility is delegated individual responsibility.

The right to privacy is a right to participate in personal experience with undivided attention—without emerging from absorption in that experience to view it from the intrusive viewpoint of another. Individual experience should unfold with the least distraction if individual testimony is to have the greatest credibility—not necessarily credibility as an expression of the truth, but as an expression of that individual's witness to the truth.

If the basic right is one of inquiry in a context of potentially universal dialogue, this right may not seem to include a right to private inquiry. Yet private inquiry is one stage in public inquiry. Freedom of thought is (1) freedom in the private formative thought process, and (2) freedom in publicizing the result of that process. The formative process may be secret without violating anyone's human right. A human right of privacy ideally exists to hold this process secret. Only its result addresses a universal audience, but a right exists to hold even this result private. Even if others think they could benefit from your private thoughts, no moral obligation exists to broadcast them.

We further justify the right to privacy insofar as exposing private thought creates the possibility of theft of the product of thought. Freedom of thought as a civil right implies a proprietary right to its product. In private thought, a person addresses at most an alter ego or a limited audience, not the universal audience. Private discussion circles include more than intrapersonal exchange between internal voices. Private but still interpersonal discussion circles also exist, and they remain private so long as they do not address the universal audience. Participants in such discussions operate as privileged observers. Yet the discussions in which they take part are for that reason less credible than inquiry before the universal audience. A private consensus whose participants allow for further appeal to the universal public is more credible than a private consensus that blocks such recourse.

Military or corporate research and development, operating in secrecy, provides only a limited check on truth. For verification, the corporation must consult a larger audience, which it can do only by sacrificing its original secrecy. It cuts short private research and development and publicizes the result to consumers in the marketplace. Discussion then takes place in public, in tacit discussions by consumers, however unequally weighted they may be by dollar-backed demand. The final check on any truth in a research and development program lies in placing the service or product on the market and allowing public consumer inquiry to take over where inquiry internal to the corporation leaves off.

We attribute "privacy" to activities of a group, not just to those of an individual. The greater the range of private topics off limits to discussion before the universal audience, the greater the restrictions placed on public inquiry. If discussion of a topic is taboo in a single group, its members do not enjoy a recognized right to free discussion of it whether within the group or outside. If a topic is private or sacred, truth seeking would not be the standard in dealing with it in that group, and universal freedom of thought would suffer restriction. Restricted freedom of thought restricts human rights in their entirety.

Egyptian priests withheld from Herodotus some secrets. Anthropologists know tribes whose members object to publication of sacred rituals, songs, and dances. Members of such tribes make no claim to being discussion partners in a quest for universal consensus regarding the presuppositions of these rituals. A private realm exists withheld from public discussion. Sometimes, the anthropologist mistakenly claims to exercise a putative right of tribesmen to have their sacred life form placed in a public gallery of alternative possible human life forms, for comparison, contrast, and inspection. The anthropologist violates a trust. As long as private or sacred matters exist which some maintain all persons should not publicly discuss, only restricted human rights can exist—rights restricted in subject matter.

The institutions of each culture draw the distinction between the public and the private differently. The boundaries of what remains private in a culture are of public concern to that culture. What one culture considers private the world human rights culture, if it knew, might even consider an atrocity. Much depends on what priests or tribesmen want to keep secret. *The human rights culture legitimately leaves only such things private whose publication would undermine dialogical freedom.* This private sphere is the kitchen in which someone prepares the communications he or she wishes to make public. Though the right to privacy, as a person rests from past public outings and prepares further ones, is heuristically crucial, private correspondence no longer serves this purpose after an author's death, and so becomes public.

By the standard of human rights ethics, tribal dances ought to remain beyond the scope of intrusive inquiry if they are a sacred source of tribal energy that would dissipate under public scrutiny, a source to which tribesmen return to renew themselves for further outings in secular dialogue. Human rights ethics advocates privacy insofar as it enhances the public exercise of freedom of thought and choice, but not insofar as privacy conceals human rights violations.

Article Thirteen: (1) Every individual has the right to freedom of movement and residence within the borders of each state. (2) Everyone has the right to leave any country, including his own, and to return to his country.

The right to freedom of movement is an application of the right to freedom of thought. The right to travel supports dialogue by expanding communication to distant persons. Yet, because of economics, not all are equally able to exercise the right. By the minimal negative interpretation, to respect a right only means to refrain from interfering in its exercise, such as not to refuse visas. On the maximal interpretation, the right to travel would be the right to the provision of resources by others with which to travel. To determine the intended interpretation in human rights ethics, we ask which interpretation must apply for the right to be a universal mode of the right to freedom of thought. Freedom of thought comes in degrees. A right to minimal freedom of thought comes with a negative right to travel, while a right to maximal freedom of thought includes a positive freedom to travel. The positive right today is an epistemological ideal, not a recognized human right. The realizable human right that the Declaration intends is a negative right to freedom of movement.

Due to contemporary media (the press, telephone, film, television, internet, fax, and other media), physical travel has become less necessary to the most extensive exercise of freedom of thought. We maintain the intent behind the right to travel by a complementary human right to receive and send communications without interference at the borders, so long as messages do not oppose human rights (Article Twenty-Nine). Though establishing a real positive human right to travel is difficult, a positive right of access to email, to fax machines, and to the internet is closer to universal recognition. A right to have the messages brought to someone technologically accomplishes much that a positive right to travel would accomplish.

Article Thirteen does not state a right to immigrate that would oblige host countries. Such a right might promote multicultural dialogue, though in European nations it has sometimes done the opposite. Yet Article Fourteen states an ideal human right to immigrate in the case of political refugees.

Article Fourteen: (1) Everyone has the right to seek and enjoy in other countries asylum from persecution. (2) This right may not be invoked in the case of prosecutions genuinely arising from non-political crimes or from acts contrary to the purposes and principles of the United Nations.

The right to freedom of thought includes, as a particular mode, a right to leave any nation that restricts self-expression by persecuting individuals for their opinions. The right of asylum is a non-universal mode of the basic right. Unlike the right to security, we do not find it to be necessary in all conceivable situations in the evolution of the international order. For the right presupposes a plurality of sovereign states.

Article Fifteen: (1) Everyone has the right to a nationality. (2) No one shall be arbitrarily deprived of his nationality nor denied the right to change his nationality.

The right to a nationality, viewed as a civil right to citizenship in a sovereign state as well as to participation in the life form of a people, again applies freedom of thought in a particular historically situated situation. National identity assigns everyone a place on the map of world history. No obligation exists to have such identity, but exercising the right enhances the ability to hold a geographical-historical perspective in discussion. It affords inter-cultural orientation, making individuals less anonymous.

We should not prevent an individual who wishes to express personal identity by a national identity from doing so. This is a negative right. Yet no one is obliged to retain her original national perspective or statehood. In exercising freedom of thought, a modal right exists in dialogue between national viewpoints to select a different nationality.

The choice of national identity is not that of state citizenship, since some states are non-national states or multinational states, and some nations are not states. The right to a nationality is not a right to a sovereign state representing that nationality. Yet the right to a nationality is a right to some state that protects the right to express national identity in the exercise of freedom of thought. Human rights ethics must in principle oppose nation states, though many still exist. Such states politicize national identity, making residents of other nationalities into second-class citizens.

> *Article Sixteen*: (1) Men and women of full age, without any limitation due to race, nationality or religion, have the right to marry and to found a family. They are entitled to equal rights as to marriage, during marriage and at its dissolution. (2) Marriage shall be entered into only with the free and full consent of the intending spouses. (3) The family is the natural and fundamental group unit of society and is entitled to protection by society and the State.

The right to marry is a right to a use of one's body as personal property. The right superficially sounds like a right to eat vanilla ice cream. Both rights remove restrictions on the right to freedom of thought and choice, serving to extend respect for human rights. If we restrain a person from eating vanilla ice cream, we seem to restrain free choice for no good reason. Since a *prima facie* right exists to free choice, a very good reason must always exist—such as the freedom of choice of others—for constraining freedom of choice. A human right worth including in the Declaration is not a right to any freedom of choice others might restrict. A right worth including is a right to a freedom of choice that historically has been restricted for no good reason.

If powerful forces repressed eating ice cream, a special rights movement among ice cream lovers might emerge. If the consensus was that exercise of this right favored the exercise of the person's basic human right and the exercise by others of their basic right, a right to eat ice cream might have been in the Declaration. Parents, religious authorities, nationalists, and racists have restricted the right to marry, which explains its inclusion in the Declaration.

No obligation to marry exists, although, as with any declared right, an invitation exists to do so. Undeclared rights like the right to divorce exist, but not as invitations. The non-obligatory, self-initiated exercise of human rights within the limits of respect for the human rights of others does not suffice to fully define the good life. No objective concept of the good life exists. One universal morality of respect for human rights exists, but endless ideas of the good life lie within the bounds of such morality. Each morally permissible vision of the good life proposes a cafeteria-style selection and prioritization among human rights as long as freedom of thought remains paramount.

We justify a human right to marry by showing that its exercise promotes exercise of the primary right to free thought. This freedom includes free choice among visions of the good life. It includes a right to choose a definition of the good life that by an alternative definition is bad. Deepening of the basic human right implies expansion of the available alternative definitions of the good life. Germans enjoy long hikes more than four-hour French meals. Such differences will not disappear in Europe under the European Convention on the Protection of Human Rights and Fundamental Freedoms.

If marriage founds families, we justify the right to marry if its exercise helps expand the freedom of choice of those entering it. We also justify marriage if it protects the future freedom of children by respect for their right to early education (Article Twenty-Six). Many exercise freedom by marrying and founding families. Though human rights documents expressly declare no right to eat vanilla ice cream, the declared right to marry extends a special invitation to marry free of traditional restrictions, in part because of the invitation's impact on the exercise of rights by offspring. Traditional restrictions of nationality, race, religion, or social class should not impede marriages from providing respect for the rights of children to subsistence, security and education.

No externally imposed obligation to marry exists. Each individual objectively justifies his or her decision to marry according to whether it expands the freedom of that individual, the partner, and children. Further, marriage is itself a form of inquiry. Some believe that the family that the Declaration asserts to be the basic unity of society is a traditional patriarchal family in which women have not enjoyed equal freedom of choice. Yet we justify the right to marry and found a family only by expanding the freedom of choice of all involved, including women. The family invoked in the Declaration presupposes the existence of human rights, and so is not just any historically existing family, patriarchal or otherwise.

Since the Declaration does not specify marriage as a relation between two sexes, we may surmise that the Declaration protects same-sex marriage. Although, barring adoption, children do not enter into such domestic partnerships, empowerment of each partner by the other may enter and serve to justify the partnership. Same-sex marriage is one among alternative concepts of the good life. We may justify it as an option for all if it enhances freedom of thought for some, and if it does not violate other human rights. Human rights ethics permits same-sex marriage, without recommending it for all, though the right to such marriage is not explicit in the Declaration.

A declared right, unlike the right to eat ice cream, is a right some have historically repressed in the pursuit by other persons of some idea of the good life. By that criterion, the right to same-sex marriage may qualify for explicit declaration as a human right, and since 1948 a new special rights movement has emerged to promote its declaration.

> *Article Seventeen*: (1) Everyone has the right to own property alone as well as in association with others. (2) No one shall be arbitrarily deprived of his property.

A right to own property can mean different things. As a civil right it is the right to own whatever is the product of one's labor. Since Article Seventeen is preceded and followed by civil rights, it itself apparently intends a civil right. But a right to own property can also mean an economic right to have property independently of one's labor. Such an economic right seems justified as a universal mode of the basic right to dialogical freedom of thought. The economic right to property places some limitation on the civil right to the product of labor. If the civil right were absolute, one would have the right by labor to own more property than what supports freedom of thought, or less. The economic right to own personal property is a universal modal right. It is the right to freedom of thought by actually owning all property necessary to the expression of thought in dialogue.

Except for ownership of one's own body, the economic right to own property is not a right to own any particular kind or amount of property. Yet given a right to life or subsistence (Article Three), a right results to own as much property as would assure subsistence. We should also read this modal right in the light of Article Twenty-Three: everyone has a right to own sufficient property to enable his or her family to live in dignity, where welfare may supplement the mere product of his or her labor as needed.

The recognition of a person's inner will by others, and of one's thought, is possible only by public recognition of the person's will or thought as expressed in bodily and personal property. Dialogue is possible only through the reciprocal recognition of another's personal property and bodily behavior as an expression of inner thought. Exercise of the right to own one's body and external property is an empirically necessary condition of the human right to freedom of thought. Unless someone owns the means of expressing a thought, the exercise of no human right is possible. The right to one's own body appropriated by both the labor of muscular coordination and the intellectual labor of reworking the neural pathways of one's brain is not an option that, like the right to marry, we may refuse while still making it possible to exercise human rights in general.

Denial of a person's right to own his or her body (or a controlling interest in it) reduces the person to slavery. If another owns the product of someone's bodily and intellectual labor, the other person can rightfully deprive the first person of this product at will. If we labor at the pleasure of another, the product of labor ceases to be a credible expression of our free choice. Others will find in us nothing but our master's voice. The epistemologically justified maximal multiplication of voices requires the elimination of servitude.

An individual has a right to own property outside his or her body that others can *damage*, but not property that others can *injure*, not the body of another person. A human body, to be a credible expression of free thought, must embody predominantly a single will. Everyone has a human right to a voice, and no one has a right to two voices, that person's own and another's.

Extensions in the range of the property one owns are justifiable as an incentive to inquiry. This consideration introduces a right to capital under Article Seventeen as a possible product of one's labor as well as personal property, so long as others are not denied the personal property needed for their exercise of the basic human right. Such extensions are justifiable by the support they lend to the exercise of the basic right by as many as possible.

From a rational dialogical point of view in which the quality of your possible responses interests me, I ought to transfer unjustifiable property ownership to those who for want of property still cannot exercise freedom of thought to their maximum ability. In human rights ethics, the criterion for the ideal distribution of property would be "to each according to what a person needs to sustain him or her in the equal exercise of the one basic right." The above Article does not expressly state this right by itself, but the Preamble implies it.

> *Article Eighteen*: Everyone has the right to freedom of thought, conscience and religion; this right includes freedom to change his religion or belief, and freedom, either alone or in community with others and in public or private, to manifest his religion or belief in teaching, practice, worship and observance.

This right to freedom of thought is a civil right, a legally protected right to use our minds as we wish. The right provides legal protection to the basic human right, which international custom helps enforce even without constitutional or positive law. It is an immediate application within the state of the basic human right, which is the right for the sake of which the exercise of modal human rights is either contingently commendable (like marriage) or obligatory (like property).

By its objective content the one basic human right to freedom of thought is *de facto* the highest human right. Yet, in interim human ethics, the subjective right to freedom of thought of this or that individual is only a *prima facie* right. When the basic human right assumes legal form as a civil right, it enjoys priority over other civil rights.

The indivisibility of human rights does not eliminate the distinction in sense between the basic human right, universal supportive or modal human rights like the right not to be enslaved or to own property, and contingently supportive rights like the right to housing or the right to marry. The indivisibility of human rights means we cannot separate respect for the basic human right from respect for "other" universal rights that are really only necessary ways of exercising the basic right. Respect for that right is also inseparable from respect for contingent ways of exercising it, ways which become necessary in particular situations. We cannot uphold the one right to freedom of thought if we ignore its modes. Respect for the basic right means respect for the exercise of all ostensibly "other" rights that are locally or universally necessary for the exercise of the basic right. Contrary to the Stoic belief that thought is purely private, freedom of thought in contemporary human rights is outwardly expressible and so can be violated. Safety, security, subsistence, political and other such rights support the external expression of freedom.

Anyone committed to truth seeking can integrate even the impulsive action of others into the life of intra- and interpersonal dialogue. Impulsive action by a person may play a part in the inquiry and reflection of a second person, or later of the same person. Persons committed to the pursuit of truth recognize a universal right to freedom of action, even impulsive, within the bounds of respect for human rights. *Because thought includes reflection on action, whether one's own action or that of others, maximum freedom of thought invites maximum freedom of action within the bounds of respect for human rights.* The narrower the range of known action on which thought can reflect, the more freedom of thought suffers restriction. The right to freedom of thought is a right to freedom of thought *and* action.

> *Article Nineteen*: Everyone has the right to freedom of opinion and expression; this right includes freedom to hold opinions without interference and to seek, receive and impart information and ideas through any media and regardless of frontiers.

A civil right to freedom of thought is a right to communicate and exchange ideas, not with all other persons, but with those whom we can recruit to show interest. A positive right to freedom of expression would imply the provision of equal access to any means of communication, e.g., equal access to broadcast time or the press. As long as this is impossible, the right will be interpreted as a negative right of non-interference in such access.

Stoic freedom of thought can remain private, but the freedom of thought asserted here is also a freedom of outward self-expression. Article Nineteen means that the freedom of thought of Article Eighteen is public. To have a right to think freely is, as stated, to have a right to "receive and impart information through any media and regardless of frontiers." The frontiers through which we must freely pass in exchanging information are national, but they are also frontiers of race, religion, social class, profession, age, and wealth. In rationally motivated discussion, anyone has a *prima facie* right to impart and receive information to and from any quarter through any medium with the least discrimination possible. The Article implies that neither government nor private parties should control the media of communication to cause the restriction or suppression of communication. If one avenue of communication does not allow communication between two individuals on a given topic, an ideal right exists to another avenue that does.

9. Political Rights

Article Twenty: (1) Everyone has the right to freedom of peaceful assembly and association. (2) No one can be compelled to belong to an association.

The two rights in this Article have non-political and political applications. They represent non-universal applications of the one basic right. Peaceful assembly is one way in which communication can occur; voluntary association lasts longer than an assembly, and can exist without it. Discussion is possible without formal membership in an association and without inclusion in any assembly. The right to join assemblies and associations is, like a right to housing but unlike the right to own your body, a contingent exercise of the basic right. That this right serves the basic right is what would justify it. A prohibition against attendance or membership should never detract from exercise of the basic human right. Since 1948, the ideal universal human right to membership in assembly has grown to include virtual assembly, conference calls and internet chat rooms. This illustrates how a general right develops to embrace new particular rights, in this case due to new technology.

Article Twenty-One: (1) Everyone has the right to take part in the government of his country, directly or through freely chosen representatives. (2) Everybody has the right of equal access to public service in his country. (3) The will of the people will be the basis of the authority of government; this shall be expressed in periodic and genuine elections which shall be by universal and equal suffrage and shall be held by secret ballot or by equivalent free voting procedures.

The nature of political human rights suggests an ordering of human rights on three levels. The first clause of this Article states a third-level political right, as does the third clause. Third-level rights sustaining a constitutional democratic political culture protect second-level legal-access human rights, which protect the basic first-level right to freedom of thought and action along with any civil rights, public service rights, public works rights, and welfare rights needed to implement that basic right.

The right to participate in government and to develop and safeguard constitutional law implies direct or indirect citizen influence over government and, ultimately, courts. This right helps prevent the abuse of state power, including interference with judicial impartiality, so that government limits itself to protecting the basic right to freedom of thought and action, along with other rights constituting universal or limited applications of the basic right. Judicial impartiality is a result of constitutional political action that is relatively untouchable by subsequent political action.

The second clause states an equal human right, without discrimination, to compete for civil service jobs. This is a political right, a right of citizens to compete on a level playing field for employment in government. All citizens have this right, which civil servants exercise. Like other modal rights, it can be limited only if it does not support but rather subverts the basic right.

Do all have a right to vote or hold office? Do severely retarded persons have this right? If not, some "human rights" exclude some human beings. The right to vote is not a necessary application of the basic human right, but it is an application of the primary right to persons of a minimal compe- tence. Different applied rights implement the basic human right for different persons in different situations. The right to housing is a non-counterfactual human right for non-nomadic persons, and the right to vote is non- counterfactual only for adults whom we presume minimally capable of grasp- ing political issues. This conclusion holds only if we remember that those who have no right to vote still have a real interest in many public issues, and have a right to competent and fair advocates.

10. Welfare Rights to Subsistence and Work

Article Twenty-Two: Everyone, as a member of society, has the right to social security and is entitled to realization, through national effort and international cooperation and in accordance with the organization and resources of each state, of the economic, social and cultural rights indis- pensable to his dignity and the free development of his personality.

This Article asserts universal applications of the right to survival and se- curity in Article Three. It includes welfare, public service, and public works rights—and different applications implementing the basic right for different groups, nations, and persons. We justify these rights wherever they are neces- sary to maintain the dignity of individuals, and to realize their rational poten- tial in the exercise of freedom of thought and choice (Article One). *Use of resources for a purpose other than implementing unimplemented human rights when we could use them to implement such rights is a prima facie vio- lation of human rights.* Today extravagant private consumption and military expenditure purely for prestige are violations of morally ideal human rights. Voluntary inefficiency in the allocation of resources for the implementation of unimplemented rights is a similar violation.

The United States contests welfare human rights as distinct from privi- leges. Whether they are ideal human rights depends on whether universally they support freedom of thought. Freedom of thought is a near categorical right, a universal condition of public inquiry among fallible human beings. Welfare rights are more hypothetical. Philosophy cannot establish them as categorical. They need the support of social science. As hypothetical, they are ideal human rights only if social science establishes them as universally necessary to optimize freedom of thought. If they are necessary to optimize such freedom only in some cultures, cultures disabled by general insecurity without welfare rights (France?), the right is not a human right, but only a local application of a human right. Human rights ethics *per se* is not socialistic. Yet, pending social science research, it does not exclude socialism.

> *Article Twenty-Three*: (1) Everyone has the right to work, to free choice of employment, to just and favorable work conditions and to protection against unemployment.(2) Everyone, without any discrimination, has the right to equal pay for equal work. (3) Everyone who works has the right to just and favorable remuneration ensuring for himself and his family an existence worthy of human dignity, and supplemented, if necessary, by other means of social protection. (4) Everyone has the right to form and to join trade unions for the protection of his interests.

The ideal right to work, to compensation if unemployed, and to health care becomes a human welfare right when we protect it by an involuntary general insurance policy drawn upon when work is not possible. It is a non-universal human right implementing a universal right to subsistence in non-traditional, market societies. If health insurance is a benefit that only some employers grant, we exercise a right to this benefit only if we exercise a right to work for such employers. We do not exercise it as a universal human right. Human rights to work, unemployment benefits, and health care apply the right to subsist to modern societies in which those who cannot work would not otherwise subsist.

Unlike the right to own some personal property, a human right to work is not universal at all times and places. In a superabundant society, no right to work would be needed. Nor would there be any if the extended family met individual needs. History also conditions the right to join a trade union. It exists only emptily, without any possible exercise of it it, in some societies and eras. Yet an unexercised right may survive if some persons periodically affirm the claim. Exercise of the right may be possible again as conditions change. Particular rights that apply the basic human right in limited conditions are hypothetical rights, or counterfactual rights which we may wish hold in reserve when those conditions are absent.

> *Article Twenty-Four*: Everyone has the right to rest and leisure, including reasonable limitation of working hours and periodic holidays with pay.

This is an actual regional right in Western Europe. We justify it as an ideal human right in part by the value of rest and leisure in enhancing inquiry and dialogue, not merely by its role in the renewal of energy for work. The case for holding that recognition of the validity of this right should be universal connects the right to rest and leisure with the right to work in Article Twenty-Three. First, the right to work implies a right to property as the product of work. Secondly, labor produces as part of its product rest and leisure, and this product belongs to the laborer who produces it. The right to rest and leisure is a consequence of the right to work. The worker earns the paid annual vacation. His or her income extends over twelve monthly installments including a vacation. We assume a disinclination to agree to a labor contract without claiming the right to enjoy rest and leisure as one product of labor.

The right to rest and leisure is a universal application of the right to dialogical inquiry, which requires periodic rest. We may grant an ideal right to rest and leisure to those who do not work, thus enhancing the quality of their "freedom of speech and belief" (Preamble). Rest and leisure not justified as part of the product of one's own labor may be supported by others if they are dialogically rational. Others may find reason to fund it out of the product of their labor. Rest and leisure are moral goods, even if not produced by the labor of those enjoying them.

Though respect for a universal human right to rest and leisure supports dialogical reason, not all nations may be able to realize this right equally. To work is to claim some rest and leisure as one of the products of labor, but in some lands they are a smaller portion of the product than in others. Regardless of the portion, we see a general claim to rest and leisure as valid. If human rights are standards, we do not dismiss them because we still cannot give them due respect. General respect for the claim to rest and leisure is on the world's moral agenda. A human right exists if it contains a claim generally recognized to be legitimate, even if respect for the claim remains purely ideal pending the expansion of resources.

Article Twenty-Five: (1) Everyone has the right to a standard of living adequate for the health of himself and of his family, including food, clothing, housing, medical care and necessary social services, and the right to security in the event of unemployment, sickness, disability, widowhood, old age or other lack of livelihood in circumstances beyond his control. (2) Motherhood and childhood are entitled to special care and assistance. All children, whether born in or out of wedlock, shall enjoy the same social protection.

This Article states quasi-universal applications of the universal right to life, liberty, and security (Article Three). Discussion rights validate welfare rights, alleviating neediness beyond individual control. The more vulnerable we are, the more welfare we merit. Mothers and young children have a right to greater assistance. Young children are vulnerable, but they are also the adult human rights bearers of the future.

11. The Right to Public Services and Works

Article Twenty-Six: (1) Everyone has the right to education. Education shall be free, at least in the elementary and fundamental stages. Elementary education shall be compulsory. Technical and professional education shall generally be made available and higher education shall be equally accessible to all on the basis of merit. (2) Education shall be directed to the full development of the human personality and to the strengthening of respect for human rights. It shall promote understanding, tolerance, and friendship among nations, racial or religious groups, and shall further the activities of the United Nations for the maintenance of peace. (3) Parents have a prior right to choose the kind of education that shall be given to their children.

The right to education is a universal application of the right to freedom of thought. Education protects persons from exclusion from discussions that concern them. It extends our knowledge of alternatives on any issue, and of the direct and indirect consequences of each proposal. We ought to give education to each to the extent that he or she can use it. Those who by ability and interests merit higher or specialized education should not lack it because of an inability to pay. Elementary education should be universal and compulsory.

A child has no right to evade education. This compulsion, though it restricts the freedom of the child, is justifiable in cost/benefit analysis by expanding its later freedom as an adult. Education expands the options available to a person as an adult. It is an end in itself in developing the personality of the individual in communication with others, and is not purely vocational. All education should be education in human rights regardless of the special subject. Education in human rights fosters peace by tolerance of different concepts of the good life, but also fosters amicable dialogue between individuals representing different concepts of the good life.

Education also includes ethnic, religious, patriotic, or other culturally based education. Parents have a human right to seek to perpetuate their cultural identity, their non-universal concept of the good life, by amplifying the basic education given to all children. This parental right perpetuates as many ways of life as possible, as a resource for future discussions. It does so by educating a new generation of individuals who represent those ways of life. Yet children, reaching adulthood, have a human right to choose their respective concepts of the good life, consistent with respect for the human rights of many as possible.

Article Twenty-Seven: (1) Everyone has the right freely to participate in the cultural life of the community, to enjoy the arts and to share in scientific advancement and its benefits. (2) Everyone has the right to the protection of the moral and material interests resulting from any scientific, literary or artistic production of which he is the author.

The first clause asserts a right to go beyond participation in a single concept of the good life (a single church, national culture, art form or science) to develop cosmopolitan interest in the full range of contemporary culture, art, and science. The ideal universal right to participate in cultural and scientific life is basic to freedom of thought and reciprocal free speech.

The right to take part in the cultural, artistic, and scientific life of the human community by enjoying its benefits is an ideal right to join today's approximation of the universal audience as the final court of appeal at the current stage of rational criticism. No one is obliged to exercise this right. Yet, if we do not exercise it, the culture of rational criticism shrinks. Though today's judgment by the universal audience is final today, we imply a right to appeal to the next generation. Public service rights implement these rights— rights to libraries, to schools, or to museums. All persons also have a *prima facie* ideal right to benefit from technological innovation.

The second clause of the Article balances a right to enjoy the fruit of culture with the right of creators to the product of their labor. Either those who enjoy culture or public funds should compensate creators of culture for their enhancement of the universal exercise of dialogical freedom of thought. We justify the right to scientific, literary, or artistic proprietorship by realizing that the rewards of proprietorship subsidize and motivate scientific, literary, and artistic creation, and new discussion. A right to participate in and enjoy discussion is not optimal unless scientific, literary, and artistic creations are made public, initiating new discussions.

12. The Civil Right to Peace

Article Twenty-Eight: Everyone is entitled to a social and international order in which the rights and freedoms set forth in this Declaration can be fully realized.

A right to live in peace is a universal ideal right based on the right to freedom of thought in the context of dialogue. War and violence disrupt discussion. Even if an individual's contribution to dialogue is not evident at present, we should nonetheless invite his or her freedom of thought if it does not violate a similar right of others. We ought to protect individual freedom for possible future contributions more than present ones. Since some suddenly make recognized contributions to discussion after having never done so, we ought not to discount anyone by his or her record as incapable of motivating future discussion. We enhance discussion by giving individuals the benefit of the doubt in this matter.

The right in this Article is an ideal right to whatever world order we need for peace. We can test whether sovereign nations today participate in such an order partly by observing current events. If we need something different, everyone has an ideal right to the cooperation of all in constructing an alternative. We can justify world governance or government, with predictable humanitarian intervention in the internal affairs of nations and in the maintenance of external peace between them, only if we can thereby more nearly respect the human right to world peace, and to a global environment supporting reason and discussion. The Universal Declaration might then authorize institutions going quite beyond the United Nations, its original sponsor.

13. Human Duties

Article Twenty-Nine: (1) Everyone has duties to the community in which alone the free and full development of his personality is possible. (2) In the exercise of his rights and freedoms, everyone shall be subject only to such limitations as are determined by law solely for the purpose of securing due recognition and respect for the rights and freedoms of others and of meeting the just requirements of morality, public order and the general welfare in a democratic society. (3) These rights and freedoms may in no case be exercised contrary to the purposes and principles of the United Nations.

Morality requires us to promote and then respect the equal freedom of all. We ought to restrict individual free choice only by the freedom of a greater number. Restricting free choice by some may help each of a greater number of persons to enjoy free choice between a greater number of alternatives. We ought to restrict the freedom of a school to limit subjects of instruction if student discussion would benefit from greater choices in life.

We need not interpret "general welfare" in a utilitarian manner. In human rights ethics, it consists, not in happiness for all, but in equal rights. We may need restrictions on individual freedom, but no *a priori* judgment is possible. Some allegedly necessary sacrifices may not be necessary. Few challenges to social science are as great as that of uncovering ideal modal rights other than freedom of thought that empower such freedom for as many as possible.

Human duties ideally exist, not just human rights. An ideal duty exists to respect human rights, to build respect, and to establish recognition of claims that, if we recognized them generally, would be human rights. Human duties, moral burdens, in the Declaration appear subordinate to rights, to moral benefits. We may see Western influence in the priority of rights consciousness over duty consciousness in the Declaration, a declaration of rights, not duties. This priority raises suspicion that the Declaration does not state a universal morality including the Orient and Africa. Only rational interpretation of the Declaration can lay this suspicion to rest.

The Confucian life form, deferring to paternalistic authority, does not privilege the right to freedom of discussion. Even if it evolved to privilege this freedom, it still might see a duty to respect individual freedom in general as superior to individual assertions of that right. The desirability of subordinating Western individualistic competition between subjective rights to Eastern and African shared human duties toward all is likely to be a major issue in this century. The best compromise would join Western individual freedom of thought to Eastern duty consciousness.

> *Article Thirty*: Nothing in this Declaration may be interpreted as implying for any State, group or person any right to engage in any activity or to perform any act aimed at the destruction of the rights and freedoms set forth herein.

This Article continues the third clause of the previous one. Human rights include no right to oppose such rights, even democratically. Speech promoting racism, servitude, or intolerance is a hate crime. Contrary to the interpretation of freedom of speech present in tolerance by United States courts of Nazi propaganda on the internet, this Article denies that hate falls under freedom of speech. Human rights are never legitimate if we use them to undermine universal dialogue. To use human rights to excite intolerance is contradictorily to both subscribe to and at once repudiate their purpose.

Fourteen

WORLD GOVERNANCE, WORLD GOVERNMENT

1. Utopian vs. Scientific One-Worldism

Ethics is not just respect in private life for rights that would be human rights if we respected them universally. It also seeks to bring the world closer to universal respect. If only world government guaranteed human rights, their creation would depend in part on world politics and only as a consequence on national politics. Germany can protect the rights of Germans, but not human rights. Despite the undeveloped state of world politics, a case for world government would lie at the heart of human rights ethics. The case would begin with the relation between world governance and world government.

World government is neither logically sufficient nor necessary for the existence of human rights. A world state can be oppressive, and sovereign nations may simultaneously respect basic rights. Germany cannot protect universal rights, but it can contribute. If all states contributed, human rights would exist. Yet all sovereign states would probably not ever simultaneously enforce human rights. Even if they did, one nation might still suddenly violate them. Only sanctions or war would return that nation to its previous respect. The chances of bringing a nation back into compliance with rights would be greater in human rights-based federal world government than in an international system binding states only subject to their discretion.

World governance, falling short of world government operating by a democratic world parliament, is the technocratic management of world problems, placing them in the hands of a global civil service. Unlike sixty years ago, such governance now exists. It performs functions of world government without regulation by such government. World governance is the decentralized action of governing without control by world government. World government would be formal, centralized, and ideally expressed in a world legislative body elected by persons, not by nations. It might be bicameral, though Hegelians would advocate a third house based on corporate representation, encompassing and regulating the inevitable lobbies that would in any case surround the world parliament. The scattered institutions of world governance today are the United Nations with the Security Council, General Assembly, Human Rights Council, the World Bank, the International Monetary Fund, the G-8, multinational corporations, the World Trade Organization, and the International Criminal Court, but also the spontaneously arising global markets for goods and services and for the exchange of information (the internet).

These institutions are economic and mediatic, not strictly governmental. They function autonomously from their position in global civil society because formal world government regulation of them is absent. Yet because of the new weight of world governance, world government—which was utopian in the 1940s and 1950s (Wendell Wilkie, Eleanor Roosevelt, or Bertrand Russell)—has gained relevance.[1] Eleanor Roosevelt displayed this utopian tendency as the United States Ambassador to the United Nations:

> Right in the middle of these deliberations [in preparation for the Universal Declaration], Eleanor Roosevelt received most unwelcome instructions telling her to focus her efforts on a declaration of principles on human rights, where the United States government felt "on safer ground," and that any discussion about legal commitments and enforcement should be "kept on a tentative level" and should not involve any commitments by the Government.[2]

Russell's plan was to threaten a nuclear attack on the Soviet Union, to enlist Stalin in world government under the United Nations. It was desperately utopian.[3] Today the growth of world governance, addressing problems neither nations nor regions can deal with, begins to call for regulation by democratic world government if we are not to lose control of our destiny to increasingly faceless bureaucracies.

In a state, some but not all directly govern, either by the power of money or of ideology. Neither all nor one can directly govern: in either case, the remote governor must delegate governance to some, typically to specialists. Government, the self-government of a democratic state, is not the equal decision making power of all, but lies in political pluralism, the power of any individual or minority to intervene in government even if by default it allows others to govern. In government by the permanent possibility of such intervention, the state exists in conformity with the concept of what a state should be. It preserves the possibility of active political participation by any in the place of rule by all, but also in the place of the political alienation of any.

A world state is ambiguous and frankly ominous, while it can at once inspire hope. Because of the rise of world governance, scientific one-worldism is beginning to replace utopian one-worldism. Scientific one-worldism is historical materialism redirected from communism as the end game of history to the universal freedom of thought by which communism, like everything in the end, must justify itself. Utopian one-worldists call for constitutional conventions to create a world parliament. Scientific one-worldists only say that, because of different growth rates between related variables in civil society, pressure to call for such a convention is predictable.

Scientific one-worldism would show a way by economic laws of getting from here to there. It would exhibit related variables with different growth rates, one growing out of proportion to the other. A proportion on which an institution depends yields, by a quantitative growth of variables, a qualitatively new proportion. Where the proportion of goods and services produced for domestic markets once exceeded that produced for foreign markets, growth reverses the proportion. A state surviving by foreign trade survives without it only by a wrenching adaptation to a reduced standard of living.

Whether we can make historical materialism relevant again based on a human rights vision of the end of history, in an era in which communism is irrelevant and in which social science has exploded, will depend on collaborative research of a magnitude of which Karl Marx never dreamed. It will depend on a new generation able to deepen Critical Theory's union of philosophical criticism and empirical social science. The authority of world governance might be informally legitimated if it laid down intelligible rules of the road toward real global human rights. Parliamentary world government, overcoming political alienation vis-à-vis impersonal global bureaucracies, might then formally legitimate it. World government would make world governance legitimate by institutions with which we could identify. Yet in the near future, no world government will cause individuals to respect, recognize as valid, or even comply with universal rights. One reason is cultural. If China is part of world government, universal respect for freedom of dissent will be difficult. World government—enforcing rights by sanctions, publicity, tribunals, the reporting system of the United Nations Human Rights Council, a human rights-based world constitution, and the threat of police intervention—awaits the universal human rights culture necessary for the actual existence of human rights. A successful world state awaits humanity's loyalty to a supranational *world nation* embracing the nations of today as so many sub-nations.

2. The Case against World Governance and Government

We must also consider the case against world government. Opponents of such government believe it is impractical and counter-productive. No emigration could check its abuses. The existing international system serves human rights better. Treaties between sovereign states are preferable to coercive world governance and the resulting need for world government. We do not hold nations friendly to individual freedom of thought to a lowest world common denominator: the international system allows states to progress at their own pace.

If Egypt or Algeria, threatened by Islamic fundamentalism, does not respect the democratic political rights that it accepts in principle through international declarations, the system of sovereign states allows derogations. More exemplary states are on public view, while nations progress towards basic rights one at a time. Asylum exists for citizens of countries that do not respect basic rights, and states unite in alliances against the worst rights violators. Yet supporters of national sovereignty must agree that sovereignty is in decline. Their program is no longer one of saving what exists, but of reversing entrenched institutions like the World Trade Organization. They must also agree that world government, if successful, alone can enforce universal rights, not just allow for local contributions that may not add up to universal enforcement. They simply doubt its possible success. The reply is that if world governance is irreversible, democracy's only hope is world democracy.

The movement for world government depends on democratic global opposition to any world governance that disregards basic rights. It depends on a perception by populations that national leaders concerned to protect privileges of office serve them ill. Realizing that they have shared interests potentially served by world governance, they will want to claim rights in governing such institutions. If people cannot take back national control of their problems, some will seek transnational control. The alternative is endless political alienation. "[C]itizens . . . need to be able to participate directly in the making of international law. . . . Individuals feeling unheard in the international system have shown themselves willing to resort to increasingly destructive acts of violence."[4]

Opponents of one-worldism doubt that world governance can extend rights around the globe. The United Nations has no duty to intervene for such rights, militarily or economically. Article 2 of its Charter respects the sovereignty of member states, though Article 24 gives the United Nations a right and responsibility to intervene to protect peace. Institutionalized human rights make possible the peace of satisfied basic moral demands. We may infer a duty of intervention on behalf of basic rights. Yet the United Nations has no mandate to intervene if permanent members of the Security Council disagree.

For victims of atrocities, United Nations intervention is an uncertain privilege. Jeffrey Whitman argues that intervention would not be justifiable because a people's rights result from its own struggle.[5] Rights won by paternalistic intervention are fleeting. When the intervening power withdraws, abuses resurface. Defending the rights of a population that does not know how to claim them creates pressure for the permanent paternalistic presence of the intervening power.

The United States was not inclined to pay the price of nation building in Somalia in 1993. If it had paid it and extended the rule of intervention applied to Somalia (or more recently, Iraq) around the world, the price would be, short of federal world government, world governance, soft empire, with scrupulous even-handedness toward the claims of client nations regardless of their cultural distance from Americans. We cannot force universal rights on the unready. Yet cultural bias can prevent the imperial nation from delivering the just peace that can alone make global empire legitimate, as we await the global extension of democratic citizenship and the dissolution of empire.

3. Oppression by World Government?

The fear of world governance and government is that they may themselves be oppressive. A Hobbesian reply is that, if a nation weighs the *risk of attack by foreign power*s in the international state of nature and the *risk of attack by* *world government*, the first risk is greater. Without world government, one nation can bet on some other nation attacking it. A chance exists that world government would stick to its task and not attack its citizens. We would reduce the risk by founding world government on a democratic constitution. Paying lip service to rights is awkward for governments that do not uphold them.

Human rights ombudsmen and world courts might further reduce the risk. A world constitution may contain a bill of rights that the parliament swears to uphold. Yet the only assurance that world government would keep its promise would seem to come from a right of revolt. The chances of successful revolt by peaceful non-cooperation, national liberation wars, terrorism, or other means appear small.

Some will prefer no world governance. They will take their chances with war and geographical restrictions on dialogical rationality if the alternative is the risk of oppression by world governance from which escape is not possible. Yet world governance may no longer be avoidable. The choice today is no longer between world governance and no world governance. World governance with some approach to world government has entrenched itself. If we make no choice, we will have world governance by obscure negotiations between the World Trade Organization, the International Monetary Fund, and other such institutions. When we do not elect the staff of such an institution, since it consists in expert appointees, democratic control is thin. Appointees have a responsibility to diverse nations, but only very remotely to the world's voters.

Instead of a Hobbesian choice between an international state of nature and world government, we face a choice between versions of world governance, between acquiescence in undemocratic world governance and struggle for global democracy. The choice is not between undemocratic world governance and democratic world government, but between acquiescence in the first and struggle for the second. We will have undemocratic world governance if we make no choice. Meaningful national sovereignty is simply less available.

Institutions restricting the arbitrary executive power of world governance also include a ministry of human rights, the subordination of the executive to a world parliament, and a chief executive rotating between world regions.[6] They also include federal institutions following a rule of subsidiarity. Federal authority is subsidiary to local authority. Issues capable of local solution, such as choice of a national language, we ought to leave to solution at the local level. External national sovereignty disappears, but internal sovereignty remains. In debating whether we need to solve a problem locally or globally, we assume first that we can handle it locally. If a medical treatment is still debatable, for world governance to impose it globally is oppressive. Yet limits on world executive power are limits on the power to do good, not just evil. Debate concerning the right limitation will be a long-standing feature of world politics. Some limitations may make world government more acceptable at its start without remaining permanent.

4. World Government as a Moral Ideal

Even if we never realize rights-based world government, it may be a moral ideal. We can never guarantee human rights if their observance anywhere remains purely voluntary. We cannot enforce morality, but successful enforcement of human rights fosters moral respect: regularly doing what is right, even for the wrong reason, instills the habit of doing it without reflection on the reason, and this disposes individuals to listen to right reason.

Among the rights legitimate world government would enforce is world peace. Peace or security is a universal mode of universal freedom of thought. Freedom of thought amidst violence succumbs to a fear of saying what one thinks, disrupted communication, reduced audiences, and the reduction of the subject of thought to the mere thought of survival.

Thomas Hobbes held the right to peace to be ultimate, appealing to it to justify the state. If we suppose the right to freedom of thought is the substantial basis of all human rights, a world state that protects universal freedom of thought must guarantee world peace and security. A right to security that ceases to be subordinate to the right to freedom of thought is no longer a *human* right to security. No state that makes a right to security ultimate has a human rights foundation. The identity of all human rights with the dialogically basic right is the most effective reply to authoritarian government.

Hobbes recognized that local sovereign states are in a state of nature relative to one another. Yet Hobbes knew nothing of missiles, whether classical missiles or terrorist human missiles, which penetrate national frontiers and create an international insecurity to match the local insecurity that concerned him.[7] International terror attacks have shown that no nation is free from attack—not even the most powerful of nations. World government worth supporting would protect world security without intimidating freedom of thought.

While we wait for world government, global insecurity already calls for its precursor, world governance. Beyond freedom of speech through peace, an ideal right to such freedom exists by regulation of the world economy, with a view to instituting global welfare, public service, and public works rights. Victims of shifts in the global economy and ecology claim a right to such regulation. The obligation of any government is, where possible, to create conditions necessary for universal freedom of thought. A local state that fails in this by declining to sacrifice some sovereignty loses legitimacy.

The institutionalization of rights by world governance and world government follows the global expansion of the exchange of goods, services, and information. If respect for dialogical rights requires global lines of communication, it requires globalization. Yet global development is uneven. Some, in or outside the world market, fall into deeper poverty, creating human rights imbalances. Yet human rights are impossible without economic globalization. Persons left in a primitive isolation, not integrated in the global economy and media, cannot actively respect universal claims or enjoy active respect by all others. World governance makes possible a correction of its abuses if those who hold power are sensitive to the need for legitimacy.

5. World Governance as Predominantly Eastern?

The emergence of the European Union shows that the sacrifice of some national sovereignty to a human rights-based supranational confederation can happen. How might it occur globally, with greater cultural diversity than in Europe? The prospect of world federation dominated demographically and economically by Eastern or Third World nations worries some Western world federalists. "Democracy as a way of organizing a polity will sooner or later reach the global level, and the First World will then run up against a very hard fact: the First World represents a small minority of the world's peoples."[8]

Some Third World nations lack individual human rights traditions. Yet, despite current American cultural and economic supremacy, we may have left an American century to enter one that will be Chinese. If the Far East should gain economic and political ascendancy, human rights need not suffer. The Eastern obligation *toward* one another may absorb the divisive Western rights defended by each *against* all. (See Chapter Two.) Suppose China's Confucian ethics of exclusive local obligation evolved toward the ethics of universal obligation that the erstwhile follower of Confucius, Mo Ti, developed, something closer to modern socialism. Suppose also that the universal obligation is not merely to respect general welfare, but to respect dissent reinforcing China's sense of its own legitimacy. Two things would follow. First, human rights would be closer to existing, as implied by a universal human obligation. Secondly, we would no longer need to defend such rights as much, since others would often automatically honor them through that ethics of obligation.

Universal human obligations preserving individual rights to freedom of thought are not yet prevalent in the East. Yet this conversion should be the goal of any Western policy more committed to human rights than to their Western form. The result would be a reconstruction of rights superior to the West. We would also have a reply to world federalists reluctant to hand power away from the Western world. Human rights would rest on a synthesis of the strength of the East with that of the West.

6. Creeping One-Worldism

World governance advances by agreements: by free or forced agreements, and other times by free agreements that later imprison the parties. Let us call this mechanism "creeping one-worldism," analogous to the "creeping socialism" of another era. The expression communicates relentless, if unheralded, movement toward world governance. Creeping one-worldism resembles the passage of the United States from a voluntary confederation at the time of the

Constitution to Lincoln's indissoluble constitutional contract. A voluntary agreement becomes an indissoluble union, not because the states consciously modified their original agreement, but because people come to take the customary union, uncontested over a period, for granted. The dissolution of such a union by a return to the original voluntary agreement, followed by dissolution of the agreement itself, becomes unthinkable.

We saw the process in 1994 when North Korea opted out of the nuclear non-proliferation treaty it had entered voluntarily. The United States tried to block its withdrawal. Entry was a one-way street. The coercion did not disappear by the offering of economic incentives to North Korea. Yet a treaty that limits the sovereignty of signatories cancels itself as a treaty, becoming world law. The United States is more or less the successful agent of world governance in matters of security. Many Americans are uneasy with the idea of world governance, even more so with that of world government. Yet if they look in the mirror, in matters of security they have been an agent of world governance.

The war in Kosovo defended rights, not to world security, but to freedom from genocide and ethnic cleansing. It implied a rule of acceptable behavior between ethic groups. If the threat of American air power were as credible elsewhere as it was in Kosovo, and if countries other than ex-Yugoslavia understood and observed the rule, creeping one-worldism in the treatment of minorities would advance with few wars. It was also credible in Kurdish Iraq, even if air power did not suffice in the Iraqi war. A creeping one-worldism consistent with human rights ethics would depend on American defense of human rights on behalf of cultures alien to its own.

Success for the United States depends on confidence in it among nations experiencing its intervention. If the United States disqualifies itself for the enjoyment of such confidence, and if no other power inspires such confidence, the United Nations becomes the only mid-term alternative to abandoning regions to anarchy or terrorism. Note that failure by the United States need not be failure of its essential strategy as the agent of world security. It easily could be a failure of execution, style, etiquette, and modesty, or a failure of true multicultural awareness in the very country that most boasts of such awareness. The accidental details then become the essence of the matter, and the original abstract essence of the policy becomes quite irrelevant.

7. World Governance Legitimated by a Rational Global Consensus

De facto and *de jure* world governance grows, if not by conquest, by accumulated international agreements which, eventually taken for granted, forge a union between nations that resists dissolution. The Security Council as we know it will not ratify world government, since the Council represents major powers that, barring catastrophe, would not abandon sovereignty in defense. Could a group of weak nations whose sovereignty carries no great weight for them or others lead the way to world government? Such a world government would initially fall short of universal government, but it could become a world government by acquiring new members. A universal state might emerge by a process of creeping one-worldism.

A world state, no matter how it emerges and how well justified, is legitimated, and thus effective through general endorsement, only if an optional global democratic assembly *recognizes* the justification. The United States is not fully legitimated without the free adherence of Southerners with a real alternative to the Union. Legitimated world government by creeping one-worldism would require a free adherence of nations (perhaps like Quebec in Canada) with a real option of succession. Expert panels may have good arguments for new world institutions. Yet only a constitution created by a democratic constitutional assembly is dialogically rational by the right to deliberate on matters of perceived concern. If we ask whether Southerners after the Civil War adhered freely to the Union, we are asking whether freedom of thought and speech have been fully real in America. Generally, people conceal thoughts that others would punish them for expressing. World government could only hope to be as well legitimated as the United States.

8. Creeping One-Worldism from Above and the United States

Major powers are all agents of world governance to some degree. Their sovereignty is worth its weight in gold. They would be reluctant to ratify a world human rights constitution if, as seen in the United States' response to the International Criminal Court, they thought the Court might find them in violation. Yet they already act as "world police" enforcing rights of which no external court is likely to find them in violation. The United States—in Bosnia, Kosovo, Afghanistan, and Iraq—has been transforming voluntary international treaties between sovereign states into a Lincolnesque union. This is creeping one-worldism from above.

The Bush Administration in 2000 at first retreated from foreign intervention, and as a result its subsequent foreign entanglements are strong evidence of the difficulty of avoiding them. The publicly posted justification for such foreign policy intervention is human rights protection. Yet, in the Gulf, human rights rode piggyback on material interests.

The United States had, and lost, an opportunity to lead the world toward one-worldism in 1945 as the sole superpower to emerge from World War II. After the Soviet Union had nuclear weapons, the United States lost the ability to lead the world toward integration. After the fall of the Soviet Union, the United States had another chance to lead. Is the United States still in the era of this second chance? After Kosovo and September 11, 2001, the American technology of airborne enforcement from a safe distance held out a promise that the enforcement of minority rights, of the sanctity of existing borders against regional wars, and universal security rights against terrorism would be as frequent as necessary to teach nations underlying rules of conduct. Ominous terrorist challenges to this enforcement were more atavistic than representative of any promising wave of the future.

In 2003, the second Bush administration increased deterrence by a willingness to commit ground troops in situations where air power is insufficient. That willingness is significant even if troops do not intervene. We should not criticize the United States military for "cowardice" when it spares American lives, although in a cost-benefit analysis by human rights ethics we may question whether the number of lost non-American lives was necessary. Once we are sure that the United States gives as much attention to the loss of non-American dialogue partners as to American ones, we may praise the United States for trying to make the enforcement of world law politically affordable and regular.

Yet an era of mutually checkmated superpowers may return. The United States' leadership will then be too late. Advance towards world governance and government will cease to have a single national agent. But in an age of globalization, such advance will not disappear. International agreements will continue to emerge, to evolve into indissoluble union, and to appear irreversible in the face of attempts to dissolve such union. For the Presidency, which Arthur Schlesinger called an Imperial Presidency, now has a global clientele.[9] Congress, like the Roman Senate under the Emperors, becomes increasingly irrelevant in foreign affairs, in part for lack of the vast information resources assumed to be at the President's disposal. The widespread unofficial involvement of the five United States military Commands in civilian problems around the world begins to resemble the role of Roman Consuls in establishing the authority of imperial Rome.[10]

A problem with creeping one-worldism under United States auspices is that there has been little national debate about the kind of world in which Americans want to live a century from now. The Clinton Presidency led the United States toward a new world order without trying to bring onboard the public whose future depends on this order. The American world presence is, except in the Middle East, often seen as benign. Yet as long as the new order and American consent to it remain unclear, foreign governments will have reservations. The lack of national debate on the issue suggests government distrust of democracy and discussion. An absence of discussion saves the republic from divisive issues of sovereignty. A fear exists that an attempt to discuss sovereignty would not remain calm, though world governance threatens the sovereignty of other nations more than the United States. Yet the lack of public discussion allows those promoting creeping one-worldism to remain safely in the woodwork, and ultimately to win by default.

9. Third World Debt and One-Worldism from Below?

Those from the Third World who favor world government often come from countries that have never had real sovereignty, in part due to debts to the First World. According to Philip Isley, the problem of Third World debt may help create world government by the very mechanism of its solution. He suggests a world currency backed by reconstruing Third World *debt* to First World countries as First World *investments* in Third World economies. Currency is a function of government, and a world currency is a function of world government. Whereas we see creeping one-worldism from above actually taking place, the creeping one-worldism from below that Isley suggests has not materialized. Yet the idea illustrates the creative thinking that might convert worldwide human rights problems into opportunities.[11]

Poor nations might accelerate creeping one-worldism by imaginatively renouncing repayment of debts in existing hard currencies. Yet indebted nations cannot unilaterally impose this debt renunciation on creditor countries. It may occur as the result of discussions in which creditor nations recognize their interest in replacing the feudal dependence of unproductive debtor countries with productive Third World enterprises that attract First World investment. Instead of rescheduling payments on debts, or asking First World nations to forgive debt, Third World states might collectively form an embryonic world government, which might then issue "earth dollars" to creditor nations in exchange for debt cancellation. Earth dollars are a stock issued by Third World nations designed to finance remunerative capital investment by the industrial world in Third World economies. Creditor nations agree to hold the stock and accept it as a universal means of exchange.

Yet success would depend on First World confidence in Third World entrepreneurship. If Third World enterprise showed promise of succeeding, First World powers, without a prospect of other forms of repayment, might agree to repayment in earth dollars. The First World would join world government in a monetary dimension. World government from above and from below would meet. The role of the Third World in world government would be to inspire confidence in a world currency.

The scenario naturally poses problems. Since stock values are volatile, earth dollars might be an unstable currency. Third world countries might try to mitigate this instability by lumping earth dollars into a basket of stock holdings of different enterprises in different countries. Earth dollars would not be the only world currency, much as the dollar competes with the Euro. Countries could trade earth dollars in a world stock market for other currencies, but nations could also use them for purchases. They would be a currency and not merely a stock issue. Mere investment by creditor nations in debtor nations would not itself produce world government, but if investment takes the form of a world currency that changes hands but that no one can withdraw from circulation, the destiny of creditor nations would come in part to depend on the fate of former debtor nations.

Even if Third World investments financed by earth dollars returned a profit, the Third World would be as economically dependent on the First World as in its indebtedness, except that it would depend on investors, not lenders. Yet this is a significant difference. Reconceptualizing debt as an investment replaces the stigma surrounding unmet obligations by shared confidence in the future. Much of Africa may be the test case. If services and products from African nations as a group inspired external investment, the proposed monetary one-worldism from below might work elsewhere. Elites in several of these countries cherish national sovereignty because of their local privileges even though sovereignty is of little value in expanding the country's real range of choice.

The most difficult thing would be to foster a climate in which a domestic entrepreneurial culture can flourish. Americans are right in believing that studying entrepreneurship, why it exists in a given environment, and how Third World environments can foster it, is crucial. We must attack corruption. Rewarding those who do not produce demotivates those who do. Equally demotivating are extended family systems in which new entrepreneurs share too much wealth to be able to reinvest. Yet such family systems go to the heart of African society.

Corruption is only partly due to Western interests corrupting local elites. The West would have to sacrifice its domination in the Third World to isolate the remaining corruption that the Third World must learn to face. Success need not depend on a strong Third World consumer market, since the main market for the Third World initially will be the First World. Industries based on value-added products with a strong component of Third World labor would prevail. Asia shows that successful entrepreneurship need not depend on an individualistic Western model. African cultures steeped in duty consciousness may learn from Far Eastern economies more than from the West.

The World Bank and International Monetary Fund pursue a policy of world governance from above. They in principle forgive debt upon proof that a Third World country is fighting poverty, not enriching local elites. Fighting poverty means using funds no longer needed to repay debt to invest in local enterprises. The formerly indebted country would own the enterprises, not industrial nations accepting the earth dollars invested in the Third World.

The World Bank plan does not lead to monetary world government. Making a country-by-country assessment of the link between debt forgiveness and emergence from poverty, the plan does not forgive the debts of countries that show little promise. In the Isley plan, Third World nations invite wealthy nations to maintain investment in a mutual fund. Companies join the fund because they are located in indebted countries, not because they are good investments. Poor countries may try to make these companies attractive investments, but their economic performance is likely to be uneven, which might be enough to dissuade wealthy nations from accepting earth dollars in the first place.

10. A Conditional Scenario for World Governance

Of the world problems listed in the next section, the source of several (economic refugees, terrorism, inequalities in social protection, over-consumption of meat, national debt, and over-population) is Third and Second World poverty. Yet poverty is not just a problem that calls for new world governance. Poverty is the problem that most blocks creation of the universal audience. Poverty in some nations, alongside extreme wealth in others, is a problem whose solution might lead to deeper world governance, requiring a transfer of growth rates and allowable carbon dioxide emissions from developed to underdeveloped economies. Only new technology compensating for the depletion of resources and reducing emissions could avoid this result.

Most world human rights problems show only that world governance is necessary to solve them. The generic problem of poverty shows that forces may be in place to produce the world governance needed to reduce the gap between rich and poor. The Third World tolerates poverty easily when the prospect of Third World economic growth creates confidence that poverty will decline. Yet ecological considerations, such as those brought forward since the Club of Rome, suggested that world economic growth will wind down due to the depletion of non-renewable natural resources, due to pollution, or due to both. The concern is that it will wind down before the attainment of even approximate economic parity between the North and South.[12]

Economic inequality that begins to appear permanent also begins to be intolerable, and violent forms of opposition to First World economic domination can then develop. In 1992, the United Nation Rio Declaration on Environment and Development reiterated the perspective of the Club of Rome, with more stress on pollution than on depleted raw materials:

> States shall cooperate in a spirit of global partnership to conserve, protect and restore the health and integrity of the Earth's ecosystem. In view of the different contributions to global environmental degradation, States have common but differentiated responsibilities. The developed countries acknowledge the responsibility that they bear in the international pursuit of sustainable development in view of the pressures their societies place on the global environment and of the technologies and financial resources they command.[13]

Domination in international civil society takes the form of systematically distorted discussion as to how to allocate scarce resources. Not all whom a discussion concerns have equal power to influence its course. Some nations control enough wealth that they determine, by enormous purchases, what the world produces. Wealthier nations are free to maintain what may appear to be indecent levels of consumption. Respect for basic rights may call for the production of more affordable food of high nutritional value and fewer luxury goods. Yet it will occur only in the form of charity if a lack of money-backed demand prevents the Third World from making the needed purchases.

We cannot say by what combination of pressure from below and reform from above world governance may manage a transition to more tolerable distributions of growth and emissions between North and South. Some one-time Third World nations have attained high growth rates. The United States, with its addiction to growth and consumerism, resists solutions perceived to be just by many nations still in the Third World. Implementation and management of a more equitable rationing of growth, natural resource usage, and emissions might require new institutions and agreements, which in time could become involuntary through creeping one-worldism.

Creeping one-worldism by itself does not suggest that the resulting world governance would be any more equitable than the existing international system. The current institutionalization of domination in the world does encourage the belief that the result would be more equitable. The reduction of domination in favor of communication between more equally empowered discussion partners is rational. The legitimacy of the industrial North requires assent by affected populations elsewhere. World economic growth, pollution, and emission levels continue to rise while reserves of non-renewable natural resources fall. The legitimacy of world institutions itself declines if domination largely excludes dissenting voices from the discussion circles of world governance.

The *Limits to Growth* became a subject of controversy in part because its thesis challenged economic assumptions in the industrial world. The North, especially the United States, feeds on a psychology of endless economic growth. Some, including the United States government, take the optimistic view of Herbert Kahn: technology will rescue us from depleted resources or the threat of pollution. Past technology caused carbon dioxide emissions that threatened to limit growth in industrial nations. More and better technology will limit or reduce carbon dioxide and global warming: "200 years from now, we expect, almost everywhere they [human beings] will be numerous, rich, and in control of the forces of nature."[14]

The First World often perceives the Club of Rome report as pessimistic. Yet others view it as optimistic in holding out the promise of a world economy more successfully meeting the basic needs of all at sustainable growth levels, with marginally raised levels of growth and consumption in the poorest regions and marginally lower levels elsewhere. The report did not advocate world government, though we may fail to see how a reduction of the growth rate and consumption levels in First World populations could be voluntary. We may expect such reduction only after intense negotiation, with poor nations applying available forms of pressure on wealthy nations. The negotiation would envisage a global social contract requiring a difficult adjustment for the United States.

If Third World growth rates with more lenient emission standards resulted in the wider satisfaction of subsistence needs, the result would hardly be unjust by human rights ethics, with its concern for equal empowerment for dialogue. Dialogical equality without domination requires the poor of the Central African Republic to have things they have not had: better education, access to the media, travel, health care, better nutrition, legal-access rights, and democratic control of their government—just to mention a few universal modes of any freedom of thought that is not abstract. Yet industrial nations, in contributing to such a transformation, and to their own legitimacy, need to know that concessions to the Third World would meet subsistence needs, reduce corruption, and increase democracy. This would require further world governance monitoring.

World governance would manage a compulsory reduction of emissions and growth rates in a growth-addicted West. If the new global contract were to become customary, if diplomacy, economic sanctions and a concern to mitigate violence originating in the Third World mitigated challenges to the contract, world governance could claim a success. The creeping one-worldism whose banner the United States has carried is one from above, addressing problems of ethnic cleansing, regional border wars, arms control, and international terrorism. Far-sightedness might permit the United States to pursue a campaign against world poverty to a conclusion with fuller world governance.

Until then, the world state for which the United States prepares us is a night watchman state, an uneasy peace without a new global social contract. New technology may well invalidate this scenario developed from *Limits to Growth*, but it might not. If the technology does not come on time, advances toward new world governance will likely bring conflict between the First World—with its power to maintain emissions, pollution, and consumption of resources—and poor nations. If the technology is on time, the wealthy nations can reassure themselves that their limitless growth is guiltless, imposing no limits on Third World growth. If Third World nations do not show economic growth, that will be their problem. Puritanism would make a comeback.

Yet even if the West does not cause Third World poverty, it still has a motive for taking some responsibility for it. The West has a rational interest in doing so in part because the economic independence of the Third World would make any Third World free speech legitimating the First World in global media credible. This source of gentle pressure for world government in the face of growing undemocratic world governance would not relent even if a global contract on emissions or pollution proves unnecessary.

11. World Human Rights Problems

The job of world governance is to solve problems of implementing respect for human rights not open to solution by local states or regional treaties. Such problems are "world problems." World problems will come and go. Not all publicized world problems may be actual ones, and some actual ones may not have received publicity. The following list is not complete. We could easily have added farm subsidies in the European Union and the United States, since they depress farm income in the Third World. We could have added trafficking in human cargo, a contemporary illegal form of slavery. The following are just examples of world problems. Terrestrial catastrophes, no matter how great, would not have been world problems in 10,000 BC, since no possibility existed then as now for a global response to the consequences of such catastrophes.

In the following list, the first four are security problems. Five through ten are subsistence problems. Problems eleven through thirteen concern both subsistence and security. Only individuals can put freedom of thought and choice in action, but world governance may help assure its universal modalities. The problems cited for consideration are (1) nuclear non-proliferation; (2) weapons of mass destruction; (3) regional wars; (4) terrorism; (5) debt relief for poor states; (6) dependence on fossil fuels; (7) over-population; (8) excessive meat consumption in the First World; (9) pollution; (10) unequal social protection between trading nations; (11) sovereignty over the high seas and space; (12) illicit drug trafficking; and (13) economic refugees. In considering each problem, we ask whether a world problem as defined exists, and if so, how world governance, if not world government, should address it.

Universal security is a civil rights problem, while subsistence is a welfare problem. If security and subsistence rights are only animal rights unless they condition freedom of thought, how can world governance support civil rights directly and not merely by supporting its modes? The United Nations Human Rights Commission (now Council) has tried to do this by assigning *rapporteurs* to nations whose records raise questions about respect for human rights. These *rapporteurs* write country reports that congratulate and prod. The reports publicize the situation of human rights in a country. They attempt to persuade the country to take seriously its ratification of the United Nations Covenant on Civil and Political Rights and to measure its own progress.

Since Saudi Arabia, Pakistan, Indonesia, Cuba, and other countries have not ratified the Covenant, attempts to cajole all countries through country reports meet with mixed success. An ideal way to protect civil and political rights would be a world human rights court system analogous to the European Union Court of Human Rights in Strasbourg—with the proviso that its decisions be enforceable. The Strasbourg Court functions because of shared European values, and it could not enforce decisions against a government that no longer shared them. A worldwide human rights court has to await a global fusion of Eastern duty consciousness and Western claims to freedom of thought and choice. It also has to await a genuine world police to enforce it in exceptional cases of non-compliance.

Most world problems lie in the area of subsistence and security rights, two universal modes of the basic right to freedom of thought. We secure thinking and choosing freely from a maximum range of options, with a maximum pooling of information, only by freedom from want and fear. Want and fear impact on freedom of thought, restricting the range of what we can think and try, ultimately reducing thought to the immediate thought of one's own subsistence and security. As long as a region of the world exists where any population is subject to the terror of possible nuclear attack, freedom of thought and action is not maximal. To cite an example, during the balance of terror between the United States and the Soviet Union, some Americans actually asked if it was worthwhile to save and plan for a future. Those who focused their lives on mere survival and tried to build and stock backyard atomic bomb shelters lost much freedom of thought to terror.

Nuclear Non-Proliferation. The extension of nuclear non-proliferation to sovereign countries that prevent inspection and to potential terrorist groups is already a world problem. If compliance were attainable by treaty, all would be well. But a treaty subject to sovereign states parties is insufficient. The urgency of the matter propels us toward world governance at the expense of the voluntary consent of sovereign nations. Formal treaties may still exist, but if a ratifying state attempts to withdraw, the treaty may become binding by the mechanism of creeping one-worldism. The treaty shows itself to be mere form without content, no longer corresponding to tacitly understood demands of an era in which a universal right to security has more authority than the will of nations. Nations that are not parties to a nuclear non-proliferation treaty may encounter pressure and enticements to renounce nuclear weapon programs, and then to abide by their word through inspections with the threat of economic or military sanctions. To avoid hit and miss world governance, the rule would have to be applicable even to states that have not ratified the treaty.

Creeping one-worldism makes sovereign nations non-sovereign prisoners of past free decisions. Accelerated one-worldism would make them prisoners of decisions forced upon them. Each nation is responsible for denying nuclear proliferation to terrorist groups on pain of losing its responsibility for action against terrorism to world governance action.

Weapons of Mass Destruction. A related problem is weapons of mass destruction, including those held by major powers other than the agents of world governance itself. Such governance now functions in nuclear arms reduction and inspection. Yet nuclear powers hesitate to surrender arms of terror. Each prefers terror to remain struck into the hearts of non-nationals. Nuclear armament is officially sanctioned terrorism used even by those who fight a war against terrorism. Each sovereign nation's fear of attack means that global civil society has no world governance to fully assure national security. Such security would lead nations with peaceful intentions to re-nounce nuclear arms gladly. The United States, which comes closest to having the power to guarantee the borders of nations, is an instrument of world security.

Loose talk about the United States as "world policeman" without a mandate from any world government has circulated widely. Worldwide nuclear disarmament would probably require a real world police force. The North Atlantic Treaty Organization, perhaps including Russia and even China, might one day acquire a monopoly in weapons of mass destruction. The carrot in nuclear disarmament would be the guarantee of current borders against aggression. The stick would be punitive action, with a possible risk of retaliation, against any country that retains nuclear weapons programs. If the world guarantees borders, the retention of nuclear weapons only arouses suspicion of aggressive intentions that would again jeopardize borders and provoke other nations to arm themselves similarly.

Weapons of mass destruction are already a world problem. To guarantee existing borders need not be to freeze the injustices of historical conquest. We may avoid such frozen injustice if we embark on a policy to depoliticize ethnic identity and promote secular human rights-based states in which no ethnic group has second-class citizenship. (The elimination of arms of mass destruction must lead governments to examine the right to bear arms for individual destruction. If the police does its job, weapons of individual or mass destruction are both without justification, while if these weapons have justification the local or world police is not doing its job.)

Regional Wars. Regional wars may not engage the self-interest of major powers, but they squander resources that could fund basic rights. A solution here is an obligation, not just a right, of world governance to intervene in making and keeping the peace. The mechanism of creeping one-worldism would undergo a test if regional wars, such as between Arabs and Israelis, or Pakistanis and Indians, again threatened after the world had accustomed itself to peace. Since regional wars jeopardize borders and create insecurity, world governance eliminating arms of mass destruction would need to halt regional wars that make a nation feel a need for such arms. Regional wars are already a world problem.

Terrorism. Terrorism is part of the problem of ensuring respect for a right to equal freedom of thought that does not succumb to fear. Eliminating terrorism is a world problem. If, after a time in which relative freedom from terrorism was customary, a terrorist organization or state shocks the world, one response is a world police force to eliminate safe havens for terrorists. Renouncing terror would not be a decision that a nation could reverse anymore than an individual can withdraw from a commitment not to murder.

In some regions today, non-state terrorism is not so rare as to have the shock value needed for the mechanism of creeping one-worldism to take over. In the Middle East and in parts of Africa, it is a daily occurrence. International police action is not yet the neutral action of formal world governance. Such police action is defective world governance executed by aggrieved parties.

Terror strikes fear in the hearts of civilians, though usually people do not include official nuclear terror for self-defense practiced by traditional great powers under this category. Revenge is part of the motive for the current war on terrorism. Yet when non-state terror reaches a certain threshold in public consciousness by targeting the most powerful state, as on September 11, 2001, that state may become an instrument of world governance as it pursues its attackers. But, to be an effective instrument of world governance against terrorism, it would have to break escalating regional and global cycles of revenge and counter-revenge that national parties cannot break. It would have to go after root causes. Yet these cycles include the one in which the United States finds itself as it awaits the next attack.

Third World Debt Relief. Until recently World Bank and the International Monetary Fund, financing Third World development and supporting its currencies, openly represented the interests of the industrial nations providing loans. A feudal regime existed in the recycling of non-payable debts. Paying the interest on existing debts reduced the ability of such nations to invest in development and subsistence rights, which reduced their ability to contribute credibly to global dialogue.

In the late 1990's industrial lender-nations officially gave the World Bank and the International Monetary Fund greater autonomy as institutions of world governance, acting in the interest of a viable economic and social world system, not in the direct interest of lenders. The World Bank tried to make debt forgiveness, new loans, and the rescheduling of payments depend on evidence that recipient countries were serious about reducing poverty, not maintaining privileged classes. Because debt undercuts Third World autonomy in global discussion, debt relief is already a world human rights problem.

Dependence on Fossil Fuels. Few now deny that increased carbon dioxide due to increased fossil energy utilization causes rising temperatures, deforestation, the exhaustion of top soils, the advance of deserts, and the shrinkage of coastal regions. The result is limits to growth by fossil fuels, even Third World growth. The Kyoto Treaty tries to moderate energy consumption in the industrial North, allowing greater development in the Third and Second Worlds. Ecological and environmental problems are not local. Solutions require binding law that optional treaties cannot provide. If the United States, consuming a quarter of the world's energy, frustrated the economic growth of poorer nations, rational discussion in the matter might halt. Forms of one-worldism from below, seeking to force concessions, might replace one-worldism from above, negotiation, and the enforcement of free agreements.

The Kyoto treaty addresses continued reliance on fossil fuels. It ultimately requires world governance to ration such fuels to keep the total amount used below levels spelling ecological disaster. If newer cleaner energy sources eliminated the need for limitations on growth in the First World, all nations, rich and poor, could envision endless growth. . If nations do not ration themselves, defenders of state sovereignty rightly fear that, because something must ration growth, a binding treaty will emerge. If voluntary restriction on energy use in the First World fails, the rationing authority—as coastal areas and cities are flooded later in the century—would be an institution of world governance, not just a treaty that nations are free to denounce. Why should nations without endangered coasts pay? The authority would need punitive power. The World Trade Organization might agree to tax the goods and services of nations found in violation of their word and the new *jus gentium*.

We have alluded to the alternative scenario of unlimited technology-driven growth attractive to First World nations: Third World growth needs no restriction of energy use in the First World by institutions of world governance. Regulation unnecessary for the protection of universal rights serves world governance poorly. Which scenario is true depends on the empirical velocity of technological innovation compared to that of climate deterioration. If the second velocity is greater, emissions are a world problem.

Third World Over-Population. If the basic human right is to contribute to dialogue in the quest for truth, the right progresses as the number of potential contributors increases. This argues against limiting births. Yet the ability to contribute to dialogue relates inversely to poverty. Unless resources increase, this is an argument for restricting births. Better to have some discussion partners of an average high quality than a greater number of a low quality. If a maximum number of high quality discussion partners calls for greater subsistence resources than are available in the short-run, it may be possible to reallocate resources used to finance other rights like consumer choice.

Over-population in Egypt is a local problem, but also a global one if poverty eliminates the voices of millions of Egyptians in dialogue with other creators and critics of cultural products. The World Bank and the International Monetary Fund recognize population control as a condition of escaping poverty and as a condition for qualifying for debt relief and loans. Economic development like tilled lands claimed from the Sahara by the Aswan Dam becomes meaningless by population growth that, except for foreign aid, leaves Egyptians poorer than before.

Excessive Meat Consumption. Meat consumption in wealthier countries is excessive alongside poverty and starvation in poorer countries. If a solution is necessary to prevent starvation, the problem is a world problem. Reallocation of land used to feed livestock or produce alcoholic beverages and drugs could result in grains and vegetables for human consumption. If a treaty to ensure this result were to go into effect through economic sanctions, world governance would advance, supporting universal subsistence rights. Enforcement could come from customs duties imposed by many nations on products and services from an offending nation, a boycott of its products, or an embargo on the sale of arms or oil. Yet a mandatory boycott or embargo would require a threat of police action.

Pollution. Pollution does not respect national boundaries. In the Rhine Valley, pollution is not a problem that one nation can solve. It requires regional governance if not world governance. Technology that does not reduce atmospheric carbon dioxide is a world problem. One approach, which the members of the World Trade Organization might negotiate, is to include worldwide costs of pollution in the price of polluting goods. A consensus of nations agreeing to prohibitive customs on dangerous imports like tobacco would reduce hospitalization within a generation.

Many nations might agree to reciprocal reimbursement of pollution costs and then enforce them by customs levied against states parties which do not comply. Sanctions would make each nation comply with its own decision to join the general agreement and accept the regime of sanctions. Sanctions might even be extended to non-signatories. A non-pollution treaty might arise in the World Trade Organization. The strength of enforcement by the Organization is that member states need not unanimously support arbitration recommendations for it to adopt the recommendations and apply sanctions. The Organization is a formal centralized institution of world governance with punitive powers in the area of trade. Nations freely join, yet joining is easier than getting out and escaping sanctions. Sanctions can apply to a polluting nation even if it withdraws. If the growth of world trade means declining prices, increased wealth and potentially decreasing world poverty, the rewards of reducing customs and of sanctions may be too great to forgo.

The enforcement mechanism of the World Trade Organization makes it a tool for the extension of world governance and human rights even without world government. The Organization now threatens nations with punitive tariffs because of sins against free trade, but might similarly threaten punishment for infringements on agreed rules restricting global warming or ensuring social protection. The lack of social protection in Asian countries appears to the European Union as violation of fair trade on a level playing field where only the quality of products manufactured by fairly compensated workers counts. China, depending on an economy growing at ten percent a year, may not be ready to agree to such protection. Yet in the nineteenth century, Western Europe had similar growth rates, and now with an affluent mature economy its social services show that it has agreed.

Outer Space and the High Seas. No nation has a recognized claim to a portion of either outer space or the high seas, the common heritage of humankind. Yet they both have potentially habitable regions and exploitable resources whose extraction could be taxable. The United Nations might protect common human ownership, assuming a further function of world governance. Outer space might be taxable in support of subsistence rights in poor countries. The assumption that the high seas and outer space belong to no nation easily goes unquestioned, until some nation invests capital and labor in appropriating a region out of the global commons. We cannot easily see today what obstacles a nation with superior technology and strong economic incentive would face in establishing property claims in the commons.

Common human ownership of the heavens and oceans could give world government its initial territory, and later they might remain world federal territory like, Washington, D.C.. Yet they would have largely symbolic value. World governance and government can prove their reality only in population centers, and would receive no deathblow through the elimination of the global commons. Ownership of the commons is not a worldwide human rights problem that only world governance can solve.

Drug Trafficking. The elimination of drug trafficking is a world problem. Drug traffic takes land away from food production, concentrates wealth in the hands of fewer, and destroys human potential. The traffic calls for police action unimpeded by national borders. If cooperation between different sovereign police agencies is unsuccessful, their legitimacy is doubtful. A United Nations treaty against organized drug traffickers would target trafficking sanctuaries in "safe" countries. Would such countries ratify the treaty? If they did, would they do so merely not to attract unwelcome attention? If they continued to protect and profit from drug traffic, would we be better off with the treaty than without it? If the treaty did not defeat trafficking in some countries, would not other countries pursue traffickers into their sanctuaries much as some countries have pursued terrorists? This intervention would accelerate one-worldism if an institution of world governance forced once safe sanctuaries to join. Intervention would illustrate creeping one-worldism if states ratifying the treaty suddenly woke up to mandatory compliance. Either way, if the results were successful, world governance would replace a regime of treaties.

Unequal Social Protection between Countries. Unequal social protection means unemployment in old industrial nations as some Third World economies grow rapidly without social protection. The transfer of employment to the developing world, and of investment to that world, is one phenomenon—expressed in wealthy countries as a threat to employment and in poor countries as an inhibition to establish social protection. This phenomenon is not a world problem, but is a result of solving the world problem of poverty. We can reach a solution only if wealth becomes so equally distributed that the transfer of production is no longer profitable, since Third World countries develop to the point that producers there may also pay for social protection.

World governance does not solve the problem, but eases transition to a free market solution. Thinking that world governance should eliminate competition between highly paid work in rich countries and the same work poorly paid elsewhere misinterprets delocalization and the function of world governance. To stop such competition blocks development, limits the creation of new wealth, and subverts possible funding of universal subsistence rights. (The rate at which new wealth actually reduces world poverty is another question.)

Economic Refugees. Economic refugees are not a world problem, but are a local problem that is part of a solution to the world problem of poverty. World governance should encourage economically motivated immigration to the different limits of host country tolerance, which we should try to increase. The poor immigrate to wealthier countries and tax the welfare systems of those countries, reducing the burden of subsidizing the poor in countries of origin. Wealth and poverty tend to equalization. Poorer regions with fewer poor are less poor. Equalization of poverty and wealth leaves a global civil society with immigrant populations in wealthier nations. The alternative is investment in poor countries to help them absorb their unemployed. Restriction on immigration to maintain high wages or ethnic purity in a host country is inconsistent with human rights.

Immigration supports diversity in multicultural society, and it enhances freedom of thought by exposure to wider alternatives. Unless virtual travel replaces actual travel, a right to emigrate is a mode of the right to freedom of thought. Today the right supposes sovereign nations ready to accept immigrants. The Universal Declaration has no positive right to immigrate, but host country demand for skilled labor amidst demographic stagnation or a geopolitical interest in population increase supports a human right to immigrate.

World governance in security and subsistence must advance, by dialogue and sanctions, in the areas of non-proliferation, disarmament, war on terrorism and drugs, an end to regional wars, controls on emissions and clean technologies, the transfer of growth to the South and labor to the North, Third World debt relief, reduced grazing, increased farming, and reduced Third World population growth. We also need lower farm subsidies that do not depopulate rural America or Europe.

A global human rights culture, with freedom of thought enshrined in a more Oriental duty consciousness, would promote voluntary compliance with world human rights courts. The existence of human rights will depend on such a culture, which will depend on merging strengths of the East and the West, duty consciousness and individual rights consciousness. World enforcement of world law and a world parliament compensating for the democratic deficit of world governance may in time need little advocacy.

Fifteen

CONCLUSION

1. Freedom of Speech and Its Conditions

Suppose a territory of some nation receives the radiation of secret atomic bomb testing in the name of national security. Suppose the government does not consult individuals in that region on a matter vital to them. They have little or no chance to propose a form of national security other than one involving their unwitting self-sacrifice. Without information, they have effectively risked their health without their consent. We might fairly say then that, regarding one crucial issue, these individuals lack locally a right that, if universal, would be a *human right*, a right of all to maximal freedom of thought, to a thought-determined choice between a maximum of knowable choices.

If we ever sacrifice freedom of thought locally, such freedom is not a universal right. We may sacrifice it on the altar of wealth, power, the greatest happiness, or another apparent human right such as security or subsistence. Yet this right, which Americans acclaim as *freedom of speech*, now appears as *the* human right—justified because without it the maximal justification of no claim is possible.

Philosophers have debated a final standard of right and wrong for over 2500 years. Still-debated theories include ethical egoism, utilitarianism, and Kantianism. The current era of human rights rhetoric occasions the thought that we have finally found the long-sought standard for a universal moral minimum, and that it lies in respect for the freedom of thought and speech necessary for maximally unrestricted inquiry.

The priority of ethical respect for human rights frees them from their isolation in international human rights law. Such law, due to the failure in large regions of the world to enforce human rights, is not true law. Until the morality of respect for rights becomes a global culture, until we see the struggle against atrocities as an extension to extreme situations of the morality regulating the most ordinary of human relationships, many will leave human rights to a litigation of horrors in a legal heaven having little hold on their daily lives. Universal international law, cut off from public support, will then inevitably fail.

International law, which requires a global consensus, cannot presuppose a still controversial ethics. Yet the hope is that some set of rules governing fair discussion between controversial positions, such as the one presented in this book or some improved variation of it, may prove uncontroversial. We should model controversy generally on disagreement between judges interpreting the law. Opposing justices can respect one another as fully rational and yet divide between majority and minority opinions, but by shared canons of argumentation the minority can become the majority and the majority the minority. The truth is objective, but the issues are often more difficult to resolve in law than those in beginning physics, where all agree. Yet if I am right that some ethics such as the human rights ethics presented here holds the promise of bringing the history of normative ethics to an end, a universal consensus with possible sources in Karl Popper, Jürgen Habermas and Georg Wilhelm Friedrich Hegel is conceivable in the theory of human rights law.

We know that some have found aspects of international humanitarian law obsolete in the war on terror. They hold that world peace and security can only rest on overwhelmingly superior power, not (as the United Nations asserts) on economically and educationally empowering a global open society for testing diverse beliefs in dialogue. If security becomes an end in itself, America faces an identity crisis over its basic commitment to freedom of speech understood in the most straightforward sense.

Differences exist between United States courts and Europe, for example, over the death penalty. Let us assume that the right to freedom of speech is uncontroversial. Controversy still exists as to whether we exercise this right optimally *by*, or *without*, a right to freedom from the threat of execution. Non-controversial human rights exist only at a high level of abstraction. Might we exercise a *universal* right to freedom of speech, with the least intimidation, by a *national* right to freedom from the death penalty in one nation and without such a national right in another? This is a question for empirical research. The rights that implement a universal right are controversial. Yet the death penalty (whatever else it does) necessarily curtails the range of discussion partners in the search for the truth. Research must still determine whether, on balance, it advances or hinders the cause of free speech in inquiry.

An ethics of respect for human rights is non-controversial only if limited to basic rights and its empirically necessary applications. Discussion might make this ethics more or less concrete. A right to life by abolition of the death penalty is not today a human right, since we do not universally recognize the right to be valid. To say that the right is "a human right" is then at most to say it ought to be one.

Some universal empirical applications of freedom of speech seem so obvious that the temptation exists to dispense with research—except for our knowledge that some have in fact denied them. Libertarians have denied that subsistence is such an application. Worlds apart, Osama bin Laden exercised freedom of speech in the global media on behalf of his cause, while subtracting thousands from his audience. We exercise freedom of thought *by* exercising a right to life, only under the description of being that right, too.

2. The Language of Rights

In the past, philosophers of international human rights law appealed to a *natural law* open to direct inspection by reason, to the law of human nature. Yet we must find the criterion of valid law elsewhere. Human nature falls under what is, not what ought to be, and so cannot legitimate law. Habermas's view that we can justify rights claims only by the requirements of reason in public discussion implies that to be rational is not to be right, but to be capable of correcting error by empowering others to reply. Whether someone is a human being or is of another species, each person capable of dialogical inquiry merits the basic right of reply.

A *right*, even if invalid, is a claim to a freedom of action, service, or good socially recognized to be valid. A claim without recognition of its validity within some community is not yet a right. A right in this minimal sense is a customary right, and perhaps not a legal or moral right. A *moral right* is a justified right. But the world might universally *recognize* a claim to freedom of thought as valid even if, whether due to willfulness or incapacity, it does not universally *respect* the claim. The existence of human rights depends on universal (or near universal) recognition, but such recognition is an empirical matter.

Human Rights Watch can investigate whether human rights exist by gauging whether they enjoy, approximately and for the most part, all possible respect. It monitors outer respect for human rights, but it is more difficult to test for the inner commitment to their validity which would be sufficient for their existence. The best test would be to demonstrate to all that the means with which to implement such rights exist, and then to observe whether or not these means are used.

Moral rights are either inclusive human rights or exclusive rights acquired by exercising inclusive human rights. I have sought to show that the apparent multiplicity of human rights stems from the empirically discoverable universal conditions of the one right of publicly exercisable freedom of thought. Moral obligations, including an ideally universal obligation to respect that basic right, stem from making, with insight into a good reason for dong so, a promise to oneself.

Those who do not know how to claim rights directly (for example, children) may eventually win them through others acting on their behalf. As for those who do not recognize the validity of rights claims, we may need to enforce compliance with them. If we are committed to human rights, enforcing some of them is more crucial than knowing that everyone complies for the morally right reason. As a method of moral education, enforcing compliance also may create habits that dispose individuals to consider the good reason for respecting rights.

The existence of rights does not imply respect for them. The rights of all over against all are claims that address three classes of persons: (1) those who have real power to *respect* the claims, (2) those who *recognize* the validity of claims while lacking the power to furnish respect, and (3) those who are forced into *compliance* while failing to recognize their validity.

The right to food might be the basic human right under one of its descriptions or modes even though we are incapable of universally respecting it, or even if some comply under duress with a rule against diverting food production to drug manufacture. Recognition of the validity of property rights may accompany compliance with laws protecting property, although it is difficult to be sure. Human rights will require compliance in some cases if universal observance is to be possible. Yet compliance precludes testing for universal recognition of a claim's validity unless we are to empty the prisons to see if this recognition is genuine?

Progress toward universal recognition of the legitimacy of a right depends on viewing compliance as moral education. We enforce compliance to instill recognition of the validity of claims. We foresee this recognition by those who now only comply as a future conclusion of such education. If some merely comply with rights claims, human rights can only be rights of all over against the present *or* incipient recognition by all. Yet the recognition incipient in this moral education may fail. Human rights are always at risk.

Human rights ethics does not claim that our only obligation is to respect rights that would be human rights if they were universal. We would even fail to have such an obligation if no persons, whether directly or putatively, staked out human rights claims open to recognition as valid rights. Our obligation is also to extend the range of rights holders by educating individuals regarding the rights which they could claim. Creating these rights here means bringing persons to lay claim to human rights. An obligation of moral education precedes the obligation to respect rights.

Even if our ability to realize human rights around the globe is limited, each one of us is capable of choosing to empower those with whom we come into direct contact with a freedom to reply to us. What we call human rights ethics can thus already be practiced as a personal ethics in local encounters.

Strictly, a Hobbesian "natural right" to life and hence to self-defense is no right at all, since biology, not voluntary respect, enforces it. Such a natural right is not even universal, since individuals sometimes lose the will to live. In the absence of any claim to the right to life, an obligation may exist in the name of our own possible enlightenment to protect life on behalf of the other person, and so to protect the possibility of a return of that claim. Persons who seem to have lost all ability to reclaim a right to life and to freedom of thought occasionally reclaim them.

3. The Argument for Human Rights

Embracing human rights is an act of reason. Good reasons may not convince all human rights offenders, many of whom have only a secondary interest in the cogency of belief. Such reasons convince only those who make this interest primary. Most crucially, we need to be able to convince ourselves in order to convince others. In humanitarian intervention, success may require that we communicate the cogency of human rights and not just feel compassion.

The main argument for creating and respecting human rights is that we have, surprisingly, learned from those from whom we least expected to learn. Once a limited audience has been convinced, voices external to it can lead its members to reflect despite themselves. We have learned from people of other religions, nationalities, and social classes, even from those considered retarded. We know by a strong induction, fallibly and yet by long historical experience, that no one exists from whom we may safely say we cannot learn. If we are fully rational, we should stake our lives on creating and maintaining a world of potential discussion partners on all sides. Doing what we can in the defense of such a world, working toward respect for all implied modes of the basic right, defines, we suggest, moral conduct.

No matter what position we adopt, we support it in a maximally rational manner only if we support dialogical human rights. We may cease dialogue and consider other action only when faced with non-dialogical opposition to the possibility of universal rights-protected participation in dialogue. Sometimes we argue against human rights violations by pointing out, to those who already implicitly accept them as presuppositions of dialogue, that they in fact do so. Civil and political rights are upheld by all who are under the spell of the modern Enlightenment in all discussion, including discussion of such rights. Yet today this is not everybody. The attempt to impose belief, forms of worship, and political loyalties by force remains all too frequent.

Yet even if every human practice presupposed human rights, this fact would not justify them. An argument for human rights as assumed by existing cosmopolitan discussion risks a confusion of *justifying rights* with *necessarily presupposing them*. A corrupt practice may presuppose that everyone is ready to sell him- or herself to the highest bidder, but that does not justify the presupposition. It would not justify the belief even if the belief were universal. A presupposed belief may be only hypothetically necessary, in a non-necessary context. A person can cease to participate in corruption, and a rational discussant may regress to addressing a merely national audience.

If we construe our presupposition of the validity of ideal human rights as an argument for their validity, the argument is circular. True, it becomes impossible to reject human rights norms by the public procedure of rational discussion. To violate them would be a *practical contradiction*: it would be a contradiction between what one implicitly claims by the violation and a presupposition of claiming it. But this not a justification of them.

Exhibition of a practical contradiction might lead those who have tacitly promised to respect freedom of thought to be consistent in upholding that promise, if indeed they still wish to uphold it. Yet this would not be a justification of human rights, since the option remains of repudiating the promise.

Yet, unless reason means a dogmatic appeal to self-evidence, a fully reasoned attempt to reject human rights still would have to appeal to a rationally motivated consensus whose credibility would depend on contradictorily assuming universal freedom of thought precisely in order to reject it.

Some suspend participation in public discussion while others never reach such participation. But if private inquiry, without presupposing the validity of human rights, can initiate a justification of them by finding its "self-evident" convictions to be surprisingly falsified by others, we may begin to justify rights to some of those who do not presuppose them, to some of very people we most want to convince. We do not want merely to lead those who already implicitly presuppose such rights to accept them explicitly.

What justifies adopting human rights norms when existing procedures do not presuppose them? If members of a group seek legitimacy through affirmation by others, affirmation of them is fully credible only if it is human rights-protected. Legitimacy exists only if their assent is credible. Further, this credibility may depend on varying mixes of civil, welfare, public service, public works, and legal-access rights as ways of exercising the basic right to freedom of thought. Without protection of such modal rights, freedom of thought may be unnecessarily limited, and assent may even occur under intimidation. Do we need to perform the experiment upon human beings to see how the deprivation of food affects the credibility of assertions?

Credible affirmation by others who now economically depend on us may require their economic independence for the sake of our own legitimacy. They may require health or unemployment insurance. If others do not enjoy rights protection, we may never enjoy legitimacy even through universal affirmation. Inquiry in which we seek no affirmation by others is private inquiry, in which we base ourselves on claims of self-evidence or insight controlled by purely internal voices. Call this *monological inquiry*. The need for affirmation by others supposes that private judgment has proven uncertain. We sometimes discover external voices to have validity. Yet dialogue remains limited until the equal rights of all potential discussion partners are established. A conversion is possible from monological to dialogical inquiry, and then from restricted or distorted dialogue circles to fully open dialogue. Such conversions point to a developmental concept of inquiry and reason.

4. Human Rights and Fallibilism

Human rights ethics justifies rights by showing how public inquiry into objective truth depends on them. Some other human rights ethics might ground them in relativism, in an equal right of everyone to express her or his personal truth. Yet a justifiable human rights ethics has its basis in *fallibilism*, not in relativistic denials of objective truth.

Relativism regarding truth allows the denial of human rights to be subjectively true for all who deny them. Yet subjective truth is either trivial or absurd. That astrological statements are true *for* astrologers means *either* that they believe them, which is trivial, *or* that believing the statements makes them objectively true, which is absurd. The second interpretation would give relativism force, but would also mean that non-astrologers can make the negation of astrological statements objectively true, so the world would contain contradictory facts.

A third human rights ethics would justify rights by invoking a divine image in each human being. Yet such theology consists in statements whose validation must presuppose human rights in dialogue. Rational theologians address our nearest approximation of the universal audience, without necessarily convincing it. Revealed theology does not even address it: it fails to limit itself to the universal logical and empirical rules of inquiry of that audience. Human rights ethics as understood here both addresses and convinces the universal audience, insofar as we have done all we can to construct it.

Realizing that we fail to know infallibly, we invite exchanges with rights-protected persons everywhere. Yet a consistent fallibilist could be wrong about fallibilism, about being possibly wrong about everything. We may only apparently have refuted a conjecture. Refutations are themselves refutable. Human rights ethics based on fallibilism is itself fallible. Yet as long as we seem to be fallible due to our own perceived past errors, the right to freedom of thought, with all the modal rights that support it, appears valid. There is no higher justification of these rights than that they still seem to be valid in the light of our experience of having been falsified by unexpectedly good critics.

With self-evident knowledge in the privacy of each person's soul on all topics, there would be no reason to respect the kind of human rights we have in mind. Yet, we have too often patently refuted claims of self-evident knowledge through the surprising turns of inquiry for us to continue to place any confidence in it. Even mathematics, once the preserve of such knowledge, has yielded to assault.

The repeated onslaughts of fallibilism since Charles Saunders Peirce have dealt a deathblow to dogmatism. They have also opened the door to ethical relations of mutual respect between all persons on a fully reasonable basis. It is safe to hold that any beliefs benefit from discussion. Healthy skepticism, based on the history of the long-surviving battlefield strewn with apparently refuted knowledge claims, leads us to base respect for rights, not on the fortunes of compassion, but on an argument that all those who argue can understand that the other person can be a source of instruction. Compassion, identification with the suffering of others, supports the advance of rights only if it is rationally regulated. Otherwise, the plight of those closer to home, or more visible in the media, may unfairly arouse it.

Dogmatism and appeals to private self-evidence are not just apparent folly in the formation of belief, not just intellectually arrogant in light of the history of science. They are the root of evil, of the supposition that persons

exist who can teach us nothing. Supporting all in their inquiries is not sentimental, it is enlightened. We do not know what questions we may one day
pose, nor of what future consensus will result from our respect for each individual's right to diverge from today's consensus.

Respect for human rights based on a cooperative quest for truth is close
to Kantian respect for persons as ends in themselves. Without human rights,
there could still be inquiring persons. Yet respect for persons without human
rights is either purely inner reverence, a feeling of being sorry for their plight,
or at most an unrealized will to construct a world order founded on these
rights.

5. The Moral Point of View as Included
by the Theoretical Point of View

For Kant those who violate human rights violate the principle of respect for
persons as ends in themselves: "[H]e who transgresses the rights of man intends to use the person of others merely as means. . . ."[1] Yet, while actual
human rights have not existed, Kant has held that the moral law of respect for
persons as ends in themselves has always been in effect. It follows that respect for others as ends in themselves is not, for Kant, identical to respect for
human rights. Respecting human rights that do not yet exist is impossible. Until we construct human rights, some persons are not credible witnesses
in inquiry.

Those who, like Kant, separate the moral point of view from that of truth
seeking give no basis from the cognitive point of view for respecting persons.
Yet the pursuit of knowledge is more reliably universal than any moral point
of view separate from it. Success in any venture is more likely if we know the
world as it is. Assimilating morality to the cognitive point of view benefits
morality.

Human rights ethics holds that we ought to respect persons as ends in
themselves with their own agendas because they are potential discussion
partners responding independently and credibly to questions that we someday
might pose. Theoretical reason gains a new primacy over practical reason.
The non-existence of human rights cancels the possibility of ideal inquiry.

6. From Recognizing the Validity of
Rights to Respecting Them

Respect for "human rights," if it is only a local practice, is respect for a privilege. The right to freedom of speech, which in global society we may recognize as a valid moral ideal that we are still powerless to respect as an actual
universal freedom, may actually be respected within a single nation as a *national right*. Globally respect for human rights would then remain merely a

project. National privileges are not human rights, even if the privileges would be human rights if globally we all recognized them to be valid. Yet *respect* for national privileges such as freedom of speech or the right to health care qualifies as *recognition* of human rights when joined by a movement to cancel privilege by universalizing it. National privileges then become prospective human rights.

Human rights can exist by universal recognition of their validity even if we do not universally respect them. Actual human rights lie in the mutual recognition by all of the validity of claims by all. Strictly speaking, we can only approach universal recognition. Still, human rights may be effective even if we do not always observe them. One dove does not make a summer, and one cold day does not annul the effectiveness of summer. An actual human right can coexist with violations so long as we initiate procedures to counter them.

7. Global Institutions

The movement to cancel national privilege by its universalization takes place within global institutions. These are institutions of economic globalization, but also of political globalization attempting a political correction of the perceived injustices of economic globalization. They include the United Nations, the United States operating in world security, the G-8, the World Bank, the International Monetary Fund, the World Trade Organization, the International Criminal Court, non-governmental organizations, world opinion forums, and organized movements as local agents for the advance of global rights. Such institutions and movements make up a new global form of *ethical life* beyond the family, market, and local state.

Market globalization creates communications industries that intensify possibilities of dialogical inquiry. The human rights movement both transcends and presupposes economic globalization in seeking to realize the cosmopolitan dream of dialogue across all barriers. The ethos of global life is not a seamless whole. The ethos of the global market does not coincide with that of the human rights movement, which intends a political check on the market, on pre-globalization nationalisms, and on archaic forms of domination.

Without the trial of the fullest possible public discussion, we have justified no belief as much as we might have. Yet maximum justification does not mean discussion with *all* persons. We scan the universal audience, not to discuss with as many as possible, but to recruit an elite of actual discussion partners from a maximal range of candidates. Conclusions enjoy less justification when they rest on discussion with persons recruited merely from a local or restricted range of potential discussion partners. We must cast the net as widely as possible.

The construction of human rights may eventually call for the construction of individual directories by which anyone can invite responses from anyone, and by which everyone is capable of unconstrained response. This

construction is also the construction of discussion directories by which anyone can join a discussion of concern to him or her. Such constructions are a
still incomplete economic, technological, political, and cultural feat.

Dialogical human rights are now emerging in part due to new global
media as the material basis of the universal audience, and of human rights
ethics. Appeal to the universal audience implies the arbitrariness of assuming
that a given thesis does not concern some people. We ought to include in the
discussion any who feel concerned. The course of discussion will put that
feeling to the test. But some ought to feel concerned who do not feel concerned, and in such cases, human rights ethics seek to raise their awareness
and, if need be, speak on their behalf. As long as some potentially affected by
the conclusion of an argument find themselves excluded from the audience to
which we appeal, we have not justified the conclusion as fully as we might
have done.

Is complete justification practical? The argument is only for approaching
as closely as possible access to a universal pool of those capable of participating in the discussion circle, actively or passively. Approaching respect for
human rights is a condition of approaching full justification of any conclusion. In the procedural division of labor in rights-protected discussion, a court
of law can appoint a jury, a university can institute a class, and a committee
can appoint a special panel. Yet the jury, research team, or panel, in reporting
back, emerges out of its temporary isolation in that division of labor. It addresses public opinion in a provincial or national audience, ultimately in the
universal audience empowered by the new global media. If the universal
audience has no appreciation of the evidence in a case, it still has the evidence
provided by the reputation of a court or panel.

8. On Asking a Question Seriously

All who *seriously* ask for justification, and who follow a maximal procedure
for obtaining it, presuppose human rights norms. To ask any question seriously and without reservation, including the question of a justification for
human rights, is to be ready to accept a good answer from any quarter—
without restriction as to ethnic or other origin. To ignore answers from a
given source is to take the *question* with less seriousness than one takes the
chosen *persons* questioned. Preservation of a limited circle of discussants
becomes more crucial than a true answer to the question. To ask while assuming everyone *could* have something to say is already to work for human
rights. This, by itself, is not to say that such rights are justifiable, but only that
we presuppose them when we attend more to the question than to the persons
whom we ask.

To pursue truth seriously is to pursue human rights. Yet such direct
justification of human rights, vindicating them ultimately before the universal
audience, presupposes their validity, the very point at issue. To avoid circular-

ity, we attempt an indirect approach, adopting the standpoint of those who in private inquiry do not endorse or even explicitly repudiate these rights. Yet there is no guarantee that we could convince Osama Bin Laden in six hours in an isolation chamber.

The rational inescapability of human rights becomes apparent only if we discover the contradiction of *both* addressing the universal audience *and* violating or denying the legitimacy of human rights. Yet assumptions that imply a contradiction do not imply that everyone will see the contradiction, or react to it by consistently adopting or rejecting human rights norms. Some have sought to vindicate themselves before world opinion by issuing videos with an air of sweet reason while subtracting thousands from the universal audience—and at once creating a climate of insecurity diminishing the ability of millions to engage in rationally motivated discussion

The passage into human rights ethics can occur only by contingent private reflection and new insight, or insight within a restricted audience. The cogency of voices external to the privacy of one's own mind, if it is recognized, comes as a shock to anyone who previously appealed only to self-evidence. Yet an individual's discovery of his or her fallibility, no matter how well justified, is difficult to predict.

Persons to whom we cannot justify universal rights are those who persist in a complete and certain system of knowledge, or in whom the admission of fallibility is less insistent than some conflicting conviction. Individuals uncommitted to human rights can begin their conversion to them, not by our realization, but only their own realization that someone has refuted their private judgment, suggesting that exposure to all others would be the best test for any judgment. Such an initial endorsement of the human rights ideal in private inquiry enjoys only weak justification to the individual. The justification can become stronger only as the experience of learning from others comes to repeat itself.

Persons committed to pleasure, power, profit, or beauty will not find human rights justified unless, at a deeper level, they commit to the full *justification* of pleasure, power, profit, and beauty. Libertarians claim that the final human right is the right to the product of the right-holder's labor. But such a right is either self-evident or discussable. If the right is self-evident, appeal to all rationally motivated inquirers and to their freedom of thought is dispensable. If the right is discussible, it is not self-evident or final.

From the standpoint of ideal inquiry, we scan and consult the universal audience established by human rights to identify discussion partners most capable of testing existing beliefs. Short of inquiry in such ideal conditions, public rationality assumes truth seeking before the widest possible audience. Even from the perspective of egoistic pleasure seeking that ignores inquiry into the truth of pleasure seeking there is reason to participate in the procedures of truth seeking. A good reason exists to have good reasons. We ought to have them to minimize the *pain* of clinging to beliefs shown to be false.

9. Non-Academic Rights-Governed Inquiry

Do human rights as a presupposition of inquiry overly intellectualize ethics, making it an appendage of purely academic endeavor? This is not the case. We do not restrict dialogue to its written or verbal form. Yet it does not exist everywhere. Human rights ethics, discussion ethics, has a cutting edge—it rules some things out. We do not practice this ethics if without further discussion we impose the conclusions of restricted discussion on others who disagree. It does exist where genuine rivalry arises as to whether someone can surpass a given achievement. One achievement calls forth a rival achievement, rivalry in the quest for truth. The competition shows what target belief we cannot currently circumvent.

Tacit discussion occurs in the arts, in the sciences, in technology, in the market, in politics, and in religion, and it stretches the range of discussion far beyond the academy. Achievement is an implicit challenge to others: "Top this, if you can!" The number of pleasure-seekers or power-seekers who are not at bottom dialogical truth-seekers drops if we reflect on the number of them who tacitly seek to test and establish the assumptions of their quest.

10. Equal Human Rights and Jürgen Habermas

The case for human rights does not presuppose that the ability to participate in a given discussion distributes itself equally. An argument is not justified by actually convincing all equally, but by excluding none from the list of potential discussion partners. Equal human rights are a test of who is superior, a way of filtering and sifting through humanity to locate talent wherever. In parts of Africa the absence of rights means that, despite appearances, one cannot tell who does not have talent. By instituting human rights, we perform an experiment upon everyone equally of seeing what she or he can achieve.

The ethics of respect for human rights is a kind of discussion ethics. Habermas does not identify respect for human rights as the sole presupposition of rational discourse, but he does use human rights to illustrate such presuppositions. Between the present human rights ethics and Habermas's discussion ethics three differences seem to exist. First, human rights ethics in this book has clearly equated the rules of conduct in dialogical ethics with nothing beyond the rules of respect for human rights largely found in international declarations and covenants.

Secondly, human rights ethics is not justifiable by appeal to the presupposed norms of rational discussion, since we circularly would have to presuppose these norms as valid even in arguing for their justification. What Habermas calls *procedural justification* sometimes seems to lie merely in noting presuppositions of existing practice, but this is to justify the presuppositions only hypothetically, only *if* the practice is justified. An individual engaged in private inquiry, not circularly presupposing human rights, justifies them to him- or herself by discovering the heuristic value of universally open channels of communication.

Thirdly, we have placed Habermas's legitimate fear of self-righteous human rights crusades, invoking human rights to serve moralistic foreign policies, alongside the equally legitimate fear of appeasing human rights violations by foregoing all politically as well as legally effective means in a world without world government. Yet the second Iraqi war suggests that powerful nations often should act for human rights, going beyond their strict self-defense, only at the request of the United Nations, which has now sprung back from its oft-cited irrelevance to a clearer world mission than ever.

However, the present formulation of human rights ethics owes much to Habermas's development of discussion ethics (*Diskursethik*). We have borrowed his analysis of the basic dialogical human right into sub-rights. The basic human right to freedom of thought in the ideal speech situation contains four sub-rights. (1) A right to discuss a claim ought to extend to all who feel concerned. This is a right of access. (2) Each dialogue partner ought to have a right to enter an agreement, accept a conclusion, without anyone preventing or forcing him or her. (3) More particularly, every dialogue partner has a right to all information available to the other partners about direct and indirect consequences of the universal observance of a norm, of an agreement, or of acting on a conclusion. (4) Likewise, before entering an agreement or drawing a conclusion, every dialogue partner has the right to know all that other partners know of alternative agreements or conclusions that he or she could have reached.

Freedoms to which we have a human right are freedoms from compulsion and restraint. A person ought to have a right to enter into a dialogue without anyone having a right to compel or prevent such a decision. A right is an option anyone may take or leave. A decision to discuss is credible only if everyone is free not to enter.

Assuming they do not exceed our ability, choices cause actions, whether or not the choices are justified. Since which choice is justified is difficult to determine, no obligation exists to make an enlightened choice, to choose governed by true insight, and no obligation exists to choose by anyone else's concept of true insight. A human right to err while respecting the rights of others is valid. Even those who violate human rights seem to have *prima facie* dialogical human rights insofar as, by a general rational consensus, their potential contribution as dialogue partners justifies those rights. If no such consensus existed, the rights of persons with unblemished moral records might exist, but human rights would fail to exist as the rights of all.

12. From Mere Tolerance to an Invitation to Diversity

Traditionally a human right to freedom of worship meant indifferent tolerance of another's faith for the sake of the common peace. Today, we begin not merely to tolerate the exercise of human rights by others with indifference to the results, but to solicit it. We ought to respect human rights as part of an invitation we extend to others to exercise them in diverse ways, out of a sense of our cognitive loss due to their non-exercise. This is the underlying identity between the human rights culture and what is currently promoted in America as the culture of diversity.

At the time of the *Declaration of Independence*, people needed protection against persecution because of diverse dogmatic expressions of their freedom of belief. Few thought of the right to be different as a gift bestowed by others for their possible instruction. Today, respect for human rights diversely exercised in dialogue requires inquiry into human constraints and restraints on thought, and of ways to remove them. Constraints and restraints on freedom of choice are physical, as in famine, but also can be informational, as in domination by restriction of the alternatives of which one knows, or by restriction of one's knowledge of direct and indirect consequences of a particular choice.

One of the greatest restrictions on freedom of thought has always come from not realizing that others believe differently from oneself. Suppose you justify belief monologically in the privacy of your mind, without entering into a discussion with other concerned individuals. Given different isolated persons, it may be reasonable for one to believe something monologically, and for another to believe its denial monologically. Yet since either the original belief or its negation must be false, if someone defending the first belief and someone else defending the second communicated in a collaborative quest for truth through their diversity, they would both have to conclude that one of them, in entering the discussion, believes a falsehood. Yet, in a collaborative inquiry, neither can rest content with such a conclusion. Those who inquire together but disagree, and who want the truth, must suspend categorical judgment and believe only heuristically until they reach a rationally motivated consensus.

Monological dialogue between private voices in one person ought, if possible, to convert to interpersonal dialogue between diverse rights holders. A flesh and blood other person protected by human rights gives a stronger impetus to discussion than an unprotected dissident inner voice.

13. Human Rights Ethics and the Eclipse of Traditional Moral Theories

We have argued that rationally human rights ethics prevails over the traditional rival theories of right and wrong in that we presuppose this ethics in trying to argue for any other theory. Religious ethics, for example, says that the will of God determines right and wrong. Yet to argue for religious ethics, or for any theory, would be to argue for *arguing* as a procedure governed by respect for the basic human right, a procedure that puts any and every theory at risk except a correct theory laying out necessary norms governing the procedure itself.

Yet any particular formulation of the presuppositions of rational discussion is itself at risk. The only available criterion of truth is an ever-fallible consensus of all concerned discussants as enabled by a fallible consensus as to the best available theory of dialogical rights. Human rights as we have formulated them are far from receiving maximally possible respect, and hence from having true existence. In the ideal speech situation, a speaker's promise that, if everybody investigated, everyone would agree would not be hollow. Until such a situation exists, until all are empowered by an actual right to investigate, the promise remains hollow. Human rights depend on institutions still under construction. The moral institution of life is not, as we often suppose, already out there merely for us to accept or not. In its particular forms, we must still invent it.

Until this construction is complete, human rights ethics takes the form of *interim human rights ethics*, which may justify sacrificing the actual human rights of some persons for more extensive present or future rights. The loss of present voices is an irremediable evil for which the bright future of human rights never compensates. For this loss is not a non-moral evil like pain. The sacrifice of any human witness is a moral evil.

The evil of believing that we have nothing to learn from one another would legitimate the sacrificing of possible witnesses to the truth. The Taliban sacrifice of the witness of Buddhist art in their midst, a violation of the right of Buddhists to speak from the past, is an example. Every witness has a ideal right to speak, though not necessarily for others to listen. Voices fallen silent from the past show that the realization of human rights will never be complete. The rights of all present persons fall short of the rights of all against all.

We may think that reducing ethics to respect for the right to be a potential partner in dialogue with other persons means that the moral law is insecure. Does it not vanish if some do not opt for the pursuit of truth as a final standard? The moral law would then cease to be categorical. Yet we cannot fully evade respect for persons as ends in themselves by choosing not to adopt the moral point of view, such as by adopting the aesthetic or egoistic point of view. For even if we turn a deaf ear to conscience by living life from the aesthetic point of view, the moral point of view remains permanently available. The moral standpoint becomes imperative as soon as we decide to test our choices. Intellectual conscience, which commands the pursuit of truth, develops into the moral conscience that commands respect for the rights of potential discussion partners. Truth seeking depends on morality.

Trying to neglect truth pursuits does not eliminate the imperative character they assume from a perspective that reason places constantly at our disposal. Hedonism, for example, as an "ism," is not just the pursuit of pleasure. Hedonism pursues a justification of the truth about pleasure pursuits. People may be oblivious to basic institutions of the modern world—to science, schools, the marketplace, the courtroom, communications, or travel—which foster truth pursuits. Yet the pursuit of truth behind successful action stems from a permanent and recurrent alternative among human perspectives invoked in the justification of all other perspectives, and in their implementation in adaptation to the real world.

Once we have made the transition to cosmopolitan dialogical reason, the argument against theories of right and wrong other than human rights ethics becomes transparent. We can maximally justify no other theory of right and wrong except by submitting that theory to discussion before a universal audience protected by human rights. The human rights ethics of dialogical justification preempts every other norm of right and wrong.

How do we know this if not by circularly assuming human rights as a presupposition of public inquiry? The answer, we have seen, is that private inquiry converts itself non-circularly into rights-based public inquiry. Others believably correct or confirm us only insofar as they are rights-protected. Private inquiry itself leads us to infer that protection of the rights of all would most believably correct or confirm the claims of private inquiry. Not everyone wants others to correct or confirm him or her on every issue, though we would want this if we were maximally rational. Human rights are a function of reason understood as the correction of error.

The argument against theories of right and wrong other than human rights ethics is a forceful argument in favor of human rights ethics. We can fully justify neither religious ethics, nor utilitarianism, nor any other traditional theory except by submitting it to discussion before the universal audience of individuals empowered and protected by human rights. To justify anything in the fullest sense is to esteem the process of justification and the accompanying human rights ethics.

An obligation to invoke law and custom, and not merely conscience, to guarantee human rights—to ensure outer observance of rights and not just inner reverence for them—has been coming to the center of normative ethics and international relations for decades. I do not say human rights "trump" other ethical considerations like the common good.[2] I say that no other ethical considerations exist—none other than human rights and their implementation by countless special rights and commitments. The rights and obligations of a spouse are not human rights and obligations, though their acquisition is an exercise of human rights (the right to marry). Special rights and commitments that are inconsistent with respect for human rights are unethical.

The alleviation of *suffering* is morally relevant because we enjoy what is finally the *only* human right—the right to dialogically situated freedom of thought—only *by* exercising a right to minimal physical comfort. Either the right to minimal comfort is a universal mode of the substantive essential right to freedom of thought or such comfort is no human right at all. Apart from its status as a mode of the basic right, cherish it as a significant animal right, but do not call it a human right.

I have written this book, in the American context, against a foil that I may identify. In 1957, one writer wrote:

> [T]he dominant approach to international politics in America has emphasized the rationality and moral capacity of man and the possibility of . . . . progress in history. . . . [T]his dominant approach has been challenged by an increasing number of theologians, students of world politics, and statesmen who . . . have emphasized the limits of man's moral capacity and the tragic character of history.[3]

Some neo-Augustinian theologians, if not St. Augustine himself, will tell us that the city of man here below can never approach the city of God. They peddle a counsel of despair in the world we know. I have not claimed that human rights will surely exist. I have only claimed that, with the greatest respect for political realism, we ought to make every intelligent effort to realize such rights. Human rational and moral incapacity should never become an incapacitating dogma.

NOTES

Chapter One

1. Friedrich Nietzsche, *Genealogy of Morals*, trans. Horace B. Samuel (New York: Random House, 1954), First Essay, §16, pp. 663–665.
2. Georg Wilhelm Friedrich Hegel, *The Phenomenology of Spirit*, trans. A. V. Miller (Oxford: Oxford University Press, 1977), pp. 43–45.
3. Myles F. Burnyeat, "Did the Ancient Greeks Have the Concept of Human Rights," *Polis*, 13:1–2 (1994), pp. 1–11.
4. John Hospers, *Human Conduct* (New York: Harcourt Brace, 1996), p. 192.
5. Cicero, *On Duties*, eds. M. T. Griffin and E. M. Atkins (Cambridge, England: Cambridge University Press, 1991), bk. 1, sec. 16.
6. Jürgen Habermas, *Faktizität und Geltung* (Frankfurt: Suhrkamp, 1992), pp. 155–157.
7. *Purdue University Faculty and Staff Handbook*, 1999–2000, p. 11.
8. Burnyeat, "Did the Ancient Greeks Have the Concept of Human Rights," pp. 1–11.
9. Jürgen Habermas, *The Structural Transformation of the Public Sphere: An Inquiry into a Category of Bourgeois Society*, trans. Thomas Burger with Frederick Lawrence (Cambridge, Mass.: MIT Press, 1989), p. 106.
10. Jürgen Habermas, *Moral Consciousness and Communicative Action*, trans. Christian Lenhardt and Shierry Weber Nicholsen (Cambridge, Mass.: MIT Press, 1993), p. 89.
11. Barbara Hernstein Smith, *The Contingencies of Value: Alternative Perspectives for Critical Theory* (Cambridge, Mass.: Harvard University Press, 1988), p. 110.
12. Robert Pippin, "Kant's *Rechtslehre*," *The Philosophy of Immanuel Kant*, ed. Rich Kennington (Washington, D.C.: Catholic University Press, 1985), p. 111.
13. Plato, *Republic*, trans. Benjamin Jowett (New York: Random House, 1991), bk. 6.
14. Karl Popper, *The Open Society and its Enemies*, vol. 1 (Princeton, N.J.: Princeton University Press, 1953), p. 162.
15. Aristotle, *Rhetoric*, trans. W. Rhys Roberts, in *The Complete Works of Aristotle*, vol. 2, ed. Jonathan Barnes (Princeton, N.J.: Princeton University Press, 1984), p. 2187.
16. Empedocles, Fragments 136, 137, *Early Greek Philosophy*, ed. John Burnet (London: Macmillan, 1930), pp. 225–226.
17. *Ibid.*, Fragment 109, Burnet, p. 221.
18. Popper, *The Open Society and its Enemies*, pp. 94–96.
19. Aristotle, *Politics*, trans. Benjamin Jowett, in *The Complete Works of Aristotle*, pp. 2039–2040.
20. *Ibid.*, p. 2040.
21. Augustine of Hippo, *On The Trinity*, *Basic Writings of Saint Augustine*, vol. 2, trans. Marcus Dods (New York: Random House, 1948), p. 675.
22. Augustine of Hippo, *The City of God*, trans. Marcus Dods (New York: Random House, 1950), bk. 19, sec. 13–14, pp. 690–693.

23. Georg Wilhlem Friedrich Hegel, *Hegel: The Letters*, trans. Clark Butler and Christiane Seiler (Bloomington: Indiana, 1984), p. 35 (letter no. 11).

24. Joseph-Marie de Maistre, *Considérations sur la France*, ed. Jean-Louis Darcel (Geneva: Skarkine, 1980).

25. Auguste Comte, *System of Positive Polity*, vol. 1, trans. John Henry Bridges (New York: Burt Franklin, 1877), p. 48.

26. *Ibid.* pp. 289–290.

27. Jürgen Habermas, *Justification and Application*, trans. Ciaran Cronin (Cambridge, Mass.: MIT Press, 1993), p. 54.

28. Jeremy Bentham, "Anarchical Fallacies," *Human Rights*, ed. Abraham Irving Melden (Belmont, Calif.: Wadsworth 1970), p. 32.

29. *Ibid.*

30. *Ibid.*

31. Jürgen Habermas, *The Philosophical Discourse of Modernity*, trans. Frederick Lawrence (Cambridge, Mass.: MIT Press, 1987), pp. 84–85.

32. Martin Heidegger, *Nietzsche I & II* (Pfullingen, Germany: G. Neske, 1961).

33. Nietzsche, *Genealogy of Morals*, First Essay, sec. 7, pp. 643–644.

34. Confucius, *The Analects*, trans. William Edward Soothill (New York: Dover, 1995), bk. 15, chap. 38.

35. *Ibid.*, bk. 1, chap. 2.

36. *Ibid.*, bk. 12, chap. 1.

37. *Ibid.*, bk. 14, chap. 29.

38. Peter Woo, "A Metaphysical Approach to Human Rights from a Chinese Point of View," *The Philosophy of Human Rights: International Perspectives*, ed. Alan Rosenbaum (Westport, Conn.: Greenwood, 1981), p. 119.

39. Theodore de Bary, "Neo-Confucianism and Human Rights," *Human Rights and World Religions*, ed. Leroy Rouner (Notre Dame, Ind.: University of Notre Dame Press, 1988), pp. 183–184.

40. Confucius, *The Analects*, bk. 12, chap. 13, p. 70.

41. *Ibid.*, bk. 15, chap. 14, p. 94.

42. *Ibid.*, bk. 14, chap. 27, p. 86.

43. *Ibid.*, bk. 16, chap. 2, p. 100.

44. *Ibid.*, bk. 15, chap. 35, p. 35.

45. *Ibid.*, bk. 15, chap. 35, p. 96.

46. Henry Rosemont, Jr., "Why Take Human Rights Seriously: A Confucian Critique," *Human Rights and the World's Religions* (Notre Dame, Ind.: University of Notre Dame Press, 1988), pp. 177–178.

47. Roger Ames, "Rites as Rights," *Human Rights and World Religions*, pp. 212–213.

48. Donald Holzmann, *La Chine et les droits de l'homme* (Paris: Harmatten, 1991), pp. 35–36.

49. Edward Allen Kent, "Taking Human, Rights Seriously," *Rationality in Thought and Action*, eds. Martin Tamny and K. D. Irani (New York: Greenwood Press, 1986), p. 36.

Chapter Two

1. Mahatma Gandhi, *All Men Are Brothers*, ed. Krhisna Kripalani (New York: Columbia University Press, 1959), p. 59.

2. *Ibid.*, pp. 139–140.

3. Micheline Ishay and David Goldfischer, "Human Rights and National Security: A False Dichotomy," *The Human Rights Reader: Major Political Writings, Essays, Speeches, and Documents from the Bible to the Present*, ed. Micheline Ishay (New York: Routledge, 1997), pp. 377–402.

4. Gregory Vlastos, "Justice and Equality," *The Philosophy of Human Rights: International Perspectives*, ed. Mortimer Emanuel Winston (Belmont, Calif.: Wadsworth, 1989), pp. 80–81.

5. Sophocles, *Antigone*, trans. Kelly Sherry, *Sophocles 2*, eds. David R. Slavitt and Palmer Bovie, (Philadelphia: University of Pennsylvania Press, 1999), 194–196.

6. A. S. McGrade, "Aristotle's Place in the History of Natural Rights," *Review of Metaphysics*, 49:5 (June 1996), pp. 816–823.

7. Richard Taylor, *Metaphysics* (Englewood Cliffs, N.J.: Prentice Hall, 1983), pp. 48–49.

8. Helsinki Accords, 1975, Principle 7.

9. United Nations Declaration on the Right to Peace, 1986, art. 8, par. 2.

10. Jürgen Habermas, "*Wahrheitstheorien*," *Wirklichkeit und Reflexion: Festschrift für Walter Schulz* (Pfullingen, Germany: Neske, 1973), pp. 215–220.

11. Thomas Hobbes, *Leviathan*, ed. Michael Oakeshott (Oxford: Basil Blackwell, 1960), chap. 14, p. 84.

12. Richard Rorty, "Human Rights, Rationality, and Sentimentality," *On Human Rights*, eds. Steven Shute and Susan Hurley (New York: Basic Books, 1993), pp. 116, 120.

13. Richard Rorty, *Philosophy and the Mirror of Nature* (Princeton, N.J.: Princeton University Press, 1979), pp. 170–171, 377–378, 389–394.

14. Charles Sanders Peirce, "The Fixation of Belief," *Collected Papers*, eds. Charles Hartshorne and Paul Weiss (Cambridge, Mass.: Harvard University Press, 1931–1958), vol. 3, p. 254.

15. Charles Sanders Peirce, "How to Make our Ideas Clear," *Collected Papers*, vol. 3, p. 273.

16. Rorty, "Human Rights, Rationality, and Sentimentality," p. 119.

Chapter Three

1. Douglas Birsch, *Ethical Insight* (Mountain View, Calif.: Mayfield, 1999) pp. 76–77.

2. Myles F. Burnyeat, "Did Ancient Greeks Have the Concept of Human Rights," *Polis*, 13:1–2 (1994), p. 6; and Ronald Dworkin, *Taking Rights Seriously* (Cambridge, Mass.: Harvard University Press, 1977), p. 171.

3. Burnyeat, "Did Ancient Greeks Have the Concept of Human Rights," pp. 3–4.

4. John Burnet, *Early Greek Philosophy*, 4th ed. (London: Macmillan, 1930), p. 225.

5. Declaration of Rights of Man and the Citizen, 1793, Article 1.

6. Compare the August 19, 1789 draft of the Declaration to the one of August 26.

7. Laurence Blum, "Antiracism, Multiculturalism, and Interracial Community: Three Educational, Values for a Multicultural Society," *Applied Ethics: A Multicultural Approach* (Upper Saddle River, N.J.: Prentice-Hall, 1998), p. 21.

8. Alasdair MacIntyre, *After Virtue* (Notre Dame, Ind.: University of Notre Dame Press, 1981), p. 67.

9. Karl Popper, *The Open Society and its Enemies* (Princeton, N.J.: Princeton University Press, 1966), vol. 1, p. 95.

10. Jacques Maritain, "Natural Law," *The Social and Political Philosophy of Jacques Maritain* (New York: Doubleday, 1965), p. 41.

11. Attributed to Hippias in Plato, *Protagoras, The Dialogues of Plato*, trans. Benjamin Jowett (Oxford: Oxford University Press, 1953), pp. 163–164.

12. Popper, *The Open Society and its Enemies*, vol. 1, p. 171.

13. *Ibid.*, vol. 1, p. 96.

14. John Burnet, *Early Greek Philosophy*, p. 200.

15. Jacques Maritain, "Natural Law," p. 41.

16. Cicero, *The Laws, De Re Publica, De Legibus*, trans. Clinton Walker Keyes (Cambridge, Mass.: Harvard University Press, 1961), pp. 343, 345.

17. Marcus Aurelius, *Meditations*, trans. George Long, in *The Stoic and Epicurean Philosophers*, ed. Whitney Oates (New York: Random House, 1940), p. 548.

18. Cicero, *De Officiis (On Duties)*, trans. Harry G. Edinger (Indianapolis, Ind.: Bobbs-Merrill, 1974), p. 26.

19. *Ibid.*

20. William K. Frankena, *Ethics* (Englewood Cliffs, N.J.: Prentice Hall, 1973), pp. 46–47.

21. John Locke, *Second Treatise on Government* (Amherst, N.Y.: Prometheus, 1986), chap. 6.

22. *Ibid.*

23. *Ibid.*, chap. 4.

24. *Ibid.*, chap. 6.

25. Jack Donnelly, *Universal Human Rights in Theory and Practice* (Ithaca, N.Y.: Cornell University Press, 1989), p. 94.

26. Locke, *Second Treatise on Government*, chap. 6.

27. *Ibid.*, chap. 11.

28. St. Thomas Aquinas, *Summa Theologica*, Dominican Translation. (New York: Benizer Brothers, 1947), vol. 2, p. 1477.

29. *Ibid.*, vol. 1, p. 1017.

30. *Ibid.*, vol. 2, p. 1467.

31. *Ibid.*, vol. 1, p. 1002.

32. *Ibid.*, vol. 2, pp. 1359–1360.

33. Thomas Hobbes, *Leviathan*, ed. Michael Oakeshott (Oxford: Basil Blackwell, 1960), pt. 2, chap. 14, pp. 84–90.

34. *Ibid.*, chap. 17, p. 109.

35. *Ibid.*, chap. 14, p. 84.

36. *Ibid.*

37. *Ibid.*, chap. 17, p. 109.

38. Hugo Grotius, *The Law of War and Peace*, trans. Francis W. Kelsey (Indianapolis, Ind.: Bobbs-Merrill, 1962), p. 13.
39. *Ibid.*, p. 38.
40. *Ibid.*, pp. 13, 42.
41. *Ibid.*, p. 13.

Chapter Four

1. Thucydides, *The Peloponnesian War*, trans. Rex Warner (New York: Penguin, 1954), bk. 2, p. 147.
2. Herodotus, *The Histories*, trans. Aubrey de Sélincourt (New York: Penguin, 1954), pp. 238.
3. *Ibid.*, p. 369.
4. *Ibid.*, pp. 574–75.
5. *Ibid.*, p. 239.
6. Democritus, quoted in Karl Popper, *The Open Society and its Enemies*, vol. 1 (Princeton, N.J.: Princeton University Press, 1963), pp. 185–186.
7. Popper, *The Open Society and its Enemies*, vol. 1, p. 185.
8. Robert Brumbaugh, *The Philosophers of Greece* (New York: Crowell, 1964), p. 78.
9. Popper, *The Open Society and its Enemies*, vol. 1, p. 185.
10. *Ibid.*, bk. 1, chap. 1.
11. *Ibid.*, bk. 2, chap. 3; bk. 4, chap. 1.
12. Immanuel Kant, *Über den Gemeinspruch: Das mag in der Theorie richtig sein, taugt aber nicht für die Praxis* (1793), *Über den Gemeinspruch: Das mag in der Theorie richtig sein, taugt aber nicht für die Praxis; Zum ewigen Frieden, ein philosophischer Entwurf*, ed. H. Klemme (Hamburg, Germany: Felix Meiner Verlag, 1992), p. 24.
13. Immanuel Kant, "What Is Enlightenment?" *On History*, trans. Lewis White Beck (Indianapolis, Ind.: Bobbs-Merrill, 1963), p. 7.
14. Immanuel Kant, *Groundwork of the Metaphysics of Morals*, trans. H. J. Paton (London: Hutchinson, 1972) pt. 1, sec. 2.,, pt. 1, sec. 2.
15. *Ibid.*, "Introduction."
16. *Ibid.*
17. Kant, "What Is Enlightenment?" pp. 3–10.
18. Immanuel Kant, *Critique of the Faculties*, trans. Mary Gregor (New York: Abaris Books, 1979), p. 153.
19. *Ibid.*, p. 159.
20. Immanuel Kant, *Perpetual Peace, On History*, trans. Lewis White Beck (Indianapolis, Ind.: Bobbs-Merrill, 1963), p. 111.
21. *Ibid.*, p. 95.
22. *Ibid.*, p. 94.
23. *Ibid.*, p. 98.
24. Georg Wilhelm Friedrich Hegel, *Philosophy of Right*, trans. T. M. Knox (Oxford: Oxford University Press, 1951), §36.
25. Johann Gottlieb Fichte, *Grundlage des Naturrechts* (1796) *Fichtes Werke*, ed. I. H. Fichte (Berlin: Walter de Gruyter, 1971), vol. 3, p. 8.

26. Hegel, *Philosophy of Right*, §36.

27. *Ibid.*, §44.

28. *Ibid.*, §48, §57.

29. Georg Wilhelm Friedrich Hegel, *Phenomenology of Spirit*, trans. A. V. Miller (Oxford: Oxford University Press, 1977), p. 43.

30. Georg Wilhelm Friedrich Hegel, *Lectures on the History of Philosophy*, trans. Elizabeth. S. Haldane (Lincoln: University of Nebraska Press, 1995), vol. 1, "Introduction," p. xiii.

31. Georg Wilhelm Friedrich Hegel, *Lectures on the Philosophy of Religion*, trans. E. B. Speirs and J. Burden Sanderson (London: Routledge, 1895), vol. 3, p. 56; and *Philosophy of Mind*, trans. William Wallace (Oxford: Oxford University Press, 1971), §564.

32. Georg Wilhelm Friedrich Hegel, *Science of Logic*, trans. A. V. Miller (Oxford: Oxford University Press, 1969), p. 824.

33. Hegel, *Phenomenology of Spirit*, p. 43.

34. Hegel, *Philosophy of Right*, §270, §316–319, §317 Addition.

35. Universal Declaration of the Rights of Man and the Citizen, 1789, Articles 2, 4, 10; Georg Wilhelm Friedrich Hegel, *The Letters*, trans. Clark Butler and Christiane Seiler (Bloomington: Indiana University Press, 1984), p. 35, (Hoffmeister letter no. 11).

36. Hegel to Creuzer, 30 October 1819, *Ibid.*, p. 451 (Hoffmeister letter no. 359).

37. Hegel, *Philosophy of Right*, §34–40.

38. *Ibid.*, §44, §45–51.

39. *Ibid.*, §148–150, §155.

40. Georg Wilhelm Friedrich Hegel, *Philosophy of History*, trans. J. Sibree (New York: Dover, 1956), p. 279.

41. Hegel, *Philosophy of Right*, §36.

42. *Ibid.*, §104.

43. *Ibid.*, §241–242.

44. Hegel, *Phenomenology of Spirit*, pp. 355–63.

45. Hegel, *Philosophy of History*, p. 447.

46. Hegel, *Philosophy of Right*, §43.

47. *Ibid.*, §40.

48. *Ibid.*, §51.

49. Hegel, *Phenomenology of Spirit*, p. 121.

50. Hegel, *Philosophy of Right*, §44.

51. *Ibid.*, §258.

52. *Ibid.*, §261.

53. Jean-Jacques Rousseau, *The Social Contract*, trans. Wilmoore Kendall (Chicago, Ill.: Henry Regnery), 1954, bk. 1, chap. 7, p. 25.

54. Hegel, *Philosophy of Right*, §100.

55. *Ibid.*, §51.

56. Hegel, *Phenomenology of Spirit*, p. 43.

57. John Rawls, "Kantian Constructivism in Moral Theory," *Journal of Philosophy*, 77:9 (September 1980), p. 519.

58. John Rawls, "Justice as Fairness: Political, not Metaphysical," *Philosophy and Public Affairs*, 14:3 (July 1985), p. 287.

59.John Rawls, "The Law of Peoples," *On Human Rights*, eds. Steven Shute and Susan Hurley (New York: Basic Books, 1993), pp. 42–82.

60. *Ibid.*, pp. 2–63.

61. *Ibid.*, p. 63.

62. Alan Gewirth, *Human Rights: Essays on Justification and Applications* (Chicago, Ill.: University of Chicago Press, 1982), p. 20.*Ibid.*, p. 19.

63. Jürgen Habermas, *Moral Consciousness and Communicative Action*, trans. Christian Lenhardt and Shierry Weber Nicholson (Cambridge, Mass.: MIT Press, 1990), p. 198.

64. Jürgen Habermas, *Justification and Applications: Remarks on Discourse Ethics*, trans. Cianan P. Cronin (Cambridge, Mass: MIT Press, 1993), p. 56.

65. *Ibid.*, p. 50.

66. Jürgen Habermas, *Moral Consciousness and Communicative Action*, trans. Christian Lenhardt and Shierry Weber Nicholson (Cambridge, Mass.: MIT Press, 1990), p. 197.

67. *Ibid.*, p. 65.

68. Jürgen Habermas, *Erlaüterungen zur Diskursethik* (Frankfurt: Suhrkamp, 1990), p. 25.

69. Habermas, *Moral Consciousness and Communicative Action*, p. 198.

Chapter Five

1. Myles F. Burnyeat, "Did the Ancients Have a Concept of Human Rights," *Polis*, 13:1–2 (1994), pp. 1–11.

2. Jürgen Habermas, *The Structural Transformation of the Public Sphere: An Inquiry into a Category of Bourgeois Society*, trans. Thomas Burger with Frederick Lawrence (Cambridge, Mass.: MIT Press, 1989), p. 106.

3. Robert Pippin, "Kant's *Rechtslehre*," *The Philosophy of Immanuel Kant*, ed. Richard Kennington (Washington, D.C.: Catholic University Press, 1985), p. 111.

4. John Hospers, *Human Conduct* (New York: Harcourt Brace, 1996), p. 192.

5. Jürgen Habermas, *Justification and Application: Remarks and Discourse Ethics*, trans. Ciaran Cronin (Cambridge, Mass.: MIT Press, 1993), p. 209.

6. *Ibid.*, p. 31.

7. Jürgen Habermas, *Moral Consciousness and Communicative Action*, trans. Christian Lenhardt and Shierry Weber Nicholson (Cambridge, Mass.: MIT Press, 1990), vol. 1, p. 205.

8. Jürgen Habermas, "Kant's Idea of Perpetual Peace with the Benefit of Two Hundred Years of Hindsight," *Perpetual Peace*, eds. James Bohman and Mathias Lutz-Bachmann (Cambridge, Mass.: MIT, 1997), p. 137.

9. Maximilien Robespierre, "*Discours sur les principes de la morale politique qui doivent guider la Convention nationale dans l'administration intérieure de la Republique*," The French National Convention, Session of February 4, 1794.

10. Habermas, "Kant's Idea of Perpetual Peace," p. 140.

11. *Ibid.*, p. 137.

12. *Ibid.*, p. 140.

13. *Ibid.*

14. Georg Wilhelm Friedrich Hegel, *The Phenomenology of Spirit*, trans. A. V. Miller (Oxford: Oxford, 1971), pp. 329–330.

15. *Ibid.*

16. Clark Butler, "Review of *The Philosophy of Human Rights*, ed. Alan S Rosenbaum," *Journal of Social Philosophy*, 18:2 (January 1983), pp. 58–62.

17. Habermas, *Moral Consciousness and Communicative Action*, pp. 6–97.

18. *Ibid.*, p. 97.

19. *Ibid.*, p. 65.

20. *Ibid.*, pp. 52, 57–62, 77.

21. Robert Pippin, "Hegel, Modernity, and Habermas," *The Monist*, 74:3 (1991), pp. 329–357.

22. Jürgen Habermas, *Theory of Communicative Action*, trans. Thomas McCarthy (Boston: Beacon, 1987), vol. 1, pp. 298–318.

23. John L. Austin, *How to Do Things with Words* (London: Oxford University Press, 1962), pp. 9–10.

24. Habermas, *Theory of Communicative Action*, p. 309.

25. *Ibid.*, p. 318.

26. *Ibid.*, p. 298.

27. Habermas, *Moral Consciousness and Communicative Action*, pp. 96–97.

28. Karl Otto Apel, *Towards a Transformation in Philosophy*, trans. Glyn Adey and David Frisby (Milwaukee, Wis.: Marquette University Press, 1998), pp. 225.

29. Habermas, *Moral Consciousness and Communicative Action*, p. 97.

30. Pippin, "Kant's *Rechtslehre*," p. 111.

31. Robert Pippin, "Hegel, Modernity, and Habermas," p. 345

32. *Ibid.*

33. Charles Sanders Peirce, "How to Make Our Ideas Clear," *Collected Papers of Charles Sanders Peirce*, eds. Charles Hartshorne, Paul Weiss, and Arthur W. Burks (Cambridge, Mass.: Harvard University Press, 1933), vol. 3, p. 273.

34. *Ibid.*, vol. 8, p. 12.

35. Richard Rorty, *Philosophy and the Mirror of Nature* (Princeton: N.J.: Princeton University Press, 1979), pp. 315–322.

36. Humphey Hawksley, "Ghana's Trapped Slaves," The BBC, 8 February 2001.

37. Douglas Birsch, *Ethical Insight* (Mountain View, Calif.: Mayfield, 1999), pp. 75–77.

38. Habermas, *Justification and Application*, p. 97.

39. Chaïm Perelman, "Can the Rights of Man be Founded?" *The Philosophy of Human Rights: International Perspectives*, ed. Alan S. Rosenbaum (Westport, Conn.: Greenwood Press, 1981), p. 50.

40. Edward Allen Kent, "Taking Human Rights Seriously," *Rationality in Thought and Action*, eds. Martin Tamny and K. D. Irani (New York: Greenwood Press, 1986), p. 36.

41. Chaïm Perelman, in "Can the Rights of Man be Founded?" p. 50.

42. Jean-François Lyotard, "The Other's Rights," *On Human Rights*, eds. Steven Shute and Susan Hurley (New York: Basic, 1993), pp. 140–141.

43. Barbara Hernstein Smith, *The Contingencies of Value: Alternative Perspectives for Critical Theory* (Cambridge, Mass.: Harvard University, 1988), p. 110.

Chapter Six

1. Clark Butler, "History as the Story of Freedom," *Theoretische Geschiedenis* 16:3 (1989), pp. 297–309.

2. Karl Popper, *The Open Society and its Enemies* (Princeton, N.J.: Princeton University Press, 1953), vol. 1, chap. 1.

3. *Ibid.*, vol. 2, p. 270.

4. Jean-François Lyotard, *The Post-Modern Condition*, trans. Geoff Bennington and Brian Massumi (Minneapolis: University of Minnesota Press, 1984).

5. Popper, *The Open Society and its Enemies*, vol. 2, p. 278.

6. *Ibid.*, vol. 1, p. 173.

7. Jürgen Habermas, *Justification and Application: Remarks and Discourse Ethics*, trans. Ciaran Cronin (Cambridge, Mass.: MIT Press, 1993), p. 85.

8. Popper, *The Open Society and its Enemies*, vol. 1, pp. 202–203.

9. Henri Bergson, *The Two Sources of Morality and Religion*, trans. Audra Ashley and Cloudesley Shovell Brereton (Garden City, N.Y.: Doubleday, 1935), p. 268.

10. Alan Sandstrom, "Prehistory and Paradise Lost in Empirical Anthropology," *History as the Story of Freedom*, ed. Clark Butler (Amsterdam: Rodopi, 1997), p. 208.

11. John R. Searle, "How to Derive 'Ought' from 'Is,'" *The "Is/Ought" Question*, ed. H. D. Hudson (London: Macmillan, 1969), pp. 120–134.

12. Popper, *The Open Society and its Enemies*, vol. 2, pp. 228–33.

13. *Ibid.*, vol. 2, p. 225.

14. *Ibid.*, vol. 1, p. 185.

15. Alan Sandstrom, pp. 206–207.

Chapter Seven

1. Richard Rorty, "Human Rights, Rationality, and Sentimentality," *On Human Rights*, eds. Steven Shute and Susan Hurley (New York: Basic Books, 1993), 111–134.

2. A. J. M. Milne, *Human Rights and Human Diversity* (Albany: State University of New York Press, 1986).

3. William Frankena, *Ethics* (Englewood Cliffs, N.J.: Prentice Hall: 1973), pp. 25–38.

4. Jean-François Lyotard, "The Other's Rights," *On Human Rights*, 135–148.

5. André Mineau, "Human Rights and Nietzsche," *History of European Ideas*, 11 (1989), p. 878.

6. *Ibid.*, pp. 879–881.

7. Georg Wilhelm Friedrich Hegel, "What Means Spirit Uses in Order to Realize its Idea," *Philosophy of History*, trans. J. Sibree (New York: Dover, 1956), pp. 20–37.

8. Clark Butler, *History as the Story of Freedom* (Amsterdam: Rodopi, 1997).

9. Jürgen Habermas, *Justification and Application: Remarks and Discourse Ethics*, trans. Ciaran Cronin (Cambridge, Mass.: MIT Press, 1993), p. 197.

10. *Ibid.*, p. 208.

11. Robert Pippin, "Hegel, Modernity, and Habermas," *The Monist*, 74:3 (1991), pp. 345–346.

12. Lawrence Kohlberg, "Moral Stages and Moralization," *Moral Development and Behavior*, ed. Thomas Likona (New York: Holt, Rinehart, and Winston, 1976), pp. 31–53.

13. Georg Wilhelm Friedrich Hegel, *The Phenomenology of Spirit*, trans. A. V. Miller (Oxford: Oxford University Press, 1971), pp. 16–17.

14. Pippin, "Hegel, Modernity, and Habermas," pp. 343–350.

15. Hegel, *Philosophy of History*, p. 447.

16. Hegel, *Phenomenology of Spirit*, pp. 356–357.

17. Georg Wilhelm Friedrich Hegel, *The Science of Logic*, trans. A. V. Miller (Atlantic Highlands, N.J.: Humanities, 1969), p. 824.

18. Hegel, *The Phenomenology of Spirit*, p. 359.

19. *Ibid.*, p. 357.

20. *Ibid.*, p. 359.

21. *Ibid.*, p. 361.

22. Pippin, "Hegel, Modernity, and Habermas," pp. 345–346.

23. Clark Butler, "Hermeneutic Hegelianism," *Idealistic Studies*, 14:2 (1985), pp. 128–129.

24. Hegel, *The Phenomenology of Spirit*, p. 109.

Chapter Eight

1. Alasdair MacIntyre, *After Virtue* (Notre Dame: Notre Dame, 1981), pp. 67–68.

2. Michael Freeman, "The Philosophical Foundations of Human Rights," *Human Rights Quarterly*, 16 (1994), pp. 491–514.

3. Jan Gorecki, *Justifying Ethics* (New Brunswick, Canada: Transaction Publishers, 1996), p. 134.

4. Immanuel Kant, *Groundwork of the Metaphysics of Morals* (1785), trans. H. J. Paton (London: Hutchinson, 1972), sec. 2.

5. *Ibid.*

6. *Ibid.*

7. Jürgen Habermas, *Erlaüterungen zur Diskursethik* (Frankfurt: Suhrkamp, 1990), p. 198.

8. W. David Ross, *The Right and the Good* (Oxford: Oxford University Press, 1930).

9. William N. Nelson, "Human Rights and Human Obligations," *Human Rights*, ed. J. Roland Pennock (New York: New York University Press, 1981), p. 286.

10. Hugo Adam Bedau, "Review of Judith Jarvis Thomson's *The Realm of Rights*," *Human Rights Quarterly*, 14 (1992), p. 540.

11. Ronald Dworkin, *Taking Rights Seriously* (Cambridge, Mass.: Harvard University Press, 1977), p. 364.

12. Judith Jarvis Thomson, *The Realm of Rights* (Cambridge, Mass.: Harvard University Press, 1990), p. 165.

13. *Ibid.*, p. 154.

14. *Ibid.*, p. 152.

15. Georg Wilhelm Friedrich Hegel, *The Phenomenology of Spirit*, trans. A. V. Miller (Oxford: Oxford University Press, 1971), p. 122.

16. William Frankena, *Ethics* (Englewood Cliffs, N.J.: Prentice Hall: 1973), pp. 43–45.

17. James W. Nickel, "Are Human Rights Utopian," *Philosophy of Public Affairs*, 11 (1982), p. 252.

18. Jürgen Habermas, *Justification and Application*, trans. Ciaran Cronin (Cambridge, Mass.: MIT Press, 1993), p. 31.

19. Jürgen Habermas, *Erlaüterungen zur Diskursethik* (Frankfurt: Suhrkamp, 1990), p. 204.

20. *Ibid.*, pp. 94–95.

21. *Ibid.*, p. 209.

22. Jürgen Habermas, "*Wahrheitstheorien*," *Wirklichheit und Reflexion: Festschrift für Walter Schulz* (Pfullingen, Germany: Neske, 1973), p. 219.

23. Douglas Birsch, "The Moral Rights Theory," *Ethical Insights* (Mountain View, Calif.: Mayfield, 1999), p. 65.

24. Steven Lukes, "Five Fables about Human Rights," *On Human Rights*, eds. Steven Shute and Susan Surley (New York: Basic Books, 1993), p. 39.

25. Douglas Husak, "Why There Are No Human Rights," *The Philosophy of Human Rights*, ed. Morton E. Winston (Belmont, Calif.: Wadsworth, 1989), pp. 234–246.

26. Georg Wilhelm Friedrich Hegel, *The Science of Logic*, trans. A. V. Miller (Atlantic Highlands, N.J.: Humanities Press, 1969), p. 824.

27. Alan Gewirth, "Why There Are Human Rights," *The Philosophy of Human Rights*, p. 255.

28. Sören Kierkegaard, "Balance between the Aesthetic and the Ethical in the Development of the Personality" *Either/Or*, trans. Howard V. Hong and Edna H. Hong (Princeton, N.J.: Princeton University Press, 1988), pt. 2, pp. 155–333.

Chapter Nine

1. Georg Wilhelm Friedrich Hegel, *The Phenomenology of Spirit*, trans. A. V. Miller (Oxford: Oxford University Press, 1971), pp. 54–55.

2. William Frankena, *Ethics* (Englewood Cliffs, N.J.: Prentice Hall: 1973), p. 109.

3. Gilbert Harman, "Moral Relativism as a Foundation for Natural Rights," *Journal of Libertarian Studies*, 4 (1980), pp. 367–371.

4. Hegel, *Phenomenology of Spirit*, pp. 217–221.

5. *Ibid.*, pp. 217–221.

6. Jürgen Habermas, *Theory of Communicative Action*, vol. 1–2, trans. Thomas McCarthy (Boston: Beacon, 1984, 1987), p. 298.

7. Robert Pippin, "Hegel, Modernity, and Habermas," *The Monist*, 74:3 (1991), p. 348.

8. Jürgen Habermas, *Erlaüterungen zur Diskursethik* (Frankfurt, Germany: Suhrkamp, 1991), p. 209.

9. *Ibid.*, p. 211.

10. Vienna Declaration and Programme of Action, adopted at the World Conference on Human Rights, 5 June 1993, *The United Nations and Human Rights: 1945–1995* (New York: United Nations Department of Public Information, 1995), p. 462.

Chapter Ten

1. Hugo Adam Bedau, "Capital Punishment Is Irreversible," *The Case against the Death Penalty*, New York: American Civil Liberties Union, 1973.

2. Alan Gibbard, "Utilitarianism and Human Rights," *Social Policy and Policy*, 1–2 (1984), pp. 92–102.

3. Richard Palmer and Kenneth Lucey, "Misguided Criticism of Utilitarianism," *Teaching Philosophy*, 15:1 (1992), pp. 57–70.

4. Edward Allen Kent, "Taking Human Rights Seriously," *Rationality in Thought and Action*, eds. Martin Tamny and K. D. Irani (New York: Greenwood Press, 1986), p. 34.

5. James Rachels, *The Elements of Moral Philosophy*, 3rd ed. (Boston: McGraw-Hill College, 1999), p. 118.

6. Confucius, *The Analects*, trans. William E. Soothill (New York: Dover, 1995), bk. 16, chap. 2, p. 100.

7. Ronald Dworkin, *Taking Rights Seriously* (Cambridge, Mass.: Harvard University Press, 1977), xi–xiii.

8. R. G. Frey, "On Human Rights," *History as the Story of Freedom*, ed. Clark Butler (Amsterdam: Rodopi, 1997), pp. 37–40.

9. Associate Justice, Sandra Day O'Connor, Majority Opinion, *Grutter vs. Bollinger*, 23 June 2003.

Chapter Eleven

1. Georg Wilhelm Friedrich Hegel, *Philosophy of Right*, trans. T. M. Knox (Oxford: Oxford University Press, 1952), §44.

2. John Locke, "Of the Beginning of Political Societies," *Second Treatise on Government* (Amherst, N.Y.: Prometheus, 1986), chap. 8.

3. Kenneth Minogue, "The History of the Idea of Human Rights," *Human Rights Reader*, eds. Walter Lacqueur and Barry Rubin (New York: New American Library, 1989), p. 14.

4. John Hospers, *Human Conduct* (New York: Harcourt and Brace, 1996), pp. 221–222, quote taken from a dialogue.

5. Douglas Birsch, *Ethical Insights* (Mountain View, Calif.: Mayfield, 1999), chap. 1.

6. Johann Gottlieb Fichte, *Fichtes Werke*, ed. I. H. Fichte (Berlin: Walter de Gruyter, 1971, vol. 3, p. 8. (Foundations of Natural Right, Part 1, 1796).

Chapter Twelve

1. Dennis Driscoll, "The Development of Human Rights in International Law," *The Human Rights Reader*, eds. Walter Laqueur and Barry Ruben (New York: Penguin, 1990), p. 43.

2. See. Patricia Werhane, Al Gini, and David Ozar, eds., *Philosophical Issues in Human Rights: Theories and Applications* (New York: Random House, 1986).

3. The Paris Declaration, adopted by The Human Rights Defenders Summit, Palais de Chaillot, Paris, 10 December 1998, Articles 7, 14.

4. John Stuart Mill, "Of the Liberty of Thought and Discussion" *On Liberty*, sec. 2.

5. *Ibid.*

6. *Ibid.*

Chapter Thirteen

1. Universal Declaration of Human Rights, United Nations General Assembly, Resolution 217 A (III), 11 December 1948.

2. Paul Gorden Lauren, *The Evolution of International Human Rights: Visions Seen* (Philadelpfia: University of Pennsylvania Press, 1998), p. 237.

Chapter Fourteen

1. Wendell Wilkie, *One World* (Urbana: University of Illinois Press, 1966).

2. Paul Gorden Lauren, *The Evolution of International Human Rights* (Philadelphia: University of Pennsylvania Press, 1998), pp. 231–232.

3. Bertrand Russell, *Has Man a Future?* (Baltimore, Md.: Penguin, 1961).

4. Richard Falk and Andrew Strauss, *International Herald Tribune*, Paris, 9 April 2002.

5. Jeffrey Whitman, "An End to Sovereignty," *Journal of Social Philosophy*, 24:2 (Fall 1996), pp. 146–157.

6. Earl Harris, "A Constitution for the Federation of Earth," *One World or None* (Atlantic Highlands, N.J.: Humanities Press, 1993), p. 119.

7. Clark Butler, "Peaceful Coexistence as the Nuclear Traumatization of Mankind," *Philosophy and Social Criticism*, 10:3–4 (Winter 1984), pp. 81–94.

8. John Galtung, "Third World and Human Rights: Post-1989," *Human Rights: Fifty Years On*, ed. Tony Evans (Manchester: University of Manchester Press, 1998), p. 227.

9. Arthur Schlesinger, *The Imperial Presidency* (Boston: Houghton Mifflin, 1973).

10. DefenseLINK, U.S. Department of Defense, Reference Number No. 066–96, 7 February 1996.

11. Philip Isley, personal communication, 1994.

12. Donella H. Meadows et al., *The Limits to Growth: A Report on the Club of Rome's Project on the Predicament of Mankind* (New York: Universe Books, 1972).

13. Rio Declaration, 1992, Principle 7.

14. Herbert Kahn, William Morle Brown, and Leon Martel, *The Next 200 Years: A Scenario for America and the World* (New York: William Marrow, 1976), p. 1.

Chapter Fifteen

1. Immanuel Kant, *Groundwork of the Metaphysics of Morals*, trans. H. J. Paton (London: Hutchinson, 1972), sec. 2.

2. Ronald Dworkin, *Taking Rights Seriously* (Cambridge, Mass.: Harvard University Press, 1977).

3. Ernest Lefever, *Ethics and United States Foreign Policy* (New York: Meridian Books, 1957), p. 22.

BIBLIOGRAPHY

Aquinas, St. Thomas. *Summa Theologica*. Dominican Translation. New York: Benziger Brothers, 1947.

Apel, Karl Otto. *Towards a Transformation in Philosophy*. Translated by Glyn Adey and David Frisby. Milwaukee: Marquette University Press, 1998.

Aristotle. *Politics*. In Barnes. *The Complete Works of Aristotle*. Vol. 2.

———. *Rhetorica*. In Barnes. *The Complete Works of Aristotle*. Vol. 2.

Augustine of Hippo. *The City of God*. Translated by Marcus Dods. New York: Random House, 1950.

———. *On The Trinity*. In *Basic Writings of Saint Augustine*. Vol. 2. Translated by M. Dods. New York: Random House, 1950.

Aurelius, Marcus. *Meditations*. In *The Stoic and Epicurean Philosophers*. Edited by Whitney Oates. Translated by George Long. New York: Random House, 1940.

Austin, John L. *How to Do Things with Words*. London: Oxford University Press, 1962.

Barnes, Jonathan, ed. *The Complete Works of Aristotle*. Vol. 2. Translated by W. Rhrys Roberts. Princeton, N.J.: Princeton University Press, 1984

Beck, Lewis White, ed. *On History*. Indianapolis: Bobbs-Merrill, 1963

Bedau, Hugo Adam. "Capital Punishment Is Irreversible." In *The Case against the Death Penalty*. New York: American Civil Liberties Union, 1973.

———. "Review of Judith Jarvis Thomson's *The Realm of Rights*," *Human Rights Quarterly*, 14 (1992), pp. 540–543.

Bentham, Jeremy. "Anarchical Fallacies." In *Human Rights*. Edited by Abraham Irving Melden. Belmont, Calif.: Wadsworth, 1970.

Bergson, Henri. *The Two Sources of Morality and Religion*. Translated by Audra Ashley and Cloudesley Shovell Brereton. Garden City, N.Y.: Doubleday, 1935.

Birsch, Douglas. *Ethical Insights*. Mountain View, Calif.: Mayfield, 1999.

Blum, Laurence. "Antiracism, Multiculturalism, and Interracial Community: Three Educational Values for a Multicultural Society." In *Applied Ethics: A Multicultural Approach*. Upper Saddle River, N.J.: Prentice-Hall, 1998.

Brambaugh, Robert. *The Philosophers of Greece*. New York: Crowell, 1964.

Burnet, John. *Early Greek Philosophy*, 4th ed. London: Macmillan, 1930.

Burnyeat, Myles F. "Did the Ancients Have a Concept of Human Rights?" *Polis*, 13:1–2 (1994), pp. 1–11.

Butler, Clark.

———. "Soft American Empire vs. Playing the U.N.-E.U. Card." In *Guantanamo and the Judicial-Moral Treatment of the Other*. Edited by Clark Butler. (West Lafayette: Purdue University Press, 2007), 1-12.

———. "Hegel and Indirect Proof," *The Monist*, 75: 3 (1991), pp. 422-437.

———. "Human Rights: The Ethics Behind the International Legality," *Philo*, 4:1-2 (2002), pp. 3-22.

———. "Hermeneutic Hegelianism," *Idealistic Studies*, 14:2 (May 1985), pp. 121–135.

———. "History as the Story of Freedom," *Theoretische Geschiedenis* (Netherlands), 16:3 (1989), pp. 297–309.

———. "Jack Donnelly on Human Rights," CLIO, 33:1 (2003), 107-113.

———. "Peaceful Coexistence as the Nuclear Traumatization of Mankind," *Philoso-*

phy and Social Criticism, 10:3–4 (Winter 1984), pp. 81–94.

_____."The Right to Freedom of Thought and its Modalities." In *Human Coexistence and Sustainable Development* (Editions Montmorency: Montreal, 2001). Vol. 2, pp 50-55.

_____. "Review of *The Philosophy of Human Rights*, edited by Alan S. Rosenbaum," *Journal of Social Philosophy*, 18:2 (January 1983), pp. 58–62.

_____. *History as the Story of Freedom*. Amsterdam: Editions Rodopi, 1997.

_____. "The Reducibility of Ethics to Human Rights," *Dialogue and Universalism* (University of Warsaw), 5:7 (1995), pp. 29-41.

_____. "Technological Society and Its Counterculture," *Inquiry,* 18:2 (Spring 1975), pp. 195-212

Cicero, Marcus Tullius. "On the Nature of the Laws." In *On the Nature of the Gods*. Translated by Charles Duke Yonge. London: George Bell, 1907.

_____. *On Duties*. Translated by Miriam Griffin and Margaret Atkins. Cambridge, England: Cambridge University Press, 1991.

Comte, Auguste. *System of Positive Polity*. Translated by John Henry Bridges. New York: Burt Franklin, 1877.

Confucius. *The Analects*. Translated by William E. Soothill. New York: Dover, 1995.

De Maistre, Joseph-Marie. *Considérations sur la France*. Edited by Jean-Louis Darcel. Geneva: Skarkine, 1980.

Donnelly, Jack. *Universal Human Rights in Theory and Practice*. Ithaca, N.Y.: Cornell University Press, 1989.

Driscoll, Dennis. "The Development of Human Rights in International Law." In Laqueur and Ruben. *The Human Rights Reader*.

Dworkin, Ronald. *Taking Rights Seriously*. Cambridge, Mass.: Harvard University Press, 1977.

Fichte, Johann Gottlieb. *Grundlage des Naturrechts* (1796). In *Fichtes Werke*. Vol. 3. Edited by I. H. Fichte. Berlin: Walter de Gruyter, 1971.

Frankena, William. *Ethics*. Englewood Cliffs, N.J.: Prentice Hall, 1973.

Freeman, Michael. "The Philosophical Foundations of Human Rights," *Human Rights Quarterly*, 16 (1994), pp. 491–514.

Galtung, John. "Third World and Human Rights: Post-1989." In *Human Rights: Fifty Years On*. Edited by Tony Evans. Manchester: University of Manchester Press, 1998.

Gandhi, Mahatma. *All Men Are Brothers*. Edited by Krhisna Kripalani. New York: Columbia University Press, 1959.

Gibbard, Alan. "Utilitarianism and Human Rights," *Social Policy and Policy*, 1:2 (1984), pp. 92–102.

Gewirth, Alan. *Human Rights: Essays on Justification and Applications*. Chicago: University of Chicago Press, 1982.

Gorecki, Jan. *Justifying Ethics*. New Brunswick, Canada: Transaction Publishers, 1996.

Grotius, Hugo. *The Law of War and Peace*. Translated by Francis W. Kelsey with A. E. R. Boak, et al. Indianapolis, Ind.: Bobbs-Merrill, 1962.

Habermas, Jürgen. *Erlaüterungen zur Diskursethik*. Frankfurt: Suhrkamp, 1991.

_____. *Faktizität und Geltung*. Frankfurt: Suhrkamp, 1992.

_____. *The Inclusion of the Other*. Translated by Ciaran Cronin and Pablo de Greiff. Cambridge, Mass.: MIT Press, 1998.

_____. "Kant's Idea of Perpetual Peace with the Benefit of Two Hundred Years of Hindsight." In *Perpetual Peace*. Edited by James Bohman and Matthias Lutz-

Bachmann. Cambridge, Mass.: MIT Press, 1997.

————. *Justification and Application.* Translated by Ciaran Cronin. Cambridge, Mass.: MIT Press, 1993.

————. *Moral Consciousness and Communicative Action.* Translated by Christian Lenhardt and Shierry Weber Nicholson. Cambridge. Mass.: MIT Press, 1995.

————. *The Philosophical Discourse of Modernity*, trans. Frederick Lawrence. Cambridge, Mass.: MIT Press, 1987.

————. *Theory of Communicative Action.* Vol. 1–2. Translated by Thomas McCarthy. Boston: Beacon, 1984, 1987.

————. "*Wahrheitstheorien.*" In *Wirklichkeit und Reflexion: Festschrift für Walter Schulz.* Edited by Helmut Fahrenbach. Pfullingen, Germany: G. Neske: 1973.

————. *The Structural Transformation of the Public Sphere: An Inquiry into a Category of Bourgeois Society.* Translated by Thomas Burger with Frederick Lawrence. Cambridge, Mass.: MIT, Press, 1989.

Harmon, Gilbert. "Moral Relativism as a Foundation for Natural Rights," *Journal of Libertarian Studies,* 4 (1980), pp. 367–371.

Harris, Errol. *One World or None.* Atlantic Highlands, N.J.: Humanities Press, 1993.

Harris, Errol, and James Yunker, eds. *Toward Genuine Global Governance.* Westport, Conn.: Praeger, 1999.

Hegel, Georg Wilhelm Friedrich. *The Encyclopaedia Logic*: Part I of the *Encyclopaedia of Philosophical Sciences* (1830). Translated by T. F. Geraets, W. A. Suchting and H. S. Harris. Indianapolis: Hackett, 1991.

————. *Lectures on the History of Philosophy.* Translated by E. S. Haldane. Lincoln: University of Nebraska Press, 1995.

————. *The Letters.* Translated by Clark Butler and Christiane Seiler. Bloomington: Indiana University Press, 1984.

————. *The Phenomenology of Spirit.* Translated by A. V. Miller. Oxford: Oxford University Press, 1971.

————. *The Philosophy of History.* Translated by J. Sibree. New York: Dover, 1956.

————. *Philosophy of Nature.* Translated by A. V. Miller. Oxford: Oxford University Press, 1970. (*The Encyclopaedia of Philosophical Sciences* (1830). Pt. 2, §§245–376.)

————. *Philosophy of Mind.* Translated by William Wallace. Oxford: Oxford University Press, 1971. (*The Encyclopaedia of Philosophical Sciences* (1830). Pt. 3, §§377–577.)

————. *The Philosophy of Right.* Translated by T. M. Knox. Oxford: Oxford University Press, 1952.

————. *The Science of Logic.* Translated by A. V. Miller. Atlantic Highlands, N.J.: Humanities Press, 1969.

Heidegger, Martin. *Nietzsche I & II.* Pfullingen, Germany: G. Neske, 1961.

Herodotus. *The Histories.* Translated by Aubrey de Sélincourt. New York: Penguin, 1954.

Hobbes, Thomas. *The Leviathan (1651).* Edited by Michael Oakeshott. Oxford: Basil Blackwell, 1960.

Holzmann, Donald. *La Chine et les droits de l'homme.* Paris: Harmatten, 1991.

Hospers, John. *Human Conduct.* New York: Harcourt & Brace, 1996.

Ishay, Micheline and David Goldfischer. "Human Rights and National Security: A False Dichotomy." In *The Human Rights Reader: Major Political Writings, Essays, Speeches, and Documents from the Bible to the Present.* Edited by Micheline Ishay. New York: Routledge, 1997.

Kahn, Herbert, William Morle Brown, and Leon Martel. *The Next 200 Years: A Scenario for America and the World.* New York: William Marrow, 1976.

Kant, Immanuel. *Critique of the Faculties.* Translated by Mary Gregor. New York: Abaris Books, 1979.

———. *Groundwork of the Metaphysics of Morals.* Translated by H. J. Paton. London: Hutchinson, 1972.

———. *Perpetual Peace.* In Beck. *On History.*

———. *Über den Gemeinspruch: das mag in der Theorie richtig sein, taugt aber nicht für die Praxis; Zum ewigen Frieden, ein philosophischer Entwurf (1793).* Edited by H. Klemme. Hamburg, Germany: Felix Meiner Verlag, 1992.

———. "What Is Enlightenment?" In Beck. *On History.*

Kierkegaard, Sören. *Either/Or.* Vols. 1–2. Translated by Howard V. Hong and Edna H. Hong. Princeton: Princeton University Press, 1988.

Kohlberg, Lawrence. "Moral Stages and Moralization." In *Moral Development and Behavior.* Edited by Thomas Lickona. New York: Holt, Rinehart, and Winston, 1976.

Laqueur, Walter, and Barry Rubin, eds. *The Human Rights Reader.* New York: New American Library, 1989.

Lauren, Paul Gorden. *The Evolution of International Human Rights.* Philadelphia: University of Pennsylvania Press, 1998.

Lefever, Ernest. *Ethics and United States Foreign Policy.* New York: Meridian Books, 1957.

Locke, John. *Second Treatise on Government.* Amherst, N.Y.: Prometheus, 1986.

Lyotard, Jean-François. *The Post-Modern Condition.* Translated by Geoff Bennington and Brian Mussimi. Minneapolis: University of Minnesota Press, 1984.

———. "The Rights of the Other." In Shute and Hurley. *On Human Rights.*

Meadows, Dennis L. et al. *The Limits to Growth: A Report on the Club of Rome's Project on the Predicament of Mankind.* New York: Universal Books, 1972.

MacIntyre, Alasdair. *After Virtue.* Notre Dame, Ind.: Notre Dame University Press, 1981.

McGrade, A. S. "Aristotle's Place in the History of Natural Rights," *The Review of Metaphysics,* 49:4 (June 1996), pp. 803–829.

Maritain, Jacques. *The Social and Political Philosophy of Jacques Maritain.* New York: Doubleday, 1965.

Mill, John Stuart. *On Liberty.* In *Essential Works.* Edited by Max Lerner. New York: Bantum Books, 1961.

Milne, A. J. M. *Human Rights and Human Diversity.* Albany: State University of New York Press, 1986.

Mineau, André. "Human Rights and Nietzsche." *History of European Ideas,* 11 (1989), pp. 877–882.

Nickel, James W. "Are Human Rights Utopian?" *Philosophy of Public Affairs,* 11 (1982), pp. 246–264.

Nietzsche, Friedrich. *Genealogy of Morals.* Translated by Walter Kaufmann. New York: Random House, 1967.

Palmer, Richard and Kenneth Lucey. "Misguided Criticism of Utilitarianism," *Teaching Philosophy,* 15:1 (1992), pp. 57–70.

Peirce, Charles Sanders. *Collected Papers of Charles Sanders Peirce.* Vol. 3. Edited by Charles Hartshorne, Paul Weiss, and Arthur W. Burks. Cambridge, Mass.: Harvard University Press, 1933.

Perelman, Chaïm. "Can the Rights of Man be Founded?" In *The Philosophy of Human Rights: International Perspectives*. Edited by Alan S. Rosenbaum. Westport, Conn.: Greenwood Press, 1981.

Pippin, Robert. "Hegel, Modernity, and Habermas," *The Monist*, 74:3 (June 1991), pp. 329–357.

———. "Kant's *Rechtslehre*," In *The Philosophy of Immanuel Kant*. Edited by Richard Kennington. Washington, D.C.: Catholic University Press, 1985.

Plato. *The Dialogues of Plato*. Translated by Benjamin Jowett. Oxford: Oxford University Press, 1953.

Popper, Karl *The Open Society and its Enemies*. Vol. 1–2. Princeton, N.J.: Princeton University Press, 1953.

Rachels, James. *The Elements of Moral Philosophy*. Third Edition. Boston: McGraw-Hill, 1999.

Rawls, John Bordley. "Justice as Fairness: Political, not Metaphysical," *Philosophy & Public Affairs*, 14:3 (July 1985), pp. 223–251.

——— "Kantian Constructivism in Moral Theory," *Journal of Philosophy*, 77:9 (September, 1980), pp. 515–572.

———. "The Law of Peoples." In Shute and Hurley. *On Human Rights*, pp. 42–82.

Robespierre, Maximilien. "*Discours sur les principes de la morale politique qui doivent guider la Convention nationale dans l'administration intérieure de la Republique*." French National Convention, Session of 4 February 1794.

Rorty, Richard. "Human Rights, Rationality, and Sentimentality." In Shute and Hurley. *On Human Rights*.

———. *Philosophy and the Mirror of Nature*. Princeton, N.J.: Princeton, 1979.

Ross, W. D. David. *The Right and the Good*. Oxford: Oxford University Press, 1930.

Rouner, Leroy, ed. *Human Rights and World Religions*. Notre Dame: University of Notre Dame Press, 1988.

Rousseau, Jean-Jacques. *The Social Contract*. Translated by Wilmoore Kendall. Chicago: Henry Regnery, 1954.

Russell, Bertrand. *Has Man A Future?* Baltimore, Md.: Penguin, 1961.

Schlesinger, Arthur. *The Imperial Presidency*. Boston: Houghton Mifflin, 1973.

Shute, Steven and Susan Hurley, eds. *On Human Rights*. New York: Basic Books, 1993.

Searle, John R. "How to Derive 'Ought' from 'Is.'" In *The "Is/Ought" Question*. Edited by W. D. Hudson. London: Macmillan, 1969.

Smith, Barbara Hernstein. *The Contingencies of Value: Alternative Perspectives for Critical Theory*. Cambridge, Mass.: Harvard University Press, 1988.

Sophocles. *Sophocles 2*. Edited by David R. Slavitt and Palmer Bovie. Philadelphia: University of Pennsylvania Press, 1999.

Tamny, Martin and K. D. Irani, eds. *Rationality in Thought and Action*. New York: Greenwood Press, 1986.

Taylor, Richard. *Metaphysics*. Englewood Cliffs, N.J.: Prentice Hall, 1983.

Thomson, Judith Jarvis. *The Realm of Rights*. Cambridge, Mass.: Harvard University Press, 1990.

Thucydides. *The Peloponnesian War*. Translated by Rex Warner. New York: Penguin, 1954.

The United Nations and Human Rights: 1945–1995. New York: United Nations Department of Public Information, 1995.

Vlastos, Gregory. "Justice and Equality." In *The Philosophy of Human Rights*. Edited by Mortimer Emanuel Winston. Belmont, Calif.: Wadsworth, 1989.

Whitman, Jeffrey. "An End to Sovereignty," *Journal of Social Philosophy*, 24:2 (Fall 1996), pp. 146–157.

Wilkie, Wendell. *One World*. Urbana: University of Illinois Press, 1966.

Woo, Peter. "A Metaphysical Approach to Human Rights from a Chinese Point of View." In *The Philosophy of Human Rights: International Perspectives*. Edited by Alan Rosenbaum. Westport, Conn.: Greenwood, 1980.

Werhane, Patricia and David Ozar, eds. *Philosophical Issues in Human Rights: Theories and Applications*. New York: Random House, 1986.

Winston, Morton E., ed. *The Philosophy of Human Rights*. Belmont, Calif.: Wadsworth, 1989.

ABOUT THE AUTHOR

Clark Butler was born in Los Angeles, California, in 1944. He attended Hollywood High School and the University of Southern California—from which he received the PhD in 1970, studying ethics under John Hospers and Dallas Willard. He also studied at the University of Strasbourg, France; at the American University in Cairo, Egypt; and at the University of Tunis, Tunisia. Since 1969, he has taught at Purdue University, at the Indiana University-Purdue University Fort Wayne Campus (IPFW). He is a past chair of the IPFW philosophy department. IPFW has served as a base for extended stays at European universities including Trent Polytechnic in Nottingham; the Ruhr University in Bochum, Germany, where he was a Fulbright Guest Researcher at the Hegel-Archiv in 1974, and in 1975–1976; the University of Zaghreb in Dubrovnik; the University of Strasbourg, France, where he taught in 1987–1988; the Institute of Political Studies (Science Po), Strasbourg, where he taught human rights ethics in the Spring 2002 Semester; and the International Institute of Human Rights in Strasbourg where he has lectured in Summer since 2006 on the philosophical fundamentals of human rights.

Since the 1980s he has directed study abroad and student exchange programs between his home institution and Strasbourg. Besides publishing over thirty articles, his books include *G. W. F. Hegel* (G. K. Hall, 1977); *Hegel: The Letters* (Indiana University Press, 1984), a life in letters supported by a major National Endowment for the Humanities grant; *Hegel's Logic: Between Dialectic and History* (Northwestern University Press, 1997); and *History as the Story of Freedom* (Editions Rodopi, 1997). His translation of *Hegel's Lectures on Logic* (1831) appeared in 2008 with Indiana University Press. He is a past Co-Editor of the journal *CLIO*. Still a Hegel scholar and self-professed Hegelian of the original Hegelian Middle, he has addressed the foundations of human rights since the early 1980s.

He lives with his wife—a native of Lille, France—in Fort Wayne and Strasbourg. He is the founding Director of the Indiana University-Purdue University Fort Wayne Institute for Human Rights and is currently completing a book manuscript on the dialectical method.

INDEX